Myth, Montage, & Visuality
in Late Medieval Manuscript Culture

Myth,
MONTAGE, & VISUALITY
IN LATE MEDIEVAL
MANUSCRIPT CULTURE

Christine de Pizan's *Epistre Othea*

Marilynn Desmond & Pamela Sheingorn

The University of Michigan Press
Ann Arbor

First paperback edition 2006
Copyright © by the University of Michigan 2003
All rights reserved
Published in the United States of America by
The University of Michigan Press
Manufactured in the United States of America
♾ Printed on acid-free paper

2009   2008   2007   2006   5   4   3   2

A CIP catalog record for this book is available from the British Library.

Library of Congress Cataloging-in-Publication Data

Desmond, Marilynn, 1952–
   Myth, montage, and visuality in late medieval manuscript culture :
Christine de Pizan's Epistre Othea / Marilynn Desmond and Pamela
Sheingorn.
      p.   cm.
   Includes bibliographical references and index.
   ISBN 0-472-11323-2 (alk. paper)
   1. Christine, de Pisan, ca. 1364–ca. 1431. Epître d'Othéa à
Hector.   I. Sheingorn, Pamela.   II. Title.
PQ1575.E53 D47 2003
841'.2—dc21   2002152246

ISBN 0-472-03183-X (pbk : alk. paper)
ISBN 978-0-472-03183-2 (pbk : alk. paper)

Preface and Acknowledgments

꘎꘎꘎

The material properties of late medieval French manuscripts testify to the power of visual images to shape both the reading experience and the reader. As a multi-disciplinary study, *Myth, Montage, and Visuality* uses Christine de Pizan's *Epistre Othea* to address broad cultural questions regarding the visual organization of knowledge. As a collaborative project, this book has incurred unusual kinds of debts. For instance, in the early summer of 1998, just after the British Library moved to its new quarters on Euston Road, we spent a month there working intensively on a portion of this book. Our work was greatly facilitated by the willingness of the staff of the Reading Room in Humanities I to allow us daily access to a small sound-proofed room where we could pursue our highly inter-active and therefore vocal method of research and writing.

In the course of our research we have also found that many libraries were willing to give us joint access to manuscripts and early printed books, so that we could pursue our inquiry as a team. We are especially grateful to librarians and manuscript curators at the Bayerische Staatsbibliothek, Munich; the Biblio-thèque de l'Arsenal, Paris; the Bibliothèque municipale Jean Levy, Lille; the Bibliothèque municipale, Rouen; the Bibliothèque royale de Belgique, Brus-sels; the British Library; the Bodleian Library; Cambridge University Library; the J. Paul Getty Museum, Los Angeles; the Koninklijke Bibliotheek, The Hague; Newnham College and St. John's College Libraries, Cambridge University; the Pierpont Morgan Library, New York; the Bibliothèque nationale de France, Paris; and Waddesdon Manor, Aylesbury. In addition to the access to original materials housed in these libraries, the photographic and slide collections at the Warburg Institute were critical to the direction of our research for this proj-ect. We began this project by viewing together a complete set of slides of the

Othea in BL, Harley 4431, a set that had been purchased through the efforts of Penelope Mayo for the Center for Medieval and Renaissance Studies at Binghamton University.

The status of the *Epistre Othea* as a highly visual text suggested how important the visuality of manuscript culture is to any study of textuality. *Myth, Montage, and Visuality* is an interdisciplinary study of the interrelationship of the visual and textual aspects of late medieval manuscript cultures; such a study demanded both multiple perspectives and a range of skills. Collaboration greatly enables multidisciplinary work, and from the start, we have pursued every aspect of this project as a joint endeavor, including its writing. We have worked together in drafting and revising every sentence. We individually brought to this project our separate training and skills in the textual and visual cultures of the Middle Ages, yet our aim has been to produce a seamless text in one voice.

Although we have benefited greatly from the long tradition of scholarship on the *Epistre Othea,* we must acknowledge the tremendous contribution of Sandra Hindman's *Christine de Pizan's "Epistre Othéa": Painting and Politics at the Court of Charles VI* (1986). Hindman's recognition that the *Epistre Othea* deserves monographic treatment laid the foundation for our inquiry into late medieval visuality. In the process, we have drawn widely from feminist theory, particularly feminist film theory, out of our conviction that premodern and postmodern cultures share a predilection for a cinematic arrangement of knowledge in a montage format.

We have been fortunate to have generous and critical readings from a large number of colleagues. Deborah McGrady, Seth Lerer, and Diane Wolfthal all read and commented on the entire manuscript; Cristelle Baskins, Reinhard Bernbeck, Glenn Burger, Charles Burroughs, Esther Cohen, George Custen, Steven Kruger, Ingeborg Majer O'Sickey, Susan Pollock, Carol Weisbrod, and Jean Wilson all read one or more individual chapters. Drawing on his immense expertise, Robert L. A. Clark carefully and thoroughly answered many questions about translations of the *Epistre Othea.* Jonathan Alexander, Adelaide Bennett, Leslie Abend Callahan, Lois Drewer, James Laidlaw, Susan L'Engle, and Christine Reno all responded cheerfully to our queries about language, manuscripts, or codicology. Joseph Pappa generously shared his knowledge and research in cultural studies. Rhonda Knight provided all sorts of research assistance at the early stages of this project. Celia Braxton, Wendy Matlock, Jenna Soleo, and Jill Stevenson all helped with the final stages of acquiring photographs and permissions as well as compiling bibliographic materials.

Material from this project was presented several times at the annual meetings of the Modern Language Association and the College Art Association, in addition to conferences sponsored by the Center for Medieval and Early Renaissance Studies at Binghamton University and the Illinois Medieval Association, as well as the Queer Middle Ages conference sponsored by the Center for Lesbian and Gay Studies at the Graduate Center, City University of New York in 1998. Many kind invitations to speak enabled us to present material during the evolution of this project. In this regard, we especially thank the following individuals and institutions for inviting one or both of us to deliver lectures based on this book: Esther Cohen and the Lafer Center on Gender Studies at the Hebrew University, Israel; Michael Curschmann, Medieval Studies, Princeton University; the graduate students in Medieval Studies at the University of North Carolina, Chapel Hill; Carmella Franklin, the Medieval Seminar at Columbia University; Elisabeth Pastan, Emory University; Miri Rubin, Oxford University; William Burgwinkle, Medieval French Seminar at Cambridge University; Anna Davin, *History Workshop Journal* Seminar in London; E. Ann Matter, Medieval Studies, University of Pennsylvania; and Thérèse de Hemptinne, University of Ghent, Belgium.

Dean Mileur of Harpur College, Binghamton University, contributed to a subvention to cover publication of photographs; several Professional Staff Congress–City University of New York Research Awards supported travel and purchase of photographs. For his consistent commitment to the project, we thank our editor at University of Michigan Press, Collin Ganio.

A portion of chapter 3 appeared as "Queering Ovidian Myth: Bestiality and Desire in Christine de Pizan's *Epistre Othea*," in *Queering the Middle Ages,* edited by Glenn Burger and Steven F. Kruger (Minneapolis: University of Minnesota Press, 2001). For electronic troubleshooting that on one particular occasion saved our manuscript from oblivion, we thank Mark Sheingorn. Although collaborative work is highly stimulating and synergetic, it is more disruptive to one's personal routine than the individual pursuit of scholarship. This has often been an exhilarating enterprise, but it has put unusual demands on Jerry Kutcher and Mark Sheingorn. During the course of this project, their understanding and support have been tremendous; they have cheerfully lived with this book much longer than they had anticipated.

Contents

ཊགྷཊ

Abbreviations   xi

Introduction   1
Visual Pleasures and
Medieval Manuscripts

1
The Cinematic Experience   23
Iconography in the Age of
Mechanical Reproduction

2
Constructing Masculinities   47

3
Envisioning Desire   99

4
Engendering Violence   157

5
Visualizing Rhetoric   195

Afterword   231

Notes   243

Bibliography   301

Index of the Works of Christine de Pizan   329

Index of Manuscripts Cited   331

General Index   335

Plates   345

Abbreviations

୧୬୨୬

Bibl. mun.	Bibliothèque municipale
BL	London, British Library
BnF	Paris, Bibliothèque nationale de France
BR	Brussels, Bibliothèque royale de Belgique
BUV	València, Universitat de València, Biblioteca Històrica
Othea	Christine de Pizan, *Epistre Othea*
PML	New York, Pierpont Morgan Library

Myth, Montage, & Visuality
in Late Medieval Manuscript Culture

Fig. I.1. Christine in the Salle de Fortune, *Livre de la mutation de Fortune,* Munich, Staatsbibliothek, Ms. Gall. 11, fol. 53r. (Foto Marburg/Art Resource, New York.)

INTRODUCTION

Visual Pleasures and
Medieval Manuscripts

> The world spectator is . . . not just someone to whom the past re-
> turns, but someone who holds [her/]himself open to the new form
> it will take—who anticipates and affirms the transformative mani-
> festation of what was in what is.
>
> —Kaja Silverman, *World Spectators*

> And meanwhile the Sphinx can only speak with a voice apart, a
> voice off.
>
> —Laura Mulvey and Peter Wollen,
> "Riddles of the Sphinx, Script"

In a miniature in the Munich manuscript of her *Mutacion de Fortune,* Christine
the poet stands in the Salle de Fortune, a room whose walls are densely covered
with a visual record of history (fig. I.1).[1] Separated by narrow bands of text, the
images stretch in registers along the entire length of the hall. The unfolding
narratives combine with the receding diagonals of the walls to create a volume
of space. The three-dimensionality of the hall envelops Christine: the quiet intensity of her demeanor, her solitude, and her contemplative expression suggest
that the texts and images of history on the walls are creating her as a spectator.
This miniature introduces the section of the text that narrates how Christine ar-
rives at the Salle de Fortune and studies the wall paintings there.[2] The allegory

of the *Mutacion* (1403) proposes that Christine as author first sees history and then renders this visual experience in language through her ekphrastic writing. The miniature thus illustrates a central premise of the *Mutacion,* that cultural memory is primarily visual. This scene in the Salle de Fortune thereby encapsulates critical aspects of the relationship between the textual and the visual in late medieval manuscript cultures.

With the publication of the *Mutacion* in four simultaneously produced manuscripts with full-color miniatures late in 1403, Christine de Pizan enters a new phase in her literary career. Early-fifteenth-century Paris, specifically around the year 1403, saw a proliferation of luxury manuscripts whose luminous illuminations situate the reader as spectator: this aspect of late medieval Parisian manuscript culture creates a readerly subjectivity that qualifies as cinematic. For centuries, manuscript decoration had played with the properties of light in painting; indeed, the word *illuminatio* denoted the decoration in manuscripts as well as the concept of "light as color." As Michael Camille observes, "Light was the inherent formal characteristic of external objects, giving them the 'color' of luminosity, and was a basic requirement for the optical theories of the perspectivists who theorized vision."[3] Ivan Illich comments on twelfth-century theories of light: "according to the spiritual optics of the early scholastics, the *lumen oculorum,* the light which emanates from the eye, was necessary to bring the luminous objects of the world into the onlooker's sense perception."[4] In this theory, known as extramission, human eyes function rather like a movie projector in casting a beam of light that renders objects visible.

Manuscript painting, particularly in the deployment of colors alongside the reflective gold and silver backgrounds, places the light-emitting object before the eyes of the reader. In a discussion of the manipulation of luminosity in film, Maureen Turim comments, "Luminosity suggests a quality of light, light emanating from its source, as in a candle flame, an ember or a light bulb. . . . The actual light we see during the film projection is also reflected light, bounced off the screen."[5] Scholars such as Patrick de Winter, Charles Sterling, and Millard Meiss emphasize that manuscript painting reaches its zenith in the exploitation of luminosity in the late fourteenth and early fifteenth centuries.[6] At the same time, as Paul Saenger has shown, reading had become an increasingly private experience. The luminous nature of the reading experience in a manuscript culture situates the reader as a spectator constructed by the luminous quality of the page.[7] This aspect of the reading experience in late medieval manuscript culture is analogous to the modern cinematic experience.

In the manuscript culture of early-fifteenth-century Paris, one text in particular manipulated the luminosity of book illustration to create a cinematic experience for the reader—Christine de Pizan's *Epistre Othea* or Letter of Othea to Hector, composed in 1400 and dedicated initially to Louis of Orleans. Forty-seven complete manuscripts of the *Othea* survive from the fifteenth century. Two of these manuscript copies appear in early-fifteenth-century luxury editions of Christine's collected works: the *Othea* in the Duke's manuscript, named for the duke of Berry, is now in BnF, fr. 606, and the *Othea* in the Queen's manuscript, named for the queen of France, Isabeau of Bavaria, is in BL, Harley 4431. The *Othea* was printed in at least five separate editions in France; of three English translations, two circulated in manuscript and one appeared in print.[8] These different versions of the *Othea* are variously dedicated to the duke of Berry, Philip the Bold, and Henry IV, king of England.[9]

Fully illustrated copies of the *Othea* consist of one hundred images accompanied by textual explanations,[10] so that the *Othea* enacts a viewing of classical myth as a constitutive text for the late medieval humanist or chivalric subject. Othea, a supposedly classical goddess and personification of wisdom whom Christine invented,[11] instructs the Trojan hero Hector in the codes of chivalric conduct by means of a letter addressed to him at the age of fifteen. The design of the book follows a pattern in which a chapter opens with a visual image of a mythological figure or event in a classical narrative (see figs. 2.17, 2.18, 3.15, 4.11, 4.12). After each miniature comes a passage of Othea's letter: a short narrative verse, often of lapidary complexity, labeled *texte* and addressed to Hector in the second-person familiar. The *texte* instructs both Hector and the reader in the politics of viewing the miniature. A prose passage labeled *glose* follows the *texte;* the *glose* may expand the narrative but primarily functions to interpret the myth as a lesson in conduct for the good knight; each *glose* ends with a tag line from an ancient philosopher. Another short prose passage, the *allegorie*, concludes the unit and draws a lesson from the myth that is applicable to the "good spirit" or soul; each *allegorie* ends with a Latin quotation from a biblical text written in red.[12] The *glose* and the *allegorie* do not always agree with each other or with the *texte,* and the narrative may remain incompletely told. The moralizing efforts do not always result in a unified reading, nor do they exhaust the interpretative possibilities of the image and the text. In the Duke's and the Queen's manuscripts in particular, the miniatures are often much more evocative than the *glose* and *allegorie* that follow. Indeed, the overall effect emphasizes the visuality of reading. In addition to the image—illuminated and framed in gold in the luxury manuscripts—the textual material is organized visually. The textual material not only juxtaposes verse and prose, but includes decorated initials and rubrics in a complex page design or *ordinatio* that combines the visual and verbal components of reading.

The *Othea* works to visualize the past in the present since the epistolary allegory of the *Othea* posits a male reader who might transform the past into agency by adopting a conduct responsive to the demands of the present. Such agency, however, does not result from an imitation of the past: instead the mythic past offers the reader an opportunity to explore the relationship between ethics and temporality. Basic to the trajectory of the *Othea* is the knowledge that Hector dies defending Troy, and the inevitability of his death imparts an urgency to the lessons Othea offers throughout her epistle to him. In the first chapter, Othea imperatively alludes to his death: "Understand and do not grieve, because I will not say anything that will not come to pass" [Or entens et ne te soucie, / Car riens ne diray qui n'aviengne] (1.69–70).[13] In mythic terms, Hector's mortality defines the significance of his conduct for the reader. Mortality places temporal demands on ethics, as Kaja Silverman observes: "Our being must . . . be defined in terms of what, from the moment of death, we will have been; it inheres in the future perfect."[14] In the *Othea,* the future perfect of Hector's death in the mythic past allows the reader to use that mythic past to negotiate the ethical demands of the present.

The mythical past was available to Christine and her readers in a variety of textual traditions; although Christine demonstrably read Latin texts, the *Epistre Othea* records her reception of the vernacular adaptations of classical texts central to late-fourteenth-century humanism.[15] All of these vernacular retellings of classical narratives belong to manuscript traditions that are frequently illustrated.[16] Much of the mythological material in the *Othea* comes from Ovid by way of the *Ovide moralisé,* a French translation and moralization of Ovid's *Metamorphoses* produced in the early fourteenth century.[17] The *Roman de la rose* likewise negotiates Ovidian myths in a highly visual format; indeed, the visual component of several chapters of the *Othea* could be viewed as a "remake" of the Ovidian interpretations in the *Rose.*[18] The historical material in the *Othea* comes from the French vernacular tradition of universal history that modern scholars have entitled the *Histoire ancienne jusqu'à César,* a prose compendium of biblical, Theban, and Trojan history drawing on Ovid, Virgil, and Statius.[19] The *Othea* engages only sporadically with Boccaccio's encyclopedic approach to mythical material, *De claris mulieribus,* which first appears in French adaptation in an illustrated format in 1402. Although Christine seems to have had some acquaintance with the Latin text of *De claris mulieribus* before it was available in French, it is her later work, the *Livre de la cité des dames*—composed in 1405—that engages specifically with the French Boccaccio, *Des cleres et nobles femmes,* and thereby undertakes a critique and revision of Boccaccio's textual misogyny. However, the illustrations in *Othea* manuscripts made after 1402 sometimes respond to the alluring and often lurid illustrations to *Des cleres et nobles femmes,* which circulated widely after 1402.[20]

In addition to the vernacular traditions of classical myth and history, astrological manuscripts in Latin and French also offered a mythical iconography for the *Othea*. In Paris, knowledge of astrology pervaded both the court and the university: in 1368, Christine's father, Tommaso da Pizzano, came to Paris from Italy, where he had been professor of astrology and astronomy at the University of Bologna, in response to Charles V's invitation that he serve as court astrologer to the French king, whose library included a wealth of astrological materials.[21] Charles's brother, Jean, duke of Berry, also showed a keen interest in astrology, a fact exemplified by a Latin astrological manuscript he received as a gift. This manuscript, a set of images with introductory texts translated from Abū Ma'šar's *Introduction to Astrology,* depicts a series of planetary deities that form an interpictorial context for the *Othea.*[22] In the *Othea*, the visual traditions of astrology intersect with the vernacular traditions of myth and history, particularly with the Ovidian narratives that offer explanations of how constellations came into being.

Taken together, these materials provided Christine with a vast repertoire of classical materials in highly visual formats. The intertextual and intervisual references restructure these received traditions so that the *Othea* confronts the spectator with a series of individually framed scenes that refuse the imposition of narrative continuity from chapter to chapter. The *Othea*, moreover, displays selected moments from classical myth and history with an almost total disregard for the narrative sequence received from tradition. Nor does the *Othea* offer any sustained narrative thread of its own; each chapter presents a fragment of an authoritative pre-text, redeployed within the context of Othea's instructions to Hector, so that the *Othea* operates as an exercise in *bricolage* on Christine's part. Claude Lévi-Strauss considered mythology to be an inherently *bricolage* project because it collects and uses elements "which are 'pre-constrained' like the constitutive elements of myth, the possible combinations of which are restricted by the fact that they are drawn from a language where they already possess a sense which sets a limit on their freedom of manoeuvre."[23] Lévi-Strauss's concept of *bricolage* has been appropriated into a variety of discourses and it has been employed to analyze both material and intellectual culture.[24]

As *bricolage,* the formal structure of the *Othea* enabled Christine to revise myths without reinscribing them as master narratives.[25] Indeed, the lack of a perceptible overall structure in the *Othea* has often been remarked upon. Some scholars emphasize the initial series of textual clues provided at the allegorical level: the four cardinal virtues (chaps. 1–4), the seven gifts of the Holy Spirit (chaps. 6–12), the theological virtues (chaps. 13–15), the seven deadly sins (chaps. 16–22), the articles of the Creed (chaps. 23–34), and the Ten Commandments (chaps. 35–44).[26] Such approaches, however, have no purchase on the *Othea* after chapter 44, and they even fail to account for every chapter before 44; for example, the allegorical message of chapter 5, that the chivalric soul should desire fame or a good reputation ("bonne renommee") among the saints in heaven, fits none of these schemes. The *bricolage* arrangement of the *Othea* ultimately works against any overall formal structure. Specific figures, such as Helen, Diana, Circe, Midas, Ino, Venus, Saturn, Mars, and Hector are treated in two or more widely separated chapters; occasionally, as in the two chapters that treat the abduction of Helen by Paris, the textual material from one chapter would seem to illustrate the miniature from another.[27] The reader/viewer of the *Othea* experiences this visual *bricolage* as montage, a visual arrangement in which meaning is derived from unexpected juxtapositions.

In his synthetic and wide-ranging analysis of the formal properties of montage, S. M. Eisenstein considers cinema to be a modern extension of a "general principle of montage," a principle that he sees operating throughout the history of painting and that is particularly evident in medieval painting. Eisenstein's theory that the montage properties of cinema make it "part of the mainstream of the development and history of painting"[28] renders montage a particularly efficacious category for the analysis of a text such as the *Othea*. In filmic terms, montage has a specific value for revisionary cinema, as exemplified in two avant-garde feminist films from the 1970s made by Laura Mulvey and Peter Wollen: *Penthesilea* (1974) and *Riddles of the Sphinx* (1976). Both of these films employ montage to intervene in the received traditions of classical mythology and thereby modify the standard Hollywood structures of visual pleasure as Mulvey originally identified and analyzed them.[29] Each film invokes a traditional narrative of a particular myth, but in each case the actual appropriation of that myth depends on the fragmentation made possible through montage. Section 3 of *Riddles of the Sphinx* presents a montage of photographs of the Sphinx: this montage is framed by Mulvey's introduction in section 2, in which she explains how the myth of the Sphinx will be appropriated in the film, an appropriation that includes reading the Egyptian Sphinx as female, since the film itself depends on the premise that "the Sphinx as woman is a threat and a riddle."[30] Only through the subversion made possible by montage can the Sphinx claim cultural authority, and even then "the Sphinx can only speak with a voice apart, a voice off."[31] In a similar fashion, the middle section of *Penthesilea* screens a montage on the theme of the Amazons. The filmmakers' description of this portion of the film reads: "A complex arrangement of images of paintings, sculptures, bas-reliefs, comic strips, etc. on the theme of the Amazons. The transitions are effected with animated wipes and maskings. The sound track presents the 'birth' of a new form of language."[32] Both films depend on the reader's existing knowledge of classical myth and the conventions of narrative and nonnarrative cinema. The redeployment of these mythic materials in a montage destroys the potential for voyeuristic pleasure and instead enables what Mulvey calls the viewer's "passionate detachment."[33]

Mulvey's practice as a feminist filmmaker reflects her theoretical concerns with the categories of visual pleasure as she originally articulated them in her 1972 polemic, "Visual Pleasure and Narrative Cinema." In this classic formulation of the voyeuristic mastery available in the "male gaze," Mulvey articulated a theory of spectatorship that has been highly productive in feminist film theory. According to Mulvey, the visual pleasure available in classic Hollywood cinema depends on a scopophilic structure of heterosexual desire, a voyeuristic economy in which men possess the gaze and women are the objects of erotic desire. Though her initial formulation of the male gaze has been extensively critiqued, even by Mulvey herself, her interrogation of visual pleasure initiated an inquiry into the gendered nature of spectatorship that remains part of the silent inheritance of film theory as well as literary studies.[34]

In Mulvey's words, feminist films such as *Riddles of the Sphinx* and *Penthesilea* succeed by "foregrounding the cinematic process privileging the signifier, [which] disrupts aesthetic unity and forces the spectator's attention on the means of production of meaning."[35] These films anxiously acknowledge their own formal structures, at times in a highly didactic framework. Such an interrogation of aesthetic possibilities is a standard rhetorical strategy in the revisionary discourses of feminisms. The *Othea* displays a similar anxiety about the aesthetic values of myth, an anxiety evident in the foregrounding of its formal epistolary structure, derived from the *ars dictaminis*. As an epistle, the *texte* of the *Othea* opens with the rhetorical flourish of the *captatio benevolentiae*, the attempt to win the recipient's attentive goodwill. In each of the short *textes*, the goddess Othea addresses Hector in an exhortatory mode; she employs the familiar form of the second-person direct address appropriate in a letter from an older, wiser interlocutor. In cinematic terms, the voice of Othea functions as a voice-off, that is, the voice of a character who is part of the filmic diegesis but not on screen when speaking. The other two textual elements, the *glose* and *allegorie,* are presented in the authorial voice of Christine, who explains Othea's meaning to the reader. This authorial voice functions as a "voice-over." As Kaja Silverman defines it, voice-over is "a voice which speaks from a position of superior knowledge, and which superimposes itself 'on top' of the diegesis."[36] The shifts in voice within each chapter demand that the reader negotiate competing levels of meaning as part of the process of interpretation.

The visual level likewise intervenes intrusively in this process. Kaja Silverman has recently argued that the visual functions as the primary arena for all psychic processes.[37] The visual program of the *Othea* depicts the psychic drama of conduct as cultural capital and rehearses the possibility that Hector might learn to perform as a good knight. The assumption that conduct could be understood as performance was central to Nicole Oresme's French version of Aristotle's *Ethics,* produced under the patronage of Charles V in 1370–72. Several illustrated manuscripts of Oresme's translation were made in Parisian workshops in the last quarter of the fourteenth century; indeed, one was made for Louis of Orleans in 1397–98.[38] At the start of chapter 2 on moral virtue, Oresme offers an explanatory gloss on the theory of conduct in the *Ethics* that emphasizes the role of habit in the acquisition of virtue.[39] In a similar way, the visual hermeneutics of the *Othea* work to elicit a habit of looking that will shape conduct, what Pierre Bourdieu would call a *habitus.*[40] The initial miniature stages Hector's acceptance of Othea's authority, a visual sign of his receptivity to the mythic lessons of her letter (fig. I.2). Othea leans down from the clouds and hands her letter to Hector, who reaches up eagerly to receive it. A group of nobles who have a stake in his education as a knight look on approvingly. In each subsequent chapter, Othea prescribes a specific physical, psychic, and moral stance and directs Hector to react to her prescription in a performative mode.

Performance theory and film theory come together in the emphasis both place on the centrality of the spectator, whether corporealized, perverse, gendered, embodied, or disembodied.[41] The current critical emphasis on spectatorship offers a theoretical paradigm for reading medieval manuscripts for their performativity. A hybrid culture flourished in early-fifteenth-century Paris in which various oral performances, what Bernard J. Hibbitts calls "the vitally communicative roles of gesture, touch, smell and taste," coexisted with exuberantly literate productions such as the *Othea.* Hibbitts draws on contemporary performance studies, especially in anthropological literature, to develop the concept of "performance culture." With its "distinctly theatric connotation," "performance culture" refers to a society in which individuals are "performers" in the sense of being culturally fluent in speech, gesture, touch, smell, and taste.[42] It is this cultural fluency that the *Othea* communicates in its images; the visual culture of the *Othea* is rich in represented gestures that could neither be communicated verbally nor effectively described in the text. Thus manuscript painting is the apparatus by which the *Othea* presents performativity, and since these images depict classical myth, the visual component of the *Othea* offers what Catherine Soussloff identifies as a feature of performance, that "iteration carries with it the past into the present."[43] According to the rhetoric of the *Othea,* the body, character, and soul of the spectator will all have been formed as a result of simultaneously reading the text and viewing the images of the *Othea.* As repeated performances, or iterations, these acts will constitute out of the young male an ideal knight: throughout the *Othea,* though, this iteration is subject to an interrogation along the lines of gender.

Fig. I.2. Othea giving her letter to Hector, *Epistre Othea*, BnF, fr. 606, fol. 1v. (Photo Bibliothèque nationale de France, Paris.) ◆

Christine's chapter on Medea illustrates the concepts of gendered performativity at work in the *Othea*. The miniature represents Medea seated on the edge of a bed and opening a strongbox before the kneeling Jason (fig. I.3). In the brief verse *texte* Othea advises:

> Do not allow your judgment to be destroyed by illicit pleasure; do not allow your possessions to be taken away, and if they are asked for, then see yourself in Medea.

> [Ne laisses ton sens avorter
> A fol delit, ne emporter
> Ta chevance, se demandee
> T'est, et te mires en Medee.]
> (58.2–5)

The *glose* describes Medea as "one of the wisest women of prophecy who ever lived" [une des plus savans femmes de sors qui oncques fust] (58.7–8), who nonetheless "let her judgment be destroyed by her desire" [laissa son sens avorter a sa propre voulenté] (58.9–10) when she gave herself and her goods to Jason, for which he repaid her with evil. The moral lesson in the *glose* states that the good knight should not permit reason to be overcome by foolish pleasure, and the *allegorie* offers the lesson for the soul that one's desire must never have mastery. In her *Epistre au dieu d'Amours,* a text she wrote before the *Othea,* Christine describes Medea:

> How did Medea act toward the false Jason? She was very loyal, and through her subtle cleverness, she enabled him to win the Golden Fleece, for which he was more famous than a hundred thousand other men. Because of her, his renown was greater than anyone else's, and he promised her that he would be her sweet, loyal love, belonging only to her; but he broke his word, left her for someone else, and departed.[44]

> [Que fut jadis Medée au faulz Jason?
> Trés loialle, et lui fist la toison
> D'or conquerir par son engin soubtil,
> Dont il acquist loz plus qu'autres cent mil.
> Par elle fu renommé dessus tous,
> Si lui promist que loial ami doulz
> Seroit tout sien, mais sa foy lui menti
> Et la laissa pour autre et s'en parti.][45]
> (437–44)

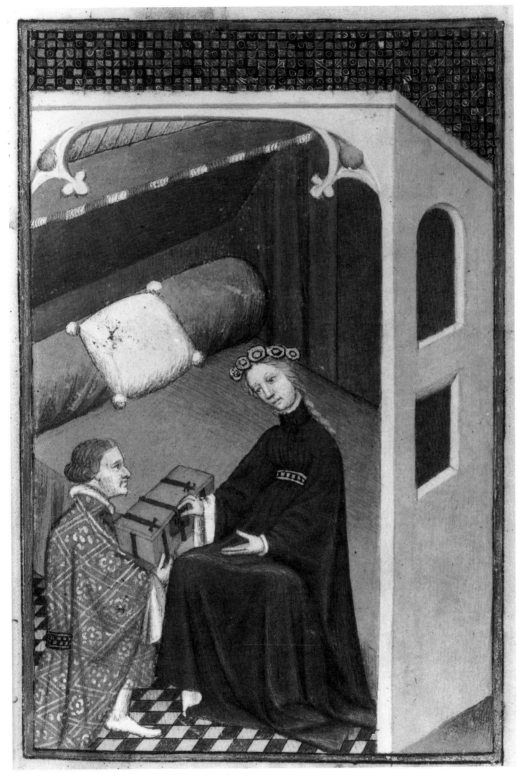

Fig. I.3. Medea, *Epistre Othea*, BL, Harley 4431, fol. 122r. (By permission of the British Library.) ☙

Fig. I.4. Medea, Boccaccio, *Des cleres et nobles femmes,* BnF, fr. 598, fol. 27v. (Photo Bibliothèque nationale de France, Paris.)

Though the textual characterization in the *Othea* corresponds closely to this description from the *Epistre,* the visual component in illustrated manuscripts of the *Othea* offers a performative level of commentary on Medea's conduct as a mythic woman.

Christine clearly knew the myth according to which Medea assisted Jason in winning the Golden Fleece, bore him two children, and murdered those children to retaliate for his betrayal and abandonment of her; in addition, she knew the visual tradition that constructed Medea as a wielder of powerful magic and a terrifying murderess.[46] Both textual and visual versions of this narrative of infanticide occur in Boccaccio's *Des cleres et nobles femmes* (chap. 16; see fig. I.4) and the *Histoire ancienne* (fig. I.5), as well as the *Roman de la rose* (ll. 13199–234; see fig. I.6). None of this narrative content of Medea as a murderess appears in the image or text of the *Othea.* As Sandra Hindman has

Fig. I.5. Medea, *Histoire ancienne,* BL, Royal 20 D. I, fol. 37v. (By permission of the British Library.) ☙

Fig. I.6. Medea, *Roman de la rose,* Oxford, Bodleian Library, MS Douce 371, fol. 87v. (Bodleian Library, University of Oxford.) ☙

demonstrated, the *Othea* miniature refers to an early moment in the *Histoire ancienne* narrative when Jason attends Medea in her room, and she offers him a charm and a ring from her jewelry box.[47] In this case, a textual tradition provides the authority to rewrite a gruesome visual tradition of infanticide. The image in the *Othea* offers a moment in the story when Medea confronts a conventional ethical dilemma: whether to resist or yield to transgressive desire. Her gestures—of opening and openness—perform her availability to Jason. The courtly context signaled by her garland and the lover bending his knee before her brings this scene into focus as a chivalric performance. Yet Othea tells Hector to identify across genders: "If this is asked of you, then see yourself [literally, "mirror yourself," *te mires*] in Medea."[48] This invitation to think through Medea's decision is remarkable for both the implied empathy and the lack of anxiety about the female power and sexuality that the figure of Medea traditionally encodes. Christine's Medea is a wise woman who made a foolish mistake, a woman with the authority to bestow her own body and goods—to be the subject of desire—but who made a bad decision when she did so and suffered as a result. The mnemonic potential of images works to substitute Christine's revision of Medea for the vicious Medea in the visual memory of her readers;[49] such a revision suggests that Christine the poet saw the visual component of the *Othea* as a critical shaper of ethical meanings for the reader/viewer.

The miniature to the Medea chapter poses important questions about authorial involvement in image making and manuscript production. Hindman cites this miniature and its relationship to the text of the *Histoire ancienne* as evidence that Christine herself must have determined the contents of the visual material throughout the *Othea*.[50] Certainly the nature of workshop production in late medieval Paris allowed for authorial supervision of manuscript design and illustration, as Claire Richter Sherman has demonstrated in the case of Nicole Oresme's translations of Aristotle.[51] Since the early illustrated manuscripts of the *Othea* all show similar visual programs, they ultimately must derive from one vision. At times the iconography in these early manuscripts appears to be highly idiosyncratic, and at times it is original to the *Othea*. The originality of these visual programs and their engagement with the textual material suggest a collaborative artistic partnership that would certainly include the author but should not be characterized as "authorial"; consequently the text-image relationship should not be considered the product of authorial intention so much as the result of workshop practice. Much like the Hollywood studio system, manuscripts emerge from multiple artistic efforts in response to some overriding vision. Throughout our analysis of the *Othea* we take up the invitation it offers the reader/viewer to consider the visual material as the primary focus of readerly interpretive activity.

Scholars have long been aware of the illuminations in many of Christine's manuscripts,[52] and some have posited Christine's central role in the production of the two extensively illustrated manuscripts of her collected works, the Duke's and the Queen's manuscripts.[53] Fundamental work on the miniatures of the *Othea* has been done by Lucie Schaefer, Rosemond Tuve,[54] Millard Meiss,[55] and Sandra L. Hindman.[56] From the earliest exemplars, the *Othea* is presented in an *ordinatio*—or layout—that directs the reader's attention to the visual organization of meaning. The images are one component of the visuality of the *Othea* manuscripts and their construction of a reading subject. The earliest surviving manuscript of Christine's *Epistre Othea* (BnF, fr. 848), which was dedicated to Louis, duke of Orleans, and presented to him in 1400 or 1401, is a small manuscript of twenty leaves.[57] The page design signals at a glance a set of relationships integral to the meaning of the text. Folio 2r, the opening of the text proper, centers on the *texte* of chapters 1 and 2, which is written in a larger script than the flanking prose passages of the *glose* on the left and the *allegorie* on the right. Above the first line of the *texte* with its decorated initial is a two-part miniature, executed in grisaille, whose subjects correspond to the topics of the first two chapters: Othea and Temperance (fig. I.7). In this clear visual separation of different kinds of representation, the poetic text in the center is framed by various supplementary materials—the image at the top of the page forms the upper segment of the frame; the prose *glose* and *allegorie* are adjusted to fill in the space at the bottom below the *texte*. The deliberate restriction of the image to grisaille facilitates the integrated exchange between text and image. The visual presentations of poetry, prose, and image work to create a harmonious effect.

In this earliest text of the *Othea*, the visual program is limited to the first four folios, a situation that James Laidlaw attributes to Christine's limited means at this early stage of her career.[58] These initial images are not neatly matched on the same page with the textual material, and in one case, that of folio 2v, the image for chapter 4 (Minos) is on the left in a double miniature in which the image for chapter 3 (Hercules) is on the right. This double miniature nonetheless presents a pleasing composition and illustrates the extent to which visual design is privileged over a tight relationship between text and image in this manuscript.[59] Even in the absence of miniatures after chapter 5, the purposeful *ordinatio* of these first few folios persists throughout the manuscript. Such an effectively balanced page visually replicates the layout of biblical, theological, and legal manuscripts and thereby evokes the authoritative status of commentary.[60] Mary Ann Ignatius observes, "The disposition of the text of the *Othea* in ms. fr. 848 . . . invites a non-linear, contemplative style of reading."[61] The *ordinatio* of fr. 848 may have been the model for two surviving single-text

Fig. I.7. Othea giving her letter to Hector; Temperance, *Epistre Othea*, BnF, fr. 848, fol. 2r. (Photo Bibliothèque nationale de France, Paris.) ❧

manuscripts of the *Othea* that arrange the three textual portions of each chapter around a centrally placed miniature: Cambridge, Newnham College Library, MS 900 (5) and Beauvais, Bibl. mun., MS 9, both of which have been dated to the third decade of the fifteenth century.[62] These three manuscripts demonstrate the potential of *ordinatio* to highlight the inherent visuality of the *Othea*.

The *Othea* takes on a different *ordinatio* when it is included in larger manuscript compilations. The earliest version of Christine's collected works, designated by Laidlaw the "Livre de Christine," now lost, included the *Othea*. In addition, two early manuscripts were copied from the "Livre de Christine": Chantilly, MS 492–93 and BnF, fr. 12779. In order to fit the *Othea* into the *ordinatio* of these collections, both of these versions employ a double-column format and single-column miniatures.[63] The miniatures cease early in both manuscripts, but the text continues with the same format. Such *ordinatio* points to the interpretive juxtaposition of texts—verse and prose, *glose* and *allegorie*—as well as a purposeful arrangement of text and image.

Just after the middle of the first decade of the fifteenth century, Christine began what would eventually become two luxury editions of her collected works. The *Othea* in each collection contains one hundred miniatures that form a new, elaborate cycle of illustration, a complete program of one image per chapter. One collection, known today as the Duke's manuscript (BnF 835, 606, 836, 605, and 607), was begun for Louis of Orleans and acquired by the duke of Berry after Orleans's assassination in 1407.[64] The other collection, known today as the Queen's manuscript (BL, Harley 4431), was presented to Isabeau of Bavaria after its compilation in 1410–11.[65] Harley 4431 and fr. 606 emerge from a patronage system that allowed Christine as author to retain some control of her work. As Deborah McGrady has shown, "Christine undertakes concurrent projects intended for individual patrons and then disseminates copies of these same works to multiple members of the nobility."[66] Having several noble patrons made possible a lavish scale of illumination in these two manuscripts. Patronage stimulated illumination but left some control in the hands of the poet, since the patron owned an illuminated exemplar, not the text itself.

As exemplars, the copies of the *Othea* in the Duke's and the Queen's manuscripts, so similar in *ordinatio* and roughly contemporary in date, are closely related, but the nature of that relationship is difficult to determine with any specificity. A folio-by-folio comparison of the six quires in each copy shows that each closely resembles the other in layout and page design until the final quire. The first three quires of eight folios each begin and end identically in both manuscripts; the quires display slight internal variations in text layout, although the images are always placed in the same position on the page. The fourth quire of fr. 606 lacks one folio, resulting in a total of forty-seven folios rather than the forty-eight found in 4431. In fr. 606 the text covers forty-six folios; in 4431 it covers forty-seven. From the fourth quire on, 4431 and fr. 606 are not identical in terms of collation, yet the miniatures fall in the same places on the page and the text breaks at the same point at the end of every eight leaves. In 4431, the *ordinatio* of the sixth quire shows a self-conscious sprawl; in comparison to the earlier quires, larger blank spaces are left between portions of the text, and these spaces are visually claimed by unusually long ascenders and descenders. After the first folio of this sixth quire, the placement of miniatures in 4431 no longer corresponds to that in fr. 606. This last quire also contains more and longer strikeouts than the earlier quires, and the size of the script grows noticeably larger, as if the scribe had determined to spread the text and layout over one more folio.

The identical breaks between folios at the end of every eight leaves suggest that each manuscript was copied from an exemplar with regular quires of eight leaves each. Had Harley 4431 been copied from fr. 606, following the usual practice of disbinding a manuscript before copying it, then the irregular quire in the middle of fr. 606 would have been copied as an irregular quire lacking one folio. The sixth quire of Harley 4431 would then be identical to fr. 606. On the other hand, fr. 606 is too regular in the last quire to have been copied from the sprawling sixth quire of Harley 4431. A more likely hypothesis is that the design of both manuscripts follows a maquette. As Jonathan Alexander observes, "[F]or more complex, lengthy, and financially burdensome projects, such as making an illuminated manuscript with new or different cycles of illustrations, which might number tens or even hundreds of miniatures, there had to be a plan. This may very often have consisted of a 'maquette,' a rough copy, perhaps on paper not parchment, which functioned as guide to both scribe and illuminator."[67] The striking similarities in page design despite the divergence in the final quire suggest that, though neither manuscript may be a copy of the other, the two are twin manuscripts.[68]

The visual program of the *Othea* in the Duke's manuscript is the work of three artists whom Millard Meiss identifies as the Epître Master, the Saffron Master, and the Egerton Master.[69] Meiss attributes the *Othea* miniatures in the Queen's manuscript to the Cité des dames Master and his workshop.[70] Both of these manuscripts follow the double-column format found in versions of the *Othea* produced for collections, and within this double-column format most of the miniatures are emphatically higher than they are wide. Such verticality may be exploited in different ways. Some miniatures feature a god or goddess enthroned in the sky of the upper portion and humans on earth below, resulting in a hieratically ordered composition; other miniatures treat the lower portion of the miniature as foreground and the upper part as background, thereby creating the illusion of spatial depth; and yet others create a continuously receding space and situate the figures within it.[71] Although the visual programs of the *Othea* in both the Duke's and the Queen's manuscripts closely resemble one another both compositionally and iconographically, they are quite distinct in style and palette. Fr. 606 exhibits a rather limited palette that includes few greens and depends on neutral colors but displays a wide tonal range that emphasizes the lighter shades. Though the skies in fr. 606 are illusionistic, the architectural settings betray the artists' lack of facility in creating the perspectival illusion of the third dimension. Individual figures in a composition tend not to overlap; placed side by side, they spread across the surface rather than occupy the space. As a result, interactions among the figures sometimes appear forced or awkward, as though the artist had not transcended the sketches in the maquette. In general, the delicate use of line results in finely detailed faces and hands, richly decorative surfaces, and patterned draperies. By contrast to fr. 606, almost all of the backgrounds in Harley 4431 are diapered in a variety of patterns dominated by blue, pink, and gold. The colors in this manuscript tend to be highly saturated, and consequently the images seem bold, so that gestures read very clearly, in part due to the strong line. Intuitive understanding of perspective results in convincingly three-dimensional boxes of space, within which figures interact dynamically. The bright reflections of the diapered backgrounds create an optical effect; against such background the illusionistic groups of figures almost appear to move.

The luminous visual programs of the Duke's and the Queen's manuscripts emerge from a world system of production and trade. Europe's location as a central node in global trade networks underlies the ideologies of medieval colonialisms, and manuscript illumination in a text such as Christine's *Othea* exemplifies the fetishlike products of western European imperialisms. New applications of pigment account for the palettes of Parisian manuscripts from 1380 onwards.[72] The generous use of gold and the intensity of blues and reds in particular mark a departure from earlier practice.[73] Since France—and western Europe in general—is poor in mineral deposits, the raw materials required to produce these pigments were imported, often from great distances, as part of a precolonizing network of economic relationships. Lapis lazuli, the mineral that was processed to produce ultramarine blue—a dominant color in some sections of the Duke's and the Queen's manuscripts—was mined in Asia, specifically in the part of Asia that is today Afghanistan. Since there were no operative gold mines in Europe during the Middle Ages, gold was imported from sub-Saharan Africa.[74] The Marxist notion of the fetish characterizes such a displacement of the commodity from the means of production: the commodity becomes a fetish precisely because it appears to be disconnected from labor. Although manuscript painting in this period depends entirely on extensive European trade with Asia and Africa, the final commodity completely disavows the global interdependence behind its mode of production. As commodity-fetishes, the Duke's and the Queen's manuscripts testify to Europe's location at the core of a world system of trade relations that prefigure the power relations of European expansionism in the early modern era.

As compellingly beautiful collections of images, the copies of the *Othea* in the Duke's and the Queen's manuscripts also display the qualities of the fetish as understood in psychoanalytic terms. These manuscripts offer rich scenarios for an analysis of sexuality and desire, identity and emotion, violence and subjectivity. As a beautiful object upon which to gaze, the illustrated *Othea* offers a range of aesthetic experiences, yet the text throughout attempts to render the aesthetic claims of the image in an ethical context.[75] It is this intersection between ethics and aesthetics that provides the focus for our study of the *Othea*. In our initial chapter we explore the cinematic structures of early art historical inquiry in order to suggest how modern scholars might realign their theoretical gaze in order to appreciate a text such as the *Othea*, a text that defies the voyeuristic mastery of the iconographic method made popular by Erwin Panofsky. In chapter 2 we demonstrate how the *Othea* works to discipline the gaze of the knightly male reader, whether Hector the addressee or his implied counterpart. As such it specifically intervenes in the text-image economy of the *Roman de la rose* and purposely deploys images to construct an alternative to the masculine subject positions created by the *Rose*. In the mid–fifteenth century the *Othea* was repeatedly copied for the Burgundian court, where the visual program underwent revision and the conception of masculinity becomes more normative in response to Burgundian culture. Chapter 3 considers how the *Othea* visually recasts mythical material drawn from the *Ovide moralisé* in order to queer the contemporary construction of sexualities. In its engagement with Ovidian myth, the *Othea* evokes knowledge about the past to critique contemporary constructions of sexuality. Chapter 4 addresses the representation of violence in historical traditions. The unfolding of history in the tradition of historical texts known as the *Histoire ancienne* was central to the royal identity of the Valois court. The *Othea* screens this history as a lesson in knightly conduct and military strategy through a visual critique of the engendering of violence. Chapter 5 examines how the eloquence of gesture in the visual program enhances the rhetorical efficacy of the *Othea*, especially in response to the visual programs of *Des cleres et nobles femmes,* the early-fifteenth-century French translation of Boccaccio's *De claris mulieribus*. In an afterword, we briefly trace the reception of the *Othea* in Burgundian court culture of the second half of the fifteenth century and in the printing houses of early-sixteenth-century Paris.

With few notable exceptions, the visuality of the *Othea* has long eluded the gaze of scholars,[76] and the complex performance of its visual and textual culture has been largely illegible. This is partly due to what Leo Steinberg would call the "textism" of literary and manuscript studies,[77] but it is also a consequence of the relation of art history to the visual regimes of the twentieth century. In order to develop a methodology responsive to the visual qualities of the *Othea*, our first chapter examines the visual regimes of the early twentieth century. Throughout the century, the production of knowledge in art historical discourse was shaped by various visual technologies such as slide projection, photographs, microfilm, microfiche, and even photocopying. The dominant visual technology of the century, however, was cinema, although the role of the cinematic experience in the formation of art history is seldom acknowledged. Yet the various methodologies of early-twentieth-century art history—particularly Aby Warburg's iconology and Erwin Panofsky's iconography—result directly from the cinematic structuring of knowledge in twentieth-century scholarship. The *Othea* demands that the reader respond to the contingent quality of images, always reading them against other images. The montage arrangement of the *Othea* refuses voyeurism and constructs a spectator who must forgo visual mastery. As we shall see, it is Warburg's *Mnemosyne,* not Panofsky's iconography, that offers the most productive methodology for an analysis of the montage structure of the *Othea*.

Fig. 1.1. Mercury and his children, *Epistre Othea*, BL, Harley 4431, fol. 102r.
(By permission of the British Library.) ☙

THE CINEMATIC EXPERIENCE

Iconography in the Age of
Mechanical Reproduction

> Montage is not only the means of *recreating the image* of an object
> or phenomenon *in general*. . . . Only montage is capable of pro-
> ducing a purposeful image.
> —S. M. Eisenstein, *Towards a Theory of Montage*

Despite the popularity of Christine de Pizan's *Epistre Othea* in the fifteenth and
sixteenth century, its use of classical subject matter in the absence of classical
form meant that it would be undervalued by twentieth-century historians of
medieval art. Erwin Panofsky and Fritz Saxl, for instance, established a hierarchy in which the "best" art was classical art—that which united classical form
with classical content—the next best employed classical form without classical
content, and the least valued used medieval form to convey classical content. In
their 1933 essay, "Classical Mythology in Mediaeval Art," they construct themselves as spectators, watching the historical reel of the classical tradition unroll
in a predictable cinematic plot:

> [I]n the period generally referred to as the high Middle Ages, the illu-
> minators ceased their faithful imitation of classical models and developed
> a new and independent manner of seeing things. Transforming the an-
> cient prototypes in such a way that they became almost unrecognizable,

they decomposed the representational tradition of mythological figures. Figures which were meant to represent Orion or Andromeda no
longer looked like the Orion or Andromeda of classical times. Thus,
like the unfortunate lovers in a moving picture who await their reunion,
classical subject matter and classical form were separated.[1]

This cinematic analogy casts the Middle Ages as the villain who obstructs the
desired reunion of the pair that Panofsky and Saxl liken to the "unfortunate
lovers in a moving picture," classical subject matter and classical form. Panofsky
and Saxl's movie has a happy ending in the return to "representational tradition," an ending that privileges the Renaissance for its reintegration of classical
subject matter and classical form.[2] But what if we interrogate the conditions
of the visible within this cinematic experience? What are the cultural norms
implicit in this moving picture? To pose these questions is to take Panofsky and
Saxl's reference to a moving picture as more than an analogy and to thereby
inquire how the experience of early-twentieth-century cinema shaped their understanding of visual cultures.

Panofsky and Saxl describe medieval representations such as the *Othea* in
the language of destruction, deprivation, and decomposition.[3] These judgments
betray a Eurocentric and orientalist perspective that was standard for their time.
Such a perspective is evident, for example, when they describe an astrological
image of Hercules as "a peculiarly degenerate descendant of the widespread
Western tradition,"[4] or when they observe that such "degenerate Western types
persisted and sometimes . . . interbred with Oriental types."[5] In his influential
study of classical mythology in medieval culture, originally published by the
Warburg Institute in 1940, Jean Seznec articulates a similar hierarchy of values:
"Italian art of the fifteenth and sixteenth centuries invests the ancient symbols
with fresh beauty."[6] To privilege the Renaissance in this way is to reify both the
ancient and Renaissance worlds as pure, uncontaminated cultures. In this model,
classical Greece and Rome are seen as the high points of Western civilization,
against which the Middle Ages is measured and always found wanting. But a
text such as the *Othea*, which (in Panofsky and Saxl's terms) uses medieval form
to convey classical content, offers an instructive exercise in cultural hybridity
and, as such, challenges the assumption that Renaissance styles constitute the
privileged vehicle for classical subject matter.[7]

In their "moving picture," Panofsky and Saxl overlook the hybridity of
the visible. Their notion that the Renaissance revives classical content creates a
Eurocentric trajectory that allows early modern Europe to participate in the
perceived greatness of the classical Mediterranean world. However, the very
category of the classical Mediterranean world does not hold up under scrutiny:

much that is classed as Greek and Roman matter is actually drawn from the African and Asian cultures with which ancient Mediterranean cultures interacted. Nothing exemplifies this better than the discourse of astrology, a Late Antique episteme that conflated classical mythology, star study, and aspects of Eastern religions. Since the *Othea* recasts the visual and textual traditions of astrology as part of its mythic framework, scholarly response to the illustrated manuscripts of the *Othea* offers a case study in the politics of the visible within the cinematic regimes of early art history.

Panofsky's Gaze

For Erwin Panofsky, often called the "father of art history,"[8] early cinema, especially Hollywood cinema, set the conditions of the visible.[9] Panofsky frequented the cinema from 1905 when he was thirteen, and throughout his career he repeatedly used film to "think with" in his art historical writing.[10] His experience of the cinema helped to shape his formulation of iconography as an art historical methodology.[11] Panofsky's iconographic method—within which, for the purposes of this book, we include iconology—posits a historical subject whose memory is saturated with visual images that function within a semiotic system.[12] Iconography assumes that symbolic meaning assigned to images can and will be uniformly decoded within a culture; the task of the modern scholar is to rediscover these symbolic meanings by surveying enough examples to establish that a specific image recurs—a survey dependent on photography—and by finding literary sources that reveal its meaning.[13] The scholar traces the signification assigned to those images within a visual tradition. The elaboration of the iconographic method signaled a methodological shift in the study of visual cultures to a paradigm that capitalized on photographic and cinematic technologies and adopted their construction of the viewing subject.

Panofsky was a cinemagoer before he was an iconographer, and he interpreted premodern visual culture "as he was habituated to look on figures and narratives in films," Willibald Sauerländer observes.[14] In his single essay on cinema, the ludic paper "Style and Medium in the Motion Pictures" first published in 1936,[15] Panofsky considers the place of cinema in relation to the arts of the past and to his own culture.[16] Troubled by expressionist and abstract forms characteristic of modern art, Panofsky sees film instead as the legitimate heir of premodern art. The two forms—film and premodern art—share the representational quality essential for the application of his iconographic method.[17] Regine Prange explains, "Panofsky recognizes narrative film as the only legitimate descendant of traditional fine art primarily because it remains semiotic, illustrates speech and action through images, and thus allows iconographic decoding."[18] The semiotics of the medium depends on what he calls "movie iconography"—something that "from the outset informed the spectator about the basic facts and characters" (112). In addition, his essay displays an awareness of the power of film as visual discourse to shape the subjectivity of the viewer: "it is the movies that mold, more than any other single force, the opinions, the taste, the language, the dress, the behavior, and even the physical appearance of a public" (94). According to the most recent editor of "Style and Medium," Irving Lavin, this essay has been reprinted at least twenty-two times and is Panofsky's most popular work.[19] "Style and Medium" helped to shape early film theory and remains a silent inheritance in film studies.[20] This essay has been much less frequently acknowledged in art historical writing, perhaps due to the disciplinary exclusion of film theory from art history proper. As Thomas Y. Levin comments, there "has been—until only very recently—a virtually complete lack of serious scholarly work on Panofsky's film essay in the art historical secondary literature. While this is perhaps to some degree a function of art history's longstanding resistance to the cinema, the failure to engage an analysis of cinema from well within the art historical ranks is curious indeed."[21]

Panofsky's essay on film not only allows us to examine the role of the cinematic experience in the structures of art history, it also locates that experience in a historically specific contract between viewer and filmic image. In this respect, Panofsky's description of his early experiences of the cinema exemplifies how film activates "modes of embodied existence," in Vivian Sobchack's terms.[22] Drawing on his early filmgoing at the turn of the century in Berlin, Panofsky characterizes the moviegoer as an implicitly male consumer of "mildly pornographic" images who frequents "small," "dingy" and "faintly disreputable" "picture theaters" (93–94)—a coded reference to the cinema's location at the outer boundaries of bourgeois respectability. This description of "going to the movies" resonates strikingly with an experience Sigmund Freud describes in his attempt to define the "uncanny."[23] Freud narrates his experience of finding himself lost in the red-light district of an unfamiliar "provincial town in Italy" whose inhabitants took him for a potential client despite his conscious resistance to that construction of his identity. His very presence in that space implicitly defined him as a consumer of commodified sex. Panofsky's experience of cinema marks a similar encounter with the uncanny; yet whereas Freud flees the sexworkers and their district, eschewing "voyages of discovery,"[24] Panofsky enters the movie house and relishes "the unique and specific possibilities of the new medium" (96), a constitutive element of which, as he repeatedly emphasizes, is pornography. Early cinema, in its visual obsession with bodies in movement, put the female body on display to such a degree that "fetishism and voyeurism gained new importance and normality," as Linda Williams has shown.[25] Throughout "Style and Medium in the Motion Pictures," Panofsky claims that a "pornographic instinct" (95) is a central element in cinema; he notes that pornography is a "primordial archetype of film production" (96) and one of the "most important folkloristic elements" (104) of cinema. He thus unwittingly celebrates the historical moment that Williams has identified as the intersection of "science and perversion."[26] Panofsky's assertions regarding the pornographic contract in the cinematic experience have proven influential: thirty years later Stanley Cavell essentially repeats Panofsky's formulation when he writes that "the ontological conditions of the motion picture reveal it as inherently pornographic."[27]

For Panofsky, the social conditions of the cinema work to shape its aesthetic possibilities and limitations, as the following anecdote from "Style and Medium" illustrates: "I remember with great pleasure a French film of ca. 1900 wherein a seemingly but not really well-rounded lady as well as a seemingly but not really slender one were shown changing to bathing suits—an honest, straightforward *porcheria*" (95). The philological glee evident in Panofsky's choice of the Italian term *porcheria* in place of its English equivalent—filth or smut—gives a European flair to the enjoyment of "mild pornography" and serves to place it beyond critique. This comment also constructs an insider language for Panofsky's learned male audience while simultaneously displaying his elite training in philology.[28] Panofsky's identity as a philologist emerges from the educational environment of the all-boys Joachimsthal Gymnasium he attended during his adolescence; in a reminiscence he celebrates the homosocial ethos of his training in philology:

> The typical German "Gymnasialprofessor" is—or at least was in my time—a man of many shortcomings, now pompous, now shy, often neglectful of his appearance. . . . But though he was content to teach boys rather than university students, he was nearly always a scholar. The man who taught me Latin was a friend of Theodor Mommsen and one of the most respected Cicero specialists. The man who taught me Greek was the editor of the *Berliner Philologische Wochenschrift,* and I shall never forget the impression which this lovable pedant made on us boys of fifteen when he apologized for having overlooked the misplacement of a comma in a Plato passage.[29]

Panofsky evokes the study of classical philology as a "performance of masculinity,"[30] an elite same-sex educational training that authorizes his homosocial enjoyment of what he celebrates in film as "honest, straightforward *porcheria,*" a usage that objectifies the female body and expresses a distaste for female sexuality in the guise of appreciation. More significantly, Panofsky's insistent characterization of film as "mild pornography" can be read as a case study of pornography as a form of sex discrimination, a formulation of Catherine MacKinnon's that Frances Ferguson has extended to consider how pornography restricts access to "value-altering groups" when it "uses an image as a conspicuous expression of the difference between parties who view it."[31]

The visual dynamic celebrated by Panofsky for its potential to articulate a gendered and erotic experience of difference has a long history in the West; indeed, this dynamic is evident in early modern exercises in perspective. For instance, Albrecht Dürer's woodcut of a draftsman peering through a reticulated net at a reclining, nude female shows the erotic potential of perspective as a methodology (fig. 1.2).[32] A woodcut illustration in Dürer's instructional manual, *A Course in the Art of Measurement with Compass and Ruler (Underweysung der Messung mit dem Zirckel und Richtscheyt)*, occurs in a section that describes devices for rendering a three-dimensional form accurately on a two-dimensional surface. Of the two woodcuts on one page, the first depicts the use of a glass plate apparatus and the second introduces a mechanical drawing aid originally described by Leon Battista Alberti and recommended by Leonardo da Vinci. In the upper woodcut, the draftsman is tethered to the wall by the string attached to his sighting device, which he must hold in position with his left hand. Because the glass plate provides the surface for inscription, his range is further limited by the length of his right arm. In the woodcut, the artist's cramped position is emphasized by the crowding of artist, apparatus, and the object being drawn, a ewer, all into the left half of the illustration.

By contrast, in the lower woodcut, the male artist sits comfortably, his arms resting on the table as he renders a perspectivally correct drawing of a woman who lies before him nearly naked, a swathe of drapery loosely folded over one thigh. The expansive space is equally divided between the artist and the model; two wide windows offer vistas onto a natural landscape. The frame of the reticulated net, which allows the artist to accurately portray the woman, also establishes his distance from the nude model.[33] The text between the two woodcuts describes the features of this apparatus; it emphasizes that the artist should arrange the model's body and then sight through the apparatus to be sure that the pose suits him: "arrange the body in a way that pleases you, so that it lies correctly according to your desire" [besich das Corpus wie es dir gefall / und ob es recht nach deinem willen lig]. The gendered representation of male artist/female nude in the lower woodcut emphasizes the scientific possibilities of the reticulated net by contrast to the glass apparatus above. Under the aegis

Item noch ein anderen brauch zu Conterfeten/dardurch man eyn yclichs Corpus mag grösser oder kleyner abconterfeten wie vil man wil/deshalben nutzlicher dañ mit dem glas darumb das es freier ist/ Darzu soll man haben ein ram mit einem gitter von starckem schwartzen zwirn gemacht/die lucken oder fierungen eine ongeferlich zweyer finger breyt/ Darnach soll man haben ein absehen oben zugespitzt/ also gemacht/ das man es höher oder niderer richten mag/ das bedeut das aug mit dem .o. Darnach leg hinaus in zimlicher weitten dz corpus so du conterfeten wilt/ rucks vnd peugs nach deinem willen/vñ gee als weg hinderstich vnd hab dein aug zu dem absehen.o. negst daran/vnd besich das Corpus wie es dir gefall/ vñ ob es recht nach deinem willen lig/ Darnach stell dz gitter oder ram zwischen dem Corpus vnd deinem absehen also/ wilt du wenig lucken oder fierungen begreiffen/so ruck es dest neher zu dem Corpus/darnach besich wie vil dz corpus im gitter lucken begreuf nach leng vñ breyten/ darnach reiß ein gitter gros oder klein auf ein bappir oder tafel darein du conterfeten wilt/ vnd sich hin vber dein aug.o. des spitz am absehen auf das Corpus/ vnd was du in oder fierung des gitters findest/ das drag in dein gitter das du auf dem bappir hast das ist gut vnd gerecht/ Wilt du aber für das spitzig absehen ein löchle machen/dardurch du sihest ist eben so gut/solcher meynung hab ich hernach ein form aufgerissen.

Fig. 1.2. Albrecht Dürer, "Draftsman Drawing a Vase; Draftsman Drawing a Reclining Nude," ca. 1527, *Underweysung der Messung mit dem Zirckel und Richtscheyt*. . . . (Washington, D.C., Library of Congress.) ✤

of perspective, the artist achieves a distance from the model that makes him at once an "objective" observer and a voyeur.

Charles Musser has contextualized cinema as a form of "screen practice"; this aspect of cinema has long been thought to have essentially evolved from perspective.[34] In his attempts to define cinema André Bazin states that "the decisive moment undoubtedly came with the discovery of the first scientific and already, in a sense, mechanical system of reproduction, namely, perspective: the camera obscura of Da Vinci foreshadowed the camera of Niepce."[35] Carl Landauer points to perspective as a critical category for Panofsky, who "defined the Renaissance by its own invention, the development of visual perspective in the arts."[36] In his discourse on film, Panofsky situates himself as an embodied male spectator, much like the draftsman in Dürer's woodcut. For example, in order to illustrate iconographic types in film narrative, he is given to assertions that identify the female by her possible sexual roles in the patriarchal economy: "the Family Man could not but yield, however temporarily, to the temptations of the Vamp."[37] The moviegoer, constructed to identify with the Family Man, yields to the seductions of film. As Panofsky indirectly reveals, the consumption of the visual in the cinematic space is simultaneously the consumption of a commodified sexuality: as "commercial art" the cinema is "always in danger of ending up as a prostitute."[38] Panofsky sees the moviegoer as a male heterosexual consumer of gendered and erotic images;[39] his understanding of film does not allow for a spectatorship outside of the regime of heterosexual perspective.[40]

In his jubilant approach, Panofsky sees cinema as plenitude;[41] by comparison, Walter Benjamin's anxious essay, "The Work of Art in the Age of Mechanical Reproduction," meditates on cinema as lack and loss.[42] Unlike Panofsky, Benjamin laments the technological advances in photography and film that made the age of cinema possible:

> Around 1900 technical reproduction had reached a standard that . . . permitted it to reproduce all transmitted works of art and thus to cause the most profound change in their impact upon the public; it had also captured a place of its own among the artistic processes.[43]

Benjamin's politically motivated resistance to mechanical reproduction exposes the extent to which Panofsky was shaped by such technologies, specifically the electric light lantern—the precursor to the modern slide projector. Like cinema, the electric light lantern depends on projection for its effect. In fact, early screen practice juxtaposed the two technologies since magic-lantern shows often accompanied early film showings.[44] In addition, in the early days before sound, film and lantern shows were explicated by a "lecturer" who instructed the early cinema audience how to interpret the projected images.[45] Thus the early art historical lecture would have been almost indistinguishable from the experience of going to the movies at the time.

The technological potential of photography and slide projection was available to Panofsky at a formative moment in his career as an iconographer, due to his association with the Kulturwissenschaftliche Bibliothek Warburg in Hamburg.[46] Shortly after Panofsky's appointment as a privatdozent at the University of Hamburg in 1920, he became closely affiliated with both this library and Aby Warburg's projects.[47] In pursuit of the "afterlife of antiquity" [das Nachleben der Antike], Warburg had established a vast and idiosyncratic library on topics ranging from astrology to the zodiac, which became the most important collection on visual materials in the context of European culture.[48] From the very start, photographs and lantern slides formed a significant component of the Warburg enterprise,[49] and they became increasingly central to the project as time went on.[50] At the time of its move to London in 1933 the photographic collection included approximately twelve thousand lantern slides.[51]

Warburg himself was a pioneer in exploiting the technology of slide projection for art history. In 1912, he attended the Tenth International Congress of Art History to deliver a plenary lecture on the Schifanoia frescoes; William Heckscher reports that in this lecture Warburg projected a color slide by means of a magic lantern, the first use of color slide technology in "a serious art historical discourse," and he comments on the effect: "As if by magic, the work of art was drawn into the lecture room."[52] In the conclusion to his plenary address Warburg himself acknowledges the cinematic quality of his methodology: "My fellow students: I need hardly say that this lecture has not been about solving a pictorial riddle for its own sake—especially since it cannot here be illuminated at leisure, but only caught in a cinematographic spotlight."[53] In characteristically condensed language, he refers both to the brevity of his lecture, which has passed by as quickly as the frames of a moving picture, and to the quick viewing of the projected slide, a substitute for the original, which could be lighted and studied at length. Heckscher identifies this lecture as the originary moment of iconology. Warburg's interests in the projection of images and in iconological analysis were completely interdependent; from the beginning iconology relies on a cinematic technology.[54]

In this 1912 paper, Warburg applied his method to the puzzling imagery of the Schifanoia frescoes in Ferrara, which represent the months of the year. He found the key to interpreting the middle zone of the frescoes in what he believed was the "twofold medieval tradition of the imagery of the ancient gods. This is source material whereby we may trace the influence both of a systematic Olympian theology—as transmitted by the learned mythographers of medieval

Western Europe—and of an astral theology, preserved intact in the words and images of practical astrology."[55] Throughout the essay, Warburg apologizes that astrology has turned out to be the interpretative key to the frescoes, and he acknowledges his reluctance to "enter the shadowy nether regions of astral superstition."[56] Despite his uneasiness, his analysis demonstrates not only the critical role that astrology played in his interpretation, but also the cultural hybridity of astrology itself:

> The firmament as described by the Greeks was the base stratum with which the Egyptian cult system of decans was established; this, in turn, was overlaid by a layer of Indian mythological adaptation before finding its way, probably by way of Persia, into Arab culture. Clouded still further by translation into Hebrew and thence into French, the Grecian firmament found its way into Pietro d'Abano's Latin version of Abū Ma'šar and, ultimately, into the monumental cosmology of the Italian early Renaissance, in the form of those thirty-six mysterious figures in the middle register of the frescoes in Ferrara.[57]

Almost despite himself, Warburg is forced to conclude that astrology, an "Oriental" rather than Western discourse, functioned as the conduit for the visual survival of the Greek deities.[58] In addition, Warburg's central premise that medieval and Renaissance astrology preserves traces of antiquity misrepresents the medieval reception of classical culture. As Hans Robert Jauss would argue, the medieval period did not preserve the Greek deities as pagan figures, but rather produced a "remythization" of antique models.[59] The Warburg project, in its focus on "the afterlife of antiquity," whether in Warburg's own writings, in the library's acquisition policies, or in its institutional identity, reveals the difficulty of sustaining the Eurocentric bias of its own workings. Indeed, as Giorgio Agamben comments on the Warburg project, "[T]he humanistic restoration of Antiquity was a restoration not of classical Antiquity but of the culture of late Antiquity, in particular of the culture of Neoplatonism and Hermeticism."[60] Panofsky, however, appears to have absorbed the Eurocentric vision of the Warburg project without the contradictions and qualifications by which Warburg himself seems to have always been troubled.[61]

Panofsky's gaze, less troubled than Warburg's, aligned such Eurocentrism with the magisterial possibilities offered by cinematic technologies. Shortly after Panofsky came to the Warburg Library, Fritz Saxl delivered an inaugural lecture that set out to explicate Warburg's iconological method in visual terms; Saxl was ostensibly speaking for Warburg, who had suffered a breakdown due to mental stress and was hospitalized. Saxl articulated the central problem of

Warburg's research as, "What did antiquity mean for people of the early Renaissance?"[62] To make an argument about the survival of antique models through the Middle Ages to the Renaissance Schifanoia frescoes (the subject of Warburg's lecture at the Rome Congress a decade earlier), Saxl used lantern slides that are still to be found in the Warburg collection. When we situate Panofsky in that room, we see how, at a particular historical moment, iconography originally authorized a particularly gendered form of embodied viewer. The published version of this lecture, which appeared in volume 1 of the *Vorträge der Bibliothek Warburg*, includes plates that match the images used in the slide lecture. Saxl projected a series of representations of mythological and biblical women in order to illustrate the disappearance and return of classicizing form (figs. 1.3, 1.4), culminating in the satisfying reunion in the Renaissance of classical style and subject matter. Images of the female body are the vehicle for the demonstration, a choice that constructs the audience as male participants in a scopic economy. As a transcript of a performance, the published lecture recalls the darkened room with its cone of light from the magic lantern and the projected images of female bodies in various stages of undress; it demonstrates the voyeuristic potential of iconography within a heterosexual, cinematic regime.[63]

If the cinematic experience of the slide presentation was a shaping principle of the Warburg project, the collection and display of photographs was a central discourse for Warburg's own methodology. By the middle of the 1920s, in the years when Panofsky was associated with the Warburg Library, the photographic archive had become the single most important aspect of the library's work. As Ernst Gombrich relates, when Warburg returned to his library in 1924 after six years in mental institutions, Saxl greeted his employer with a new visual aid:

> He had welcomed Warburg on his return with a display of . . . photographs of works of art which had figured in Warburg's researches, eagerly counting on the impact of such a panorama on the scholar eager to take up the threads of his work. Large but light wooden frames over which black hessian was stretched served as a background to photographs suspended on the cloth by light clips. Warburg, it seems, immediately responded and used this tool to assemble such motifs as had engaged his interest. Moreover, in the new public role which the library had assumed, this method was a welcome aid in explaining the scope and purpose of the library's research. . . . [T]he project in which Warburg's life work was intended to culminate grew out of this technique.[64]

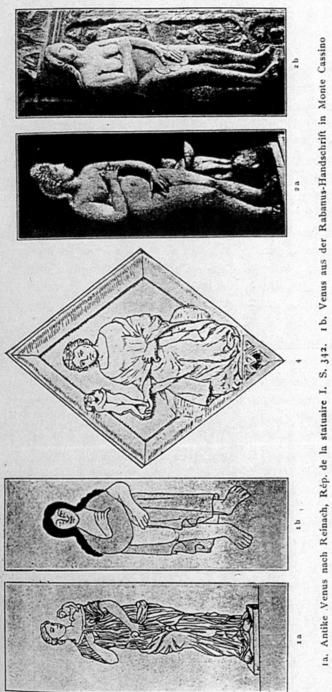

1a. Antike Venus nach Reinach, Rép. de la statuaire I. S. 342.   1b. Venus aus der Rabanus-Handschrift in Monte Cassino

2a. Antike Venus aus Lucera.   2b. Eva vom Dom von Traù

4. Venus vom Campanile in Florenz

Fig. 1.3. The survival of antiquity as illustrated in representations of the female form, in Fritz Saxl, "Die Bibliothek Warburg und Ihr Ziel," *Vorträge der Bibliothek Warburg* 1 (1921–22), pl. 1. (Copyright The Warburg Institute, University of London.) ☙

3. Venus und der Liebende. Miniatur aus dem Rosen-Roman

6. Raffael. Drei Grazien (Chantilly, Musée Condée)

Fig. 1.4. The survival of antiquity as illustrated in representations of the female form, in Fritz Saxl, "Die Bibliothek Warburg und Ihr Ziel," *Vorträge der Bibliothek Warburg* 1 (1921–22), pl. 2. (Copyright The Warburg Institute, University of London.)

Kurt Forster points out that such a methodological device resulted in "montages of images" Warburg collectively called *Mnemosyne*. The possibilities offered by this process so captivated Warburg that his research from then on depended on his ability to continually rearrange groupings of photographs.[65] This approach enabled a cinematic vision; Agamben comments that

> the atlas *Mnemosyne* that he left incomplete and that consists of almost a thousand photographs is not an immovable repertoire of images but rather a representation in virtual movement of Western humanity's gestures from classical Greece to Fascism (in other words, something that is closer to De Jorio than Panofsky). Inside each section, the single images should be considered more as film stills than as autonomous realities.[66]

In its formal arrangement and its emphasis on gesture, Warburg's *Mnemosyne* exemplifies what Eisenstein terms the "general principle of montage" that requires the "creativity of the spectator."[67] A photograph of a page entitled "The Nymphs" from the picture atlas (fig. 1.5) illustrates the visual dynamics inherent in this method. Warburg focused on the swiftly moving female figure as a vehicle for a specifically Renaissance recovery of ancient grace and movement; as he puts it in his lecture on the Schifanoia frescoes: "From the tight Burgundian cocoon springs the Florentine butterfly, the 'nymph,' decked in the winged headdress and fluttering skirts of the Greek maenad or of the Roman Victoria."[68]

In his history of the German years of the Warburg Library, Karl Landauer notes that Warburg was obsessed with the nymph from the time he was a student.[69] Although Warburg's interest shows traces of eroticism, he repeatedly seeks an intellectual paradigm within which to study his fluttering nymph. As he writes to his fellow student André Jolles, "You feel prompted to follow her like a winged idea through all the spheres in a Platonic frenzy of love; I feel compelled to turn my philologian's gaze to the ground from which she rose and to ask with surprise: 'Is this strangely delicate plant really rooted in the sober Florentine soil?'"[70] With his philologian's gaze Warburg arranged photographs of artistic representations of "nympha" to create one montage page of his *Mnemosyne* in which the nymph becomes a vehicle for his exploration of the connection between represented motion and implicit emotion. *Mnemosyne* constructs a disembodied viewer ultimately concerned not with viewing but with culture, what Agamben terms "the incessant symbolic work of social memory."[71] By contrast, the cinematic slide show of Saxl's lecture appears to construct a corporealized male spectator.

Fig. 1.5. "The Nymphs," Warburg's *Mnemosyne*, panel 46. (Copyright The Warburg Institute, University of London.) ❧

At his death in 1929, Warburg left behind forty screens filled with photographs,[72] as well as at least one hundred lantern slides recording varied arrangements of photographs on these screens to be projected in lectures.[73] This methodology allowed Warburg to manipulate a vast amount of visual material without ultimately claiming the mastery of any one authoritative arrangement.[74] Warburg relied on photographic technology to capture a variety of arrangements, and he employed slide projection to choreograph these arrangements for viewing. The lack of closure in Warburg's late research ultimately disavows the voyeuristic mastery offered by photographic spectatorship.[75] It would appear that Panofsky absorbed the Warburgian method of working with a massive amount of visual material in a format that allows for flexible juxtaposition and projection of images; Panofsky, however, exploited photography to achieve the critical closure that eluded Warburg.

Although scholars acknowledge the role of photography in late-twentieth-century art history, its importance to the formation of the discipline and especially to iconography is fundamental. As Barbara Savedoff observes with regard to "the New Art History":

> These approaches allow scholars and critics to concentrate on those properties of artworks (such as representational content and compositional relations) which can be transmitted by photographs and to neglect those which cannot. These approaches are not only fostered by research practices which have come to depend more and more on photographs, they are well suited to a readership which is often wholly dependent on photographs for its knowledge of the works discussed.[76]

Far from being restricted to current or contemporary scholarship, this observation holds true as well for a foundational discourse such as iconography.

From its inception, iconography as a methodology was "wholly dependent on photographs" for juxtaposing representational content in order to allow scholars to find relationships that became the basis for a trajectory of a tradition. Michael Ann Holly paraphrases a lighthearted comment in one of Panofsky's unpublished letters: "everybody knows that iconology can be done when there are no originals to look at and nothing but artificial light to work in."[77] Panofsky used photographs to juxtapose objects in a way that emphasizes their similarity in composition and content while erasing their difference in size and medium, and he subjects to one disciplinary view artifacts that in their original contexts were shaped for distinctly different kinds of viewing. For example, in his essay "Blind Cupid," Panofsky demonstrates a particular visual tradition of Cupid from the classical period to the baroque through the use of thirty-nine black-and-white photographs.[78] The media of the originals include ivory, manuscript illustration, woodcut, engraving, architectural sculpture, tapestry, wall painting, panel painting, and mosaic. In its original medium and as an individual artifact, each of these offers a highly distinctive sensorial experience. The photographs in an essay such as "Blind Cupid" reduce such difference to sameness both in scale and in tonal range; further, through careful selection, Panofsky restricts our vision to the details he isolates as relevant. His argument in this essay does not rest on historicist relations between the images; rather photography allows him to discover or invent an iconographic tradition.[79]

Modern art historians follow Panofsky's lead in their reliance on photography, and they likewise exploit the cinematic experience of spectatorship that he celebrated in "Style and Medium." Whether in the classroom, the lecture hall, or the conference session, the privileged mode of communication is the slide presentation,[80] which captivates and focuses an audience and disciplines its gaze. As Donald Preziosi puts it: "Modern art history has been a supremely cinematic practice. . . . The art history slide is always orchestrated as a still in a historical movie."[81] This captivating quality of the slide presentation depends upon the aura that Kaja Silverman attributes to film when she emphasizes "the illumination of the screen and the darkness of the auditorium. . . . [T]he beam of light through which filmic images are conveyed to us is more than a practical necessity; it also imparts to those images a pulsatile and dazzling quality which photographs conventionally lack, a quality which is perhaps irreducibly 'auratic.'"[82] Film theorists identify projection as the constitutive quality of the cinematic experience. As Gerald Mast defined cinema more than twenty years ago:

> An essential condition of the cinema experience is viewing flickering light in an enveloping darkness. This piercing of darkness by projected light is the source of cinema's hypnotic power. . . . We both sit in darkness and are bathed in light; the experience is both private and public at the same time; the projected images both speak to our personal dreams and fantasies and seem to depict the most public and familiar realities.[83]

In its performative modes, art history depends on the aura of slide presentation in order to create the subjectivities the discipline requires.

Benjamin insists that "the original" has "authenticity," an "aura," that "withers" in the age of mechanical reproduction. This aura powerfully directs attention to questions of physical condition and provenance, both of which enhance the "authority" of the original. But in order to study artifacts in Panofsky's comparative method, the compelling "aura" of the original has to be deleted, that is to "wither." Only when the "quality of its presence is . . . depreciated" is it possible to study an artifact analytically. But in presenting the results of such research, art historians, following the lead of Warburg and Panofsky, employ the "dazzling quality" of the slide show to create an experience for the audience that is, as Kaja Silverman might say, "irreducibly 'auratic.'" It is now the projection of the mechanical reproduction, not the object, that has the aura. Benjamin complains that the photograph removes the work of art from a functional context within a specific culture: "The technique of reproduction detaches the reproduced object from the domain of tradition."[84] Similarly, the iconographic method, following Warburg's lead and Panofsky's contribution to North American art history, relies upon the technique of reproduction to extract and collect images that propel a vision of continuity between the classical past and the European present.[85] This Warburgian goal is especially evident in the article by Panofsky and Saxl (researched in the Warburg before they left Hamburg) entitled "Classical Mythology in Mediaeval Art." In this article, written in English just after Panofsky's move to North America, the sixty images are extracted from their original, highly diverse contexts and arranged so that they function as a Eurocentric narrative of the survival of the classical tradition. At its basis, the critical desire of iconology is to weave the visual material of the classical tradition into a unified fabric.

Mechanical reproduction functions for Panofsky as a means of fulfilling that desire: photography allows him to remove images from their context and re-embed them in a narrative of the European visual tradition that only becomes visible, as Panofsky himself remarks, at a distance from Europe. Settled in North America and thereby freed from "deep-rooted emotions" connected to "national and regional bias" of European art historians, Panofsky comments, "the whole of Europe from Spain to the Eastern Mediterranean merged into one panorama the planes of which appeared at proper intervals and in equally sharp focus."[86] His relocation likewise enabled his writing on cinema. Sauerländer remarks that "the chaired professor [of] Art History in Hamburg had never written a line on cinema. It was only the 'second' Panofsky who—liberated from the fetters of German academic respectability—felt free to publish his famous paper on 'Style and Medium in the Moving Pictures.'"[87]

This essay was not, however, the only trace left by the cinemagoer in Panofsky's written work. As a scholar writing about manuscripts, he often sounds like a spectator in the cinema. For example, the chapter "French and Franco-Flemish Book Illumination in the Fourteenth Century" in *Early Netherlandish Painting* shows that lurking behind the iconographic method is a reader constructed by the images, a spectator-position, a spectatorship, that is evident in his writing on manuscripts:

With honest, straightforward veracity, Biblical events, legends of the saints—or, for that matter, scenes from Roman history—are staged in a bourgeois or rustic environment portrayed with a keen, observant eye for landscape features and such homely details as casually draped curtains, seats and couches with wooden overhangs shaped like diminutive barrel vaults, and crumpled bed clothes.[88]

This chapter ostensibly discusses style, yet its exuberant ekphrastic language constitutes a telling response to the captivating quality of the "dynamic contract" between reader and image. His description of book illumination could easily be mistaken for a description of a movie.

In "Style and Medium," Panofsky asserts, "It is the movies, and only the movies, that do justice to that materialistic interpretation of the universe which, whether we like it or not, pervades contemporary civilization."[89] Early cinema clearly shaped Panofsky and his methodology of iconography, and in developing a theoretical approach to the history of art, Panofsky assumed that a meaningful continuity existed between premodern visual culture and modern film.

Astrology, Iconography, and the Legibility of the Othea

Given the interests of Aby Warburg in "the afterlife of antiquity" through the medium of astrology, it is not surprising to find that photos of illustrations from Christine's *Othea* were acquired for his photo archive during Warburg's lifetime.[90] In fact, one of Warburg's *Mnemosyne* panels includes an illustration from a fifteenth-century Burgundian manuscript of the *Othea*.[91] Working in this archive on what would become "Classical Mythology in Mediaeval Art," Panofsky and Saxl identified the illustrated versions of the *Othea* as the first examples of the iconography known as the "Children of the Planets," the iconography over which Warburg had puzzled in his studies of the Schifanoia frescoes. For Panofsky and Saxl, Christine's use of the Children of the Planets offered the solution to a visual puzzle, but they failed to investigate Christine's intellectual milieu, in which knowledge of astrology circulated.

Christine assigned chapters 6 through 12 of her *Othea* to the planetary deities—Jupiter, Venus, Saturn, Phoebus Apollo, Phebe/Moon, Mars, and Mercury. The images in these chapters bear a highly specific relationship to one particular tradition of illustrated Latin astrological treatises based on Georgius Fendulus's translation of Abū Maʿšar's authoritative text on astrology.[92] A manuscript version of one of these treatises entered the duke of Berry's collection on 7 June 1403, as a gift from Lubertus Hautschild, abbot of an Augustinian abbey in Bruges and Berry's official counselor. This early-fifteenth-century Flemish manuscript, now PML, M. 785, is a copy of a fourteenth-century Italian manuscript, now BL, Sloane 3983, itself a copy of an early-thirteenth-century Italian manuscript, BnF, lat. 7330.[93] This tradition is distinguished by a sequence on the seven planetary deities that appears to be unique in Western astrological traditions; this representation of the planetary deities draws on the topos of medieval representations of earthly rulers to visualize each planet as a ruler in the sky.

Each planetary deity appears in four separate images, each of which represents a specific position of the planet in the sky. As the planets move along the ecliptic, they pass through twelve constellations, the signs of the zodiac. According to astrological lore, each planet gains particular powers from two constellations specific to it, called its day and night houses *(domus* or *domicilia),* and the influence of these powers on earthly events is intensified when the planet is in the relevant house. Miniatures in lat. 7330 and its copies represent this relationship by showing the personified planet frontally enthroned and flanked by the two signs of the zodiac that signify its day and night houses. When the planet passes through the two constellations opposite its day and night houses on the ecliptic, its counterhouses *(oppositiones* or *contrarietates),* the powers of the day and night houses become their opposites. To visualize a planet in its counterhouse, the miniaturists painted the personified planet in a diagonal, falling position, as if toppling from the throne. At another specific point on the ecliptic each planet goes through its ascendancy *(exaltatio),* the point of its orbit at which its power outweighs all the other planets. A planet's ascendancy was represented by means of an enthroned planetary deity displaying as attributes those aspects of human life most strongly under the planet's influence. Opposite the position of ascendancy on the ecliptic is the position of least influence *(deiectio),* at which the planet's power to influence human affairs is minimal.

In both the Queen's and the Duke's manuscripts, the *Othea* depicts all seven planetary deities sitting, frontally posed, in the star-studded sky; this composition directly cites the visual astrological tradition of the ascendant phase of the planet's motion. In these two manuscripts, this section of the *Othea* is prefaced by a long rubric in purple, the language of which is highly indebted to astrological discourse. This rubric explains the visual conventions common to the group: "And it is to be understood that because the seven planets in the sky are turning on the circles which are called zodiacs, the images of the seven planets are depicted here seated on circles" [Et est a savoir que pour ce que les .vij. planettes ou ciel sont tournans autour des cercles que on nomme zodiaques, sont les ymages des .vij. planettes ycy figurees assis sur cercles] (6.1–4). Emphasizing the astrological content of the representations, the rubric goes on to insist that the sky be filled with stars, a reference to the fixed stars interpreted as constellations and against which the planets move. As the rubric notes, the planets are turning on circles, a visual acknowledgment of the astrological understanding of planetary orbits (see figs. 1.1 and 2.10). The rubric for each planetary deity specifies the influence on humans exerted by that planet and states that this influence is depicted by the "children" of the planet situated on the ground below, who appropriately exhibit behaviors congruent with the influence of that planet.[94] The *texte* in Othea's voice below each image of a planetary deity and his or her children exhorts the reader/viewer either to resist the planet's influence or succumb to it, and the *glose* and *allegorie* describe the specific nature of the planet's influence and explain whether the knight/soul will suffer harm or improve himself under that influence.

For example, the *glose* to the chapter on Mercury, god of eloquence, states, "Mercury is the planet that exerts the influence of beautiful language embellished with rhetoric" [Mercurius est planette qui donne influence de beau lengage aourné de rethorique] (12.15–16). The rubric introducing the chapter stipulates that the planetary god holds a flower because "just as a flower is naturally pleasant to see, so language beautifully embellished is pleasing to hear" [ainsi comme la fleur naturellement plaist a veïr, aussi lengage bien aourné plaist a ouir] (12.3–4).[95] The full purse at Mercury's belt signifies the wealth that accrues from the use of beautiful language. In the miniature, Mercury, flower in hand, sits on a golden arc encircled by starry sky. A band of clouds separates the deity from his "children" below, that is, those humans especially under his influence because the planet Mercury in its ascendancy appears in their birth horoscopes.[96] The astrological tradition associates Mercury with eloquence, and Christine's *texte* urges the reader/viewer to follow Mercury's teachings.

The eloquence practiced by Mercury's children is visually encoded in a variety of distinctive gestures signaling that the seven men below are speaking together. In her *Livre du corps de policie*, written within a few years of the *Othea*, Christine describes eloquence as rhetoric and emphasizes the role that gestures play in rhetoric: "When eloquence is combined with gentle movement of the body, it affects the listeners in three ways: it affects the spirit of some and the ears of others, and it seduces and sweetens the eyes of others. Gestures affect the spirit" [quant grant eloquence est conduite par sage ordre avec le deu mouvement du corps, elle envaist les oyans par trois manieres. Car elle prent les couraiges des uns et les oreilles des autres, aux autres elle adoulcist et atendrist les yeulx. Elle envayst les couraiges] (1.26).[97] The gestures in the image are the visual equivalent of eloquence; the expressive white hands silhouetted against the strong colors of the speakers' garments attract the viewer's attention and serve as a reminder that eloquence will be gained by accepting Mercury's influence.

The astrological tradition represented in the *Othea* appears to have been illegible to Warburg, Saxl, or Panofsky. Warburg was working backward from the early modern Schifanoia frescoes, and although he correctly saw the Latin translations of Abū Maʿšar as their ultimate textual source, he mistakenly concluded that he had traced their visual sources to classical antiquity.[98] Panofsky and Saxl knew that the Arabic images of the planets did not derive from classical sources and did not influence medieval images; they were unaware of the visual tradition initiated by the *Liber astrologiae* of Georgius Fendulus that stands behind the planetary images in the *Othea*.[99] Working with the assumptions of iconography as a methodology, they identified sources for the "Children of the Planets" in Christian iconography: "it is obvious that the scheme of the composition has been assimilated to those of religious representations, such as the Last Judgment, some scenes from the Apocalypse, and the Descent of the Holy Ghost."[100] Panofsky and Saxl conclude their inquiry when they have identified this source: "Having been assimilated to a type that was familiar to the popular mind, this compositional scheme was universally accepted."[101] Although Christian formulas circulated as part of the visual language of the time, classical traditions and classical deities would be understood in humanist circles as part of a distinctly pre-Christian tradition. In addition, the iconographic method, especially when reduced to a source-hunting technique, too easily becomes the goal of the interpretive process. This approach to the *Othea* has a legacy in the work of several other scholars, who start from the position that the textual *allegories* represent the primary level of meaning and that this Christian meaning must therefore be visualized in the miniatures. In order to find it there, these scholars must assume a detailed knowledge of religious symbolism that is quite unlikely either on the part of Christine, the artists responsible for the miniatures, or fifteenth-century readers.[102]

What finally mattered to Panofsky and Saxl, however, was the recognition on the part of some artists that "it was incongruous to represent a classical deity, such as Mercury or Mars, in so non-classical a manner as was usual in late mediaeval illustrations" and that the "definitive reintegration of the genuine classical types" was on the way.[103] Their essay demonstrates the extent to which the iconological method is invested in tracing the specific trajectory of origin in classical antiquity, decline or misunderstanding in the Middle Ages, and full recovery in the Renaissance. Since the *Othea* does not preserve classical forms, its status as a conduit for astrological discourse is not visible within such methodologies.

For Christine, astrology was both a vehicle for allegoresis and a discourse in its own right. In her articulation of an iconography for the "Children of the Planets" in the rubrics to the chapters on the planetary deities, she validates the wisdom of astrology as a learned science. The miniatures offer a space to envision astrology as an authoritative discourse that the text can then manipulate.

The polysemous result offers us a view of astrology as a legitimate medieval doctrine, not an element of "the afterlife of antiquity." Although Warburg, Saxl, and Panofsky all acknowledged the importance of astrology, they failed to appreciate its medieval significance; they were likewise drawn to the illustrated manuscripts of the *Othea* but failed to understand the synthesis of mythology and astrology brought together in the allegorical program of a female author.[104]

The hybridity of astrology as a medieval discourse is difficult to ascertain within the Eurocentric bias of "the survival of antiquity" model that structured the Warburg Library.[105] Despite the richness of the resources for the study of illustration in manuscripts of the *Othea*, the Warburg Library authorized certain research trajectories that worked to limit the uses of those resources. The Warburg Institute, with its extensive publications on astrology, similarly positions the study of astrology within a Eurocentric paradigm. As one of several influential institutes established early in the twentieth century, the orientalism and Eurocentrism of the Warburg has left traces throughout twentieth-century thought.

Montage and iconography both owe their structures to the cinematic shaping of spectatorship that organized knowledge in the twentieth century. Warburg's methodological apparatus—his interest in the montage effect of the *Mnemosyne* project—has not had a marked influence on the study of visual cultures. Instead, Panofsky's articulation of iconography as a magisterial discourse has overshadowed Warburg's more decentered approach. Nonetheless, Warburg's *Mnemosyne* has the potential to undermine the claim to cultural trajectories of mastery, even those proposed by Warburg's own "survival of antiquity" model. Montage, in its refusal to authorize a linear argument in visual terms, offers a critical category for exploring the decentering possibilities of visual experience. In the case of a text-image montage such as the *Epistre Othea* in the Duke's and the Queen's manuscripts, the image along with the lapidary verse of the four-line *texte* defies the closure to which mythographic interpretation aspires.

The *Othea* is written and illustrated in a cultural context obsessed with the mythic and historical texts of antiquity. To the extent that these texts "survive" into the Middle Ages, they do so as texts that resist neat Christian categories. The enormous effort at remythization represented in a text such as the *Roman de la rose,* the *Ovide moralisé,* or even Boccaccio's *De claris mulieribus* points explicitly to the powerfully non-Christian character of classical myths. Especially in the visual experience of vernacular manuscript cultures, classical myths screen terrifying narratives of displacement, transgression, and transformation. In addition, these myths emerged from an entirely different sex-gender system than the late medieval Christian world of the *Othea*. The montage of mythic and historical texts in the *Othea* envisions the differences of this past in the present, so that new performances of masculinity and gender might be envisioned.

Fig. 2.1. Cupid and a young nobleman, *Epistre Othea*, BL, Harley 4431, fol. 117r.
(By permission of the British Library.) ❧

Constructing Masculinities

࿇

The above-mentioned ladies complain of the many clerks who
accuse them in prose and verse books, defaming their morals in
varied words; and they give these books as school texts to their
young, beginning students, by way of example and doctrine, to be
retained into adulthood.

[Si se plaignent les dessusdittes dames
De pluseurs clers qui sus leur mettent blasmes,
Dittiez en font, rimes, proses et vers,
En diffamant leurs meurs par moz divers;
Si les baillent en matiere aux premiers
A leurs nouveaulx et jeunes escolliers,
En maniere d'exemple et de dottrine,
Pour retenir en age tel dottrine.]
     —Christine de Pizan, *Epistre au dieu d'Amours,* ll. 259–66

In Christine's *Epistre au dieu d'Amours* (The God of Love's Letter, ca. 1399),
Cupid, the God of Love and king of lovers, addresses the noble and aristocratic
males of France.[1] Motivated by repeated complaints from women, Cupid dic-
tates a royal letter in which he banishes all disloyal lovers from his kingdom. In
both the Duke's and the Queen's manuscripts, the *Epistre au dieu d'Amours*
opens with a miniature in which Cupid hands his letter to the messenger kneeling before him (fig. 2.2). The winged Cupid holds the bow and arrows that identify him as God of Love. In his speech quoted above, Cupid traces misogynist
behavior to the misogyny espoused in the texts in the school curriculum, texts
boys read from their earliest days at school. Cupid speaks of masculinity as a

Fig. 2.2. Cupid sending his letter, frontispiece to *Epistre au dieu d'Amours*, BL, Harley 4431, fol. 53r. (By permission of the British Library.) ❧

construct specifically created by pedagogical practices: the schoolboy, tutored through the effective deployment of exempla and authoritative doctrines, is persuaded to think the worst of women. Cupid laments that the young male student who absorbs such purposeful training retains his scornful disregard for women into adulthood, when he will slander and betray them: Cupid thus connects the reading of misogynist texts with the performance of a misogynist masculinity.

Among the offending schooltexts, Cupid singles out Ovid's *Remedia amoris*:

Clerks are taught this book from their earliest youth, in their beginning grammar classes, and they teach it to others, so that none will undertake to love a woman.

[Si ont les clers apris trés leur enfance
Cellui livret en premiere science
De gramaire, et aux autres l'aprenent
A celle fin qu'a femme amer n'emprenent.]
(291–94)

Having pointedly criticized Ovid, Cupid extends his critique to Jean de Meun as though this French vernacular poet enjoyed the same privileged authority as Ovid. In a passage rich in rhetorical indignation, Cupid characterizes the *Roman de la rose* as an excessively elaborate exercise for the deception of women, whose supposed frailty and weakness should require no such stratagems. According to Cupid's exposition, the rhetoric of the *Rose* undermines its putative point and proves the converse: the enormous effort needed to seduce women shows that they are more resistant to flattery and seductive guile than the misogynist tradition would have it. Christine's poem thus characterizes the *Roman de la rose* as an authoritative vernacular text responsible for the dissemination of both classical and clerical misogyny to a courtly audience.[2]

Between the writing of the text of the *Othea* in 1400 and the production of the illustrated versions in the Duke's and the Queen's manuscripts seven to ten years later, Christine engaged in an exchange of views on the *Roman de la rose* known as the *querelle de la Rose*.[3] Her three epistles on the *Rose* express her anxieties about the misogynist interpretations available to its readers. Another participant in the debate, Jean Gerson,[4] took up the most extreme anti-*Rose* position and located a primary source of the *Rose*'s dangerous power in its illustrations. In his allegorical treatise against the *Rose*, Gerson creates a court of Christianity over which Canonical Justice presides. To this court Chastity brings articles of complaint against the *Fol amoureux*—a reference to Jean de Meun— for seducing readers into accepting the erotic visions of the *Rose*: "he had them written and painted carefully and powerfully according to his ability in order to draw all people into seeing, hearing, and accepting these things" [les a fait es-cripre et paindre a son pouoir, curieusement et richement, pour atraire plus toute persone a les veoir, ouÿr et recepvoir].[5] Later in the treatise the personi-fication Theological Eloquence castigates illustrated manuscripts of the *Rose:* "But what burns up and inflames [human] souls more than lewd words and lecherous writings and pictures?" [Mais qui plus art et enflemme ces ames que paroles dissolues et que luxuryeuse escriptures et paintures?] (68).[6] By contrast, Christine never comments directly in her letters on the illustrations in *Rose* manuscripts; nevertheless, the miniatures in the Duke's and Queen's copies of her *Othea* purposely cite and revise *Rose* iconography. The fact that the Duke's and the Queen's manuscripts both include the *Epistre au dieu d'Amours* and the *querelle* dossier as compiled by Christine, as well as the fully illustrated *Epistre Othea*, testifies to the centrality of the *Rose* to her literary vision. In a move be-yond the disputation of the epistolary *querelle*, the illustrated *Othea* represents Christine's attempt to resituate the male reader in relation to the mythical tradi-tions enacted by the *Rose*.[7]

Like most French vernacular texts produced for courtly readers, the *Roman de la rose* was frequently and sometimes lavishly illustrated. Every manuscript of the *Rose* exhibits a unique set of visual and material qualities such that each man-uscript produces a distinct reading experience; as Sylvia Huot has thoroughly demonstrated, there is no one authoritative exemplar.[8] Among the possible reading experiences are particular performances of masculinity, each shaped by the program of illustration that accompanies the text in any particular manuscript. Christine knew the *Rose* as a text available in several different manuscripts, each with a different program of illustration, rubrication, marginalia, and borders. To Christine, the *Rose* would have seemed a text open to both visual and verbal reinterpretation that could lead to distinctly different readings over time.

The visual programs of *Othea* manuscripts appear to cite and revise the iconography of *Rose* manuscripts produced just a few years earlier. Christine had access to *Rose* manuscripts in the libraries and manuscript workshops she fre-quented. Under Charles V, the royal library acquired four copies of the *Rose*, and an equal number were to be found among the holdings of the duke of Berry, a major bibliophile.[9] For instance, PML, M. 48 would appear to have been pro-duced for Charles V or a member of his court.[10] BnF, fr. 380 includes an ex lib-ris of Jean, duke of Berry, from 1403,[11] and BnF, fr. 12595 contains the duke's signature.[12] In addition, *Rose* manuscripts were produced in the same workshops as Christine's illustrated manuscripts; BUV, MS 387 was made for Philip the Bold, duke of Burgundy, in the same atelier that produced two manuscripts of Chris-tine's *Chemin de long estude* and possibly the earliest illustrated *Othea*.[13] Douce 371 in the Bodleian Library, Oxford, was made in another workshop by the same scribes and artists responsible for a copy of Christine's *Chemin* made for Philip the Bold in 1402–3.[14] It is specifically the iconography typical of these five *Rose* manuscripts that early-fifteenth-century *Othea* miniatures appear to revise.

Of the *Rose* manuscripts produced in Parisian workshops at the beginning of the fifteenth century, Douce 371 and BUV, MS 387 contain different visual programs and represent two distinct readings of the *Rose* available to Christine. Since both manuscripts are dated between 1402 and 1404, they would have been under production in workshops Christine engaged during the years that the letters in the *querelle* were authored. In addition the dossier of the *querelle* continued to circulate during the first decade of the fifteenth century. These two *Rose* manuscripts form a pertinent background against which to read the documents in the *querelle;*[15] they also offer an explanation for various visual details in the *Othea* in the Duke's and the Queen's manuscripts.[16] Douce 371 consistently illustrates moments from the text in a homoerotic tone. As Simon Gaunt has shown, at the level of allegory, the *Rose* relentlessly depicts homoerotic desire between men.[17] The artist has chosen to depict Amant and his interlocutors in a series of images that emphasize the homosocial world of the *Rose* allegory. The initial interaction between Amant and Cupid is densely illustrated; the final scenes in which Amant claims the rose show the potential of the rose to function as the conduit for male desire.[18] First, on folio 141v, as Bel Accueil looks on, Amant plucks the rose (fig. 2.3). On the facing page, the last miniature in the manuscript depicts Amant kissing Bel Accueil on the mouth while Venus, the God of Love, and the barons form an audience (fig. 2.4). Though the text says that Amant thanks Bel Accueil and the others "between the delicious kisses" [antre les besiers savoureus] (21728) he gives to the rose, the artist paints over the heterosexual script with a homoerotic depiction.[19]

By contrast the València *Rose,* the most densely illustrated *Rose* manuscript of its day,[20] exploits the violence and fetishism inherent in the narrative of the heterosexual quest. The subject matter selected for illustration often has a shockingly gruesome quality, as we shall see. Although the text of the *Rose* offers a potential for fetishizing the female body as the object of desire, the artistic program of the València *Rose* visualizes the female body in an economy of violence that is striking even for *Rose* illustration. For example, in the miniature to the text passage in which Amant reaches the end of his quest, the female object of desire, the rose, is depicted as a statue whose legs are pillars of the Castle of Love (fig. 2.5). The Castle has fallen due to Venus's attack, and the toppled statue retains the rigid line of an inert object. A grotesquely hybrid form, the statue consists of a female head and nude torso joined at the groin to architectural pillars that replace human legs. In one miniature, Amant thrusts his staff into the loophole between the two pillars; in the next, his staff remains in place and

Fig. 2.3. Amant plucking the Rose, *Roman de la rose,* Oxford, Bodleian Library,
MS Douce 371, fol. 141v. (Bodleian Library, University of Oxford.)

his pilgrim's scrip hangs below (fig. 2.6). This miniature chillingly renders the
completion of Amant's quest by juxtaposing his triumphant grasp of the rosebush with his sexual assault on the penetrated statue.[21]

The images in several chapters of the *Othea*—particularly those that treat
the God of Love, Saturn, Atropos, Narcissus, and Pygmalion—explicitly revise
the visual material in *Rose* manuscripts. The *Othea* thereby attempts to intervene in the visualizations of gender, sexuality, and desire in the *Rose,* and to
offer alternatives to the castration crisis, the death drive, and the fetishism of
the female body that are enacted in contemporary *Rose* manuscripts. Yet this
intervention is only evident in the versions of the *Othea* in the Duke's and the
Queen's manuscripts, so that the reception of the *Othea* in the later fifteenth
century demonstrates the unique quality and historical specificity of this early
vision. Indeed, as we shall see, the visual program in one later Burgundian manuscript, the exemplar produced by Jean Miélot and illustrated by Loyset Liédet

Fig. 2.4. Amant kissing Bel Accueil, *Roman de la rose,* Oxford, Bodleian Library, Douce 371, fol. 142r. (Bodleian Library, University of Oxford.) ☙

for Philip the Good circa 1460, offers a distinctly different performance of masculinity. Although the court of Philip the Good showed significant interest in the *Othea* as a handbook for chivalry, Loyset Liédet's illustrations to Jean Miélot's version of the *Othea* in the manuscript made for Philip emphasize the status of masculinity as masquerade.

Male Subjectivity and the Castration Crisis

Christine's appropriation of the God of Love demonstrates how the *Othea* replies to the clerks who composed "tales in rhyme, in prose, in verse" against women. As a composition in rhymed verse and prose commentary, the *Othea* offers a counterargument to the misogynist texts critiqued in the *Epistre au dieu d'Amours.* The God of Love, one of the central figures in the allegory of the *Rose,* dramatizes Amant's desire in its earliest manifestations. As Amant wandered aimlessly through the garden, "Bow in hand, the God of Love then began to follow me at a distance" [Li dex d'Amors tantost de loing / me prist a sivre l'arc ou poing] (1311–12). The God of Love pursues and shoots Amant,

Fig. 2.5. Amant penetrates the Rose, *Roman de la rose*, BUV, MS 387, fol. 147v, 1.
(Universitat de València, Biblioteca Històrica.) ☙

then claims him as his liegeman. In a miniature in the Bodleian manuscript (Douce 371), Amant and the God of Love seal the pact with a kiss. Then Amant appears to perform the technical gesture of homage, the *immixtio manuum,* kneeling on one knee and extending his joined hands, but the God of Love, instead of enclosing Amant's hands with his own to complete the gesture, acknowledges Amant's gift of his heart by locking it with a golden key (fig. 2.7).[22] Amant began his allegorical quest as the object of pursuit; having enfeoffed himself to the God of Love, he becomes a predator himself.[23]

In her *Epistre au dieu d'Amours,* as we have seen, Christine purposefully evokes the figure of the God of Love from the *Rose* and uses him to condemn the deviousness with which men pursue women.[24] Christine's God of Love mocks the idea that men need to be deceptive and aggressive in order to succeed with women.[25] At the end of the poem, the God of Love expels all predatory lovers from his kingdom. In the miniatures that accompany the *Epistre au dieu d'Amours* in the Queen's manuscript (fig. 2.2), the God of Love resembles his counterpart in *Rose* illustrations. His bow and arrow and his crown are stan-

Fig. 2.6. Amant plucking the Rose, *Roman de la rose*, BUV, MS 387, fol. 147v, 3. (Universitat de València, Biblioteca Històrica.) ৩৯

dard features of *Rose* iconography; in addition the fountain, which recalls the fountain of Narcissus, specifically connects this scene to the *Rose*.[26] This image demonstrates the extent to which Christine's God of Love is a revision of the figure in Jean de Meun's text.

Cupid, the God of Love, has a prominent role in the *Othea*. The miniature in chapter 47 depicts Cupid floating down from a cloud; both his crown and the spring flowing at the left edge mark him as a visual descendent of the *Rose* Cupid. In the Queen's manuscript he carries his bow and arrows as well (fig. 2.1). A young nobleman stands next to the spring, extending his right hand, which touches palm-to-palm the right hand of Cupid. This handshake differs in its import from the gesture of homage as found in the *Rose*. The handshake is the same for both participants even when their positions or other signs show that

Fig. 2.7. Cupid kissing Amant. Amant swears fealty to Cupid, who locks his heart,
Roman de la rose, Oxford, Bodleian Library, MS Douce 371, fol. 14r.
(Bodleian Library, University of Oxford.) ☙

they do not have the same rank; when it functions as a gesture of welcome, the handshake commonly represents the reciprocal good intentions of those who meet each other, but it does not establish a permanent bond between them. For example, in an image of the future Charles V greeting a man from Vienna in the late-fourteenth-century *Fleur des Chroniques* (fig. 2.8), this gesture expresses reciprocity.[27] In the *Othea* miniature, the God of Love and the young man clasp hands in a show of welcome reciprocity, but the lover does not become enfeoffed to Cupid the way Amant specifically subjects himself in the *Rose*. Consequently, Cupid in the *Othea* offers an alternative to Cupid in the *Roman de la rose*. In the *texte* and *glose* of chapter 47, Othea explicitly approves of the young knight's acquaintance with Cupid so long as it is measured. The *glose* specifies that "it is not at all unseemly for the young knight to be amorous toward an honorable and wise lady" [il ne messiet point a jeune chevalier estre amoureux de dame honoree et sage] (47.7–9), because true love expresses a nobility of heart. This chapter on Cupid illustrates a central premise of the *Othea*: masculinity is a contract for a particular kind of measured conduct.

In a discussion of the cinematic constructions of masculinities, Kaja Silverman identifies the castration crisis as an enduring threat to "the male subject's

Fig. 2.8. The dauphin of France, the future Charles V, greeting a man from Vienna, Bernard Gui, *Fleur des Chroniques*, Besançon, Bibl. mun., MS 677, fol. 93v. (Bibliothèque Municipale de Besançon.)

aspirations to mastery and sufficiency."[28] Silverman analyzes classic Hollywood cinema as a site where the audience confronts the castration crisis and its role in the construction and maintenance of masculinities. In Silverman's terms, the visual cultures of twentieth-century cinema both acknowledge male lack and demonstrate the cultural efforts required to deny it: "Our dominant fiction calls upon the male subject to see himself and the female subject to recognize and desire him only through the mediation of images of an unimpaired masculinity. It urges both the male and the female subject, that is, to deny all knowledge of male castration by believing in the commensurability of penis and phallus, actual and symbolic father."[29] Far from originating in twentieth-century culture, the castration crisis is a cultural constant in the West, negotiated and renegotiated in each era, particularly by reference to ancient mythic representations of castration.[30] In its cinematic economy, the visual culture of the late medieval manuscript performs a function for Christine's audience similar to the one that Silverman recognizes as the function of cinema in 1940s Hollywood.

Early in the *Roman de la rose* the castration of Saturn poses the psychic reality of male lack.[31] In the València *Rose,* a manuscript that displays a specific interest in the mythological allusions in the text, a miniature confronts the reader with the castration of Saturn (fig. 2.9).[32] Jupiter stands in the foreground with a knife in one hand and Saturn's excised genitals in the other. As if to underscore the mutilation, the artist renders the severed organs a second time at the far left of the miniature, where they engender Venus. Three men function as the audience; one of them points at Saturn's wound in a direct confrontation of the castration crisis. In the text, when Raison explains to Amant the role of Justice during the Golden Age, she mentions the castration of Saturn in a casual aside:

> Justice reigned formerly, in the days when Saturn held sway, Saturn, whose son Jupiter cut off his testicles as though they were sausages (a harsh and bitter son indeed) and flung them into the sea, whence sprang the goddess Venus, as the book says.[33]

> [Joutice, qui jadis regnot,
> au tens que Saturnus regne ot,
> cui Jupiter coupa les coilles,
> ses filz, con se fussent andoilles,
> (mout ot ci dur filz et amer)
> puis les gita dedanz la mer,
> donc Venus la deesse issi,
> car li livres le dit issi.]
>
> (5505–12)

In the València manuscript, the graphic illustration of this passage requires the reader to visually as well as textually negotiate the castration crisis.

Toward the conclusion of the *Rose* allegory, Genius returns to the myth of the Golden Age and in the process produces a forty-six-line tirade against castration as a practice:

> It is a great sin to castrate a man. He who does so robs him not only of his testicles, of his sweetheart whom he loves so dearly and who will never smile on him again, and of his wife: that is the least of it. He also takes from him his courage and the way of life that valiant men should follow, for we can be sure that castrated men are cruel, perverted cowards, because they have feminine characteristics.

> [Granz pechiez est d'ome escoillier.
> Anseurquetout cil qui l'escoille
> ne li tost pas, san plus, la coille

Fig. 2.9. Castration of Saturn, *Roman de la rose*, BUV, MS 387, fol. 41r. (Universitat de València, Biblioteca Històrica.)

ne s'amie que tant a chiere,
don ja mes n'avra bele chiere,
ne sa moillier, car c'est du mains,
mes hardemant et meurs humains
qui doivent estre en vaillanz homes;
car escoillié, certain an somes,
sunt couart, pervers et chenins,
por ce qu'il ont meurs femenins.]

(20020–30)

Genius insists that the physical loss of male genitalia results in a psychic re-alignment that threatens masculinity. In this passage, he instructs Amant that he must disavow male lack. Amant then proceeds to fulfill the reproductive imperative Genius praises at such length, and he concludes his quest with the violent conquest of the rose. Thus the narrative ends with what Silverman would call an elaborate "fiction of phallic masculinity."[34]

In the *Othea,* Christine employs the myth of the castration of Saturn in order to posit an alternative male subjectivity. Two separate chapters on Saturn pose the importance for the male subject of "learn[ing] to live with lack," as Silverman would say.[35] Early in the *Othea,* Christine uses the myth of Saturn's castration to tutor the youthful male reader/viewer in the importance of careful judgment (fig. 2.10). As one of the seven planetary deities, the aged Saturn appears in the upper portion of the miniature, seated on concentric arcs representing the planets and holding up a sickle as his attribute. Following the idea of the Children of the Planets that Christine adapted from the astrological tradition, a group of judges and lawyers on earth below "speak together about wisdom" [parlent de sagece ensemble] (8.7–8). The *glose* characterizes Saturn as a king "whose son Jupiter cut off his genitals, which is to be understood as meaning that he took away the power that he had, and disinherited him, and drove him out" [son filz Jupiter lui coppa les genitaires, qui est a entendre que il lui toli la poissance qui il avoit et le desherita et chaça] (8.23–25). The *glose* and *allegorie* connect Saturn's castration to his acquisition of wisdom and explicitly instruct the male reader to resemble Saturn in being slow to judge and in considering carefully before rendering a judgment.[36] Saturn's right hand rests between his legs as though to signify his lack, further signaled by the deep folds of the gray drapery that create a dark void. This early chapter does not represent castration as a cultural scandal as does the *Rose:* through a recognition of male lack, Christine's chapter on Saturn constructs masculinity in an altogether different register than the *Rose.*

Halfway through the *Othea,* Christine returns to Saturn in order to reiter-

Fig. 2.10. Saturn and his children, *Epistre Othea*, BL, Harley 4431, fol. 100v.
(By permission of the British Library.)

ate the lesson to be learned by the youthful knight. Whereas the first image of Saturn in the *Othea* represents him as an ascendant planet, the image of the deity leaning headfirst out of his cloud in chapter 51 cites the visual tradition for representing the planet in its *deiectio* (figs. 2.11, 2.12). In the astrological manuscript given to the duke of Berry, for instance, the image of Saturn *deiectio* plunges headlong, which is the typical pose for the planetary deity when the planet is at its position of least influence. Although it is not an exact copy, the *Othea* Saturn further resembles the astrological depiction of Saturn in the Morgan manuscript in the angle of the head, placement of the arms, and form-fitting drapery.[37] One Latin adaptation of Abū Ma'šar's text on Saturn states that he is "prone to silence" [taciturnus].[38] In the *texte* of chapter 51, Othea tells Hector, "Let your tongue be saturnine" [Ta lengue soit saturnine] (51.2), and the *glose* explains, "The tongue must be slow in that it not speak too much and wise that it not speak ill of anyone" [lengue doit estre tardive en ce que elle ne parle trop et sage que de nul ne mesdie] (51.9–10). The earlier chapter attributed Saturn's slowness to his castration, which Othea cites in this chapter with her comment, "as I've said before" [comme j'ay dit devant] (51.6); in this chapter slowness of language becomes a desirable trait. In the miniature in this chapter in both the Queen's and the Duke's manuscripts, Saturn emerges from a cloud in the upper left and raises an index finger to his lips to signal his message. Below him a group of three men and one woman sitting on the ground mimic his action. Although this miniature is not in the series on the planets, it employs the iconographic formula of the Children of the Planets, with the interesting twist that, since a planet in its *deiectio* is least able to exert influence, the burden of responsibility for guarded speech falls especially heavily on the reader/viewer. The image visualizes "saturnine" speech with a gesture that cautions against the dangers of rash and hasty speaking.[39] The *allegorie* quotes Hugh of St. Victor on the effects of unguarded speech: "The tongue poorly guarded slips like an eel; it pierces like an arrow. . . , it sows discord; and with one blow it strikes and kills several people" [Le lengue mal gardee glisse comme l'anguile, perce comme sayete, . . . seme discorde, a un coup frappe et tue plusieurs personne] (51.21–24). By linking Saturn's castration with his modeling of careful judgment and considered speech, the *Othea* posits an alternate to the "images of unimpaired masculinity" central to "our dominant fiction," as Silverman frames it. Tutored by Othea in the importance of slow and wise speech, the good knight should reform himself and abandon the scandal-spreading gossip so harmful to women that Christine had decried in her *Epistre au dieu d'Amours.*

As an elaborate and interpretive engagement with the *Roman de la rose,* the *Othea* is not so much a critical reading of Jean de Meun's text as a remake of it.

Fig. 2.11. Saturn encouraging slowness of speech, *Epistre Othea*, BnF, fr. 606, fol. 24v. (Photo Bibliothèque nationale de France, Paris.) ❧

Fig. 2.12. Saturn *deiectio* (*casus*), astrological treatises. (The Pierpont Morgan Library, New York. MS M. 785 fol. 35v.) ☙

The textual portion of the *Othea* dates from circa 1400, within a year of the composition of the *Epistre au dieu d'Amours*. In the middle of the next year, 1401, Christine composed her first prose letter in the *Rose* debate, a response to Jean de Montreuil's praise of the *Rose*. In this letter she criticizes Jean de Meun's description of the castration of Saturn:

> He sets [this] forth too indecently in some parts—and likewise in the character whom he calls Reason, who plainly names the private parts by name. As you support him in that opinion and write that it is reasonable that it be done this way and allege there is no ugliness in the things that God has created and consequently the name need not be shunned, thus I say . . . that in the state of innocence it was not ugly to name them, but by the pollution of sin man became unclean.

> [trop traicte deshonnestment en aucunes pars—et mesmement ou personnage que il claime Raison, laquelle nomme les secréz membres plainement par nom. Et a ce que son oppinion soustenéz et communiqués qu ainsi doye raisonnablement estre fait, et alleguéz que es choses que Dieu a faictes n'a nulle laidure et par consequent n'en doit le nom estre eschivé, je dy . . . n'adonc en l'estat d'innocence ne eust esté laidure les nommer; mais par la pollucion de pechié devint homme inmonde]. (13)

Helen Solterer comments that in this passage, "Christine is concerned with the way significance is determined socially. . . . Speaking the words for genitalia is not shameful. Rather, what is shameful is the fact that their articulation in this particular society can realize the symbolic form of violence against women."[40] Indeed, in the *Othea* Christine has taken Jean de Meun's line of verse "cui Jupiter coupa les coilles" (5507) and rendered it in prose: "que son filz Jupiter lui coppa les genitaires" (8.23–4). The language in the *Othea* is also reminiscent of the description of the castration of Saturn in the *Ovide moralisé*.[41] As a result, Christine's passage strikes a different register than the *Rose*. By taking her cue from the *Roman de la rose* in her description of Jupiter's action, Christine demonstrates her ability to engage the same subject matter, but in a level of language that is rhetorically appropriate. The issue of Raison's word choice animates the epistolary debate on the *Rose* as well as modern scholarship on the *Rose* debate; the fact that in the *Othea* Christine quietly deployed appropriate rhetoric to rewrite Jean de Meun suggests that she takes up a disputational position in the *Rose* debate not out of moral prudery but because she is caught in the rhetoric of her interlocutors. To Christine the issue is one of poetic decorum, not moral correctness.

Masculinity and the Death Drive

In a chapter on Atropos, the *Othea* offers a subtle commentary on the sexual discourse of Genius in the *Rose*. In the *Othea* miniature Atropos, loosely wrapped in gray drapery that exposes her emaciated body and one pendulous breast, rides on a ragged gray cloud (fig. 2.13).[42] As an agent of death, she looms over a group of men below; some just begin to apprehend the dangers of their situation, others raise their arms in helpless terror. Two fall backward as if stunned, one of them with eyes closed, and the last lies stiff on the ground. At the left the men are falling in a heap; at the right Atropos aims a large dart at two more victims. The miniature thus depicts the stages a sentient being passes through in the process of dying. Headgear and costume signify that these are elite males, among them a king, a pope, a cardinal, and a prince. The textual material in this chapter provides no physical description of Atropos; however, in the *Mutacion de Fortune,* completed in 1403 before the production of the Duke's or the Queen's manuscript, Christine describes Atropos in passing (2791–2816). Two details in the narrative of the *Mutacion* reappear in the visualization in the *Othea:* her earth-colored skin and her emaciated body.

A highly unusual figure in both textual and visual traditions, Atropos does not appear at all in the *Ovide moralisé* or the *Histoire ancienne*.[43] The visualization of Atropos-Death as a single-breasted female figure wielding her darts is unprecedented,[44] a fact that led Millard Meiss to conclude that Christine's Atropos is indebted to an unknown Italian trecento model perhaps drawn from Boccaccio's and Petrarch's texts.[45] Christine's pictorial Atropos, however, emerges from her engagement with the *Rose*, especially with the illustrations in the València manuscript. Genius's sermon, with its praise of human reproduction, includes a long, vivid description of Atropos as one of the Fates; he tells Amant:

> Concentrate upon multiplying; in that way you will trick cruel, cantankerous Atropos, who hinders everything.

> [Pansez de vos monteplier,
> si porrioz ainsinc conchier
> la felonesse, la ruvesche
> Atropos, qui tout anpeesche].
> (19771–74)

Following this line in the València manuscript, a miniature represents Atropos with three breasts nursing the three-headed Cerberus (fig. 2.14); she simultaneously holds two bodies over her head, as if in the act of casting them into the

Fig. 2.13. Atropos, *Epistre Othea*, BL, Harley 4431, fol. 111r. (By permission of the British Library.) ❧

Fig. 2.14. Atropos feeding Cerberus, *Roman de la rose*, BUV, MS 387, fol. 135r. (Universitat de València, Biblioteca Històrica.) 🏵

"triple maw" of a second representation of Cerberus ("et el li giete homes et fames / a monceaus en sa triple gueule" [19796–97]).[46] The miniature faithfully renders the gruesome details of the text. By contrast, the *Othea* miniature cites the Children of the Planets iconography, so that Atropos is positioned as though she were a deity; that is, she is placed on a cloud above a group of mortals whom she claims as her "children."

The visual prominence of the breast in both miniatures suggests that it carries symbolic meanings. The exposed breast of Atropos in the *Othea* serves to identify her as the figure who nurses Cerberus and therefore as the Fate who cuts all lives short. Taking the perspective of stylistic analysis, Meiss noticed the importance of the breast in the composition: "The pendant breast is one of the most conspicuous verticals in a mobile field, seeming to acquire, therefore, a special though uncertain significance."[47] The compositional prominence of the exposed breast renders it phallic, a visual sign that Atropos has power over life and death. Whereas Genius urges his male audience to use phallic power to defeat Atropos through heterosexuality and reproduction,[48] Christine's interpretation accords phallic power to Atropos.

The *texte* tells the reader:

Keep watch at all times for Atropos and her spear, which strikes and spares no one; This will make you think of the soul.

[Ayes a toute heure regart
A Atropos et a son dart
Qui fiert et n'espargne nul ame;
Ce te fera penser de l'ame.]
(34.2–5)

This *texte* interpellates the reader/viewer into the miniature as one of Atropos's potential victims. This visual and verbal rhetoric of memento mori challenges the invocation of Atropos by Amant in the *Roman de la rose;* Amant makes this protestation of his fealty to Amours in a conversation with him:

May Atropos deign not to take my life except when I am engaged in your work; instead may she take me in the very act that Venus performs most willingly, for I have no doubt that no one has such delight as he does in this. As for those who should mourn me when they see that I am dead, may they be able to say, "Fair sweet friend, who now find yourself in this situation, it is no tale but the plain truth that your death was appropriate to the life you led when you held body and soul together."

[Atropos mourir ne me doigne
fors en fesant vostre besoigne,
ainz me praigne en meïsmes l'euvre
don Venus plus volentiers euvre,
car nus n'a, ce ne dout je point,
tant de delit conme an ce point;
et cil qui plorer me devront,
quant ainsint mort m'apercevront,
puissent dire: "Biaus douz amis,
tu qui t'iés en ce point la mis,
or est il voirs, sanz point de fable,
bien iert ceste mort convenable
a la vie que tu menoies
quant l'ame avec ce cors tenoies."]
(10341–54)

Amant baldly calls upon Atropos to cut him down while he is engaged in sexual intercourse and thus at the height of physical ecstasy. Christine's *glose* explicitly evokes this passage from the *Rose* in order to direct the "good knight" in his contemplation of Atropos: "Thus he must have more care of the virtues of the soul than to take pleasure in the delights of the body, and every Christian must think about this, so that he have in mind the care of the soul, which will endure without end" [Si doit plus avoir cure des vertus de l'ame que soy delicter es delices du corps; et a ce doit tout crestien penser, affin que il ait a memoire la provision de l'ame qui durera sanz fin] (34.10–13). Christine's play on Jean de Meun's use of "delit" ("delicter es delices du corps") signals her pointed rejoinder to Amant's conception of memento mori: Christine's exhortation to the good knight to remember the soul's eternal fate exposes Amant's eroticized appeal to Atropos as a reckless disregard for his soul. Rather, as Christine explains in the *allegorie*, a proper regard for Atropos leads to a Christian awareness that death can result in the resurrection of the flesh. She closes the *allegorie* with the last article of the Apostles' Creed: "Resurrection of the flesh, eternal life" [Carnis resurreccionem vitam eternam] (34.26–27). In place of the earthly body of Amant's shortsighted sexual fantasies, Christine's view of Atropos privileges the glorified body.

Narcissus and Pygmalion

In the *Roman de la rose*, Guillaume de Lorris evokes the Narcissus myth as a programmatic site. When Amant comes upon a fountain in the forest, he learns by reading its inscription that Narcissus perished there, and Amant's negotiation of the fountain and the myth initiates his engagement with the *Rose*. Despite his misgivings, Amant reenacts the Ovidian myth by looking into the fountain, a performance that culminates in the sight of the crystals and the rose reflected in the waters. Guillaume de Lorris's Amant imitates Ovid's Narcissus with a difference: in his action he resembles Narcissus; in the construction of his desire that resemblance functions to enable the ostensibly heterosexual quest allegorized in the pursuit of the rose.[49] In Douce 371, the four illustrations that accompany Amant's negotiation of the Narcissus myth visually equate Amant and Narcissus. At the moment in the narrative when Amant approaches the fountain of Narcissus, a miniature depicts Amant, arms folded, standing before a rectangular stone fountain (fig. 2.15). Pausing, he recalls the myth of Narcissus. Forty-three lines later, the next image depicts Narcissus dressed in hunting garb and leaning over a fountain that reflects his own face back to him (fig. 2.16). Narcissus models the dangerous behavior of gazing into the fountain that Amant himself performs a few lines later, again illustrated, first in a miniature in which Amant repeats the action of Narcissus, and then in a miniature that allegorizes Amant's quest by depicting Amant and the rose. In BnF, fr. 12595 a series of five images in the course of six pages articulates a similar distinction between Narcissus and Amant in order to emphasize Amant's imitation of Narcissus.[50] The sequences of illustration in Douce 371 and fr. 12595 emphasize Amant's resemblance to Narcissus even as the text of the *Rose* points to the differences between Amant and Narcissus.

The miniature that introduces the chapter on Narcissus in the *Othea* offers a generic treatment of its subject, even to the extent of including visual details that are part of the Ovidian and *Rose* pre-texts, but are not mentioned in the *Othea*'s textual material (fig. 2.17). For instance, Christine does not say that Narcissus has grown thirsty while hunting, though the images signal such a context through the presence of a hunting dog and a deer in the forest, as well as a hunting horn suspended from his belt. The miniature is almost compositionally interchangeable with the standard depictions of Narcissus in *Rose* manuscripts.[51] In citing Narcissus illustrations in *Rose* and *Ovide moralisé* manuscripts, the image in the *Othea* critiques the presentation of Narcissus's fountain as a danger to be negotiated in the *Rose*.[52] Immediately below the miniature of Narcissus, the *texte* warns the reader/viewer, "Do not wish to resemble Narcissus" [Narcisus ne vueilles sembler] (16.3). The *glose* echoes the verses of the *Rose* as well as the *Ovide moralisé*: Christine characterizes Narcissus by his "overweening nature" [oultrecuidance] and his "pride" [orgueil], categories drawn from the *Ovide moralisé*.[53] Christine's knight, unlike Amant in the *Rose*, should heed the warning at Narcissus's fountain and disavow both the self-love of Ovid's

Fig. 2.15. Amant at fountain of Narcissus, *Roman de la rose,* Oxford, Bodleian Library, MS Douce 371, fol. 10v. (Bodleian Library, University of Oxford.) ✤

Fig. 2.16. Narcissus looking in fountain, *Roman de la rose,* Oxford, Bodleian Library, MS Douce 371, fol. 11r. (Bodleian Library, University of Oxford.) ✤

Fig. 2.17. Narcissus looking in fountain; Athamas and Ino, *Epistre Othea*, BL, Harley 4431, fol. 104r. (By permission of the British Library.) 🖙

Narcissus and the courtly redefinition of self-love in its homoerotic manifestations as heterosexual desire in the *Rose*. The *glose* explicitly admonishes the knight: "Therefore it is forbidden for the good knight to admire himself in his good deeds at all, on account of which he may be overweening" [Pour ce deffent au bon chevalier que il ne se mire point en ses bienfais par quoy il en soit oultrecuidez] (16.14–16). The *allegorie* asserts that Narcissus must be understood as the sin of pride. Quoting Origen, the *allegorie* rhetorically characterizes Narcissus's self-love as dangerous delusion because it arises from pride in physical beauty, in a body that is not only subject to decay but never ceases to throw unclean matter from its conduits ("en quelles ordures il est plungié et quelles nettayeures il ne cesse de giter de sa char par tous les conduis de son corps" [16.27–29]). All parts of the text consistently work to characterize the gorgeous Narcissus of the miniature as a negative exemplum; unlike the reader of the *Roman de la rose*, who participates in Amant's renegotiation of the Narcissus myth, Christine's implied reader/viewer is directed away from the Narcissus narrative and the dangerous fountain.

Given the programmatic status of the Narcissus myth in the *Rose*, Christine's reinterpretation of this myth suggests that the *Othea* be read as her continuation of the critique she had begun in the *Epistre au dieu d'Amours*. When she returns to the Narcissus story in the chapter on Echo, the nymph who loved Narcissus (fig. 2.18), Christine uses Echo's story to further undermine the authority of Guillaume de Lorris's version of the Narcissus myth. Echo seldom appears in *Rose* illustration,[54] but the miniatures in the *Ovide moralisé* illustrate her pursuit of Narcissus (fig. 2.19); a subsequent miniature in the same manuscript depicts Echo and Narcissus at the fountain. The miniature in the *Othea* draws on this Ovidian pre-text to counter the *Rose*. Set at the fountain, this miniature depicts Echo's amorous approach to Narcissus with a prayerlike gesture that simultaneously seems to plead with him and with the gods to punish him. Narcissus's fashionably ornate costume includes a belted tunic with wide sleeves, dagged hems, and bells—he epitomizes the courtly lover. With his right arm he gestures toward the fountain in a proleptic reference to his episode of fatal self-love, and with his left hand he eloquently expresses his disdainful rejection of Echo.

The visual analogue in the Rouen *Ovide moralisé* portrays Echo as a predatory lover and Narcissus as her fleeing prey; Narcissus looks back at Echo as she attempts to grasp him from behind. By contrast, Christine's restrained Echo pleads with rather than pursues Narcissus, whose costume and gestures recall the earlier chapter on Narcissus at the fountain as the exemplum of the deadly sin of pride. The *texte* warns:

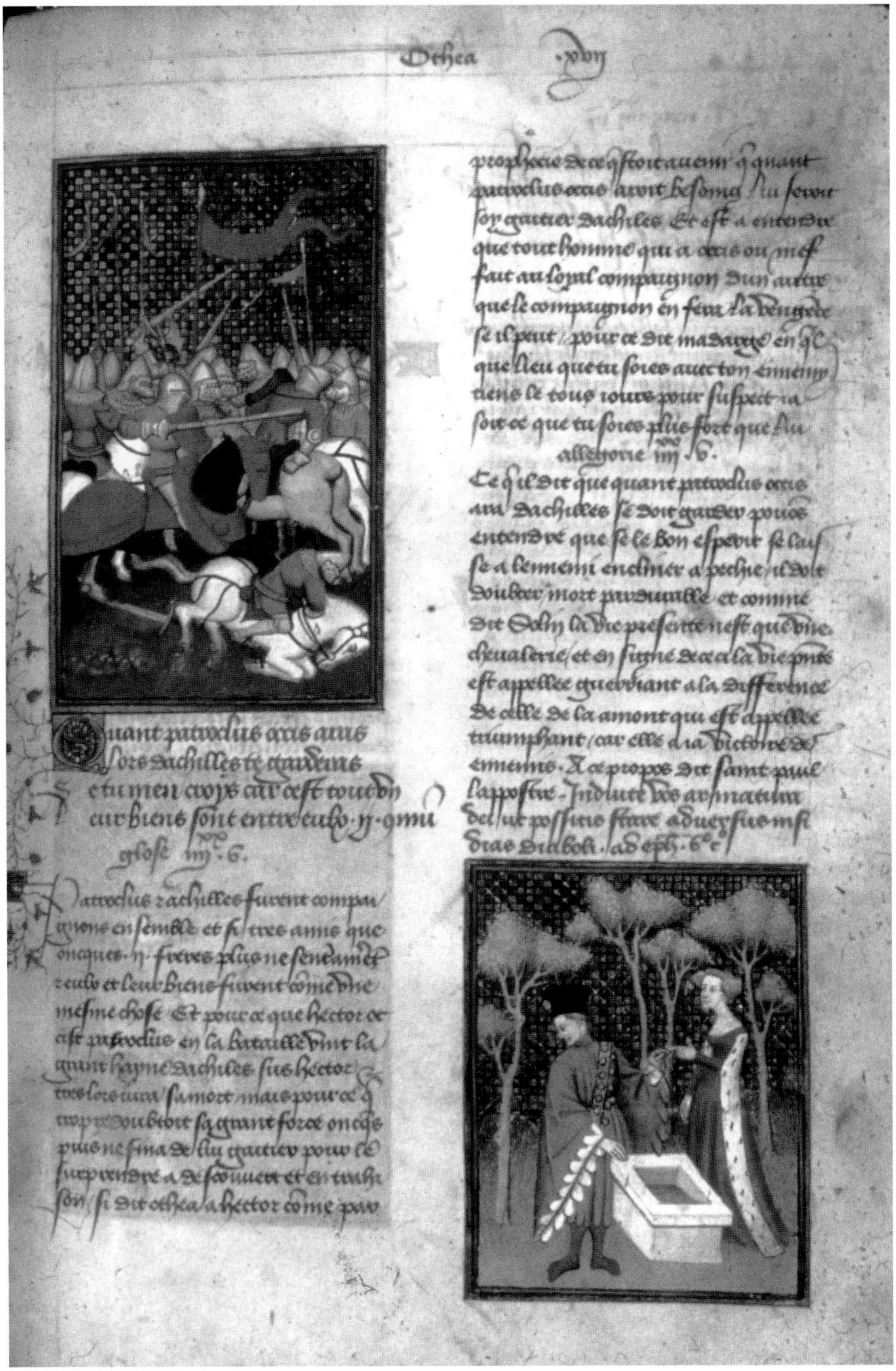

Fig. 2.18. Hector killing Patroclus; Narcissus and Echo; *Epistre Othea*, BL, Harley 4431, fol. 134r. (By permission of the British Library.) ☙

Fig. 2.19. Echo pursuing Narcissus, *Ovide moralisé,* Rouen, Bibl. mun., MS O.4, fol. 8or. (Collections de la Bibliothèque municipale de Rouen. Photographies Thierry Ascencio-Parvy.) ❧

Watch that you do not reject Echo nor despise her piteous complaints; if you can hold out against her desire, you do not know what will happen to you.

[Gardes qu'Echo tu n'escondises
Ne ses piteus plains ne desprises;
Se son vueil tu peus soustenir,
Tu ne scez qu'il t'est a venir.]
(86.2–5)

The *glose* instructs the reader to interrogate the courtly script's preoccupation with romantic love and to view Echo as a sign of those in need of charity rather than as an unwelcome suitor.

Just as Narcissus is the mythological figure who initiates Amant's quest in

Fig. 2.20. Venus attacking the Castle, *Roman de la rose*, Los Angeles, J. Paul Getty Museum, 83.MR.177 (Ms. Ludwig XV 7), fol. 129v. (The J. Paul Getty Museum, Los Angeles.)

the first part of the *Roman de la rose*, Pygmalion stands at the end as the mythological lover who models a particular desire for Amant to imitate.[55] Pygmalion's desire for his statue functions as an idealized exemplum; the narrator cuts to this exemplum in the midst of the final scene, freezing the frame to leave in the reader's visual imagination the image of Venus aiming her arrow at the loophole hidden between the two small pillars of the castle tower (fig. 2.20).[56] While the allegorical narrative about Amant and the rose is thus suspended, the digression on Pygmalion, a mythological flashback of sorts, focuses the reader/ viewer's attention on an icon of heterosexual male desire that objectifies and ultimately denies the feminine. The erotic plot of the Pygmalion narrative becomes the script Amant will follow to create (and possess) the female object of his desire.[57]

Fig. 2.21. Pygmalion carving his statue, *Roman de la rose*. (The Pierpont Morgan Library, New York. MS M. 48 fol. 142v.) ☙

Although the Pygmalion story is a relatively short digression at the end of the *Rose*, the episode is frequently illustrated in *Rose* manuscripts, often as the final image.[58] PML, M. 48, for instance, represents the Pygmalion story in two images that conclude the visual program of the manuscript. In the first, Pygmalion wields hammer and chisel to cut into the block of stone from which he is fashioning his ideal woman (fig. 2.21). The half-formed female figure lies prone on a workman's table, its lifeless inertia in sharp contrast to Pygmalion's creative agency. As he carves, the form takes on the appearance and form of a funerary effigy: closed eyes and arms lying limp across the body encode death. According to the narrative, this is a preanimate form, yet the visual rendering suggests a corpse. In the second miniature, three folios later, Pygmalion has clothed

Fig. 2.22. Pygmalion dancing with his statue, *Roman de la rose*. (The Pierpont Morgan Library, New York. MS M. 48 fol. 145r.)

his image and propped her up in an attempt to dance with her (fig. 2.22). As Virginia Wylie Egbert notes, *Rose* illustrations depict Pygmalion carving a life-sized stone statue despite the text's specific designation of the statue as a work in ivory, which would have been limited by materials to a much smaller scale.[59] All five of the *Rose* manuscripts to which Christine had access exhibit this visual preoccupation with Pygmalion's statue.[60]

The València *Rose* contains the most elaborate illustration for the Pygmalion episode of any manuscript in this group. The double-column Pygmalion illustration includes several scenes that represent the range of subjects visualized in *Rose* illustrations of this narrative (fig. 2.23). At the left Pygmalion sculpts the statue lying horizontally before him with arms crossed; reading counterclockwise, a series of three scenes depicts his desire to bring the statue to life: in the lower left he genuflects before it; in the center he cavorts before the statue he has dressed in fine blue garments, but it fails to respond; at the lower right he attempts to dance with the statue. In all three vignettes Pygmalion's excessive activity contrasts with the statue's persistent rigidity. In the upper right corner of the miniature, Pygmalion kneels before a cult statue of Venus in a temple, imploring her to bring his statue to life. Finally in the upper left Pygmalion courts his statue, which should be living by now, but retains its rigidity.

79

Fig. 2.23. How Pygmalion made love to the statue that he had made, *Roman de la rose*, BUV, MS 387, fol. 142r. (Universitat de València, Biblioteca Histórica.)

The Pygmalion myth brings closure to the narrative of the *Rose* by connecting heterosexuality and artistic desire, femininity and fetishism. Pygmalion's creative ability to fashion a woman as the object of his desire suggests the fetishism inherent in male heterosexuality as it is constructed in this text. The lifeless status of his love object aestheticizes femininity as death and thereby enables the agency of masculine artistry.[61] In visual terms the València manuscript signifies the aestheticized femininity of the rose by depicting her as a statue whose lifeless form substitutes for Pygmalion's object of desire. The allegorized rose is fetishized in the same libidinal economy that constructs Pygmalion's beloved as a fetish. As the narrator of the *Rose* turns from the Pygmalion story back to the allegory proper, the attack of Venus and the fall of the castle, he assures the reader: "You will certainly hear what this signifies before my work is finished" [Bien orrioz que ce senefie / ainz que ceste euvre soit fenie] (21183–84). This closing assertion signals that the trajectory of the Pygmalion myth extends to the closing lines of the *Rose*.

The chapter on Pygmalion in the *Othea* intervenes in the matrix of voyeurism, heterosexuality, and artistic agency in the *Rose*. The *texte* directs the reader:

If you are wise, do not become besotted with Pygmalion's image, because the beauty of such a decorated image is too dearly bought.

[Ne t'assottes pas de l'image
Pymalÿon, se tu es sage,
Car de tele ymage paree
Est la beauté trop comparee.]
(22.2–5)

The miniature immediately above these lines depicts the moment in the story when Pygmalion visits the temple of Venus and pleads with the goddess to bring his statue to life (fig. 2.24). He kneels, palms joined in a gesture of prayer, while Venus, enthroned beneath an elaborately carved Gothic canopy, listens attentively to his plea. This moment is illustrated in the *Ovide moralisé* (fig. 2.25), and it frequently occurs in *Rose* manuscripts as one of several illustrations of the Pygmalion story. In the *Othea*, the selection of this subject, to the exclusion of Pygmalion carving, or cavorting with, his statue, illustrates Christine's turn away from the Pygmalion myth as an allegorization of fetishism.[62] The miniature refers neither to Pygmalion's artistry nor to his statue: consequently the *Othea* does not offer an image with which the reader/viewer might become besotted.

The *glose* similarly refuses to extol the fetishism in the myth and instead offers the interpretation that the statue stands for a beautiful but unresponsive

Fig. 2.24. Pygmalion and Venus, *Epistre Othea*, BL, Harley 4431, fol. 106v. (By permission of the British Library.) ❧

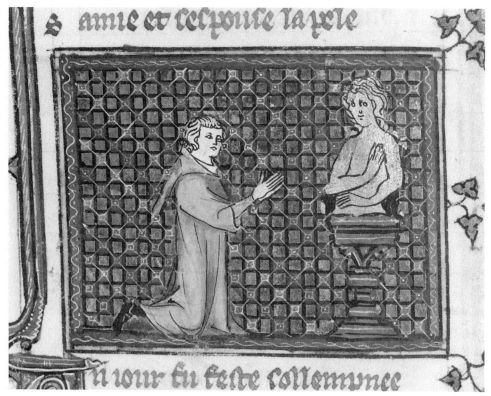

Fig. 2.25. Pygmalion kneeling before Venus, *Ovide moralisé*, Rouen, Bibl. mun., MS O.4, fol. 252v. (Collections de la Bibliothèque municipale de Rouen. Photographies Thierry Ascencio-Parvy.) ☙

woman "who would not or could not hear [Pygmalion's] piteous complaints, any more than if she herself had been a statue" [la quelle ne vouloit ou ne pouoit entendre ses piteux plains, ne que se de pierre fust] (22.30–31). The *allegorie* furthers the point of the *texte* and *glose* by identifying Pygmalion's voyeurism as lechery. Whereas the *Rose* incites readers to participate in the voyeurism of the Pygmalion myth and thus prepares them to be complicit with the violent eroticism of the end of the allegory, the *Othea* directs readers away from violence and voyeurism toward moderation and wisdom.

In a Latin letter in defense of Jean de Meun, Jean de Montreuil describes the defenders of the *Rose:* "For they are shining with golden spurs and empowered by higher rank" [Sunt enim quorum calcaria auro fulgent magnisque dignitatibus potiuntur] (38). Here and elsewhere he writes as though interpretation were a tournament and male readers in their chivalric roles were the best defenders of Jean de Meun and his allegory; as Karen Sullivan has pointed out, the defenders of the *Rose* speak as though they were knights.[63] With the writing of the *Othea,* Christine had begun to address the conduct of the ideal knight;

several years later and after the epistles on the *Rose* debate had already been put into public circulation, the production of the visual programs in the Queen's and the Duke's manuscripts was undertaken. In both text and image, throughout the first decade of the fifteenth century, her *Othea* questions the categories of chivalric conduct, poetic interpretation, and their connection to masculinity.

Chivalry and Masculine Anxieties

An intervention in specific aspects of normative constructions of masculinity, the *Othea* treats the code of chivalry as a script that can be revised. In the initial chapter of the *Othea* Christine asserts, "we may call human life true chivalry" [nous pouons appeler la vie humaine droite chevalerie] (1.134–35). The goddess Othea interrogates categories of masculinity, particularly as they are promoted in the *Rose,* and she appeals to chivalry as a moral standard. Measured against the ideals of chivalry, the masculinity championed by the *Rose* could be seen as predatory and denigrating to women. The status of the *Othea* as a handbook of chivalry accounts for its enthusiastic reception in the fifteenth-century court of Philip the Good (1419–67). Yet the popularity of the *Othea* in Philip's court ironically testifies to the failure of its original program, since Burgundian productions of the *Othea* reinscribe the categories of normative masculinities under critique in the Duke's and the Queen's manuscripts.

From early in her career as a writer, Christine found ready patrons in the dukes of Burgundy. During the first decade of the fifteenth century, she presented copies of several of her works to Philip the Bold (1364–1404), who in reciprocity commissioned Christine to write a biography of his brother, Charles V. Charity Cannon Willard suggests that the Burgundian interest in history, education, and political reform helped to shape Christine's literary agenda after 1405.[64] John the Fearless, son of Philip the Bold and duke of Burgundy from 1404 to 1419, continued to act as Christine's patron and is credited with encouraging her to write her treatise on warfare, the *Livre des fais d'armes et de chevalerie.*[65] By the time Philip the Good became the third duke of Burgundy in 1419, the ducal library already contained at least one copy of each of Christine's works. During his reign, Flanders became the cultural center of Burgundian court life, which took on an increasingly flamboyant and stylized character. A major feature of Burgundian court culture in this period was the prolific production of luxury manuscripts, both of newly commissioned works and of texts originating in earlier periods that held appeal for Philip and his court.[66] Among the earlier texts that gained popularity and saw new productions in Flanders during this period were the works of Christine de Pizan, especially her *Epistre Othea.*

Philip the Good's patronage of the *Othea* illustrates his investment in chivalry, which led to his founding of the Order of the Golden Fleece in 1430.[67] A late manifestation of a movement on the part of European monarchs to found secular orders of chivalry, the Order of the Golden Fleece, like all chivalric orders, was ostensibly dedicated to furthering the goals of the Crusades. The Golden Fleece, however, exemplified the nostalgic irony of all the late orders in its preference for crusading rhetoric over actual crusade activity, its interest in tournaments over actual warfare, and its promotion of courtly conduct rather than religious zeal.[68] Philip the Good and his wife, Isabelle of Portugal, eagerly acquired illustrated books treating various aspects of the Holy Land, apparently in lieu of mounting an actual crusade.[69] The Order of the Golden Fleece embraced all the trappings of chivalry and displayed them in a glittering masquerade of knighthood. The Burgundian court cultivated masculinity as a theatrical performance of chivalric values no longer responsive to the realities of combat, whether secular or religious.

Paintings suggest the self-consciousness with which Philip the Good and his court embraced masculinity as performance. In the well-known miniature that represents the presentation of Jean Wauquelin's *Chroniques de Hainaut,*[70] Philip, dressed in black from head to toe, stands silhouetted against the pink and gold canopy of his throne (fig. 2.26). His elongated figure is unnaturally slender and demonstrates what Margaret Scott has called the "obsession for underfed male bodies" evident in visual representations produced in Flanders in this period.[71] His extremely broad shoulders, perhaps due to the new fashion for stuffed sleeves, are set off by his long, slim legs and narrow waist.[72] Disciplined to fashion, the body of Philip the Good becomes the spectacle of chivalry. Self-consciously striking a pose, Philip the Good "disavows passivity" by the control necessary to maintain his elegant posture,[73] so that his potential for activity codes his masculinity. Though his subordinates surround him attentively, he claims enough space that no figure overlaps his. Prominent against the black costume, the chain around his neck displays the chivalric emblem of the Order of the Golden Fleece. All of the courtiers on Philip's left, including his son and heir, wear the same symbol, identifying them as knights in this order. As a presentation image, this frontispiece depicts a set of courtly relationships in their semiotic richness. For Philip's court, chivalry, replacing the traditional feudal hierarchy, provides the script for what Norman Bryson has termed the "masquerade of the masculine."[74] This frontispiece demonstrates Bryson's paradox according to which this privileged form of masculinity requires "being at the same time the subject of the male gaze and its object," with the inevitable result of "intermale surveillance, constant monitoring, controlling, and inspection."[75]

The most lavish Burgundian manuscript of Christine's *Othea,* produced

Fig. 2.26. Philip the Good receiving Jean Wauquelin's *Chroniques de Hainaut*, Jacques de Guise, *Chroniques de Hainaut*, BR, MS 9242, fol. 1r. (Art Resource, New York.) ❧

about 1460 under the patronage of Philip the Good, was made in Jean Miélot's workshop in Lille and illustrated by Loyset Liédet.[76] Miélot designed a uniform presentation for each chapter so that the miniature always appears on the upper third of a folio verso. The text of each chapter fills all the remaining space in the opening. Since Christine's chapters are not uniform in length, Miélot added material to the *gloses* in some chapters in order to expand the textual material so that it would fill in what would otherwise be empty spaces.[77] The additional information develops the mythological narrative, not its allegorical interpretations. In Liédet's miniatures, the visual program from the Queen's and the Duke's manuscripts is easily recognizable, and Liédet's images often cite this iconography. In scenes from myth, Liédet attempts to render narratives, often by repeating the same figures more than once to convey action, a visual technique Eisenstein specifically identifies as montage. In episodes from the history of the Trojan War, Liédet's miniatures frequently shift the focus from issues of conduct to the visualization of military power and its trappings.

Liédet's interpretation of the episodes from the Trojan War situates Burgundian masculinity as fashion and spectacle. For instance, the miniature of Ulysses' discovery of Achilles depicts knighthood as a costume (fig. 2.27). To avoid fighting, Achilles hid in a convent, disguised as a nun. Since the Greeks needed him to win the war, Ulysses went to the convent and identified Achilles among the nuns by offering objects to the assembled group, whose individual choices betrayed their genders. In the Queen's manuscript, the group of nuns all reach eagerly for brightly colored items with feminine appeal except Achilles, who grasps a helmet with one hand and a dagger with the other (fig. 2.28). His choice of these military objects belies the feminine identity he attempted to claim by cross-dressing. The dagger in his right hand accords him the phallic identity necessary to perform as a warrior, even as Ulysses aggressively grabs him by the wrist and reinstalls him in normative masculinity. Like the necessity of learning to live with lack posed by Saturn as a figure of the castration crisis, the lesson of this chapter on Achilles does not depend on a notion of essentialized phallic masculinity.

Liédet's miniature of this subject exhibits an iconographic similarity to the miniatures in the Duke's and the Queen's manuscripts, yet the shift in focus exposes the status of masculinity as masquerade. In the foreground, Achilles in a nun's habit appears enthralled by a piece of body armor, which he leans over to claim with both hands. Arrayed beside it are gauntlets and a sword; at the left, Ulysses offers the helmet. The armor, with its nipped-in waist and V-shaped torso, offers its wearer the same fashionable silhouette that Ulysses displays. Garbed in the latest courtly fashion, Ulysses exhibits the broad shoulders, slender waist, and long legs of the masculine prototype set by Philip the Good in the

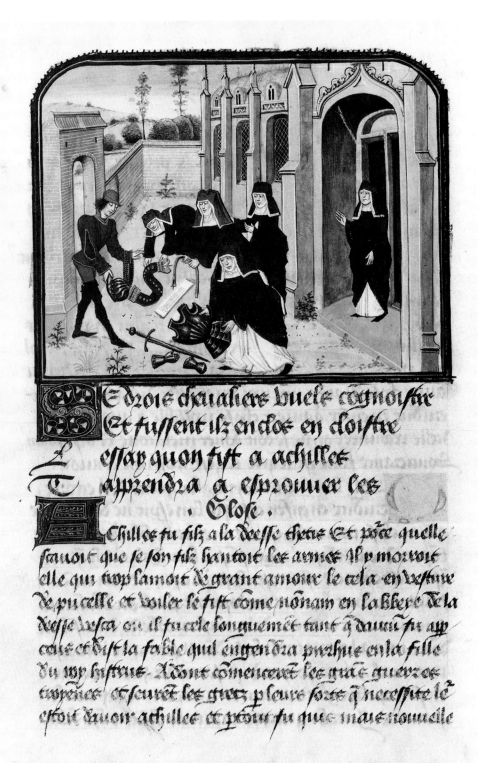

Des chevaliers vueil congnoistre
Et fussent ilz enclos en cloistre
essay quon fist a achilles
apprendra a esprouuer les
. Glose .

Achilles fu filz a la deesse thetis Et pour ce quelle
sauoit que se son filz hantoit les armes il y mourroit
elle qui trop lamoit & grant amour le cela en vesture
de pucelle et voiler se fist come nonnain en labbeye de la
deesse dyana ou il fu cele longuemet tant q dauen fu ap
cele et dist la fable quil engendra pirrhus en la fille
du roy lyttaire Adont comencerent les grãc guerres et
tuproies et sceurt les grecs y soure soste q necessite le
estoit dauoir achilles et pour fu que mare nouuelle

Fig. 2.27. Achilles discovered by Ulysses, *Epistre Othea*, BR, MS 9392, fol. 74v. (Brussels, Royal Library of Belgium.)

Fig. 2.28. Achilles discovered by Ulysses, *Epistre Othea*, BL, Harley 4431, fol. 127v. (By permission of the British Library.) ☙

Chronique de Hainaut presentation miniature (see fig. 2.26). Whereas the earlier miniature could represent Achilles' masculinity by his selection of the dagger, Liédet shows Achilles' choice of armor in preference to the sword that lies directly in front of him. Liédet's Achilles does not achieve a masculine identity through the equivalence of the sword and the phallus; rather, he will masquerade as masculine through the assumption of armor.

The aspect of warfare most highly valued in the cultural productions of the Burgundian court was individual combat.[78] In a chapter on the death of Patroclus, Othea addresses Hector as though the narrative of the Trojan War is unfolding in the present: "When you have killed Patroclus, watch out for Achilles" [Quant Patroclus occis aras, / Lors d'Achillés te garderas] (85.2–3). In the miniature in the Queen's manuscript, two knights engage at the forefront of a battle, one unhorsing the other with a lance; in the foreground a knight and his horse fall to the ground (fig. 2.18). The banners and the helmeted heads filling the background impart the sense of a suffocatingly close battle between two large armies. The *glose* encourages Hector to avoid individual combat with Achilles if at all possible. As Charity Cannon Willard observes, "Christine understood the dangers of the traditional chivalric ambition to indulge in shows of individual prowess."[79] By contrast, the Liédet miniature and the Miélot addition to the *glose* in the Burgundian manuscript glory in the drama of one-on-one combat (fig. 2.29).[80] Liédet creates a spacious, tree-filled landscape in which the conflict between Patroclus and Hector takes place in two episodes: first, Patroclus strikes Hector's shield; then Hector kills Patroclus with a swordblow to the head. Liédet has lovingly detailed every feature of the armor-clad knight, as well as the accoutrements of his horse. The armor accentuates his long, slender legs, narrow waist, and broad shoulders—the preferred proportions for the male body in Burgundian court culture. This image depicts a fantasy of warfare as a homoerotic display of male bodies locked in single combat.

Christine uses the figure of Helen of Troy to instruct her male reader/viewer that masculinity should not be based on the theft of women. She describes a negotiation between the Greeks and the Trojans for the return of Helen to her Greek husband Menelaus (fig. 2.30). In the miniatures in the Queen's and the Duke's manuscripts, the diminutive figure of Helen occupies the far right edge of the council chamber scene, which focuses on the Trojan refusal of the Greek request that Helen be yielded to them. The direct address of the *texte* instructs Hector to "return Helen if one demands her, because in a great misdeed lies reparation" [Rens Helayne s'on la demande, / Car en grant meffait gist amende] (43.2–3). Othea tells Hector that, rather than fighting a war over an abducted woman, the Greeks and Trojans should have resolved the conflict peacefully. She considers the Trojan War a folly and questions whether

Fig. 2.29. Hector killing Patroclus, *Epistre Othea*, BR, MS 9392, fol. 88v. (Brussels, Royal Library of Belgium.)

the Trojans could gain glory through the theft of women and whether keeping Helen is worth launching a war.

By contrast to this sober and ultimately negative assessment of war in the text, the Liédet miniature for this chapter celebrates the glory of warfare by fetishizing military combat: gleaming armor, swords, spears, and caparisoned horses are all displayed (fig. 2.31). Liédet's composition faithfully renders the *glose* in the *Othea:* "And when the Greeks had come upon Troy with a large army for the vengeance of this deed, before they did any damage to the land they demanded that Helen be returned to them" [Et quant les Grieux furent venus sus Troye a grant armee pour la vengence d'icellui fait, ains que ilz meffeissent a la terre, ilz requirent que Helayne leur fust rendue (43.8-11)]. In the miniature the Greek army masses outside the walls of Troy in full array, their

Fig. 2.30. Greek messengers asking Trojans to return Helen, *Epistre Othea*, BL, Harley 4431, fol. 115r. (By permission of the British Library.) ☙

Fig. 2.31. Greek messengers asking Trojans to return Helen, *Epistre Othea*, BR, MS 9392, fol. 46v. (Brussels, Royal Library of Belgium.) ❧

banners waving above countless heads. On the foremost banner the word "Menelaus" can be deciphered. The messenger, shown three times, first rides through the city gate, then approaches the palace, and finally receives Priam's negative answer. Helen appears nowhere in this image. Liédet emphasizes military force; whereas the earlier images in the *Othea* had just as appropriately rendered the narrative of the *glose* by focusing the viewer's attention on issues of negotiation rather than military display. Miélot's addition to this chapter explicates the Trojan decision to abduct Helen by describing the earlier abduction of the Trojan princess Hesione by the Greek Telemon. Miélot's *glose* implicitly characterizes the abduction of Helen as a matter of strategy; whereas the *Othea* originally uses the contest over Helen to critique warfare, the Miélot interpretation sees the traffic in women as a standard component of warfare.

In Liédet's chivalric fantasy, women such as Helen are the spoils of war, a

93

Fig. 2.32. Diomede, Troilus, and Briseyda, *Epistre Othea*, BR, MS 9392, fol. 87v.
(Brussels, Royal Library of Belgium.)

fantasy reenacted in Liédet's depiction of the transfer of Briseyda from the Trojan prince Troilus to the Greek knight Diomede (fig. 2.32). Outside the walls of Troy, the three figures are triangulated. The rear view of Diomede on horseback displays his ideal, armor-clad figure. By contrast, Troilus, in courtly dress, is half-screened from view by Briseyda's horse. Briseyda herself, enveloped in heavy fabric, exhibits a vacant look that indicates her status both as object of exchange between the Trojans and the Greeks and as the object of Troilus's and Diomede's desire. In depicting this triangle as the exchange of Briseyda between two men, Liédet's image draws upon the historical tradition from the *Histoire ancienne* in which Briseyda is traded from the Trojans to the Greeks and passes from the hands of Troilus to Diomede (fig. 2.33). Liédet thus overwrites the

neur: œfu oyomeæs 7 vhues
li rois thalamon anæ liour
antHxnes 7 tuuh plus pro
fies de lost des gregiois la
anmoifele ploroit fi ou iemt
q̃ mils ne la pou reco foiwr.
·tdatreparit avilus fen rewr
ne mlt deſcofoitez. Et mian
tenant q̃ la damoifele fu en
tre fes chiens amis dvoinrear̃
femiſt decoſtelie aliouſt. be
le diſt bien fe ponont prifier

amour·7 oie uoi que amour
ma du tout dnez a uous et
œne me femble pas muelle
q̃ir ie remir la g̃iebiauæ de
uous de quoi uous eſtes en
lumnee. Et pur œ uuil ie q̃
uous fachnes q̃ iamais negoer
auou autre ioie deuãt q̃ ie fo
te feur amour uiramour et
q̃ie me deuous enterine ioie
Et pur dieu uous priq̃i lne
uous foit grief ne ne me ton

Fig. 2.33. Briseyda being given to Diomede, *Histoire ancienne jusqu'à César*, BL, Royal 20 D. I, fol. 101v. (By permission of the British Library.)

representation in the Duke's and the Queen's manuscripts of the *Othea*, in which the triangle consists of the God of Love, Troilus, and Briseyda (fig. 2.34).

In the Queen's manuscript, the miniature to this chapter emphasizes Troilus's agency and responsibility. He looks and reaches up, as if to clasp the extended hand of Cupid, who is hovering in the sky above. The handclasp, similar to that in the miniature depicting the God of Love (see fig. 2.1), expresses a potential relationship of mutual respect between Troilus and Cupid, into which Troilus might enter willingly. Simultaneously Troilus reaches back with his left hand to Briseyda, who stands behind him. Troilus thus hovers between two mutually exclusive options. As the *texte* says:

> If you wish to give your heart and abandon it completely to Cupid, keep yourself from acquaintance with Briseyda.

> [S'a Cupido tu veulx donner
> Ton cuer, et tout habandonner,
> Gard toy Briseyda n'acointier.]
> (84.2–4)

Fig. 2.34. Briseyda, Troilus, and the God of Love, *Epistre Othea*, BL, Harley 4431, fol. 133v. (By permission of the British Library.) ❧

Although the *glose* goes on to discuss the triangle of Troilus–Diomede–Briseyda, the image omits Diomede and puts Cupid into the picture, where he functions as a personification of true love, not a cause of Briseyda's betrayal of Troilus. Unlike the traditional version of the Troilus and Briseyda story, which places the blame on Briseyda's fickleness, Christine's chapter, although it acknowledges Briseyda's tendency to be "fickle and seductive" [vague et attrayant] (84.7), places the overall emphasis on Troilus's choice and on how important it is for the reader/viewer to exercise judgment when faced with a similar choice. In visualizing the God of Love, the chapter on Troilus and Briseyda encapsulates the central concerns of the *Othea* as an exploration of the ethical constructions of masculinity. By drawing upon the visual tradition of the God of Love from *Rose* manuscripts in order to reinterpret a moment in the Trojan story, this chapter does not resort to the conventional misogynist explanation for Troilus's disappointment in love. That this version of an ethical masculinity is later overwritten in the Burgundian reception of the *Othea* demonstrates its uniqueness, its departure from normative constructions of heteronormative masculinity, and even the radical edge of its vision.

The Duke's and the Queen's manuscripts, through their inclusion of the letters in the *querelle* and the *Epistre au dieu d'Amours,* offer eloquent testimony to the highly dynamic nature of literary cultures in early-fifteenth-century Paris. In this context, the *Othea* in its fully illustrated copies emerges from a culture in which critique could have a highly literary value. When read against the *Rose* and critiques of the *Rose,* the texts and images of the *Othea* in the Duke's and the Queen's manuscripts intervene in normative constructions of gender, particularly in constructions of masculinity. The reception of the *Othea* in the Burgundian court reinscribes a highly normative masculinity. In this later context, the *Othea* was not read in relation to the *Rose* and the *querelle,* but rather as a vehicle for transmitting the values of Philip the Good, duke of Burgundy. The *Othea* as reshaped by Miélot and Liédet addresses issues of power and its display rather than structures of conduct. By contrast, the manuscript culture of early-fifteenth-century Paris created a space in which myth might be employed not only to critique the structures of masculinities but also to envision desire as a critical category.

Fig. 3.1. Orpheus enchanting trees and animals, *Epistre Othea*, BnF, fr. 606, fol. 31v. (Photo Bibliothèque nationale de France, Paris.) ᛒᛋ

3

ENVISIONING DESIRE

ᴥᶘᶅᴥ

How do I look? This question implies several: How do I see—
what are the modes, constraints, and possibilities of my seeing,
the terms of vision for me? How am I seen—what are the ways in
which I'm seen or can be seen, the conditions of my visibility? And
more—how do I look *on*, as the film unrolls from reel to reel in
the projector, as the images appear and the story unfolds up on
the screen, as the fantasy scenario unveils and the soundtrack plays
on in my head? For the question is, To see or not to see, to be seen
(and how) or not to be seen (at all?): subjective vision and social
visibility, being and passing, representation and spectatorship—the
conditions of the visible, what can be *seen,* and eroticized, and on
what *scene.*

—Teresa de Lauretis, *The Practice of Love:*
Lesbian Sexuality and Perverse Desire

Erwin Panofsky's insistence that "mild pornography" is a constitutive feature
of film suggests that the filmic process of envisioning desire often eroticizes it.
Since the "erotic organization of visibility"[1] in film tends to replicate the power
relations of the ambient culture, feminist film theorists have found in pornographic film the means to interrogate the politics of visual culture, specifically
around the issues of sexuality and desire.[2] Pornography thus emerges as one example of the ways in which visual culture attempts to construct subjectivities
along the lines of "generic and gendered cultural forms," in Linda Williams's

phrase.[3] Yet the stark extremes of pornographic performance result in what Judith Butler terms "the text of gender's unreality, the impossible norms by which it is compelled, and in the face of which it perpetually fails."[4]

Ovid's *Metamorphoses* offers the reader a sustained commentary on the erotic organization of visibility in Roman culture. Though not specifically a pornographic text, the *Metamorphoses* obsessively stages scenes of desire as excess in a starkly performative context that is similar to pornographic representation. And in response to the cultural organization of desire in the Roman world, heterosexuality emerges as an unstable category in the *Metamorphoses*. With the manuscript production of the *Ovide moralisé*, a moralized and illustrated vernacular Ovid in the early fourteenth century, the Ovidian obsession with sexuality and desire becomes legible in a medieval context.[5] But the categories of sexuality in Ovid's Latin text are not compatible with the heteronormative reproductive imperative of late medieval Christian culture. The author of the *Ovide moralisé* addresses this incompatibility through his extensive moralizations, which append Christian allegories to pagan myths of rape, seduction, same-sex desire, incest, bestiality, and so forth.[6] In the face of the competing sexualities of the *Ovide moralisé*, which highlight gender's unreality, the *Othea* appropriates the "frenzy of the visible"[7] from the *Ovide moralisé* in order to suggest an alternative program for the "erotic organization of visibility."

As we have seen in chapter 2, the critique of the *Roman de la rose* enabled Christine to address the particular conduct of heteronormative masculinity. The *Othea* also explores the instability of heterosexuality as it is represented in the texts and images of the *Ovide moralisé*. In the course of the *Othea*, Christine depicts mythic figures associated with male same-sex desire, such as Orpheus and Ganymede. Although she does not identify female same-sex desire as a category of identity, she nonetheless represents Diana and her followers as an exclusively female, homoerotic community. The *Othea* also includes women associated with bestiality, most obviously Pasiphaë, as well as Andromeda and Circe. By comparison to such nonnormative categories of desire, the exploration of heterosexuality in the *Othea* takes on a particular queerness, as evident in Christine's refusal to validate the conventional politics of heterosexuality represented by Paris's abduction of Helen. Christine instead offers the queer Hermaphroditus as a figure for an ideal heterosexual relationship. Since the highly transformative qualities of Ovidian myth suggest that human form as well as human conduct are subject to metamorphosis, the *Othea* uses Ovidian myth to denaturalize the categories of desire as envisioned in late medieval culture.

Orpheus and the Rhetoric of the Closet

. . . when they decide to follow Orpheus, who could not plough or write
or forge on the right forge (may he be hanged by the neck for invent-
ing such rules for them; he did Nature a disservice).

[quant Orpheüs veulent ansivre,
qui ne sot arer ne escrivre
ne forgier en la droite forge
(panduz soit il par mi la gorge!
quant tex regles leur controva,
ver Nature mau se prova).]
　　　　(*Roman de la rose*, 19621–26)

In this passage on the reproductive imperative from his sermon near the end of
the *Roman de la rose*, Genius denounces the followers of Orpheus for their
refusal to plow, write, or forge "correctly," metaphors taken from Alan de Lille
to characterize nonnormative sexual practices. Such an understanding of Orpheus derives from the Ovidian tradition of Orpheus as a lover of boys, a singer
whose songs celebrate same-sex desire, including the pederastic exemplum of
Jupiter and Ganymede.[8] Genius viciously denounces Orpheus and his followers for their sexual practices,[9] and he repeatedly insists that the followers of
Orpheus should be castrated: "may they also lose the purse and testicles that
are the signs of their manhood!" [puissent il perdre / et l'aumosniere et les
estalles / don il ont signe d'estre malles!] (19636–38); even in the ironic mouth
of Genius, this comment enacts a chilling gesture of disciplining desire.

As we have seen in the last chapter, Christine depicts the castration crisis—
so punitively evoked by Genius—as an opportunity for the male subject to
negotiate among competing masculinities. Christine's chapters on Orpheus
likewise explore desire and identity; although Christine avoids the violent de-
nunciations of Genius, her representation of male same-sex desire nonetheless
reflects cultural anxieties regarding nonnormative sexualities. The *Othea* chapters on male same-sex desire—on Orpheus and Ganymede—derive from book
10 of Ovid's *Metamorphoses*, known to Christine in the illustrated, translated,
and moralized version, the *Ovide moralisé*.

The *Ovide moralisé* preserves the idea that Orpheus invented homosexuality.
As Ovid tells it, Orpheus's loss of his wife Eurydice inspired his misogyny, and
his misogyny motivated his same-sex desire. In Ovid's terms, he was "auctor
amorem / in teneros transferre mares" (10.83–84). The *Ovide moralisé* expands
on Ovid's description of Orpheus's response to the loss of Eurydice:

He remained three years without a woman, without a wife, and with-out a concubine, so he fled from all feminine love; he refused all women. Now I do not know why this was—whether because he had made a promise to the one whose love he was, or whether because of a mis-fortune that had befallen him—but he hated all women for it. . . . He was the one who first taught Thracian men to retreat from feminine love and to take their pleasure with young men.

[Trois ans s'est sans feme tenus,
Sans epouse et sans concubine,
Si fuit toute amour femeline.
Toutes femes mist en refu.
Or ne sai ge pour quoi ce fu:
Ou pour ce qu'il eüst promis
A cele cui tant fu amis,
Ou pour ce que mal l'en cheï,
Mes toutes femes en haï.
. . . .
Ce fu cil qui premierement
Aprist ceulz de Trace à retraire
D'amour femeline et à faire
Des joennes malles lor deduit.]
                    (10.177–85, 191–94)

Subsequently Orpheus shifted the subject of his song to "the loves of great gods of the sky who loved young boys" [Les amours des grans dieux des cieulz / Qui amerent les jovencieulz] (10.720–21).

The song of Orpheus structures most of book 10 in the *Ovide moralisé,* as it does in Ovid's *Metamorphoses.*[10] Given Orpheus's stated interest in singing about sexualities, the mythic material in book 10 centers on stories of sexual transgression even more pointedly than does the rest of the *Metamorphoses.* In the course of book 10, Orpheus loses rhetorical control of his song, and the myths of desire that he narrates toward the end of the book escape his stated purpose. Consequently, *Metamorphoses* 10 presents narratives of sexuality deeply embedded in ironic and contorted narrative contexts. When the *Ovide moral-isé* author came to appropriate Orpheus's song in *Metamorphoses* 10, the *Ovide moralisé* poet encountered a complex exploration of sexualities that emerge from classical Roman culture and represent an economy of desire consistent with Augustan Rome. The *Ovide moralisé* author, of course, worked within late medieval Christian attitudes toward sexuality that derive from an altogether different social and cultural organization of desire. The author of the *Ovide moralisé* also participates in a tradition of Christian commentary on Ovid's *Meta-morphoses*. The texture and paradoxes of book 10 in the *Ovide moralisé* result from these conflicting cultural constructions of sexuality and desire and the competing textual traditions designed to address that conflict.

The *Ovide moralisé* offers an elaborate interpretive framework for Orpheus's songs of same-sex desire and pederasty: the moralizing gestures of the *Ovide moralisé* draw on a venerable tradition that interprets Orpheus's journey into Hades as Christ's descent into Hell and identifies Orpheus the musician both as David the Psalmist and as Christ whose harp plays the music of Christian doctrine. In the long allegorical passages of the *Ovide moralisé* that are stitched into Ovid's mythic narratives, Orpheus initially signifies "correct understand-ing," or the rational soul, and Eurydice figures the sensuality of the soul that must be brought under the control of reason. Orpheus's stated preference for same-sex love is twice moralized (10.205–19, 10.2521–39) and once allegorized as Christ's hatred for those who delight in the world—those of feminine nature—and his love for those who live virtuously—males of young age (10.556–77). Throughout the Orpheus narrative, the *Ovide moralisé* poet emphasizes the misogyny inherent in the Ovidian text by correlating it with Christian misogyny. Consequently, the misogyny expressed in the problematic and contested irony of Ovid's Latin text becomes authorized as legitimate discourse in the moral-ized French text. In adapting the *Ovide moralisé* material on Orpheus to the *Othea*, Christine confronts Orpheus's virulent misogyny; as we shall see, in order to exclude Orpheus's misogyny, she excludes his identification with same-sex desire. As a result, the rhetoric of the closet structures the representation of both Orpheus and Ganymede in the *Othea*.

The visual programs in *Ovide moralisé* manuscripts chart the reception of its moralizations. The earliest surviving manuscript, Rouen, Bibl. mun., O.4 (1315–20), contains the most extensive program of illustration—453 minia-tures.[11] About 90 of the Rouen miniatures illustrate the long allegorical pas-sages that the author appended to the mythological narratives; in the case of the Orpheus myth, 2 of the 8 miniatures visualize Christian allegorical interpreta-tions. Book 10 in the Rouen manuscript opens with a miniature of Orpheus's bride Eurydice bitten by a serpent whose poisonous venom kills her (fig. 3.2). According to the text, Orpheus then descends into Hades to ask for Eurydice's return, and the next miniature depicts Orpheus singing to the rulers of Hades—represented as the Hellmouth of Christian iconography—to persuade them to release Eurydice (fig. 3.2). The gods grant Orpheus's request on the condition that he not look back at Eurydice as she follows him up to the world from Hades, but when Orpheus breaks this contract, he loses Eurydice and returns alone, embittered. The accompanying illustration focuses on Orpheus's loss of

Fig. 3.2. Eurydice bitten by poisonous serpent; Orpheus singing in Hades, *Ovide moralisé*, Rouen, Bibl. mun., MS O.4, fol. 246v. (Collections de la Bibliothèque municipale de Rouen. Photographies Thierry Ascencio-Parvy.)

Fig. 3.3. Eurydice's return to Hades, *Ovide moralisé,* Rouen, Bibl. mun., MS O.4, fol. 247r. (Collections de la Bibliothèque municipale de Rouen. Photographies Thierry Ascencio-Parvy.) 🐿

Eurydice, who returns to Hades as if drawn by an invisible force (fig. 3.3). A miniature of Hellmouth (fol. 248) then signals the start of the first extensive allegorical interpretation.

The narrator of the *Ovide moralisé* relates that in bitterness and grief Orpheus decides to sing about nonnormative love. His music enchants both trees (fig. 3.4) and beasts, and his song rehearses a series of myths about desire and transgression, which we discuss later in this chapter. At the conclusion of Orpheus's song, the *Ovide moralisé* offers a long allegorical commentary on it, starting on a folio with three miniatures (fig. 3.5). An image of Orpheus surrounded by animals introduces these allegories. At the bottom of the same text column, a miniature of Orpheus speaking with two young men illustrates a highly moralistic passage on the dangerous example set by Orpheus in his celebrations of same-sex desire (10.2509–39). A miniature of the Crucifixion in the next column marks a segment of the allegory on Orpheus as Christ. The

Fig. 3.4. Orpheus enchanting trees, *Ovide moralisé*, Rouen, Bibl. mun., MS O.4, fol. 250r. (Collections de la Bibliothèque municipale de Rouen. Photographies Thierry Ascencio-Parvy.) ☙

Orpheus story concludes at the start of book 11 when the Ciconian women kill Orpheus for his repeated refusal of heterosexual love (fig. 3.6). The Orpheus sequence is typical of illustrations in the Rouen manuscript: miniatures densely punctuate the narrative episodes of the Ovidian myths and also act as markers for various phases of allegorical interpretation.

A second *Ovide moralisé* manuscript, Arsenal 5069 (ca. 1325–50) originally contained 340 miniatures, of which one-tenth illustrated the allegorical segments of the poem.[12] The Arsenal manuscript has a diminished program of illustration compared to the Rouen manuscript, and a smaller percentage of Arsenal miniatures illustrate the allegorical passages. The latest of the three *Ovide moralisé* manuscripts, Lyon, Bibl. mun., MS 742—made about 1390 for the duke

Fig. 3.5. Orpheus enchanting animals; Orpheus enchanting young men; Crucifixion (allegory of Orpheus), *Ovide moralisé*, Rouen, Bibl. mun., MS O.4, fol. 261v. (Collections de la Bibliothèque municipale de Rouen. Photographies Thierry Ascencio-Parvy.)

Fig. 3.6. Orpheus beaten to death by Ciconian women, *Ovide moralisé,* Rouen, Bibl. mun., MS O.4, fol. 271r. (Collections de la Bibliothèque municipale de Rouen. Photographies Thierry Ascencio-Parvy.)

of Berry—has only 57 miniatures, of which only 2 illustrate allegorical material.[13] The reception of the *Ovide moralisé* in the course of the fourteenth century shows both a noticeable decrease in the number of miniatures and a simultaneous shift in their content away from the moral allegories and toward the myths themselves. In the case of Orpheus, Arsenal 5069 has 5 illustrations of which 2 are allegorical, and Lyon's 5 Orpheus miniatures are all visual renderings of the mythic narrative.[14] Since miniatures functioned as visual markers for medieval readers seeking particular passages in a manuscript, Lyon 742 presupposes a readership whose interest focused on the mythological narratives of the *Ovide moralisé* rather than the appended allegories.

The Orpheus chapters in the *Othea* (67 and 70) are similarly focused on the narrative rather than the allegorical possibilities of the myth. The miniature of Orpheus and Eurydice in chapter 70 cites two of the *Ovide moralisé* manuscripts (fig. 3.7; compare fig. 3.3). The image in the *Othea* depicts a courtly couple in front of the gates of Hell guarded by two demons. The miniature evokes the

Fig. 3.7. Orpheus leading Eurydice from the underworld, *Epistre Othea*, BnF, fr. 606, fol. 32v. (Photo Bibliothèque nationale de France, Paris.) ✑

very moment of Orpheus's transgression; as the subject of the gaze, Orpheus had been forbidden from making Eurydice its object, but he "could not keep himself from turning back toward his love, at whom he wished to gaze" [ne se pot tenir de retourner pour s'amie que a regarder desiroit] (70.30–31). In the *texte* below the miniature, Othea warns the implied reader, Hector, not to imitate Orpheus's quest in the Underworld: "For Orpheus won little there for all his harping" [Pou y gaigna a tout sa lire / Orpheüs] (70.4–5). The *texte* has an ironic undertone: with his harping Orpheus gained exactly what he wanted, but he lost it again through his failure to discipline his gaze. The *glose* relates at some length how Orpheus and Eurydice marry, how Orpheus breaks the pact he made with the rulers of Hades, and then concludes with the interpretation:

"he who seeks Eurydice in Hell seeks an impossible thing; and in order to retrieve these things one must not become melancholic. Solon precisely says, 'It
is the height of folly to seek that which it is impossible to have'" [quiert Euridice en enfer qui quiert chose impossible, ne pour ycelles recouvrer on ne se
doit donner merencolie. Ce meismes dit Solon: "Somme follie est de querre ce
qui est impossible a avoir"] (70.37–40). With a consistency not frequently found
in the *Othea*, the *allegorie* repeats the same interpretive point: "That he ought
not go to seek Eurydice in Hell means that the good spirit must not aim for
nor ask from God a miraculous or marvelous thing" [Que il ne doie aler querre
Euridice en enfer pouons entendre que le bon esperit ne doit tendre ne requerir
a Dieu chose miraculeuse ne merveillable] (70.41–44). This *allegorie* directly
contradicts the standard Christian moralizations in the *Ovide moralisé* that
identify Orpheus with Christ and interpret his descent into Hell as the rational
part of the human soul seeking control over the sensuous part. By visualizing
the moment of Orpheus's look back at Eurydice, the miniature exposes his in-
ability to discipline his gaze in order to achieve the object of his desire. The textual insistence that Orpheus's failure is inevitable thus evokes a critique of
courtly love as a structure in which male lovers wield power over women.[15] In
reshaping the Orpheus myth into a critique of courtly love in chapter 70,
Christine discards the Ovidian conclusion that Orpheus's failure to retrieve
Eurydice motivates his turn to misogyny.

In a disregard for narrative sequence typical of the montage format of the
Othea, an earlier chapter depicts Orpheus performing as a musician after he has
lost Eurydice (fig. 3.1). Othea instructs Hector:

> Do not become too infatuated with the harp of Orpheus; if you wish
> to choose arms for your principal profession, you have no need to fol-
> low the profession of instruments.
>
> [Trop ne t'assottes de la lire
> Orpheüs; se tu veulx eslire
> Armes pour principal mestier,
> D'instrumens suivre n'as mestier.]
> (67.2–5)

Although this passage literally warns Hector against overindulgence in music,
it also warns against the attractions Orpheus represents. The *glose* expands on
the dangers of Orpheus's attraction:

> Thus it is to be understood that he played so well that all people, of
> whatever social status they were, took delight in hearing the poet play.

And because such instruments often seduce the hearts of men, this says to the good knight that he ought not delight too much in them, as it does not suit the sons of knighthood to amuse themselves either with instruments or in other idle activities.

[Si est a entendre que il tant bien jouoit que toute gent, de quelconque condicion que ilz fussent, se delittoient a escouter le poete jouer. Et pour ce que tieulx instrumens assottent souvent les cuers des hommes, dit au bon chevalier que trop ne s'y doit deliter, comme il n'affiere aux filz de chevalerie eulx amuser en instrumens ne autres oysivetez.] (67.11–18)

The juxtaposition of the admonition of the *texte* and the explanation of the *glose* implicitly evokes Orpheus's identification with same-sex desire, to which the miniature may refer as well. Due to the Ovidian association of Orpheus the harpist with same-sex desire, the verb *to harp* could refer to sodomy in medieval clerical culture, as evidenced by a thirteenth-century Middle High German poem about Orpheus the harpist:[16]

Oh, woe, that he has human form
Who plays his harp in such a way and allows himself to be played like
   a harp!
Enemy of nature—may the devil curse him!

[owê, daz er mannes bilde hât,
der alsô harphet únde an im harphen lât!
nâturen vîant—daz in der tiuvel hône!]

In the veiled discourse of the *Othea,* however, Christine neither denounces Orpheus as a sodomite—as does the *Rose*—nor literally identifies Orpheus as a homosexual, as does the *Ovide moralisé.* Although homosexuality enjoyed a relative tolerance on the part of the Church until the twelfth century, that attitude later shifted to open hostility and persecution.[17] Simultaneously, there is a textual closeting of same-sex desires, so that in the *Confort d'ami* (1357), Guillaume Machaut, whose work Christine admired,[18] describes Orpheus's desire only elliptically:

[He became] a man of such condition
I haven't the will to speak of him,
For it would corrupt and pollute the very air
To bring up such a disgusting story.

Now afterward he would never call any woman
Beloved, nor would he love a lady.

[Et devint homs de tel affaire
Que ne le vueil mie retraire,
Car le airs corront et empire
De parler de si vil matyre.
Mais onques puis ne volt clamer
Dame amie, ne femme amer.]
(2585–90)[19]

The *Othea* thus participates in a cultural shift in attitudes toward same-sex de-sire: by the late fourteenth century within the rhetoric of the closet, the nature of Orpheus's desire need not be named to be understood.

Of all the stories Orpheus tells, that of Ganymede is the best known. In medieval clerical and vernacular cultures the name *Ganymede* came to refer to pederasty, since the story of Jupiter's abduction of Ganymede had become a mythic exemplar of man-boy love.[20] In the *Othea*, a figure identified as Gany-mede appears in chapter 53, but the brief narrative in the *glose* does not tell Ganymede's story. The Ganymede chapter in the *Othea* conflates the first two narratives, the stories of Ganymede and Hyacinth, that Orpheus sings to illustrate his chosen topic—stories of boys loved by gods.[21] The *glose* in the *Othea* relates:

> Ganymede was a youth of Trojan lineage, and a fable says that Phoebus and he were competing with each other one day at throwing an iron bar, and as Ganymede was no match against the power of Phoebus, he was killed by the rebounding of the bar, which Phoebus had hurled so high that he had lost sight of it.

> [Ganimedés fu un jouvencel de la lignee aux Troyens, et dit une fable que Phebus et lui estrivoient un jour ensemble a gitter la barre de fer, et comme Ganimedés n'eust peu contre la force de Phebus, fu occis par le rebondissement de la barre que Phebus ot si hault balanciee que il en ot la veue perdue.] (53.6–12)

In the miniature to this chapter (fig. 3.8), Ganymede falls backward under the impact of a long iron bar that pierces him in the eye, a visual reinterpretation of the Hyacinth text and image in the *Ovide moralisé*, which reports, as does Ovid, that Hyacinth was killed by a discus. The *Othea* image of Phoebus Apollo hurling the iron bar that penetrates Ganymede's eye cites the frequently illus-trated moment in the *Roman de la rose* when the God of Love shoots an arrow

Fig. 3.8. Ganymede killed by Phoebus Apollo, *Epistre Othea*, BnF, fr. 606, fol. 25v. (Photo Bibliothèque nationale de France, Paris.) ❧

Fig. 3.9. God of Love shooting Amant in the eye, *Roman de la rose*, BUV, MS 387, fol. 13v. (Universitat de València, Biblioteca Històrica.) ☙

through Amant's eye (figs. 3.9 and 3.10). These images visualize a premise of medieval optics that desire enters through the eye,[22] and both the *Othea* and the *Rose* depict the piercing of the eye as the marker of desire. As Apollo throws and Ganymede falls, their pelvises thrust toward each other; Ganymede's back arches gracefully, and his arms open at his sides in a gesture of vulnerability. The short, tight-fitting tunics and parti-colored hose emphasize Ganymede's slender torso and Apollo's perfect male beauty; the costume follows the curve of his back and outlines his buttocks. Wide sleeves underscore their gestures and impart a dancelike quality to their poses. By the standards of the time such tight-fitting, revealing garments were considered suggestive, if elegant: the parti-colored hose and the garter worn by Apollo are the accoutrements of a courtier.[23] Both costumes represent the extremes of fashion; no other figure in the *Othea* program of illustration wears such excessively elegant costume. The combination of pose and costume offers the reader/viewer a spectacle of erotic grace.

Fig. 3.10. God of Love shooting an arrow at the fleeing Amant, *Roman de la rose*, BnF, fr. 380, fol. 12r. (Photo Bibliothèque nationale de France, Paris.)

In the Rouen manuscript of the *Ovide moralisé*, the illustrations for the stories of Ganymede and Hyacinth appear on facing folios, a layout that explains how Hyacinth's story from the *Ovide moralisé* could have been substituted for Ganymede's. The miniature that introduces Orpheus's song depicts Jupiter in the form of an eagle abducting the boy Ganymede in order to install him as the cupbearer of the gods (fig. 3.11). On the facing page, after an interval of forty-six lines, Hyacinth's story appears beneath an image of Phoebus Apollo holding the mortally wounded boy Hyacinth after he has accidentally struck him with a discus while they were playing together (fig. 3.12). The images suggest the similarities in the stories of these two boys who attracted the erotic attention of male deities: held from behind, each hangs limply in the grasp of the large, powerful god; their arms droop at their sides, their eyes are closed. The two figures are visually interchangeable. Though neither of these images appears in the Arsenal or the Lyon manuscript, the Arsenal manuscript introduces the moralization of

Fig. 3.11. Ganymede seized by Jupiter as eagle, *Ovide moralisé*, Rouen, Bibl. mun., MS O.4, fol. 250v. (Collections de la Bibliothèque municipale de Rouen. Photographies Thierry Ascencio-Parvy.) 🕮

the Ganymede story with a rubric that explicitly states the relationship between Jupiter and Ganymede: "How the king of Crete conquered the Trojans and found there a very beautiful boy and then he committed sodomy with him" [Comment le rois de crete vainqui ceus de troyes et trouva i petit enfant tres bel et ot afaire a li par bougrerie] (fol. 142r). The *Ovide moralisé* text goes on to explain Jupiter's abduction of Ganymede by euhemeristically making him a victorious king who carried off a boy named Ganymede as part of his spoils: "And many times he played with him by way of *luxuria* against law and against nature" [Et mainte fois se deporta / Avuec lui par non de luxure, / Contre droit

116

Fig. 3.12. Phoebus and the mortally wounded Hyacinth, *Ovide moralisé*, Rouen, Bibl. mun., MS O.4, fol. 251r. (Collections de la Bibliothèque municipale de Rouen. Photographies Thierry Ascencio-Parvy.) ✍

et contre nature] (10.3383–85). Such rubrication and moralizing euhemerism clarifies the nature of Jupiter's desire for Ganymede.

In the "Ganymede" chapter in the *Othea*, the status of Ganymede's story as a narrative of same-sex desire is more veiled than in any of the *Ovide moralisé* versions. In addition, the conflation of the Ganymede and Hyacinth stories confuses the categories of desire even further. Othea's voice in the *texte* draws a lesson more suited to the Hyacinth story:

> If you exert yourself against someone stronger than you in many games of strength, withdraw so that no misfortune befalls you: Remember Ganymede.

[S'a plus fort de toy tu t'efforces
A faire plusieurs jeux de forces,
Retray toy que mal ne t'en viengne;
De Ganimedés te souviengne.]

(53.2-5)

This moral fits the circumstances of the Hyacinth narrative since Hyacinth participated in the sport that led to his death. By grafting Hyacinth's story onto the name of Ganymede, the *Othea* conflates two narratives of man-boy love without naming them as such. Yet the "Ganymede" image in the *Othea* cites the iconography of the *Rose* to offer a graceful visualization of same-sex desire despite the admonitions of the *texte*. The *Othea* offers Ganymede as an exemplum of the possibilities of same-sex eroticism despite the rhetoric of the closet that accounts for the occlusion of desire in the textual material of the "Ganymede" chapter.

Eroticizing Chastity

Ovidian myth portrays the goddess Diana as a chaste huntress who shuns the company of men and surrounds herself with maidens who have forsaken traditional women's roles in favor of the hunt. Although the chastity of her followers marks them as women who have renounced heterosexuality, their allegiance to Diana shows that they have not disavowed desire—or sexuality. Medieval culture projected Christian anxieties about women and female sexuality onto this "goddess of the pagans."

Medieval popular culture preserved a notion of a "Cult of Diana" explicitly described in a tenth-century document, the *Canon Episcopi:*

> [S]ome wicked women perverted by the devil, seduced by illusions and phantasms of demons, believe and profess themselves, in the hours of night to ride upon certain beasts with Diana, the goddess of the pagans, and an innumerable multitude of women, and in the silence of the dead of night to traverse great spaces of earth, and to obey her commands as of their mistress, and to be summoned to her service on certain nights.[24]

The highly influential trajectory of the *Canon Episcopi* in legal discourse and penitential literature demonstrates that the notion of women following Diana on a "night ride," "wild ride," or "wild hunt" persisted into the early fifteenth century.[25] Though other names are attached to the female leader of the night ride, such as Abundia, Habonde, or Abonde in France, Diana is the classical deity associated with this medieval belief in "a primarily female ecstatic religion, dominated by a nocturnal goddess with many names," as Carlo Ginzburg puts it.[26] For example, the *Roman de la rose* refers to a "dame Habonde" as the leader of the night ride (18397–468); in the *Cité des dames* (1.41.1) Christine states that the Ephesians worshipped the goddess Diana. In his *Caccia di Diana,* Boccaccio characterizes Diana as a goddess "who keeps the tepid fire in chaste breasts" [che 'l tiepido foco / ne' casti petti tien].[27] In medieval popular religion as well as classical myth, the goddess Diana stands for the possibility of female resistance to heteronormativity; in both contexts she is a queer figure.

The *Epistre Othea* treats Diana in three separate chapters, all of which emphasize her queer status as a chaste goddess. In chapters 63 and 69, Diana performs her role of huntress. According to the Ovidian tradition, Diana and her huntress-companions are bathing in the woods when the hunter Actaeon accidentally stumbles upon them. Angered at finding herself the object of Actaeon's intrusive gaze, Diana punishes him by transforming him into a stag; his own pack of hunting dogs then pursues and devours him. The *Ovide moralisé* miniature for this narrative (fig. 3.13) rather crudely juxtaposes the vulnerability of the bathing women's nude bodies to the phallic masculinity of Actaeon, a stag with large antlers. This moment in the Ovidian story of Actaeon and Diana forms the content of chapter 69 of the *Othea* (fig. 3.14). In the miniature Diana's companions attempt to protect her nude body from Actaeon's gaze. Actaeon appears as a hunter in the foreground; the stag in the background signals his imminent transformation. The textual material in this chapter stresses the negative valence of hunting; the *glose,* following the *Ovide moralisé,* states that Actaeon is a young man devoted to idleness who dissipates his resources in the pleasures of the body and the activities of the hunt; his idle retinue may, like Actaeon's own hunting dogs, devour him. This means that "he was hated by Diana, who signifies chastity, and devoured by his own people" [il fu haÿs de Dyane, qui notte chasteté, et devourez de sa propre gent] (69.41–43).

Whereas the chapter on Actaeon depicts the invasion of Diana's female community by a male hunter, an earlier chapter portrays this community undisturbed. In chapter 63 Diana and three of her companions engage in a range of activities associated with the hunt (fig. 3.15). The textual material warns the reader that the hunt is an idle pursuit; although it does not condemn Diana and her followers for engaging in the hunt, the *glose* advises the aspiring knight to consider the delights of the hunt as idleness, to which the *allegorie* contrasts the "wise woman" [sage femme] of Proverbs 31:27: "She has looked after the

Fig. 3.13. Diana transforming Actaeon into a stag, *Ovide moralisé,* Paris, Bibliothèque de l'Arsenal, MS 5069, fol. 29r. (Photo Bibliothèque nationale de France, Paris.)

Fig. 3.14. Actaeon surprising Diana bathing, *Epistre Othea*, BL, Harley 4431, fol. 126r. (By permission of the British Library.) ❧

Fig. 3.15. Diana and her nymphs hunting; Pallas Athena and Arachne, *Epistre Othea*, BL, Harley 4431, fol. 124r. (By permission of the British Library.)

paths of her house and she has not eaten her bread idly" [Consideravit semittas domus sue et panem occiosa non commedit] (63.19–21).

In contrast to the two chapters on Diana and her female followers as huntresses, chapter 23 depicts Diana and her followers as readers (fig. 3.16); in addition, this image appears to lack any connection to the textual material of this chapter. In the miniature, the goddess Diana emerges from a cloud above a group of women, each of whom concentrates on an open book. Compositionally, Diana occupies the place of a planetary deity in the "Children of the Planets" iconography that structures the sequence of the planetary deities in the *Othea* (see, for example, fig. 1.1). The scheme of the planetary deities included Phoebe, the goddess of the moon, an identification shared with Diana in this chapter, so that this image cites rather than extends the group of planetary deities. The *glose*, in fact, associates Diana with the moon: "Diana is the moon, and since there is nothing so evil that it does not have some good property, the moon confers a chaste condition; and they named it after a lady so called, who was very chaste and always a virgin" [Dyane, c'est la lune, et comme il ne soit rien tant mauvais qui n'ait aucune bonne propriété, la lune donne condicion chaste, et la nommerent d'une dame ainsi nommee qui fu moult chaste et tous jours vierge] (23.6–11). In the miniature, Diana's "children," the women below her, focus their eyes on open books, intently studying the written word. This image of Diana and her followers reading has no known textual or visual source; Hindman even argues that it was invented by Christine, rather than by a miniaturist.[28] The *texte, glose,* and *allegorie* to this chapter do not mention reading and offer no narrative explanation for this image of a community of women readers.

The action in the miniature evokes the classroom, since a scene in which both professor and students hold open books was a standard way of representing a university lecture.[29] In many educational contexts, students brought relevant books to a lecture; as Paul Saenger observes: "visual reading by the listener was essential for comprehension. While the professor read aloud from his autograph commentary, the students followed the text silently from their own books."[30] This image envisions not only female literacy, but the full ability of women to participate in the intellectual and interpretive act of reading under the patronage and influence of Diana, the pagan goddess.

Late medieval humanism offered Christine a vision of reading that betrayed a cultural anxiety about the female reader and the sexual temptations to which she is prone as a result of literacy;[31] this anxiety was visualized in illustrated copies of Laurent de Premierfait's French translation of Boccaccio's *De claris mulieribus*. As we have seen, the text of the French translation of Boccaccio would not have been available at the time Christine was composing the text of

Fig. 3.16. Diana and her followers reading, *Epistre Othea*, BL, Harley 4431, fol. 107r. (By permission of the British Library.)

Fig. 3.17. Leonce, Boccaccio, *Des cleres et nobles femmes,* BnF, fr. 598, fol. 92v.
(Photo Bibliothèque nationale de France, Paris.)

the *Othea;* however, the images in fr. 606 and Harley 4431 postdate the circulation of the French Boccaccio in illuminated manuscripts. In its focus on the
dangers of female literacy, Boccaccio's text articulates the medieval assumption
that reading and female sexuality are closely linked. Several images in the program of illumination for *Des cleres et nobles femmes* depict women and books;
the illustration to the chapter on Leonce (Leontium), for example, visualizes
the connection between reading and sexuality (fig. 3.17). Poised between her
bookstand and an amorous embrace, Leonce's identity as a reader appears to

125

render her susceptible to sexual advances. On the other hand, Christine's jux-taposition of women and books occurs in the context of textual material that emphasizes the importance of chastity. Thus Christine's choice of Diana for the visualization of women reading in the *Othea* forges a link between literacy and chastity that directly counters humanist anxieties about educated women.

Christine reinforces the identification of Diana with chastity elsewhere in the *Othea*. She assigns to Diana the role of defending chastity in her unique re-visions to the stories of Daphne (chap. 87) and the Gorgon (chap. 55).[32] The act of reading in the *Othea* image of Diana and her followers (fig. 3.16) may be interpreted as the visualization of Diana's identification with chastity, as the *glose* emphasizes. Given Christine's deliberate linkage of Diana and chastity, a ho-mosocial hunting community becomes a homoerotic textual community, and Diana's band of chaste huntresses becomes a group of chaste women readers. The association between same-sex community and same-sex desire that is visu-alized here is made explicit in the story of Callisto, one of Diana's nymphs, a myth that has a prominent place in the *Ovide moralisé*, but is excluded from the *Othea*. The textual material in chapter 23 of the *Othea*, however, could have been written for a chapter on Callisto. Likewise, Callisto's story reads as a com-mentary on the queerness of Diana's women readers.

The *Ovide moralisé* identifies Callisto as Diana's favorite follower, a maiden who abandoned the womanly task of weaving in order to join Diana's band. But Callisto's beauty attracts the attention of Jupiter, who appears to her in the form of Diana in order to seduce and ultimately rape her:

> He approaches the maiden; he kisses her on the mouth more volup-tuously than a virgin should. And he began to draw her toward him more than Diana was accustomed to do. While she was wishing to tell him where she had been hunting, Jupiter ran to embrace her, he threw her into the bushes, and he took her maidenhead.

> [Vers la damoisele s'aprouche;
> Saffrement la baise en la bouche,
> Plus que vierge ne deüst faire,
> Et vers lui se commence atraire,
> Plus que Dyane ne soloit.
> Tant dis comme elle li voloit
> Dire ou elle ot esté chacier,
> Jupiter la court embracier,
> Si l'a jetee sus l'erbage,
> Et li toli son pucelage.]
> (2.1475–84)

Fig. 3.18. Jupiter seducing Callisto; Diana confronting Callisto; *Ovide moralisé*, Rouen, Bibl. mun., MS O.4, fol. 50r. (Collections de la Bibliothèque municipale de Rouen. Photographies Thierry Ascencio-Parvy.) ☙

On the left side of the two-part miniature to this passage in the Rouen *Ovide moralisé*, one woman—an exceedingly tall "Diana," who is actually Jupiter—is about to kiss Callisto on the mouth (fig. 3.18).[33] With her right hand, Diana/ Jupiter grasps Callisto's chin in a gesture with both amorous and erotic significance.[34] On the right side, Callisto rejoins Diana's band.

According to the Ovidian narrative, Jupiter's rape of Callisto results in her pregnancy, which she hides from Diana for some time. Once her condition is exposed, however, Diana expels her from the community because she ascribes to Callisto a heterosexual performance that marks her as no longer "chaste" and thus violates the homosocial pact of Diana's huntresses. In the illustration to this scene in the Rouen manuscript (fig. 3.19), Diana looks on as three of her chaste huntresses inspect Callisto's body; one places a hand on her belly and detects her pregnancy. Diana's pointing gesture encodes her immediate response: she sends Callisto away from the female community. In the miniature in the Lyon

Fig. 3.19. Callisto expelled by Diana when her pregnancy is discovered, *Ovide moralisé*, Rouen, Bibl. mun., MS O.4, fol. 52r. (Collections de la Bibliothèque municipale de Rouen. Photographies Thierry Ascencio-Parvy.)

Ovide moralisé (fig. 3.20), Callisto's nude body exposes her pregnancy to the reader/viewer as well as to the gazes of Diana and her nymphs. In undressing for the bath, Callisto has revealed the bulging curve of her abdomen to her companions, who respond to what they see by separating her from their company. As we have seen, in the *Ovide moralisé* Diana's punishment of Actaeon clarifies the exclusively female status of her hunting community; when she expels the pregnant Callisto, she polices the sexuality as well as the gender of her band of followers.

Although Callisto does not appear in the *Othea*, the *texte* that accompanies the image of Diana and her women in chapter 23 offers a commentary appropriate to the Callisto story when it admonishes the reader:

Fig. 3.20. Diana expelling Callisto, *Ovide moralisé*, Lyon, Bibliothèque municipale de Lyon, MS 742, fol. 30r. (Photo Cliché Bibliothèque municipale, Didier Nicole.)

Remember Diana for the integrity of your body, because the unclean life does not please her, nor the immodest nor the defiled.

[De Dÿane soies recors
Pour l'onnesteté de ton corps,
Car ne lui plaist vie soullee
Ne deshonneste ne toullee.]
(23.2–5)

Even without naming Callisto, this *texte* reads as though it refers to Diana's banishment of the dishonored Callisto in the *Ovide moralisé*, where the women allowed to affiliate with Diana are known by the corporeal integrity they preserve. In the image of Diana and her followers reading, this affiliation is depicted through group reading, and the sexual implications of reading open a space for female same-sex eroticism, a desire that is almost impossible to visualize in medieval culture.[35] In regard to early modern Italian visual culture, Patricia Simons observes, "Diana, the very goddess of chastity and leader of an all-woman band, could in imaginative and visual terms sometimes be a sign for *donna con donna* relations of a decidedly embodied kind."[36] In strong contrast to the hunting nymphs in the image for chapter 63, the women in the image of Diana and her women reading follow a feminine code in their dress, hairstyles, and deportment. They evoke the category of the "femme" as discussed by Valerie Traub:

> Conventionally "feminine" and yet not strictly heterosexual, her presence disarticulates the equation between (feminine) gender and (hetero)-sexuality that has governed the terms of female embodiment. Sexually deviant and yet not in the ways that traditionally signify—neither temptress nor butch—the femme embodies a transgressive potential that paradoxically elicits silence rather than censure.[37]

What the *texte* of chapter 23 calls *onnesteté* (bodily honor or integrity) is not described in words but visualized as a same-sex, homoerotic community of readers over which Diana presides.

The *Roman de la rose* offers further evidence of the complex of associations that Christine brings out in her chapters on Diana. In her lengthy discussion of cosmology, Nature invokes the "wild ride" or the "night ride" as a false belief; though Nature refers to the leader as "dame Habonde," not as Diana, the description (ll. 18397–468) includes the standard features from the description of "following the goddess" in the *Canon Episcopi*. Although Nature criticizes the popular belief in the wild ride, she praises reading as a noble activity and comments that a clerk might acquire nobility through reading, a pastime much more advantageous than the stereotypically noble activity of hunting:

> In short, he finds everything that we should avoid or cultivate written in a book, as a result of which all clerks, whether masters of disciples, are noble, or should be so. Those who are not should realize that it is because their hearts are evil, for they have far more advantages than those who hunt the wild stag.
>
> [briefmant il voit escrit en livre
> quan que l'an doit foïr et sivre,
> par quoi tuit clerc, deciple et mestre,

sunt gentill, ou le doivent estre.
Et sachent cil qui ne le sont,
c'est por les queurs que mauvés ont,
qu'il an ont trop plus d'avantages
que cil qui queurt au cers sauvages.]
(18621–28)

The image of Diana and her followers incorporates this set of assumptions from the *Roman de la rose* that privileges books as ethical guides in preference to hunting, since it transforms Diana's huntresses into readers. Given that this passage in the *Rose* occurs in Nature's paean to reproduction, the identification of Diana's followers as chaste readers in the *Othea* offers a rather ironic commentary on the erotic politics of the *Rose*. The *Rose* testifies to the pervasive awareness of the "wild ride" or "night ride" among literate cultures. If Christine's Diana participates equally in the popular notion of the "wild ride" as well as the classical mythological understanding of the goddess, then the image of Diana's followers reading envisions the erotic possibilities of chastity in the context of a female same-sex community.

Outlaw Sexualities

In offering the visual possibility of female homoeroticism, the *Epistre Othea* exploits the disruptive quality of the visual to queer the textual. By contrast, in the chapters that work with the Ovidian tradition of metamorphosis from human to animal, the visual tends to offer a normative space to a queer text. The horror of transgressing the boundary between the species takes on a lurid quality in the extensive visual program of the *Ovide moralisé*, a program that revels in images of hybrid beings, half human and half beast. The *Othea* refuses to explore this visual feast of human transformation; instead, the visual programs of the *Othea* address this captivating quality of the Ovidian tradition by re-visioning several myths of bestiality and desire in the stories of Andromeda, Pasiphaë, and Circe. The images respond to the queer space the Ovidian text offers by using the Ovidian narrative to interrogate heteronormative paradigms for female desire. As such, Christine's deployment of visual material exemplifies a methodology "that deconstructs categories of sexuality," as characterized by Sally O'Driscoll:[38]

> Outlaw theory encompasses any sexual practice that is a challenge to whatever a particular society has marked out as the preserve of the "normal." I am suggesting *outlaw theorizing* as a term that follows the

original impetus of queer theory—a liberating deconstruction of sexual ideology and categories—without the problematic terminology confusion that negates the insistence on the material reality of specific sexual practices and their consequences.[39]

Christine's explorations of female sexuality and desire in the cases of Andromeda, Pasiphaë, and Circe cannot be fully understood in terms of mainstream Christian attitudes toward women. Rather, the text and images of the *Othea* restructure the dynamics of the gaze as it operates in the *Ovide moralisé*, so that Christine's Andromeda emphasizes the erotic agency of the heroine rather than her sexual vulnerability in the face of the sea-beast. Likewise, Pasiphaë's serene caress of the bull counteracts the transgressive implications of her desires, and Circe's regal stature and demeanor shift emphasis away from her terrifying ability to transform her suitors into beasts. These images focus on bestiality even though it is a desire that the dominant culture marks as beyond the law. In her formulation of outlaw theory O'Driscoll directs attention to the "focus on the outlook of the interpreter . . . and the text . . . [that] becomes the object of the outlaw gaze."[40] In the visual dynamics of the *Othea*, the goddess Othea directs the implied male reader to look differently on these images of bestial desire and to see in their outlaw status an alternate economy of female desire, one that is not paradigmatically heterosexual but draws instead on female agency and authority. In addition to the outlaw image, the textual material in the *Othea* marks a significant revisionary departure from the moralizations and allegories in the *Ovide moralisé*. In the received mythological versions of their stories, these three women dance dangerously into the border region where human and beast mate. The *Othea* re-visions female sexuality at the boundary of bestiality as a performance constitutive of the power of female desire.

The text and image of the story of Andromeda and Perseus (chap. 5) illustrate how Christine restructures Ovidian material to explore the politics of the male gaze. The *Ovide moralisé* details Perseus's first sighting of Andromeda tied to a rock and describes her as "soft and slender" [tendre et deliee] (4.6623). Much of the Ovidian text concentrates on Andromeda's beauty in the eyes of Perseus and gives him particular access to that beauty by graphically emphasizing her nudity ("toute nue" [4.6643]) as part of the visual experience for both Perseus and the reader/viewer.[41] Perseus studies Andromeda as though she were a polychromed statue:

> He would have thought she was a form in marble, that she was painted, an image made in the likeness of a woman, if he had not seen her tears and her hair blowing in the wind.

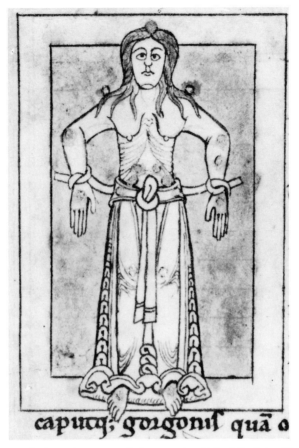

caputq; goigonis quã o

Fig. 3.21. Andromeda, astronomical manuscript, Oxford, Bodleian Library, MS Bodley 614, fol. 26v. (Bodleian Library, University of Oxford.) ◆

[Cuida que fust forme mabrine
Qu'en eüst la painte et portraite
Et en semblant de feme faite,
S'il ne la veïst larmoier
Et les crins au vent baloier.]
(4.6629–33)

The penetrating gaze of Perseus fetishizes Andromeda's vulnerable nudity in an erotic appeal to the reader.

The emphasis in the *Ovide moralisé* on a sexualized depiction of Andromeda's nude body demonstrates its participation in the astrological tradition that frequently depicts the constellation Andromeda as a nude or partially nude woman bound at the hands.[42] Images of Andromeda in astrological treatises such as the one in Bodley 614 (fig. 3.21) focus the viewer's attention on the

Fig. 3.22. Andromeda tied and Perseus, *Ovide moralisé*, Rouen, Bibl. mun., MS O.4, fol. 128r. (Collections de la Bibliothèque municipale de Rouen. Photographies Thierry Ascencio-Parvy.) ✺

mechanism by which her arms are stretched and her hands tied.[43] The textual and visual representations in the *Ovide moralisé* share an iconographic interest in the bound Andromeda. Rouen O.4 illustrates the story of Perseus and Andromeda with three miniatures (figs. 3.22 and 3.23) that form the visual pre-text for the *Othea*'s treatment of this material. The first of these miniatures translates into visual language the focus of the narrative on Andromeda as the object of desire. With her white body silhouetted against the dark rock and the ropes visibly outlined against her flesh, Andromeda's bondage encodes her exposed vulnerability. The sadistic sexual economies suggested by this representation of Andromeda bound and nude are entirely revised in the *Othea* image.[44]

Christine's *texte*, which ostensibly presents the received story from the *Ovide moralisé*, directs the young male reader/viewer not to a portraitlike

Fig. 3.23. Perseus slaying the monster and rescuing Andromeda, *Ovide moralisé*, Rouen, Bibl. mun., MS O.4, fol. 129r. (Collections de la Bibliothèque municipale de Rouen. Photographies Thierry Ascencio-Parvy.) ☙

image of a nude Andromeda but to a mirrorlike image of Perseus: "Model yourself on Perseus" [Aprés te mire en Perseüs] (5.2). The miniature immediately above these words shows Andromeda on the cliff facing the sea monster, with Perseus on the winged horse Pegasus hovering overhead (fig. 3.24).[45] Although urged by Othea's voice-off to focus on Perseus, the viewer's gaze is instead attracted to the sexually charged confrontation between Andromeda and the monster. Fixated on the resolutely poised Andromeda, the sea-beast threatens to devour her with its huge mouthful of razor-sharp teeth. The monster poses a sexual threat; as Marina Warner observes, "In myth and fairy tale, the metaphor of devouring often stands in for sex."[46] Although endangered, Andromeda exerts a powerful agency in her gaze, as though by directly staring at the monster she forcefully holds the predatory beast at bay. Perseus's chivalric rescue further situates the monster as a rival for the possession of Andromeda; Perseus's performance is the topic of the *glose*, which states explicitly that the good knight should imitate his action. The *glose* details the chivalric qualities

A près te mue en perseus . texte . b .
de qui le hault nom est sœus
par my le monde en toutes pars
pegasus li chevaulx appers

Fig. 3.24. Andromeda, the monster, and Perseus, *Epistre Othea*, BL, Harley 4431, fol. 98v. (By permission of the British Library.) ❧

inherent in Perseus's actions, particularly the nobility represented by his rescue of Andromeda from the threat of bestial aggression since, according to Christine, the chivalric knight should provide assistance to women in need.[47] The image, however, does not depict the vulnerability traditional to the Andromeda story; rather than needing aid, in the *Othea* Andromeda appears steadfastly to hold her own.

The *Ovide moralisé* text chronicles Perseus's arrival at the scene; he greets Andromeda, asks her why she is tied to a rock, and decides to rescue her. As a marital suitor Perseus negotiates with Andromeda's father for her hand in marriage before proceeding to slay his rival who threatens her. The episode concludes with a lengthy description of the marriage between Andromeda and Perseus, an event that reinscribes Andromeda's sexuality within the patriarchal order. As O'Driscoll reminds us, "The regime of 'normal' or normative sexuality is defined in the discourse of 'in-law' practice: such sexuality falls within the bounds of law, and, as 'in-law' suggests, the discourse rhetorically and legally binds sexuality to marriage, family, and reproduction."[48] Two fourteenth-century manuscripts of the *Ovide moralisé* reinforce the "in-law" emphasis of the narrative by visualizing the wedding of Perseus and Andromeda.[49] The *Othea*, on the other hand, specifically directs the reader/viewer to look at a different moment. Although the *texte* details Perseus's agency in this tale,[50] the image freezes the narrative at the particular moment of Andromeda's confrontation with the beast: Andromeda's gaze constitutes her sexual power. Unlike the images in the *Ovide moralisé*, the *Othea* image depicts Andromeda without bonds and clothed rather than nude so that the visual economy denies the specularity of the received Ovidian tradition. Instead of being the object of the male gaze, Andromeda powerfully deploys her own gaze. Likewise, the *Ovide moralisé* tale of marriage and traffic in women is completely excluded from the *Othea*. In its emphasis on Andromeda rather than Perseus, the image differs from the text and thereby queers the patriarchal and heterosexual assumptions inherent in the Andromeda myth as it had been transmitted in the *Ovide moralisé*.

Christine's chapter on Pasiphaë (45) exemplifies how the text-image relationships of the *Othea* deploy the outlaw gaze to subvert cultural assumptions about female sexuality. The received narrative of Pasiphaë explicitly presents her story of bestiality and desire as one of sexual transgression: to satisfy her desire for a handsome bull she commissions the craftsman Daedalus to construct a wooden heifer as a disguise through which she might attract the animal's attentions. The Minotaur, a half-human, half-bull, results from their sexual union. In medieval texts, the name Pasiphaë is synonymous with bestiality; for instance, in Dante's *Purgatorio* those guilty of bestiality identify themselves by calling out, "Pasiphaë," "the name of her who bestialized herself in the beast-shaped planks."[51] Modern critical responses likewise find the figure of Pasiphaë legible only as a cipher for the pejorative category of bestiality.[52] Christine's recuperation of Pasiphaë for outlaw theory so distressed Erwin Panofsky that he assumed that Christine misunderstood her subject: "poor, blue-stockingish Christine de Pisan, always prepared to take up arms in defense of her sex, found it hard to fit Pasiphae into a feminist scheme of things."[53] For medieval and modern readers alike, Pasiphaë's bestial desire has placed her beyond the law.

Christine's *texte, glose,* and *allegorie* work to bracket Pasiphaë's story as a fable of bestiality, while the image dramatically depicts her erotic embrace of the bull (fig. 3.25). The textual material explicitly subverts the mythographic traditions of Pasiphaë. First, the *texte* refuses to legitimize the standard use of the Pasiphaë story to equate female desire with degraded lust:

> For all that Pasiphaë was *fole,* you shouldn't read in your school that all women are such, for there are many worthy ladies.

> [Pour tant se Phasiphé fu fole,
> Ne vueilles lire en ton escole
> Que teles soient toutes fames,
> Car il est maintes vaillans dames.]
> (45.2–5)[54]

This comment refers to the centrality of Latin texts of Ovid in the grammar curriculum; educated males—such as the implied male reader of Othea's epistle— would have read Ovid in the privileged and homosocial space of the classroom.[55] The Pasiphaë in the *Othea* stands as a countermemory to Ovidian versions of the story, whether the Latin text authorized by the schools or the vernacular adaptation that circulated more widely, the *Ovide moralisé.*

The fable in the *Ovide moralisé* lingers for over two hundred lines on the dissolute nature of Pasiphaë's desire, which is condemned as transgressive:

> She loved the bull against nature. Loved? No, she didn't. It wasn't love at all. What was it then? Debauchery.

> [Le buef contre nature ama.
> Ama? Non fist! Ce ne fu mie
> Amours! Quoi donc? Forsenerie.]
> (8.718–20)[56]

One day Pasiphaë, seated at the window, sees "a particularly spectacular bull" [Un fier tor merveilleusement] (8.727), whose sheer masculinity inflames her:

Fig. 3.25. Pasiphaë embracing the bull, *Epistre Othea*, BL, Harley 4431, fol. 116r. (By permission of the British Library.) ✍§

"Pasiphaë passionately looked at the beauty of the bull, taking in his body, his eyes, and his cock" [Pasiphé curieusement / La biauté dou buef avisa; / Son cuer, ses iex et son vis a] (8.728–30).[57] Since Pasiphaë's sighting of the bull inevitably leads to bestial desires, the author expansively describes the dangers of female desire when a woman possesses the gaze. The *Ovide moralisé* devotes considerable attention to the symptoms of Pasiphaë's desire and the elaborate artifice of the cow she has Daedalus build so that she can satisfy her desires.[58]

The *texte* of the *Othea* refuses to read Pasiphaë's story as proof that women are generally dissolute; this refusal is further intensified in the *glose,* which refuses to retell the literal terms of the myth. The bestiality of the Ovidian tale is avoided in the *Othea glose:* "And some fables say that she was a very dissolute woman, especially because she loved a bull, by which is to be understood that she had relations with a man of base rank" [et dient aucunes fables que elle fu femme de grant dissolucion, et mesmement que elle ama un thorel, . . . qui est a entendre que elle acointa un homme de vile condicion] (45.6–11).[59] This insistence that "some fables" offer an interpretation of the bull as "a man of base rank" repeats a mythographic explanation of the Pasiphaë story. As Renate Blumenfeld-Kosinski traces it, this explanation originates in Hellenistic texts, is later echoed by Servius, and appears in commentaries ranging from William of Conches on Juvenal to commentaries on Dante.[60] According to this explanation, the word for bull, *taurus,* is understood as the proper name of the secretary to Pasiphaë's husband, Minos, so that she mates not with a bull but a socially inferior man. In her phrase, "some fables say," Christine appeals to the authority of the mythographic tradition to undermine the Ovidian tradition that associates Pasiphaë with transgressive bestiality and all women with excessive sexuality. Such an authoritative revision invites the reader to contemplate a wider range of interpretive possibilities for female sexuality.

If read apart from the image, Christine's text would appear to defend women from misogynist charges of excess sexuality. The Pasiphaë miniature, however, offers a tranquil composition suffused with a gentle sensuality (fig. 3.25). Set in a pastoral atmosphere, the scene represents cows grazing in the foreground and the bull of the herd in the background, a depiction that situates Pasiphaë harmoniously within the natural world and refutes the accusation of the Ovidian text that her actions are "against nature." Her purposeful embrace of the bull expresses Pasiphaë's eroticism in visually pleasing terms, and Pasiphaë's stroking of the bull's neck eroticizes her agency and thereby constructs her as the subject of desire.

By contrast, the combination of the image and the hundreds of lines of narrative in the Rouen manuscript of the *Ovide moralisé* relentlessly presents Pasiphaë's desire as grotesquely transgressive (fig. 3.26). The single miniature

Fig. 3.26. Pasiphaë embracing the bull, *Ovide moralisé*, Rouen, Bibl. mun, MS O.4, fol. 204r. (Collections de la Bibliothèque municipale de Rouen. Photographies Thierry Ascencio-Parvy.) ᮗ

used to illustrate the Pasiphaë narrative isolates the encounter between the bull and Pasiphaë against the patterned background typical in this manuscript. The absence of signs of nature, combined with the pillowed bench on which Pasiphaë sits, suggests a courtly setting that the bull has penetrated. The glistening white of the bull's rolling eye, his wildly disordered forelock, and the disappearance of his left front leg behind Pasiphaë's body depict the initial moment of embrace between beast and woman. Pasiphaë sits demurely, the heavy folds of her garment signaling her immobility; she responds to the bull's sexual advances with a gesture of submissive embrace that acknowledges the bull's dominance.[61] By focusing the viewer's attention on the excited bull's lunge toward the seated Pasiphaë, the *Ovide moralisé* miniature reinforces the text's insistence that the transgressive nature of Pasiphaë's desire exemplifies the excessive tendencies of female sexuality overall.

The Ovidian Pasiphaë is seated and nearly overpowered by the lunging bull;

in the *Othea* image Pasiphaë asserts her dominance by her upright posture and her possessive gesture of embrace. In validating Pasiphaë's agency, Christine's revision of this myth directly contradicts the standard cultural purpose of bestial myths; as J. E. Robson comments: "Bestial myths . . . have the effect of defining what sexual behaviour is suitable for a woman: a woman must submit to an appropriate male, and must not herself be the instigator of the sexual act."[62] Even in glossing the object of Pasiphaë's desire as a man rather than a bull, Christine does not suggest that Pasiphaë should have been submissive. In the *Othea*, neither *texte, glose,* nor *allegorie* invites the reader to be disturbed by this image. Indeed, the *glose* assures the good knight that he need not be disquieted by Pasiphaë's story, since women are generally not like this. Both the *Ovide moralisé* and the *Othea* allegorize Pasiphaë as the soul. In the *Ovide moralisé* this soul is sent to the devil; Christine, on the other hand, reads Pasiphaë tropologically as the wayward soul whose return to God creates great joy in heaven. Christine's allegory recuperates Pasiphaë from the condemnation associated with sexual sin.

Pasiphaë's desire for the bull stands in stark contrast to a vision experienced by the twelfth-century mystic Christina of Markyate when she was faced with a culturally accepted rape in a forced marriage. In her vision Christina "saw herself standing on firm ground before a large and swampy meadow full of bulls with threatening horns and glaring eyes." This vision appears to express the more normative view of sexuality and power relations ("She woke up, and interpreted . . . the bulls [as] devils and wicked men").[63] By contrast, in the *Othea* the dreamlike image of Pasiphaë stroking her bull emphatically envisions Pasiphaë's erotic agency in a visual medium that goes beyond the language of the text and its mythographic revision, so that the image enables the viewer to read the textual material as a critique of heteronormative stereotypes.

In the course of the *Othea*, the myth of the bestial encounter allows Christine to interrogate cultural assumptions regarding female desire. Early in the *Othea*, Andromeda faces an encounter with the predatory beast, and in the middle of the text, the Pasiphaë story recuperates the allure of the beast. Toward the end of the text, Circe appears as a powerful and effective queen who has mastered the bestial encounter (chap. 98). The mythical Circe marks a stopover for both the Trojans and the Greeks in the aftermath of the Trojan War. In Homer, Circe poses a threat to Ulysses on his way home to Ithaka; in Virgil, Circe threatens to enchant and divert Aeneas from his founding of Rome. Circe is the classic figure who embodies what Elizabeth Grosz terms the cultural fantasy and cultural projection that women's sexuality provides them with a terrifying power:

The fantasy of the *vagina dentata*, of the non-human status of woman as android, vampire or animal, the identification of female sexuality as voracious, insatiable, enigmatic, invisible and unknowable, cold, calculating, instrumental, castrator/decapitator of the male, dissimulatress or fake, predatory, engulfing mother, preying on male weakness, are all consequences of the ways in which male orgasm has functioned as the measure and representative of all sexualities and all modes of erotic encounter.[64]

The *Ovide moralisé*, following Ovid, embellishes the Virgilian treatment of Circe's story as an example of what Grosz would call a narrative of the "amorously imperilled male."[65] Aeneas is warned by one of Ulysses' men to avoid Circe's territory. The elaborate description that follows recounts Circe's abilities as a sorceress. The Ovidian text vividly renders the dangers of her seductive hospitality in its graphically detailed description of the process by which a human is transformed into a pig. The miniature in the Arsenal *Ovide moralisé* shows men half transformed into beasts, literally visualizing the text's elaborate description of the moment—typical in Ovid—of human terror at the dawning awareness of metamorphosis (fig. 3.27). The *Ovide moralisé* proceeds from this passage to describe Circe's frightful powers of sorcery.

The image, *texte, glose,* and *allegorie* in Christine's chapter on Circe display an unusual consistency.[66] The *texte* warns the reader/viewer:

> You ought to avoid the port of Circe where the knights of Ulysses were all turned into pigs. Remember her coasts.

> [Eschever dois le port Circés,
> Ou les chevaliers Ulixés
> Furent tous en porcs convertis;
> Souviegne toy de ses partis.]
> (98.2–5)

This elliptical comment alludes to the narrative tradition of the Circe episode as part of the Troy story transmitted from Homer's *Odyssey* (which was, of course, unknown to the medieval West) through Virgil's *Aeneid*, only to be reworked in Ovid's *Metamorphoses*.[67] The warning in Othea's *texte* that Hector should avoid the port of Circe very closely echoes the *Ovide moralisé* passage in which Eneas is warned that he should avoid transgressing the shore of Circe's island: "You will act wisely to guard against entering Circe's shore" [Garde toi, si feras que sage, / D'entrer ou circien rivage] (14.2359–60). The

Fig. 3.27. Circe welcoming Ulysses' men, *Ovide moralisé*, Paris, Bibliothèque de l'Arsenal, MS 5069, fol. 204v. (Photo Bibliothèque nationale de France, Paris.) ☙

Othea thereby locates its mythical focus in this moment of advice that the knight avoid the dangerous shore; the *texte* suggests that Circe indeed exemplifies the predatory nature of female sexuality.

The *Othea* illustration of Circe's encounter with Ulysses' men stages the scene outside a strongly walled city, its entrance blocked from the viewer's gaze by the overpoweringly large and regal figure of Circe herself (fig. 3.29). Ulysses' men have just disembarked from the ships in the foreground and requested safe haven, and Circe has turned two of them into swine.[68] This representation of Circe appears in the same opening and opposite the illustration to the *Othea* chapter on the fall of Troy (chap. 97). The illustration to this chapter depicts a dense mass of Greek warriors penetrating the burning city, an image that emphasizes Troy's vulnerability (fig. 3.28). By contrast, the placement of Circe's body at the entrance to her city renders it impenetrable and thereby envisions Circe's easy thwarting of male aggression.[69] Circe's crown clearly signals that the responsibility for defending her city is hers. Circe, a woman on her own, succeeds; the great warriors of Troy fail.

The *Othea glose* includes a description of Circe as a queen *(une royne)* who received Ulysses' knights under the guise of *courtoisie* and served them an appetizing beverage of such power that they were transformed into pigs. Christine's *glose* spells out several possible meanings for the figure of Circe: she might stand for a land or country where knights are placed in a vile and wretched prison; she might also represent "a woman of instability and fickleness" [une dame plaine de vagueté] (98.23). Yet the *allegorie* reads the port of Circe as hypocrisy. Although both the *glose* and the *allegorie* acknowledge the tradition of Circe as a terrifying enchantress whose seductive dangers threaten the knight's masculinity, this commentary must be contextualized within the entire chapter on Circe. The warning against the port of Circe in the initial *texte* becomes a warning against the life of hypocrisy by the time the reader has completed the *allegorie*. The ships in the foreground of the illustration emphasize the navigational decisions of Ulysses' men, which are analogous to the interpretive responsibilities of the reader/viewer. The Circe chapter ultimately places the responsibility on the reader/viewer to steer carefully through images and texts rather than to rely on received tradition. The relationship between text/image and reader/viewer creates a queer space, a queer desire; as Elspeth Probyn argues, "Following queer desire turns us into readers who make strange, who render queer the relations between images and bodies."[70] The interplay between text and image in the chapter on Circe in the *Othea* suggests that it is not female sexuality that is inherently dangerous, but the unchecked aggression of the male voyager. Christine's Circe is no longer an exemplum of the terrifying power of female sexuality but a figure who validates female desire outside the heteronormative paradigm.

In the myths of the bestial encounter, the *Othea* contradicts the standard disciplinary gestures of medieval mythography that attempt to shape and control female sexuality. Instead, Othea recuperates the gaze of Andromeda, the bestial desire of Pasiphaë, and the sexual power of Circe in order to articulate an outlaw theory, that is, in O'Driscoll's terms, to "investigate the ways in which the breaking of sexual taboos can call identity categories into question without necessarily constituting an identity."[71] The category of the bestial encounter allows the construction of an outlaw gaze, and through that outlaw gaze sexuality in general, including heterosexuality, appears queer.

Fig. 3.28. Burning of Troy, *Epistre Othea*, BL, Harley 4431, fol. 139v. (By permission of the British Library.) ❧

Fig. 3.29. Circe welcoming Ulysses' men, *Epistre Othea*, BL, Harley 4431, fol. 140r. (By permission of the British Library.)

Envisioning Heterosexual Performances

The text-image dynamic of the *Othea* ultimately interrogates heterosexuality, itself an unstable category in Ovidian myth, where stories of one mortal's heterosexual desire for another usually end in death, as is the case for Pyramus and Thisbe, Hero and Leander, and Ceyx and Alcyone. The *Othea* offers only a few performances of heterosexuality that Othea wishes to endorse, such as the myth of Ceyx and Alcyone, which Christine elsewhere uses to describe her own subjectivity as a widow.[72] In the *Othea,* the difficulty of envisioning heterosexual performance within the Ovidian tradition illustrates the queerness of heterosexual desire for the female subject. For example, Othea reads the hermaphrodite as an ideal of heterosexual performance. The image of Hermaphrodite (chap. 82) subtly but clearly reconfigures the power politics that flaw the heterosexual romance even as it revises the story of Hermaphroditus (fig. 3.30). In the image, two nude figures stand in a forest pool, each turned toward the other. The male extends his left arm and the female extends her right, so that each touches the shoulder of the other. This form of embrace, in which embracer and embraced cannot be distinguished because neither dominates, encodes a loving relationship between equals.[73]

The *glose* to this chapter retells an Ovidian story in which the nymph Salmacis loves the handsome youth Hermaphroditus so much that she jumps into the pool where he is bathing in order to embrace him. When Hermaphroditus rejects her, she asks the gods to assure that she would never be parted from him, and the gods respond by joining their two bodies into one body with two sexes. This etiological myth explains the origin of the hermaphrodite.[74] The interpretive material in the *glose* reminds the reader/viewer that there are multiple ways of understanding myth, and that the love story was frequently employed as the "cover of fable" [couverture de fable] under which writers hid "their great secrets" [leur grans secrés]:

> And because the matter of love is more pleasant to hear than another [matter], they often made fictions on love in order [for their stories] to be more enjoyable, especially to the ignorant people, who take nothing except the rind, and more pleasing to the learned, who suck the juice.

> [Et pour ce que la matiere d'amours est plus delitable a ouÿr que d'autre, firent communement leurs ficcions sus amours pour estre plus delitables mesmement aux rudes qui n'y prennent fors l'escorce, et plus agreable aux soubtilz, qui en succent la liqueur.] (82.30–35)

Fig. 3.30. Hermaphroditus and Salmacis, *Epistre Othea*, BnF, fr. 606, fol. 38v. (Photo Bibliothèque nationale de France, Paris.) ☙

What this "fiction of love" means has already been made clear by the voice of Othea in the *texte:*

> Do not be hard in granting that which you can use well. See yourself in Hermaphroditus, who suffered ill effects for refusing.
>
> [Ne soyes dur a ottroyer
> Ce que tu peus bien emploier;
> A Hermofrodicus te mire
> A qui mal prist pour escondire.]
> (82.2–5)

Both *glose* and *allegorie* return to this lesson of empathy:

> For just as one could not join one piece of iron to another unless both pieces are heated and softened by fire, so we cannot reform others if our heart is not softened by compassion.
>
> [car ainsi comme l'en ne pourroit joindre l'un fer a l'autre se tous les .ij. ne sont eschauffez et amoliez au feu, ainsi ne pouons nous autrui redrecier se nostre cuer n'est amoli par compassion.] (82.48–52)

This Ovidian story of excessive sexual desire is illustrated in the *Ovide moralisé* with an explicit image of a copulating couple that visualizes the message of the myth that the price of union is loss of subjectivity (fig. 3.31). According to some medieval writers, the dual nature of the hermaphrodite provided access to the secrets of women, a notion that spawned a genre of misogynistic writing whose ostensible purpose was to help men by exposing these secrets.[75] The reference in the *glose* to the "great secrets" that "subtle learned philosophers" hide in love stories indicates that Christine knew and rejected such an interpretation. In the *Othea*, Hermaphroditus is a figure for empathy, a metaphor for the union of souls. The image, which emphasizes sexual difference, strikes a balance between union and individuality, even as it represents heterosexual love as both sex and subjectivity.[76]

Paris and Helen, the most paradigmatic and problematic couple in the *Othea*, offer the originary script for performing heterosexuality in Trojan history. In the tradition, this story of seduction/abduction stands as both the cause of and the ongoing justification for the Trojan War and even the eventual destruction of Troy. The image of heterosexual embrace that opens chapter 75 (fig. 3.32) visualizes the power relations of this most notorious heterosexual

Fig. 3.31. Hermaphroditus and Salmacis, *Ovide moralisé*, Paris, Bibliothèque de l'Arsenal, MS 5069, fol. 47r. (Photo Bibliothèque nationale de France, Paris.) ☙

couple in a sharp contrast to the Hermaphrodite image: enveloped in Paris's dominant embrace, Helen demurely acquiesces.

The story of Paris and Helen comes from book 12 of the *Ovide moralisé*, which vastly expands the few lines in Ovid. The *Ovide moralisé* often attempts to provide a more extensive script for heterosexuality than the classical text of the *Metamorphoses* offers. The expansion develops at great length and in explicit detail Helen's complicity in her abduction. Even as Menelaus entrusts his wife to the keeping of his guest Paris, Helen secretly laughs at his naïveté and encourages Paris first with her glance and then with her responses to his long love speeches. She reciprocates his desire, yet she tells him that he must pretend to

Fig. 3.32. Paris embracing Helen, *Epistre Othea*, BL, Harley 4431, fol. 129r. (By permission of the British Library.) ✐

abduct her so that she can avoid public responsibility for her adultery. In agreeing to her own abduction Helen enacts the cultural assumption that women want to be physically overpowered: Paris attracts her precisely because of his willingness to use force. Even though she consents, they go through the charade of the abduction. After reading the love speeches, the reader/viewer of the Arsenal and Rouen manuscripts understands the image of the violent abduction as a staged performance (fig. 3.33).[77] In the Rouen miniature, Helen kneels before a golden idol, while Paris leads armed Trojans into the temple, where he half-embraces, half-seizes her in his mailed arms. In a pretense of being startled, Helen throws up her arms and looks over her shoulder at Paris with a complicitous glance. In emphasizing that Helen flirts and invites Paris's attentions, the

Fig. 3.33. Paris abducting Helen from the temple, *Ovide moralisé*, Rouen, Bibl. mun., MS O.4, fol. 300r. (Collections de la Bibliothèque municipale de Rouen. Photographies Thierry Ascencio-Parvy.) ☙

Ovide moralisé depicts her as a willing partner who responds to his seduction rather than a victim of his aggression. The images in the *Ovide moralisé* depict the abduction of Helen as a violent act, but the text's insistence that this abduction was staged erases the violence of the scene. The narrative concludes after the lovers have been welcomed into Troy; in the Rouen manuscript this narrative is punctuated with a final image of Paris and Helen (fig. 3.34). Now in courtly dress, Paris encircles Helen with his arms and kisses her as she sways toward him so that their bodies meet in a lovers' embrace.

The image of Paris and Helen embracing in the *Othea* differs subtly from the image of the same subject in the *Ovide moralisé*. The outline of Paris's taller and broader form encloses and controls Helen. His hands claim her languid body with their eloquent gestures of possession; her hands by contrast are not

Fig. 3.34. Paris embracing Helen, *Ovide moralisé*, Rouen, Bibl. mun., MS O.4, fol. 300v. (Collections de la Bibliothèque municipale de Rouen. Photographies Thierry Ascencio-Parvy.) ☙

even visible. Helen has been seduced by the courtly attentions of Paris and visibly yields to him. This image offers an enthralling version of "the fantasy of primal seduction, of meeting the other, seducing or being seduced by the other in an ideal pornotopia," in the words Linda Williams uses to describe the "original fantasy" that structures pornography.[78] The *texte* instructs the young knight, "Don't start out like Paris" [Ne fay pas Paris commencier] (75.3), and the *glose* adds, "Paris was not at all conditioned to arms but completely to love" [Paris ne fu mie condicionné aux armes, mais du tout a amours] (75.7–8). The text-image relationship turns the story of Paris and Helen into a critique of courtly love, since both text and image assign all of the responsibility and blame to Paris. In refusing to validate the fantasy in the *Ovide moralisé* that Helen duplicitously plotted with Paris to stage her abduction, the *Othea* rejects the notion that women always already consent to seduction if not rape.[79] This miniature of Helen seduced by Paris visualizes the seductiveness of courtly love; yet this courtly vision masks the originary violence of the Trojan War. This conventional representation of power relations in the *Othea* thus exposes the violence of heterosexuality even when it is not fully legible as violence. As we will see in the next chapter, the category of violence is gendered throughout the *Othea*.

4

ENGENDERING VIOLENCE

When violence is unloosed . . . blood appears—on the ground, underfoot, forming great pools. Its very fluidity gives form to the contagious nature of violence. Its presence proclaims murder and announces new upheavals to come. Blood stains everything it touches the color of violence and death.

—René Girard, *Violence and the Sacred*

The representation of violence is inseparable from the notion of gender, even when the latter is explicitly "deconstructed" or, more exactly, indicated as "ideology" . . . violence is engendered in representation.

—Teresa de Lauretis, "The Violence of Rhetoric: Considerations on Representation and Gender"

Illuminated manuscripts testify to the late medieval reader's thirst for graphic depictions of violence. No manuscript reveals this more vividly than the extensively illustrated copy of the *Histoire ancienne jusqu'à César* (BL, Royal 20 D. I) made in Naples around 1340 for a member of the Anjou court; this manuscript passed into the library of Charles V and later came into the possession of the duke of Berry. Royal 20 D. I today shows signs of avid and repeated readership: the upper margins bear the grime left as the fingers of readers turned its pages, and the pigments on many of the paintings in the lower margins have been rubbed away. More than most medieval books, Royal 20 D. I bears the marks of its consumption. Not only did a succession of distinguished bibliophiles

Fig. 4.2. Hector killing Patroclus in battle, *Histoire ancienne jusqu'à César*, BL, Royal 20 D. I, fol. 72v. (By permission of the British Library.) ❧

acquire this manuscript, but Royal 20 D. I also served as a workshop exemplar for two extant manuscripts of the *Histoire ancienne* and possibly for further copies that have not survived. It thereby supplied a vocabulary of violence for Parisian books made around 1400.[1]

A large percentage of the more than three hundred illustrations in this manuscript depict violent encounters, both on and off the battlefield (fig. 4.2). The unframed scenes fill the deep margin at the bottom of each page and extend beyond the width of the text columns. Each illustration disposes composition, gesture, and glance to propel the reading experience swiftly forward, from left to right and from page to page. This sequence of lower marginal illustrations creates a virtually continuous narrative that screens the violent episodes of Theban, Trojan, and Roman history narrated in the text so that the events unroll on a shallow stage before the reader's gaze. On many folios, the palette is limited to shades of red, blue, brown, and gray in broad washes of color. The thicker red pigment for blood is applied in narrow strokes. The contrast of the thick strokes of blood against the background washes of color heightens the visual impact of blood; indeed, the red pigment denoting blood adds a three-dimensional quality to the illustrations as blood streams, spatters, and even sprays from arterial wounds.

Until the late fourteenth century, medieval manuscript illustration rarely indulges in depictions of blood. As Christiane Raynaud has shown, to depict blood—even on the battlefield—was to violate a cultural taboo that saw blood as polluting.[2] The increasing visibility of blood in late-fourteenth-century French manuscripts results indirectly from the expanding networks of trade and exchange that brought a wider range of minerals into Paris from increasingly distant regions beyond western Europe. Louisa Dunlop identifies the frequent use of vermilion pigment in Parisian ateliers at the end of the fourteenth century as the consequence of its greater availability;[3] at the same moment, artists begin to depict blood more frequently in images of combat and execution. Nonetheless, the depiction of blood, often in a pigment distinct from other shades of red in a manuscript, always retains a sense of transgression; as Raynaud observes, "Le tabou existe toujours mais l'interdit qui pèse sur sa représentation est transgressé. Le sang suscite une fascination quasi-obsessionnelle."[4] Royal 20 D. I was influential in this regard: it and its copies—BnF, fr. 301 and BL, Stowe 54—revel in the visualization of blood, especially on the battlefield. In fr. 301, for example, blood is ubiquitous in battle scenes. Even before the armies have gone into battle, the artist depicts head wounds on the helmet of each combatant; small brushstrokes of vermilion pigment indicating blood are applied over the blue pigment of the helmets. These head wounds rather eerily predict the carnage to come during the battle.[5]

A marginal note on folio 8v of Royal 20 D. I contains the instruction that a portion of the manuscript be given to a producer of books, an indication that 20 D. I had been disbound so that it would be available for copying one quire at a time. The two extant copies of Royal 20 D. I, that is, fr. 301 and Stowe 54, probably result from this particular copying activity.[6] Fr. 301, made in Paris circa 1400 for the duke of Berry, largely preserves the program of illustration in Royal 20 D. I, though fr. 301 does not maintain the *ordinatio* of that manuscript. Rather than reproduce the strips of images that appear on the lower margins of Royal 20 D. I, the designer of fr. 301 inserted 228 square miniatures into columns of text and separated each image from the surrounding text by a frame and a rubric. Fr. 301 thus visualizes the violence of narrative through a different mechanism than its model, Royal 20 D. I: instead of the scroll-like strip in the lower margin, fr. 301 frames sequences of images as though each were a still, illustrating a violent moment in a montage sequence of individual scenes. For example, in narrating Penthesilea's final battle and death, fr. 301 offers five miniatures over the course of six pages, each of which marks a slight advance in the action that culminates in her final fall from her horse (figs. 4.3 to 4.6).[7] The two initial images in this sequence have gold backgrounds that reflect the light and give the impression that the figures move as the pages are turned. In the final miniature, Penthesilea has lost her helmet, and the artist has painted a bloody gash over her crown. This sequence achieves a cinematic effect in its slow-motion look at Penthesilea's death on the battlefield. This montage

Fig. 4.3. Penthesilea in battle, *Histoire ancienne jusqu'à César,* BnF, fr. 301, fol. 135v. (Photo Bibliothèque nationale de France, Paris.) ❧

supports Eisenstein's observation that "to seize a 'fragment' of movement in momentary immobility mankind did not have to wait for the invention of the camera."[8] Stephen Prince has suggested that the "graphic imagery of blood-letting and the montage aesthetic"[9] together make possible the "ultraviolence" of modern cinema; the violent visual program of fr. 301 likewise depends on a montage effect and the highly vivid depiction of blood.

The aesthetic impact of violence in these *Histoire ancienne* manuscripts results from the display of action over time: swords penetrate, blood flows, horses and their riders collide and fall.[10] Just as violence depends on action, the representation of violence has to overcome stasis to be effective. At one point, the text of the *Histoire ancienne* states that the illusion of movement increases the efficacy of images. Early in the manuscript, just before the rubrics for the Theban portion of the historical narrative, the text evokes Daedalus: "In this time lived Daedalus, about whom authors speak and recount their fables. And they say

Fig. 4.4. Penthesilea in battle, *Histoire ancienne jusqu'à César,* BnF, fr. 301, fol. 136v. (Photo Bibliothèque nationale de France, Paris.) ☙

that he made images move and go. But this is not true; I will tell you how this could be" [En ce temps fu Dedalus dont le aucteur dient et content leurs fables. Et dient quil faisoit les ymages mouvoir et aler. Mais c'est mensonge, avis vous diray comment ce pouoit ester].[11] The narrative then debunks this myth by explaining the mechanics behind the illusion of movement, so that an aesthetic ideal based on the notion that Daedalus produces an image of movement rather than makes images move emerges from the myth of Daedalus. As Eisenstein reminds us, "in cinema, the movement is not actual, but is an image of movement."[12] The artist in fr. 301 deploys montage in the Penthesilea sequence to produce an image of movement. As in cinema, manuscript painting evokes movement in order to visualize the instrumentality and impact of violence.

If the representation of violence implies action and impact, the image of a violent encounter consequently imparts a vision of agency inherently dependent on cultural notions of gender. This dynamic potential of images to engender

Fig. 4.5. Penthesilea wounding Pyrrhus, *Histoire ancienne jusqu'à César,* BnF, fr. 301, fol. 137r. (Photo Bibliothèque nationale de France, Paris.)

violence often exceeds the textual possibilities for articulating the gendered grammar of violence. For example, the illustration of the abduction of Helen (fig. 4.7) exemplifies the violent tenor of the visual program in Royal 20 D. I, which envisions violence by portraying action, and the portrayal of action genders agency. The accompanying text briefly describes how the Trojans enter the Greek temple with swords drawn and despoil it, while Paris accosts Helen and then carries her off. The image in the lower margin of the folio interprets these events as a scene of struggle and carnage. At the left, Helen and her female attendants huddle near the altar of Venus as Paris and his men in full armor advance upon them. Paris reaches out to grasp Helen's arms, though she futilely attempts to pull away from him. In the tightly compressed space at the right, the Trojans defeat the Greeks in a gruesome battle. The composition signals the Trojan victory through the contrast between orderly Trojan aggression—depicted as forward motion—and disorderly Greek defense; Greek corpses heaped

A denrenere lutaille qui
fu faite des tioiens + des
gregiois fu a un iour no
me. si sassemblerent les

Fig. 4.6. Pyrrhus cutting off Penthesilea's arm and killing her in battle, *Histoire ancienne jusqu'à César*, BnF, fr. 301, fol. 138r. (Photo Bibliothèque nationale de France, Paris.)

in the foreground bleed profusely. This image represents violence performed around two articulations: male–male or subject–subject violence and male–female or subject–object violence. As Teresa de Lauretis formulates this grammar of violence:

> [T]here seem to be two kinds of violence with respect to its object: male and female. I do not mean by this that the "victims" of such kinds of violence are men and women, but rather that the object on which or to which the violence is done is what establishes the meaning of the represented act; and that object is perceived or apprehended as either feminine or masculine.

She adds further, "For the subject of the violence is always, by definition, masculine; 'man' is by definition the subject of culture and of any social act."[13] In

antes sceu nos plaist nosyor epuo
toons.de celemerae pans.et
lien renr gces-1 menis 1lifaut
autresi present de ses biez-1 de
son fuice. Et que uos duvie pl'
ap̃s ces puroles se purtnet. Et
pans sousp̃us amours-1 en

Es armes prenentersa
tournent comunemēt
ant al devoies-1 estoit 1a la
nunit si fuier regie-1 serie ais
que la lune fust leuee-1 fuier
enpics sans tumulte-1 sans
noise se sont en semble adie

Fig. 4.7. Paris's abduction of Helen, *Histoire ancienne jusqu'à César,* BL, Royal 20 D. I, fol. 49v. (By permission of the British Library.)

the miniature, Paris's abduction of Helen constitutes subject-object violence since Paris and Helen are unequally situated; at the right, the Trojan-Greek engagement constitutes subject–subject violence, despite the Greeks' lack of armor and the surprise of the Trojans' attack. Although Royal 20 D. I contains numerous illustrations of both subject–subject and subject–object articulations of violence, the inclusion of both in this one miniature elides the difference between them and implies that they are equally justified.

The male–male violence of warfare is exhaustively visualized throughout Royal 20 D. I. For instance, the scene of Patroclus's death at the hands of Hector situates the fatal encounter between these two warriors in the midst of an intense engagement between the Greek and Trojan armies (fig. 4.2). In the foreground, just to the right of center, Patroclus and his horse fall backward as blood streams from the lance wound in his chest. Hector charges triumphantly toward Patroclus, sword bared. A sea of overlapping helmets suggests the density of the massed warriors; swords and lances aimed in all directions evoke the claustrophobic chaos of the battlefield. Discarded shields and swords, as well as a bleeding corpse, lie on the ground. At the far left, one warrior splits another's head, his sword severing the helmet in an image that renders visible the great force of the blow.[14] Blood flows from the prominent wounds, especially Patroclus's. As William Ian Miller observes, "We tend to perceive violence when blood flows outside its normal channels."[15] In these images the presence of blood signifies that these images depict not just movement but violence. The prominence of blood makes legible the violence of the battlefield.

A large number of the miniatures in *Histoire ancienne* manuscripts visualize battle scenes between armies, scenes that by their nature depend on the containment of violence within warfare. In Johann Huizinga's classic formulation, "Fighting, as a cultural function, always presupposes limiting rules. . . . We can only speak of war as a cultural function so long as it is waged within a sphere whose members regard each other as equals or antagonists with equal rights."[16] René Girard furthers this notion of warfare as a violence of reciprocity; Girard's cultural theory of violence assumes that all the participants are subjects who direct their aggression at other subjects.[17] Teresa de Lauretis teases out the gendered terms of such violence: "The distinctive trait here is the 'reciprocity' and thus, by implication, the equality of the two terms of the violent exchange, the 'subject' and the 'object' engaged in the rivalry; and consequently the masculinity attributed, in this particular case to the object."[18] The representation of violence in the setting of a battlefield, however "reciprocal" it may be, nonetheless deploys agency to envision a gendered relation of subject and object.

The visual programs of the *Othea* in the Duke's and the Queen's manuscripts frequently respond to the violence represented in the manuscripts of the *Histoire ancienne* available in Christine's milieu, such as those made in the mid–fourteenth century—Royal 20 D. I, BnF, fr. 246, and Copenhagen, Thott 341—which were in the ducal and royal libraries, as well as in manuscripts such as fr. 301 and Stowe 54, produced in Paris in the first years of the fifteenth century. The reader/viewer of the *Othea* is repeatedly offered a grammar of violence that revises the ideology of warfare as represented in the *Histoire ancienne* tradition. As part of this process, the *Othea* juxtaposes the grammar of violence in the domestic sphere to the grammar of violence on the battlefield; as a result, warfare and violence against women become legible as performances of the same cultural activity.

The Violence of Gender

Manuscripts of the *Histoire ancienne* were not the only vehicles for envisioning violence in fifteenth-century Paris. Manuscripts of the *Ovide moralisé* and the French translation of Boccaccio's *De claris mulieribus, Des cleres et nobles femmes,* also display a marked interest in the possibilities for visualizing violence. The miniatures in the *Ovide moralisé,* particularly in the Arsenal manuscript, draw out the Ovidian obsession with the grotesque implications of the process of transformation from human to beast, a violence worked upon the human form. In addition, the French manuscripts of Boccaccio's *Des cleres et nobles femmes* relentlessly depict the female as the object of violence. Boccaccio's text takes women as its subject and focuses obsessively on their violent deaths: the illustrated French translations repeatedly visualize women being stabbed, hanged, poisoned, abducted, and beheaded. Although it draws visual material from all three traditions, the *Othea* usually revises or disavows the context and tenor of the visual scandal of violence. In its versions of Ovidian narratives of transformation, the *Othea* only once depicts a body halfway through the metamorphosis; this image—the transformation of Daphne—is highly aestheticized. Consequently Christine's text offers none of the grotesque pleasure of the Ovidian spectacle found in manuscripts of the *Ovide moralisé*.[19] Though it shares topics with Boccaccio's *Des cleres et nobles femmes*, the *Othea* contains only a few images of violence against women, and these images avoid indulging in the grotesque or lurid possibilities of depicting violence. These images would consequently appear to be all the more political.

In juxtaposing images of domestic or erotic violence to images of warfare, the *Othea* implicitly comments on the organization of violence in the texts and mythologies inherited from the classical world, specifically the Ovidian tradition transmitted in the *Ovide moralisé* and the epic tradition as transmitted in the *Histoire ancienne*. Giorgio Agamben identifies the social order of the Roman world as the originary site of a notion of sovereign power and juridical violence in relation to *bare life*—a life that may be killed but not sacrificed—so that the "first foundation of political life is a life that may be killed, which is politicized through its very capacity to be killed."[20] Furthermore, when a sovereign power takes the life of someone classified as bare life, that death is not classed as homicide. The deaths and violence of the Ovidian world depicted in the *Ovide moralisé* exemplify this aspect of Roman social order, and Christine de Pizan's *Othea* explicitly comments on this organization of Roman values. When the *Othea* juxtaposes violence in the military and domestic contexts—the battlefield and the household—the category of bare life takes on the theoretical significance of gender. As Agamben's paradigm of bare life illustrates, Roman law does not identify patriarchal power in the household as an instance of sovereign power over bare life. Nonetheless, the political vision of the *Othea* explicitly situates women as objects or subjects of violence and thereby incorporates the female into the sphere of the political.[21] In addition, the *Othea* emphasizes the strategic performances of warfare so that the Trojan battlefield offers lessons in military strategy rather than models of chivalric heroism. As Hector's own story eventually illustrates, the defeated warrior becomes a figure of sexual vulnera-

Fig. 4.8. Cephalus killing Procris, *Ovide moralisé,* Paris, Bibliothèque de l'Arsenal, MS 5069, fol. 104r. (Photo Bibliothèque nationale de France, Paris.) ☙

bility, and as a result, he shares the political implications of his status as bare life with Ovidian heroines such as Procris and Coronis.

The *Othea* treats two Ovidian narratives of domestic violence in which the female victims are implicitly categorized as bare life, given that their murderers are not judged guilty of homicide. Chapters on Cephalus and Procris (chap. 76) and on Phoebus and Coronis (chap. 48) demand an analysis of violence against women as subject–object violence. Cephalus mistakenly kills his wife Procris while he is out hunting, and the god Phoebus brutally slays his lover upon hearing a report that she has been unfaithful. Despite the differences in the narratives, the miniatures in the Arsenal *Ovide moralisé* visualize both Cephalus and Phoebus as performers of deadly male aggression against defenseless females (figs. 4.8 and 4.9). These Ovidian images closely resemble one another in their compositions. Procris, crouching in leafy foliage in the left foreground, looks up and to the right at Cephalus in profile, who stares at her as he aims his arrow. Not only does his looming height embody male power, but his taut

Fig. 4.9. Phoebus Apollo killing Coronis, *Ovide moralisé,* Paris, Bibliothèque de l'Arsenal, MS 5069, fol. 18r. (Photo Bibliothèque nationale de France, Paris.) ☙

bowstring specifies the moment that power becomes force as he shoots her. In the same manuscript, the miniature depicting the murder of Coronis places Phoebus in the same position that Cephalus occupies. Phoebus stands at the right, purposefully staring at Coronis; the arrow has just left his bow. At the left, Coronis's limp body falls away from Phoebus under the impact of the arrow. Phoebus's bow and arrow seems to have been the model for Cephalus's weapon on folio 104: his bow and arrow overwrites the javelin described in the text. Just as the dynamic poses of the two males code their murderous agency as subjects, the frozen helplessness of Procris and the dead weight of Coronis's corpse communicate their status as objects. As powerful statements that equate domestic violence with subject–object violence, these images interpellate the viewer as agent in the effective deployment of violence against an object.

The text of the *Ovide moralisé* (7.2759–3282) complicates the issues of violence and subjectivity treated in such a monolithic way in the miniature of Procris's death. The text specifies that Cephalus kills his wife by accident and that her death could have been avoided if husband and wife had trusted each other more. In the narrative of Phoebus's murder of Coronis in the *Ovide moralisé* (2.2121–454), Phoebus intentionally murders Coronis when he hears of her infidelity, and though he immediately regrets killing her, the Ovidian text nonetheless sanctions violence against women believed guilty of a "sexual transgression" such as infidelity. Despite these differences, the deaths of both women are described in equally graphic, bloody detail, and the miniatures suggest that the women die similar deaths. The visuality of the *Ovide moralisé* implicitly naturalizes violence against women as an unquestioned performance of male agency. As bare life, Procris and Coronis validate the sovereign status of Cephalus and Phoebus.

The *Othea* chapters on Procris and Coronis do not critique the violence of these stories, but neither do they naturalize it. In the process, violence becomes legible without becoming alluring. In the Queen's manuscript, the miniature to the chapter on Cephalus and Procris (chap. 76) apparently takes its basic composition from the *Ovide moralisé* illustration: Procris sits on the ground, hidden in foliage, and Cephalus stands in profile (fig. 4.10). He has just pierced Procris with his magic javelin; she raises her open hands in surprise and turns her head so that her startled glance meets his. The miniature depicts the moment that their identities are constituted by mutual recognition; Procris's wimple signals her primary identity as a married woman. The brief narrative in the *glose* explains that Cephalus's habit of going out to hunt early in the morning prompted his wife's jealousy; when she surreptitiously followed him, he heard the leaves rustle where his wife was hidden, thought it was a wild animal, and thrust his javelin. Because of its magic power, its touch was enough to kill her. According to the *glose*, Cephalus regretted this mishap but had no remedy. This schematic outline in the *glose* omits the broader context from the *Ovide moralisé* and concurs with the instruction of the *texte* that the reader not stalk or spy on anyone. The combination of image, *texte,* and *glose* in the *Othea* avoids assigning Procris the responsibility for her own death; indeed, the *Othea* miniature foregrounds the accidental nature of the event and the couple's dawning awareness of its tragic consequence for both of them.

The *texte* to the *Othea* chapter on Phoebus's murder of Coronis unambiguously assigns responsibility to Phoebus:

Do not kill the beautiful Coronis on account of the raven's report and news. Because if you were to kill her, you would afterward repent of it.

[N'occis pas Corinis la belle
Pour le rapport et la nouvelle

text · hople ·

De te chulle de mul gautier
Mais ten va touidis ton sentier
Cephalus o son clauellot
e tauzent et la femme loth

Fig. 4.10. Cephalus killing Procris, *Epistre Othea*, BL, Harley 4431, fol. 129v.
(By permission of the British Library.)

Du corbel, car se l'occïoyes,
Aprés tu t'en repentiroyes.]
(48.2–5)

The *glose* tersely states that Phoebus killed Coronis as soon as he saw her, and the image depicts this death as murder, implicitly calling into question the Ovidian classification of Coronis as bare life. The miniature in the Duke's manuscript offers a rendition of Coronis's murder that is unusually sensational for *Othea* illustration in this period, a sensationalism especially evident by comparison to the same image in the Queen's manuscript. In the Duke's manuscript (fig. 4.11), Coronis's body begins to fall under the impact of Phoebus's arrow. Its winged shaft projects from her wounded breast as blood drips heavily down the front of her pale gray gown. Unlike the *texte*, the image dwells on the moment that the arrow penetrates Coronis's breast and invites viewers to align their gazes with its trajectory; as a result, the *Othea* image preserves and even heightens the visual statement in the *Ovide moralisé* that renders this event as subject–object violence. The miniature's focus on the gruesome details of the murder is consistent with the description in the *Ovide moralisé* (2.2370–79). The brutal Phoebus in the *Ovide moralisé* miniature (fig. 4.9) points his index finger accusingly and strides forward so vigorously that he breaks the frame, actions that effectively convey his crazed anger. But the same murderer in the Duke's manuscript floats gently above the horizon, his body forming a series of lyrical curves. The beauty of this image belies its violence, and the representation consequently aestheticizes and eroticizes violence against women.

The aesthetic pleasure offered by the image of Coronis's murder in the Duke's manuscript is not evident in the same chapter in the Queen's manuscript (fig. 4.1). In the Queen's manuscript, Phoebus's solid body and thick brocade costume are drawn in straight, not curving lines; the slender arrow does not penetrate Coronis's body so visibly, nor does the blood read so dramatically against the deep blue of her gown. Heavy fabric encases Coronis, and the details of her costume—the high white collar and the wide ermine-lined sleeves—shift attention from her corporeal vulnerability to her social status. The overall effect is much less violent than in the Duke's manuscript and generates no aesthetic pleasure; as a result, the image more effectively emphasizes the imperative of the *texte:* "do not kill Coronis." In the Duke's manuscript, the chapter on Phoebus and Coronis appears to have been illustrated by an artist whose work occurs only in the third quire (fols.17r to 24v). Millard Meiss attributes most of the miniatures in this quire to an artist he calls the "Saffron Master" for the painter's idiosyncratic use of a rather acid yellow pigment in these images. Though Meiss does not assign this particular image to the Saffron artist, its presence in this quire

et sa plume qui estre souloit blanche
comme noif lui mua phebus en noire
en signe de douleur, et si lor dena tire lor
porteur et nonceur de mauuaises nouel
les/et puet estre entendue ceste posicion
que le escriuteur auenir poissant homme
lui raporta semblables nouuelles dont il
il fu chacies et deffais. pour ce veult dire
que le bon cheualier ne se doit auancier de di
re a son prince nouuelles qui le meust
a yre ne courrou p flaterie contre le bien
dautrui car en la fin de te tels raport sont
communement les yuerdne petis et aussi
ne doit croire raport alui fait p flaterie
A ce propos dit le philosophe hermes
en raporteur ou controueur de nouuelles
ou il ment a cellui de qui il les raporte ou
il est faulx a cellui de qui il les dit

Texte ·xliiij·

Coronis pues comme la beste
pour le raport z la nouuelle
du corbel car se l'occiopes
Apres tu ten repentiroies

Glose ·xliiij·

Coronis fu une damoiselle que dit
une fable que phebus ama par amours
le corbel qui adont le seruoit lui rapor
ta que il auoit veu la belle coronis samie
gesir auec un autre damoisel de celle
nouuelle fu tant dolent phebus que
il occist samie apres aussi tost que elle
fut deuant lui mais merueilles sen
repenti apres/dont le corbel qui cuia
son attendroit la nour de son seigneur
pour ce bien fait en fu maudit releuee

Allegorie ·xliiij·

Coronis qui ne doit estre occise non ente
dions nostre ame que nous ne deuons oc
cire par pechie mais bien la garder et dit
saint augustin que lame doit estre garde
comme le coffre qui est plein de tresor comme
le chastel qui est assise des anemis et co
me le roy qui se repose en sa chambre de
retrait et doit estre ceste chambre close de
vj portes qui sont les vj sens de nature
z nest autre chose clorre ses portes mais
que retraire les delectacions des vj sens: sil
auient que lame doye yssir par ces portes
a ses operacions foirmees elle doit me u
rement et rassisement et en discrecion
yssir et aussi comme les princes quant
ilz veulent yssir de leurs chambres ou
ilz ont huissiers deuant eulx tenans
maces pour faire voye + en la presse

Fig. 4.11. Phoebus Apollo killing Coronis, *Epistre Othea,* BnF, fr. 606, fol. 23v.
(Photo Bibliothèque nationale de France, Paris.)

and the characteristics it shares with the miniatures attributed to the Saffron artist place it in this separate idiom. For example, the miniature of Pasiphaë in the third quire of the Duke's manuscript is more lurid than the miniature of Pasiphaë in the Queen's manuscript (fig. 3.25); the depiction of Thisbe's death is much more bloody than in the Queen's manuscript since Thisbe's wound is much more evident; and the depiction of Hector's attack on Achilles is more graphic.[22] The images in this quire of the Duke's manuscript exhibit voyeuristic attitudes toward women and violence that eroticize subject–object violence and invite viewers to identify as the subjects of violence. The images in the Queen's manuscript and elsewhere in the Duke's manuscript do not generally enter into such a contract with the viewer. In spite of this one quire in the Duke's manuscript, the *Othea* as a whole exhibits an awareness of the implications of violence and representation in the reading process. Furthermore, the *Othea* holds both Phoebus and Cephalus responsible for their violent agency, so that the *Othea* ultimately questions the Ovidian inscription of the female victim as bare life—life that one can take without committing homicide.

These two chapters on domestic violence do not stand as the synthetic statement on violence and gender in the visual and textual programs of the *Othea*. Instead of rhetorically situating women as always the victims or objects of violence, the *Othea* systematically envisions the possibility that women can intervene in subject–subject violence or even occupy the position of subject in subject–object violence. The chapter on the death of Achilles (chap. 40) offers a particularly clear example of visual play with the gendered discourse of violence. The *glose* recounts the events leading up to Achilles' murder; in the course of the Trojan War he had "treacherously" killed several of Hecuba's sons. Both the *texte* and the *glose* suggest that for this reason Achilles should have been wary of Hecuba. However, giving no heed to the risks involved, Achilles goes to the temple to meet Hecuba and request permission to marry her daughter Polyxena. As the *glose* explicitly states, there Hecuba orders her son Paris to murder Achilles in revenge for the deaths of her other children. In the *texte*, Othea warns Hector not to make the same strategic error that Achilles made and not to trust an enemy he has grievously wronged.

In the illustration to this chapter in the Duke's manuscript, Hecuba stands in a prominent position at the far left and points emphatically toward Achilles, who kneels at an altar (fig. 4.12). At her right stand three armed men, one of whom looks to her as if to obey her instructions. The other two assault Achilles while he prays: one stabs him in the back with his sword while another strikes his head. Blood from these wounds pours down his back. Such a composition locates Achilles in the position of victim in a scene of Christian martyrdom.[23] Read from left to right, the image visualizes the unfolding of Hecuba's will.

Fig. 4.12. Death of Achilles; Busiris's human sacrifices, *Epistre Othea*, BnF, fr. 606, fol. 20r. (Photo Bibliothèque nationale de France, Paris.)

Fig. 4.13. Death of Achilles, *Histoire ancienne jusqu'à César*, Copenhagen, Kongelige Bibliotek, MS Thott 431, fol. 73v. (The Royal Library.)

Though Achilles' death at the hands of the Trojan soldiers literally comes about through subject-to-subject, that is, male-to-male, violence, Hecuba sets the murderers in motion. In both the image and the text of the *Othea*, her status as a grieving mother ultimately dominates. In her vengeance, Hecuba claims agency and implicitly occupies the masculine subject position; by contrast, Achilles, as the object of violence, becomes metaphorically feminized. In this interpretation of the death of Achilles, the *Othea* moves away from the visual tradition. Pictorial variations of this subject appear in all the *Ovide moralisé* manuscripts and the copies of the *Histoire ancienne* identified as part of the collections in the ducal or royal libraries. Of all of these, a miniature in the copy of the *Histoire ancienne* in Thott 431 (fig. 4.13) provides the closest analogue.

Like the *Othea* miniature, the miniature in Thott 431 also positions Hecuba at the far left and the armed men to her right carrying out her orders by attacking the kneeling Achilles. However, by contrast, the Hecuba in the *Othea* wears her crown and stands proportionately larger than the other figures. In the *Histoire* image, the glances of Hecuba and Achilles meet, creating a moment of revenge and personal accountability, but in the *Othea,* Hecuba's regal presence performs the political authority of a grieving mother. In the miniature's version of the story, by entering her city and asking for her daughter's hand, Achilles has subjected himself to Hecuba's sovereign power—he has voluntarily become bare life. Thus the sovereign Hecuba, in ordering that he be killed, neither performs a sacrifice nor commits a homicide. Though it is a scene of violence, this image does not simply revise the gendered terms of subject–object violence, but claims instead an ethical justification for Hecuba's action, which the text, in stressing Achilles' responsibility for his own death, ultimately endorses.

In the layout of the *Othea* in the Duke's and the Queen's manuscripts, the miniature of Hecuba appears on the same folio as a miniature of King Busiris offering severed human heads as sacrifices to his gods (chap. 41).[24] These paired images are set in temple interiors with almost identical idols on the two similarly placed altars, before which kneel Achilles and Busiris respectively. By contrast to Hecuba's ethical agency, Busiris, alone in the temple, indulges in the pleasurable outcome of his violence as he lovingly offers a third head to the deities (fig. 4.12). Behind him lie three headless torsos; two of the bloody stumps confront the viewer. Busiris's face reveals an expression of rapt devotion and satisfaction. The *glose* identifies him by his bloody appetite: "Busiris was a terribly cruel king and he delighted greatly in the murder of men" [Busierres fu un roy de merveilleuse cruauté et moult se delictoit en occision d'ommes] (41.7–8). Taken together, the *texte, glose,* and *allegorie* direct the reader to avoid the cruelty depicted in the repellently gruesome image.

The image of Busiris's sacrifices in the *Histoire ancienne* focuses on the moment of violence (fig. 4.14).[25] In the miniature, a regal Busiris gestures toward his victims while an executioner swings a large ax that strikes the neck of a kneeling figure with hands folded together as if in prayer. The image captures the moment when ax cuts into flesh. Although the miniature of Busiris in the *Histoire ancienne* contains no altar or other religious detail that would suggest human sacrifice, the miniature in the *Othea* centers on the ritual moment of offering the severed heads as sacrifice, rendering visual the textual comment, "Busiris, who was a homicide" [Busierres, qui fu omicides] (41.17).[26] Revising what reads as a standard scene of legal execution in the *Histoire ancienne,* the *Othea* offers a chilling image of homicidal fetishism that visualizes the textual identification of Busiris as a cruel king. In the *Othea* the act of sacrificing defines

Fig. 4.14. Busiris's human sacrifices, *Histoire ancienne jusqu'à César*, Copenhagen, MS Kongelige Bibliotek, Thott 431, fol. 46v. (The Royal Library.)

Busiris as a homicide. As sacrificial victims, the dead bodies do not constitute bare life, and the sacrificial status of his victims ultimately exposes the cruelty of Busiris's sovereignty.

By contrast to Busiris as an example of cruelty, the *Othea* treats Thamyris as a sovereign who justifiably executes her enemies and consequently exemplifies effective military and political leadership. According to the *glose* to this chapter (57), when Cyrus, king of Persia, was waging a war of conquest, he set out to overrun the "kingdom of *Femmenie*" ruled by Thamyris, queen of the Amazons. Underestimating her strength and skill, Cyrus led his army directly into the ambush she had laid for him. The queen took Cyrus captive, had his leaders decapitated in his presence, and ordered their blood collected in a barrel. After his decapitation she addressed him: "Cyrus, you were never sated with human blood—now you can drink your fill" [Cirus, qui oncques ne fus saoulé de sanc humain, or en peus boire ton saoul!] (57.23–24). The *glose* summarily concludes the narrative at this point: "And thus Cyrus came to an end, the great king of Persia, who never before had been conquered in any battle" [Et ainsi fina Cirrus, le grant roy de Perse, qui oncques n'avoit esté vaincu en nulle bataille] (57.24–26).

The miniature to this chapter depicts the moment when Thamyris speaks to the lifeless head of Cyrus (fig. 4.15). Thamyris's Amazon lieutenants focus the viewer's gaze on the executioner who holds Cyrus's head over the barrel. Their armor-clad presence queers the scene by demonstrating the same-sex composition of the army as well as the military potential of the female warrior. The bloody, headless stumps of Cyrus's barons confront the viewer with the gruesome physical details of decapitation. Thamyris, the executioner, and the three Amazons loom over their vanquished enemies. Framed by the tent behind her, Thamyris glances down at Cyrus's head; its profile presentation contrasts with the full frontal presence of Thamyris, which expresses her royal status as well as military superiority. Meyer Schapiro identifies such frontality as marking "the theme of state" and credits "the face turned outward" with "intentness, a latent or potential glance directed to the observer [which] corresponds to the role of 'I' in speech."[27] Thamyris holds her mail-encased hand to her chest in a gesture that may allude to her bodily status as a single-breasted Amazon; such a gesture underscores the taunt she addresses to Cyrus at the moment of his punishment. In the center of this dramatic execution scene, Thamyris's sovereign pose and gesture enact her agency as the subject of violence and her prerogatives as a sovereign executing a defeated enemy.

The conflict between Thamyris, queen of the Amazons, and Cyrus, the great king of Persia, offers a paradigm of subject–object violence within a colonizing framework. This conflict originated in warfare and should have been governed

by the rules of the battlefield, which identify Thamyris as a leader responsible for defending her country from invaders. But since Cyrus had no justification for his aggression against *Femmenie,* he did not merit the respect that would otherwise be due to a captured enemy leader. His humiliation after death figures him as the object of violence and confers on Thamyris the status of subject. An astute ruler, Thamyris uses her triumph over Cyrus to warn off other potential invaders. Like the image, the text emphatically presents Thamyris as a powerful female who conquers an Asian despot through her shrewd deployment of military strategy. The textual material directs the reader/viewer's interpretation when it demands recognition and respect for Thamyris. According to the *glose,* the defeat of Cyrus "says to the good knight that he should never be so presumptuous as not to fear that some misfortune could happen to him by some turn of events and by something less than he is. And in this regard Plato says, 'Do not undervalue anything for its small faculty, because its powers could be great'" [dit au bon chevalier que ja ne soit se oultrecuidez qu'il n'ait doubte que mescheoir lui puist par aucune fortune et par mendre de soy. A ce propos dit Platon: "Ne desprises nul pour sa petite faculté, car ses vertus peuent estre grandes"] (57.26–31). The *allegorie* explicitly comments on the gendered grammar of violence when it states that Thamyris "must not be disparaged even though she is a woman" [ne doit estre desprisee pour tant se elle est femme] (57.33–34).

This inversion of the standard paradigms of gender and violence, however, can only occur in the Eastern setting of this narrative: the text characterizes the ill-fated Cyrus as a Persian conqueror filled with imperial hubris, and the image signals the Eastern location of the Amazon kingdom. The executioner wears a turban, and a band of exotic script decorates Thamyris's tent. Such details remind the reader/viewer to identify both Thamyris and Cyrus with the East, its cultural differences of language and costume, and its implied excesses. The visual register enhances the orientalizing context described in the text. Likewise, the visual component fleshes out the violent narrative with gruesome details that emphasize the sovereign status of Thamyris as a leader who rightfully executes Cyrus.

Thamyris's sovereignty derives from her role as an Amazon. From the time of Homer's *Iliad,* the Amazons have been an acknowledged feature of the Western imaginary. Pliny groups the Amazons with the monstrous races, a classification that became widely diffused in the Middle Ages.[28] This mythological tradition always places the Amazons at the borders of the known world and characterizes them primarily by their practice of amputating one breast to facilitate their performance as warriors.[29] The one remaining breast takes on the status of the phallus so that the single-breasted woman enjoys a phallic presence

Fig. 4.16. Amazons fighting in Troy, *Histoire ancienne jusqu'à César*, BL, Royal 20 D. I, fol. 25r. (By permission of the British Library.) ✍

that enables her to perform the masculine function of warrior (see figs. 4.3 to 4.6). The Amazon queers the heterosexual paradigm by her affiliation with the same-sex nation of Amazonia or *Femmenie*. She likewise disrupts the patriarchal claims of reproduction by her refusal to acknowledge the paternity of her off-spring after the moment of conception. A monstrous female warrior inhabiting the borderlands, the Amazon figures a gendered, sexualized difference as the orientalized Other.

Both text and image of the *Histoire ancienne* record the place the Amazons were thought to have in Western history.[30] Since the French nobility claimed Trojan ancestry, French crusader ideology constructed the Amazons as imag-ined allies for the Christian cause despite their monstrous, pagan identity.[31] French manuscripts of the *Histoire ancienne* in the royal and noble libraries of Paris represent Amazons as figures assimilated to Western Christianity despite their cultural difference. For example, in Royal 20 D. I, only braids distinguish an Amazon engaged in combat from her Trojan enemy (fig. 4.16); her differ-ence from the male warriors is represented solely as a matter of gender. In her construction of Thamyris in the *Othea*, Christine exploits this paradoxical sta-tus of the Amazon as simultaneously same and other in terms of gender, sexu-ality, and racialized identity. Early-fifteenth-century French texts do not always identify Thamyris as an Amazon, a fact that highlights Christine's interpre-tive decisions in this chapter. In his *De claris mulieribus*, Boccaccio identifies Thamyris only as a Scythian called upon to defend her kingdom against Cyrus. By contrast, the tradition of Thamyris in the *Histoire ancienne* emphatically rep-resents her as an Amazon and thereby claims for her a significant role in relation

Fig. 4.17. Thamyris ordering Cyrus executed, *Histoire ancienne jusqu'à César*, BnF, fr. 246, fol. 81v. (Photo Bibliothèque nationale de France, Paris.) ✒

to French history and culture. A miniature in fr. 246 shows an extremely regal Thamyris gesturing toward the crowned Cyrus as the executioner, axe raised, stands over him (fig. 4.17). The artist took pains to depict the mechanics of this imagined execution, which required a barrel with a bunghole, a trestle table to elevate the executioner, and a chopping block erected over the barrel to facilitate the beheading. The representation in the *Othea* draws specifically on this treatment of Thamyris, which is conventional in *Histoire ancienne* illustration.[32] Indeed, the miniature in the *Othea* follows sequentially in the narrative of execution after the heads have been severed and the barrel filled with blood, the collection and display of which consolidate the connection between power and the legitimate violence of the sovereign Thamyris.

As the reader of fr. 246 of the *Histoire ancienne* turns the page with its image of Thamyris (fig. 4.17), an image of the biblical story of Judith's decapi-

Fig. 4.18. Judith decapitating Holofernes, *Histoire ancienne jusqu'à César,* BnF, fr. 246, fol. 83r. (Photo Bibliothèque nationale de France, Paris.) ❧

tating Holofernes immediately comes into view (fig. 4.18). Illustrations usually set this event, as here, in the opening of a tent, and such depictions of Judith frequently occur at this point in the *Histoire ancienne* narrative.[33] Fr. 246 is unusual, however, in juxtaposing Thamyris and Judith, a visual pairing seldom found in *Histoire ancienne* manuscripts. In the Thamyris image, a queen orders a beheading; Judith carries out the beheading of her victim herself. Christine's *Othea* appropriated the iconography of the biblical heroine Judith from fr. 246 for her visualization of Thamyris.[34] In the *Othea* miniature, Thamyris's placement in front of a tent may claim for Thamyris the righteousness of Judith, the savior of her people.[35] Thamyris's victory over Cyrus, like Judith's defeat of Holofernes, identifies the phallic woman warrior with the Western cause and glories in female conquest, even as it exports the male Asian despot to the hinterland.

With her icy gaze, the triumphal Thamyris exacts the price of their defeat from the imperial Asian invaders. The *texte* below the miniature directs the reader/viewer to respect Thamyris's power and by extension to acknowledge the possibility of female rule:

> Do not disparage Thamyris even though she is a woman, and remember the pass where Cyrus was taken, for he paid dearly for his disrespect.

> [Thamaris ne desprises pas,
> Pour tant se femme est, et du pas
> Te souviengne ou Cyrus fu pris,
> Car cher compara le despris.]
> (57.2–5)

The visuality of the *Othea* renders Thamyris legible as a legitimately violent, sovereign woman. William Ian Miller points to the difficulty of representing the violent woman: "The deviance of violent men is one of excessiveness within type. The deviance of violent women is one of appropriation of an inappropriate type. The result is that violent women are 'incomprehensible' in a way that violent men are not."[36] In working to comprehend Thamyris, the *Othea* reverses the hierarchy of gender that existed in medieval Europe: Christine employs orientalism to claim female agency so that the western European Christian woman can be identified with the same-sex queerness of the Amazon. Power relations and gender intersect and yield a racist formulation, since in this scene female agency is constructed only through an orientalist vision. As Christine negotiates the cultural values of early-fifteenth-century identities, she is often complicit with French ethnocentrism to the extent that she is revisionary in relation to gender.

In the mythic narratives of domestic violence and violent women in the *Othea*, violence is paradigmatically organized around cultural assumptions of gender, so that it enhances the gendered performance of agents and victims. The battlefield offers an alternative location for engendering violence, even within the masculine economy of subject-to-subject violence, the most legible category of warfare. The death of Hector illustrates this gendered economy of violence in the text-image relationships of the *Othea*. Since Hector is both the addressee of Othea's letter and the Trojan hero who figures as the protagonist in the narrative of the *Othea*, his death points to the interpretive crux of the visual and textual program. According to Othea, on the day of his death Hector's father warns him not to go into battle, and his wife pleads with him not to fight that day. Hector's death is staged in two chapters: chapter 91 speaks generally of Hector's death, and chapter 92 describes Achilles' spearing of Hector through a gap in his armor when Hector leans over to despoil the fallen

Polybetes. Both chapters blame Hector for his death: in the first because he left himself open to attack and in the second because he coveted the armor of a fallen enemy. Although these two chapters appear to be repetitive, the division of narrative material between the two distributes Hector's failings in order to critique his error in judgment regarding Achilles separately from his unchivalric pillaging of Polybetes.

The miniatures to chapters 91 and 92 appear on the same folio in the Duke's manuscript and on the same opening in the Queen's manuscript (figs. 4.19, 4.20). The miniature in chapter 91 emphasizes Hector's vulnerability: while he is preoccupied with grasping another knight at the neck, Achilles, in a plumed helmet, approaches. The second miniature depicts Hector's death in detail: as he leans forward, intent on his spoils, his body armor rides up in back and leaves a gap; Achilles, gripping his lance with both hands, drives it into Hector's body just beneath the edge of the armor. This two-part representation of Hector's death in the *Othea* follows the visual record of Hector's death in BnF, fr. 301, which would appear to be the model for this sequence of miniatures. Both images in fr. 301 make extensive use of gold, and they illustrate two distinctive stages in Hector's last battle. In the first, Hector rides sheathed in gold (fig. 4.21). On the next page Achilles' lance penetrates Hector from behind (fig. 4.22). Stylistically distinct from the other illustrations in this section of fr. 301, these two images were clearly executed by a different artist than the rest of the program.

The *glose* to chapter 92 describes the circumstances surrounding Hector's death: "And thus Achilles, who followed him from behind with the purpose of catching him exposed, struck him from underneath the gap in his armor and killed him with a single blow" [et adont Achilés, qui par derriere le suivoit tout de gré pour le prendre a descouvert, le feri par dessoubz en la faute de ses armeures et a un coup le gita mort] (92.12–15). This version of Hector's death closely follows the text of the *Histoire ancienne*, which is even more graphic: "Achilles did not watch for or plot anything else, but urged his horse on with his spurs; and he struck Hector from behind with his uncovered lance, so that he put more than three feet of it into the body because his hauberk was slightly raised" [Achilles qui ne guatoit ne ne porpensoit autre chose brocha le cheval des esperons; si feri Hector par derriere de son glaive en descouvert, si l'en mist plus de III pies ou cors, quar li aubers li estoit un petit souleves].[37] The sodomitic suggestions of both text and image in the *Othea* take their cue from the *Histoire ancienne*. Within the violent economies of sex and gender illustrated in the *Othea*, the ignominious death of Hector-the-protagonist offers Hector-the-addressee a lesson in the gendered implications of violence: to be the victim of violence, even on the heroic location of the battlefield, is to undergo a form of sexual assault that renders its victim abject.

Fig. 4.19. First miniature of Hector's death, *Epistre Othea*, BL, Harley 4431, fol. 136v. (By permission of the British Library.) ❧

Fig. 4.20. Second miniature of Hector's death, *Epistre Othea*, BL Harley 4431, fol. 137r.
(By permission of the British Library.)

Fig. 4.21. Hector in his final battle, *Histoire ancienne jusqu'à César,* BnF, fr. 301, fol. 98r. (Photo Bibliothèque nationale de France, Paris.) ☙

Fig. 4.22. Hector's death, *Histoire ancienne jusqu'à César*, BnF, fr. 301, fol. 98v. (Photo Bibliothèque nationale de France, Paris.) ❧

The Uses of History

The chapters in the last quarter of the *Othea* increasingly address the behavior of the knight on the battlefield by focusing on the Trojan War. In chapter 85, Hector views the episode in his life that depicts his killing of Patroclus. Othea tells him: "When you have killed Patroclus, / Watch out for Achilles" [Quant Patroclus occis aras, / Lors d'Achillés te garderas] (85.2–3). Rather than address Hector in heroic terms, the *texte* and *glose* emphasize the strategy and skill that he will need to avoid Achilles once he has killed Achilles' friend Patroclus. The image to this chapter in the Queen's manuscript visualizes the skill needed to unhorse a knight in armor (fig. 2.18). Hector overcomes Patroclus by striking his shoulder with a lance and throwing him off balance, a maneuver that is more appropriate to a joust than a battle. In the foreground a knight and his horse fall forward, but unlike the battle scenes in Royal 20 D. I, the foreground of this miniature is not awash in the debris of battle: no shields, bodies, swords, or helmets are strewn on the ground. This image does not depict the death of Patroclus as an incident that gratifies either the warrior's or the reader's lust for bloodshed and carnage. In a similar fashion, the chapters on the Trojan War illustrate the rules of engagement in warfare designed to contain the subject-to-subject violence of battle. The *Othea*, however, consistently emphasizes thought rather than action in the interpretation of the heroes of the Trojan War such as Hector, Patroclus, Achilles, and Ajax. Each of these heroes exemplifies the strategic errors that led to his death. The *texte*, *glose*, and *allegorie* of each chapter direct the knightly reader to learn from these errors, a transformation of the narratives of glory from the *Histoire ancienne* into lessons in military conduct.

For example, in her *texte* on the death of Ajax (chap. 94), Othea calls attention to Ajax's foolishness in going into battle without his armor, and she warns the knight that such conduct is not honorable. The narrative in chapter 90 treats Priam's appeal to Hector not to enter the battle that day, an appeal that Hector ignored. From this, the knight should take the lesson that he always obey his lord. The stratagem of the Trojan horse, as narrated in chapter 96, reminds the knight to suspect his enemies at all times. In the illustration to this chapter, the Trojans are shown destroying the gate of their city in order to admit the gigantic wooden horse, thereby colluding in their own destruction (fig. 4.23). The final chapter on the Troy story, the fall of Ilion, warns the good knight against pride and a false sense of security based in his own strength (fig. 3.28). Several chapters offer instruction in the use of arms: chapter 92 warns Hector not to covet the arms of Polybetes; chapter 94 presents

Fig. 4.23. Trojans bringing the wooden horse into Troy, *Epistre Othea*, BnF, fr. 606, fol. 44v. (Photo Bibliothèque nationale de France, Paris.) ☙

the story of Ajax to demonstrate that a knight should not go into battle without arms; chapter 91 warns Hector to deploy his arms effectively. Chapter 89 on the fall of Babylon and chapter 97 on the fall of Troy warn the knight not to trust in the strength of a castle alone, but to make sure it is well defended and provisioned. These chapters evoke the Troy story neither to revel in the images of violence nor to contemplate the glory of warfare, but to draw strategic lessons from the fall of Troy. The violent panorama of the Troy story in the *Histoire ancienne* becomes a handbook for military strategy and knightly conduct.

The urgent need to provide military and political guidance during the conflicts of the Hundred Years' War animates the text of the *Othea,* composed around 1400; this urgency likewise shapes the representations of violence in the images produced several years later for the *Othea* in the Duke's and Queen's manuscripts. The *Othea* urges the ideal chivalric male subject to adopt strategies that will allow violence to be deployed effectively and justly. In 1408–10, Christine addressed very similar issues when she composed the *Livre de les fais d'armes et de chevalrie,* a compilation, translation, and adaptation of Latin military treatises designed to assist French knights in their engagements with the English on the battlefields of the Hundred Years' War. The *Fais d'armes,* which builds on the *Othea*'s interpretation of the Trojan War as a set of specific lessons, contributed to the "resumption of theoretical studies of warfare" in the early modern period, as Charity Cannon Willard has shown.[38]

The epistolary allegory of the *Othea,* in which Christine invents Othea, goddess of wisdom, to function as the voice-over for a montage of images, creates a gendered perspective on the violence of history and myth. Likewise, in the *Fais d'armes,* Christine invokes the goddess Minerva to justify her agency as a female author concerned with warfare:

> As this is unusual for women, who generally are occupied in weaving, spinning, and household duties, I humbly invoke, in speaking of this very high office and noble chivalry, the wise lady Minerva, born in the land of Greece, whom the ancients esteemed highly for her great wisdom.

> [Et pource que cest chose non accoustumee et hors vsage a femme qui communement ne se seult entremettre ne mais que nouilles fillasses et choser de mesnage, Ie supplie humblement audit treshault office et noble estat de chevalerie que en contemplacion de la soye dame minerue, nee du pais de grece, que les anciens pour son grant scauoir reputerent deesse].[39]

In the *Othea*, Christine had explored the issues in the representation of violence against a mythographic landscape. Later when she invokes Minerva at the start of the *Fais d'armes*, Christine draws on that mythographic landscape to bolster her authority as she attempts to intervene in contemporary military practices. The wisdom of classical women such as Othea and Minerva enabled Christine's feminist gestures and her rhetorical agency.

tepte · Cent

Cent auctoritez tay escriptes
si ne soient de toy despites
Car Augustus de femme apprist
Qui deffir adouer te reprist

Fig. 5.1. The sibyl instructing Augustus, *Epistre Othea*, BL, Harley 4431, fol. 141r. (By permission of the British Library.) ☙

5

Visualizing Rhetoric

❧❧

[A] certain kind of *ligatio,* a paralyzing power whose spell we need
to break, is continuously at work in every image; it is as if a silent
invocation calling for the liberation of the image into gesture arose
from the entire history of art. . . . Cinema leads images back to the
homeland of gesture.

— Giorgio Agamben, "Notes on Gesture"

The miniatures in both the Duke's and the Queen's manuscripts of the *Othea*
ask to be set in motion: the lithe, graceful figures radiate a visible presence by
implying the motion inherent in their poses. Specific gestures and facial expressions communicate nonverbally. Such gestures signify a range of emotions, interpretations, and persuasive actions that impart a rhetorical eloquence to
images.[1] By visualizing action, they perform agency for the viewer, just as the
textual level of the epistle performs a particular subjectivity for the reader. Although early-fifteenth-century texts often invite *disputatio*—as the *querelle de
la Rose* so dramatically demonstrates—images can be more difficult than texts
to dispute or critique because their impact transcends language. And in a tradition such as mythology, it is only through new images that received images
might be effectively revised. Since the Duke's and the Queen's manuscripts
emerge during an unprecedented decade of book illustration in late medieval
Paris, the *Othea* in these manuscripts capitalizes on the extraordinary confluence
of artists, patrons, and illustrated vernacular texts at that particular historical

moment. Indeed, the sheer proliferation of nonreligious texts being illustrated for the first time generated images of unique rhetorical and gestural fluency.

The miniatures in the *Othea* enable representation of emotion not filtered through language, and the fluency of the gestural language in these miniatures gives emotions a vivid performativity.[2] Images also convey the gendered implications of emotions and, when communicated in gestures, an emotion such as anger gains a rhetorical intensity and even efficacy that verbally expressed anger might lack. The *Othea* explores the emotion of anger particularly in relation to the performance of gender. In this process, the *Othea* returns to issues initially addressed in the *Epistre au dieu d'Amours* (1 May 1399), where Christine articulates the reasons for women's anger toward men.[3] As we discussed in chapter 2, she appropriates the figure of the God of Love from the *Roman de la rose* to function as the author of the *Epistre au dieu d'Amours*, which he addresses to his loyal followers. The epistle stages a hearing in a juridical format to consider the accusations of women, both married and unmarried, that men "blame and defame and deceive" them. The God of Love rehearses the complaints of women angry with false and deceptive lovers, and as King of the Court of Love he issues a judgment banishing such lovers from his realm. Within the epistolary structure of the poem, Christine uses the God of Love's voice to express outrage toward men who treat women badly. In delivering his judgment, the God of Love angrily and vengefully denounces men who blame women as an excuse for their own failures:

> I certainly hate such people more than anything, and I often pay them back as they deserve. For despite their slanderous words, I make them fall hopelessly in love with foolish women.
>
> [Si hé tel gent trop plus que'autre riens, certes,
> Et les paye souvent de leurs dessertes;
> Car, en despit de leurs males paroles,
> Eulx assoter d'aucunes femmes foles.]
>
> (509–12)

Throughout the *Epistre*, the God of Love repeatedly expresses indignation at the plight of women. Despite the playfulness of its allegorical structure, Christine's *Epistre au dieu d'Amours* ridicules the *Roman de la rose*. When Jean de Montreuil, secretary in the royal chancery, wrote a treatise in praise of the *Rose* in mid-1401, Christine quickly wrote a public letter in response to him.[4] The ensuing *querelle* documents a formative period in Christine's experience as a female reader and writer. Although postmodern theorists such as Joan Scott have taught us to see experience as constructed and therefore not foundational to identity,[5] recent critical interventions have recuperated experience as a significant form of knowledge. Satya Mohanty's "realist view of experience" emphasizes that experience, though constructed, also responds to "causally significant features of the social world."[6] Christine learned from her experience in the *querelle de la Rose* that it was difficult for a woman's criticism of literary values to be heard.

Responses to Christine's letters show that her critique was interpreted as anger and that, despite her careful argumentation, she was dismissed by her interlocutors as an angry and therefore irrational female. In her first epistle on the *Rose,* a response to Jean de Montreuil's treatise of mid-1401, Christine offers a carefully constructed argument.[7] She questions the ethics discernible in the text of the *Rose,* and she consistently refers to the language of the poem to advance her argument. Christine's "assumed modesty"[8] rhetorically frames the entire epistle and eloquently closes it with a flourish: "And may it not be imputed to me that I, a woman, dared by folly, arrogance, or presumption to reprimand and refute so skilled an author, and to diminish the praise of his work when he single-handedly dared to harm, by defaming and blaming, an entire sex without exception" [Et ne me soit imputé a follie, arrogance ou presompcion d'oser, moy femme, repprendre et redarguer aucteur tant subtil et son euvre admenuisier de louenge, quant lui, seul homme, osa entreprendre a diffamer et blasmer sans excepcion tout un sexe] (22).[9] Although the rhetorical polish of this first epistle suggests that Christine took pains to approach the *Rose* analytically, Gontier Col almost immediately characterized her letter as an "invective to some extent against my master" [invettive aucunement contre ce que mon maistre] (9), referring to Jean de Meun, and throughout the exchange her interlocutors speak of her as a "woman impassioned in this matter" [femme passionee en ceste matiere] (23). Indeed, they frequently denigrate her analysis by labeling it the opinion of an angry woman: "O foolish overweening pride! O word too quickly coming unadvisedly out of the mouth of a woman who condemns a man of such high intelligence" [O tres fole oultrecuidance! O parole trop tost yssue et sans avis de bouche de fame, qui condampne home de si hault entendement] (100).

This dynamic animates the entire *querelle;* although Christine adopts a self-effacing position and presents a thoroughly developed and critical argument, her interlocutors dismiss her as an impassioned woman who has penned a thoughtless invective. As Helen Solterer concludes, however, "[T]he fact that all of Christine's interlocutors interpret her critique of Maistre Jean de Meun's writing as a transgression from without suggests just how defensive they are about their own clerico-humanist domain."[10] For her part, Christine experienced their attack as anger; in two ballads (*Autres Balades* 36 and 37) she interprets this rhetorical attack as abuse, and she comments:

> But for that opinion, many would leap at my eyes.
> One is often beaten for speaking the truth.
>
> [Mais pour ce mot maint me sauldroit aux yeux
> On est souvent batu pour dire voir.]
> (*Autres Balades*, 37.26–27)

The *querelle de la Rose* tutored Christine in the gendered politics of criticism and dissent: feminist critique was interpreted as anger, and female anger was dismissed as lacking in authority. The *querelle* was a constitutive experience for Christine as a writer: she learned that, if read as angry, her attempts to intervene in the political and social issues of her day would have little effect. The codicological record documents the relationship between the *querelle* and the *Othea*. In her collected works, Christine compiled the letters in the *querelle* and introduced them with dedicatory letters to Queen Isabeau and Guillaume de Tignonville. She included the *Rose* dossier in both the Queen's and the Duke's manuscripts, thereby inviting a reading of the *Othea* in direct contrast to the rhetoric of the *querelle*.[11] The letters in the *querelle* illustrate the cultural gendering of rhetoric and the rhetorical constraints on the expression of female anger.[12] The visual program to the *Othea* in both the Duke's and the Queen's manuscripts responds to the gendered politics of anger evident in the *querelle*.

In her composition of the *Othea,* which was written before the *querelle* got underway, Christine evacuates the category of female anger almost entirely. After introducing herself as female wisdom in the first chapter, in the second chapter, Othea describes her sister Temperance, who personifies the second of four cardinal virtues. Temperance's most important quality, which Hector should acquire, is an internal equilibrium or balance never disturbed by rage:

> But above all other special qualities [she] is gentle, calm, and moderate,
> nor is she ever struck by anger; she thinks of nothing except moderation; this is the goddess of temperance.
>
> [Mais sur toute especiaulté
> Est doulce, quoye et attrempee,
> Ne de yre n'est nul temps frappee;
> A rien fors mesure ne pense,
> C'est la deesse d'atrempance.]
> (2.18–22)

The miniatures to the chapter on Temperance in the Duke's and the Queen's manuscripts depart from the composition in BnF, fr. 848 (see fig. I.7), which shows Lady Temperance adjusting the gears of a mechanical clock; this illustration directly visualizes the long rubric describing "the clock that has many wheels and measures" [l'orloge qui a plusieurs roes et mesures] (2.4); the clock is a figure for the human body that is composed of diverse things and should be regulated by reason. The two later manuscripts expand the idea of Temperance as an abstraction by employing the iconography of the Children of the Planets to depict a group of women under the influence of Temperance (fig. 5.2). The eloquent gestures of the women articulate the lesson of desirable internal equilibrium much more fully: a group of women sit beneath Temperance, their bodies and arms arranged in a balanced and harmonious rhythm, immune to the rage that would destroy their embodied moderation.[13]

If the illustrations to the *Othea* in the Duke's and Queen's manuscripts respond to the issues raised in the *querelle,* these visual programs also engage with the illustrated translations of Boccaccio's *De claris mulieribus.* With the translation of this work into French as *Des cleres et nobles femmes* in 1402 and the production of two luxury editions, one purchased in 1402 by Philip the Bold (BnF, fr. 12420) and the other given to Jean de Berry in 1403 (BnF, fr. 598), Italian humanism gained a significant presence both visually and textually in Parisian manuscript cultures. Although Christine's *Livre de la cité des dames* (1405) offers her most sustained response to the authority Boccaccio's project had attained in the vernacular humanist culture of Paris, the visual program of the *Othea,* begun after the production of these two Boccaccio manuscripts, often contests the interpretive authority of Boccaccio's rewriting of mythic women.

Boccaccio's version of the Arachne myth follows cultural norms for the gendering of rhetoric. In the Ovidian story, Pallas Athena hears of Arachne's boasts about her skill in weaving and challenges her to a contest. When Arachne produces a tapestry that depicts deities in an unfavorable light, Pallas becomes enraged and punishes her by transforming her into a spider. Boccaccio's *De claris mulieribus* omits Pallas Athena's anger and revises the Ovidian account of Arachne's metamorphosis into a spider. Boccaccio blames Arachne's pride in her work for her self-destruction: because she cannot resign herself to her loss of the weaving contest with Athena, Arachne commits suicide. In the miniature to Jean de Berry's manuscript of the *Des cleres et nobles femmes* (fig. 5.3), Arachne hangs just behind her vertical loom so that her hands appear to continue weaving, a detail that reinforces the thematic link between Arachne's pride in her work and her suicide. Arachne's fate exemplifies the consequences of female speech that is not carefully shaped by the rhetorical device of "affected modesty." By contrast, the *Othea* depicts Arachne and Pallas Athena in a tense

Fig. 5.2. Temperance, *Epistre Othea*, BL, Harley 4431, fol. 96v. (By permission of the British Library.) ✌

Fig. 5.3. Arachne's suicide, Boccaccio, *Des cleres et nobles femmes*, BnF, fr. 598, fol. 29r. (Photo Bibliothèque nationale de France, Paris.) ✒

confrontation across Arachne's loom (fig. 5.4; see also 3.15). Arachne's weaving has challenged the authority of Pallas, whose gestures signify engaged speech. Arachne responds aggressively, leaning toward Pallas and pointing at her. The large spider hanging over the loom foretells Arachne's punishment. By visualizing this encounter across the loom, the miniature emphasizes Arachne's status as an artist.

In the *texte*, Othea uses the example of Arachne's misjudgment ("qui tant mesprist") to instruct Hector not to boast. The *glose* briefly and selectively summarizes the story from the *Ovide moralisé* (6.1–316), which ends with Arachne's metamorphosis into a spider. Departing slightly but significantly from the Ovidian pre-text in its treatment of Pallas's curse, the *glose* states, "Since you boast so much of your spinning and weaving, you will forever more spin and weave work of no value" [Puis que tant te vantes de filer et tyssir, a tous jours mais filleras et tistras ouvrage de nulle value] (64.11–13).[14] Though

Fig. 5.4. Pallas Athena and Arachne, *Epistre Othea*, BnF, fr. 606, fol. 30r.
(Photo Bibliothèque nationale de France, Paris.)

this myth is richly illustrated in two manuscripts of the *Ovide moralisé,* these manuscripts visualize neither the confrontation across the loom nor Arachne's defiance. Rather, both attend carefully to the process of metamorphosis brought about by Pallas's anger (fig. 5.5). Whereas Arachne's punishment in the *Ovide moralisé* is her transformation into a spider, the *glose* in the *Othea* transfers that punishment to Arachne's work: she loses the interpretive authority that her weaving had represented before her transformation. As a spider she will continue to weave, but her work will be devoid of meaning. Christine's version of this myth demonstrates how carefully the female artist must negotiate the register of her rhetoric.

The *Othea* does not emphasize Arachne's status as the victim of Pallas's anger but rather focuses on Arachne's misjudgment in boasting about the artistic qual-

Fig. 5.5. Two stages of Arachne's metamorphosis, *Ovide moralisé*, Rouen, Bibl. mun., MS O.4, fol. 157r. (Collections de la Bibliothèque municipale de Rouen. Photographies Thierry Ascencio-Parvy.) 🐚

ity of her work to Pallas, the patron goddess of weaving. This chapter on Arachne crystallizes a set of issues around anger and the efficacy of interpretation that animate the *Othea* as a whole. The *Othea* miniature stages a confrontation between two women apparently equal in power; Arachne's artistry and skill—what Christine calls in the *glose* her "savoir"—empower the mortal. Ultimately, however, the divine Pallas will win any confrontation with a mortal, no matter how gifted and accomplished. According to the *glose*, "The goddess became furious with her" [la deesse s'aÿra contre elle] (64.10), but Pallas's gestures in the miniature signal eloquent rather than frenzied anger, especially by comparison to the imperious and vengeful Pallas represented in the *Ovide moralisé* illustrations. Boccaccio, by contrast, is interested neither in Pallas's agency nor in Arachne's artistry. In the *Othea* miniature, Pallas Athena offers an eloquent performance of anger that is not destabilizing to the female subject.

Even when the plot of a myth motivates anger as an appropriate response to abuse, the *Othea* de-emphasizes female anger. As we discussed in the introduction, Christine's Medea is not the frenzied, angry woman of myth but a woman negotiating a complex set of demands. Like the myth of Medea, the story of Latona in the *Ovide moralisé* (6.1634–1772) offers a standard mythic exemplum on the frenzy of angry women. Fleeing from a vengeful Juno, Latona pauses to slake her thirst at a shallow lake where peasants are gathering reeds. The peasants block her access to the water and mock her by muddying it so that it is undrinkable. In such a rage that she forgets her thirst ("telle ire ot, sans faille, / Que toute a sa soif oubliee" [1742–43]), Latona condemns them to stay in that marshy place forever; as her curse takes effect, they turn into frogs. The *Othea* chapter on Latona (20) makes several changes to the Ovidian pre-text. First, according to the *Ovide moralisé*, Latona was fleeing with her infant twins, Phoebus and Phoebe, the children of Jupiter; in the *Othea*, Latona is still pregnant with the twins. In addition, according to the *Othea*, the peasants are in the water because they are bathing on a hot day, not because they are gathering reeds; consequently they are not engaged in productive labor. In illustrating the confrontation between Latona and the peasants, the miniatures in all three *Ovide moralisé* manuscripts deploy gestures and postures that communicate the loutishly aggressive behavior of the peasants in addressing their insults to Latona (fig. 5.6). By contrast, the miniature to this chapter of the *Othea* in the Duke's and the Queen's manuscripts shows the heavily pregnant Latona kneeling awkwardly at the water's edge (fig. 5.7). Positioned in the foreground and facing toward the viewer, Latona's extended arm breaks the picture plane and appears to enter the viewer's space in a plea for pity and sympathy. Rather than expressing her anger, her gestures embody her thirst. Oblivious to her presence, the peasants frolic in the water, where they are joined by jumping frogs. Juxtaposing the peasants' thoughtless spoiling of the water with Latona's piteous thirst, the *Othea* miniatures imply that bodily transformation inevitably follows the peasants' bad behavior, and the textual material ascribes this behavior to their class.

In the *texte* Othea advises Hector not to sully himself in the marsh, and the *glose* explains that the marsh refers to the marsh of "villenie," the baseness of the lower classes; those born noble should not associate with the peasantry but cultivate habits that will fittingly complement their nobility. Nowhere does the textual material comment on Latona's anger with the peasants; rather it reads their transformation as a consequence of their innate nature—they are a lower class of being—and warns readers that if they associate with such creatures, they will become like them. Since the nude peasants jumping about in the water are already behaving like frogs, their metamorphosis has no significance.[15] Christine's version of Latona in the *Othea* erases Latona's rage and presents an ethical commentary about class.

Several chapters in the *Othea* revise traditional narratives of women as the frenzied subjects of rage, and the *Othea* offers in their place the possibility of female agency that goes beyond anger. The story of King Athamas and his wife Ino appears in two widely separated chapters of the *Othea* (17 and 99). The first of these, which depicts Athamas's rage, forms part of a sequence of chapters

Fig. 5.6. Latona attacked by peasants, *Ovide moralisé,* Rouen, Bibl. mun., MS O.4, fol. 164v. (Collections de la Bibliothèque municipale de Rouen. Photographies Thierry Ascencio-Parvy.) ◆§

that illustrate the seven deadly sins, as the *allegorie* to the preceding chapter directly states.[16] In such a context Christine had the opportunity to treat both Athamas and Ino as exempla of the vice of anger. Instead, she revised the version of the myth found in the *Ovide moralisé* and made Athamas alone representative of the vice of anger in the form of frenzied madness. This revision results in a significant reshaping of the myth both visually and textually in order to avoid depicting Ino as a woman frenzied by anger (fig. 2.17). According to the *glose,* Ino, a stereotypically wicked stepmother, has grain seed secretly boiled before it is sown as part of a plot to rid herself of her two stepchildren. She then suborns priests to interpret the inevitable crop failure as a sign that the gods want her stepchildren to be removed from the country. Her plan succeeds: "And because the king consented to the exile of his two children, even though he did it reluctantly and had great sorrow, the fable says that the goddess Juno wanted to take vengeance for it" [Et pour ce que le roy consenti l'exil de ses .ij.

Fig. 5.7. Latona, *Epistre Othea*, BnF, fr. 606, fol. 11v. (Photo Bibliothèque nationale de France, Paris.) ❧

enfans, tout le feist il moult envis et a grant douleur, dist la fable que la deesse Juno en volt prendre vengeance] (17.16–19). Juno sends "the goddess of fury" [la deesse de forcennage] (17.20) to punish Athamas. The miniature that opens this chapter depicts this intervention and its disastrous results. The Fury casts her spell, creating a visual force field across the diagonal of the image that engulfs Athamas. Driven mad as a result, Athamas has killed Ino, who lies dead on the ground, and he holds his two children by the neck as he strangles them to death. He stands over the dead body of Ino, one child hanging limply in his grasp while the other is in its death throes. In the *texte* Othea tells Hector to protect himself from such anger:

> The goddess of fury made Athamas, full of great rage, strangle his two children; because of this I forbid great rage to you.
>
> [A Athamas, plain de grant rage,
> La deesse de forcennage
> Fist estrangler ses .ij. enfans,
> Pour ce grant yre te deffens.]
>   (17.2–5)

Both text and image emphasize that the rage belongs to Athamas alone and that he bears sole responsibility for his children's murder.

Both text and miniature diverge powerfully from the presentation of the Athamas and Ino story in the *Ovide moralisé*, where both come under the spell of madness and anger. The *Ovide moralisé* narrates how Athamas runs berserk, grabs one child by the arms, and kills him by throwing him down; equally crazed, Ino takes the other child and climbs a high cliff overlooking the sea. With the child in her arms she leaps into the waves. Both the Rouen and Arsenal manuscripts (figs. 5.8 and 5.9) include a single illustration to this story, placed at the same line (4.3922) in each manuscript. In the Rouen manuscript, Ino stands on a sharp incline, her swaddled child held before her. The unrealistic angle of her stance conveys the inevitability of her plunge into the waves of the sea that fill the lower third of the miniature. In the Arsenal manuscript the artist selected a slightly earlier moment in the narrative: the parents face away from one another, although Ino looks back at Athamas, who murderously dangles a nude child. Ino cradles a swaddled child in her arms as she strides away. Whereas the Ovidian tradition casts both parents as equally murderous, the *Othea* text and image depict Athamas alone as the crazed murderer, and his anger becomes the topic of the chapter. Ino is the victim, not the subject, of rage. Like Medea in chapter 58 (fig. I.3), Ino is removed from any narrative context that would articulate her rage and assign her to a category of women deranged by anger to

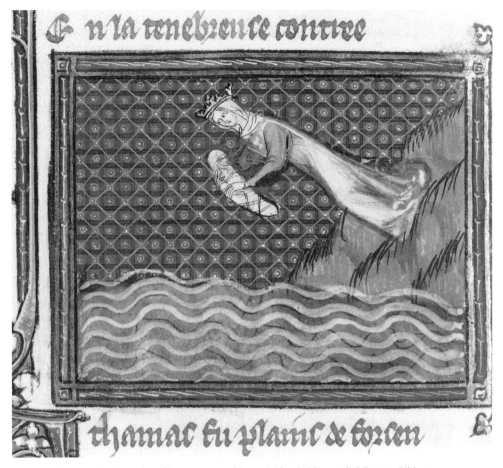

Fig. 5.8. Ino's murder of her stepson and her suicide, *Ovide moralisé,* Rouen, Bibl. mun., MS O.4, fol. 112v. (Collections de la Bibliothèque municipale de Rouen. Photographies Thierry Ascencio-Parvy.)

commit horrible acts. In the *Othea* image, moreover, Athamas literally resembles Medea in *Rose* illustration. Medea's murder of her children is a frequent topic in medieval texts (see figs. I.4 and I.5), but she is usually described as killing them with a sword. Only in *Rose* illustration is she depicted strangling them. The composition of Athamas's murder of his children in the *Othea* closely resembles the miniature of Medea strangling her children in Douce 371 (fig. I.6), a manuscript of the *Rose* produced in 1402–3 in a workshop that at about the same time was engaged in producing Philip the Bold's copy of Christine's *Chemin*. The pose of Athamas closely reproduces in reverse the pose of the Douce Medea, which suggests that the workshop used preexisting patterns that might be reversed for the sake of economy and variety.[17] The frenzied anger of Medea has been transferred across genders to Athamas.

Fig. 5.9. Ino and Athamas, *Ovide moralisé*, Paris, Bibliothèque de l'Arsenal, MS 5069, fol. 53v. (Photo Bibliothèque nationale de France, Paris.) ❧

The penultimate chapter of the *Othea* returns to the Ino story in order to pose a hermeneutic puzzle in visual form (fig. 5.10). The illustration to this chapter depicts Ino, a sower's cloth tied around her body, standing next to a large cooking pot filled with grain seed. A peasant pours seed into Ino's cloth, and in the foreground another peasant sows the boiled seed in the plowed furrows.[18] As the earlier chapter has already explained, Ino has the seed boiled in a plot to rid herself of her two stepchildren. However, the *allegorie* to this chapter shifts the focus away from Ino and explains "that beautiful words shouldn't

Fig. 5.10. Ino sowing boiled seed, *Epistre Othea*, BL, Harley 4431, fol. 140v. (By permission of the British Library.)

be spoken to simple or ignorant people who cannot understand them" [Que belles paroles ne soient dites aux rudes ne aux ignorans qui ne les saroient entendre] (99.16–17). The montage presentation, which divides the Ino story into two chapters widely separated in the *Othea*, fractures the narrative and complicates any single moralizing reading. In addition, chapter 17 visualizes Ino's death and Athamas's madness, while chapter 99 depicts an earlier moment in the narrative when she sows the boiled corn; indeed, the image to chapter 99 could have been used as illustration for chapter 17. Both chapters devoted to Ino's story deflect responsibility from her; in chapter 17 on the deadly sin of anger, Athamas is seen as culpable, and in chapter 99 the reader is enjoined not to be illiterate.

In addition to avoiding the depiction of women as the subjects of frenzied anger, the *Othea* categorizes motivated anger—such as Latona's—as an emotion rather than a vice.[19] In this respect, Christine draws on the Aristotelian understanding of anger in the *Ethics,* a text translated into French by Nicole Oresme under the patronage of Charles V.[20] Oresme's text reproduces and extends the passage in which Aristotle praises the man who is angry at the right things and with the right people and at the right time. Such anger responds to situations in which it is justified, and it does not lead to passion. In Aristotle's context, anger would belong only to the citizen of the *polis,* who is by definition an elite male. Oresme's version draws on the medieval concept of the estates and declares that the person who does not get angry at injuries is "of a miserable and servile condition."[21] As we have seen in her chapter on Latona, Christine shared this elitist view of the estates, but her understanding of anger marks a departure from the Aristotelian tradition that excludes the possibility of the female subject. In the *Epistre au dieu d'Amours,* Christine offers a list of the "natural" attributes of women, among which is "Et en courroux tost appaise son yre" [an anger that is quickly appeased] (677). Although this assertion employs Aristotelian categories, it extends to women the possibility of experiencing anger as an emotion.

In the *Othea*, Christine revises the representation of mythical women such as Medea and Ino who would contradict this category of motivated or justified anger. Pallas Athena in the Arachne story is one of the few women who act out of a controlled and justified anger. Women such as Hecuba and Thamyris act forcefully but without anger, according to Christine's text, and as we saw in the last chapter the miniatures in the Queen's and Duke's manuscripts reinforce that perception. Whereas the *Othea* refuses the tradition of women frenzied by anger, it claims that women experience justified anger, seen as an emotion, not a vice. Given Christine's careful negotiation of frenzy versus justified anger, of anger as a vice versus anger as an emotion, it is ironic that the reception of her work in the twentieth century so often reads her as a furious woman, reiterating Jean de Montreuil's characterization of her in the *querelle de la Rose*. For example, in his *Preface to Chaucer*, D. W. Robertson Jr. called Christine an "irate woman" with "frenzied observations."[22] As Christine's experience in the *querelle* shows, women's unwelcome criticism is often interpreted as anger.

Montage and Heroic Gestures

In what Susan Noakes has called its "'dismemberment' of the story of Troy,"[23] the *Othea* does not rehearse the tale of Hector's life and death as a linear development.[24] Instead the moments in Hector's last days are illustrated with images that isolate and then freeze the action, often at a highly emotional and decisive moment. The chapters on Hector focus on the rhetorical moments that the miniatures render in their own eloquent idiom of gesture. For instance, in the illustration to chapter 90 (fig. 5.11) Hector rides at the head of a troop of cavalry and foot soldiers; the banners outstretched overhead and the soldiers massed behind him emphasize his determined forward motion. His father, Priam, intercepts him and attempts to halt his progress toward the battlefield by forcefully grasping the reins of his son's charger. Priam leans forward in the saddle as a suppliant; in contrast, Hector's rigid upright posture and gesture communicate his decision to ignore Priam's request that he not go into battle. The *texte* announces Hector's death as a direct consequence of his refusal to attend to Priam's warning, and the *glose* narrates an event different from that in the image or *texte:* "Hector stole away from his father and went forth from the city by a tunnel and went into the battle, where he was killed" [Hector se embla de son pere et sailli de la cité par une soubzterraine et ala en la bataille ou il fu occis] (90.15–17). The *allegorie* draws the lesson that "the good spirit must have in continual memory the hour of his death" [le bon esperit doit avoir en continuelle memoire l'eure de la mort] (90.28–29). Thus, the miniature, *texte, glose,* and *allegorie* all focus differently on this one moment, and the *allegorie* stresses the apparently paradoxical but orthodox Christian tenet that one should always remember one's death, an event that has not yet happened. This image does more than freeze the narrative moment; rather, through a set of gestures it communicates the ethical richness of this encounter so that the implications of all that follows are contained within it. As Agamben observes, "The gesture . . . opens the sphere of *ethos* as the more proper sphere of that which is human."[25] For a narrative as well known as the fall of Troy, each moment implicitly contains the entire story. In the *Othea* miniature, the position of Hector's

Fig. 5.11. Priam asking Hector not to fight, *Epistre Othea*, BL, Harley 4431, fol. 136r.
(By permission of the British Library.)

hand signifying his refusal of Priam's plea, though Hector himself is unaware of it, gestures relentlessly toward his certain death.

The *Othea* arranges the entire Trojan story as a montage of heroic gestures that insistently violate the chronology of the Trojan War. In addition, throughout the last section of the *Othea*, these historical chapters are interspersed with material drawn from myth (Narcissus and Echo, chap. 86; Apollo and Daphne, chap. 87) and from other historical traditions (the fall of Babylon, chap. 89). The juxtaposition of mythic and heroic material further dislocates the moments of the Troy story so that each chapter appears to be temporally isolated and to refuse the ideological comforts that heroic chronologies offer. In the process, the reader's temporal location in the present often overrides the image of the past. For example, Achilles is killed in chapter 40 of the *Othea,* and yet in chapter 93 he attends Hector's funeral. Despite the significance of Hector as both the central hero of the Trojan War and the addressee of Othea's epistolary admonitions, the *texte* and *glose* of chapter 93 emphasize Achilles' presence at Hector's funeral and his foolhardy love for Polyxena, which led to his downfall. From the point of view of the textual material, Hector's funeral serves merely as the backdrop for the fated meeting between Achilles and Polyxena, yet the image (fig. 5.12) places Hector's coffin monumentally in the center of focus: it is draped with a black pall marked by a red cross, protected by a wooden canopy covered with burning candles, and flanked by groups of mourners, women shrouded in black. In its attention to details of Christian funerary practice, this image directly cites the visual tradition of the Office of the Dead in books of hours. Since by this period the Office of the Dead was commonly recited by laypersons every day, this image specifically evokes a contemporary devotional context. For the fifteenth-century reader/viewer it functions as a memento mori that is echoed in the injunction of the *allegorie,* which quotes Augustine's dictum: "Le monde passe et sa concupiscence" [The world and its lusts shall pass] (93.38–39). Thus, the funeral of Hector does not illustrate the heroic values of the Trojan past but the ethical urgency of the Christian present.

Such a montage of history and myth exploits the Trojan material for more than the political allegory that Sandra Hindman proposes.[26] The individual chapters all present the possibility that events could have happened otherwise and the death of Hector and the fall of Troy could have been avoided. As Othea tells Hector when she presents her epistle to him:

> Now then, remember well the sayings that I wish to write to you, and if you hear me recount or say anything that is to come to pass and I tell you to remember it as if it had already happened, know that these are in my thoughts in the spirit of prophecy. So understand and do not

Fig. 5.12. Hector's funeral, *Epistre Othea*, BL, Harley 4431, fol. 137v. (By permission of the British Library.) 🐌

grieve, because I won't say anything except what will come to pass if it hasn't happened yet. So remember this.

[Or mets dont bien en ta memoire
Les dis que je te vueil escripre,
Et se tu m'os compter ou dire
Chose qui soit a avenir
Et je te dis que souvenir
T'en doit, com s'ilz fussent passees,
Saches qu'ilz sont en mes pensees
En esperit de prophecie.
Or entens et ne te soucie,
Car riens ne diray qui n'aviengne,
S'avenu n'est, or t'en souviengne]
(1.61–71)

The relationship among the past, present, and future of mythic time—and its interpretation—enables the reader/viewer to intervene through interpretive decisions that would reverse or redirect the course of history. In more conventional uses of the Trojan material as history, as Gabrielle Spiegel observes, "The recuperation of the ancient past becomes . . . a process of self-definition."[27] By fragmenting the ancient past, the *Othea* attempts to disrupt this familiar process in order to urge the reader/viewer to reconsider the implications of such a heritage for the construction of masculinities, the economies of violence, and attitudes toward sexualities. Nevertheless, in its local interpretive contexts, the *Othea* repeats rather than revises the orientalism of the Thamyris chapter, the homophobia of the Orpheus and Ganymede chapters, and the class bias of the Latona chapter. Such oppressive discourses, however, are confined to individual chapters, and the overall possibility that the past need not be reinscribed in the present keeps these discourses from achieving a dominant authority.

The Gestures of Feminist Interpretation

Hector's death and the fall of Troy ultimately render futile the heroic gestures of the Trojan warriors. In her gesture of handing her letter to Hector, Othea gives him the opportunity to benefit from her wisdom and to adjust his conduct to the ethical implications she draws from the lessons of the past. For Othea to claim such interpretive agency, she has to identify women from the classical past whose gestures precede and authorize hers. Early on in the *Othea* the trinity of Diana, Ceres, and Isis offers the reader the chance to identify a category of wise women, as Hindman has demonstrated.[28] In addition to the female deities whose wisdom is made available to Hector, the wise women of Troy such as Cassandra and Andromache are invoked in the segments devoted to the Trojan War, though the failure of the Trojans to heed their wisdom is part of the larger failure of the heroic gestures in the text. According to Christine's construction of identity, these wise women of history collectively offer a fantasy scenario of ideal conduct that Christine would like to see realized in her world.[29] Such idealism requires an essentializing vision; the case of Io illustrates how much interpretive effort is required to make classical myth fit Christine's fantasies regarding the possibilities of female interpretive authority.

Christine uses the mythical figure of Io to engender knowledge of letters as a female attribute (fig. 5.13). The image to chapter 29 of the *Othea* represents a scriptorium in which Io is depicted as a woman supervising several male scribes. The miniature initiates a two-chapter discussion of Io that connects the story of Jupiter's rape of Io to the myth that Io invented letters. The latter detail is drawn from the *Histoire ancienne,* which summarizes the mythographic tradition that Io—in her alternate identity as Isis—taught the Egyptians the letters of the alphabet.[30] Thus this image of Io in her scriptorium, like the image of Diana and her women reading in chapter 23, has no visual precedent. As inventions these images offer a fantasy of female authority. Although the *Histoire ancienne* states only that she "gave letters to the Egyptians," the image in the *Othea* interprets this concept in terms of the workshop practices of scribal production.[31] In both the Duke's and the Queen's manuscripts this miniature occurs in the lower right corner of a folio recto, at the start of a new chapter whose text is available only after the folio is turned. The *glose* on the next folio allusively treats the myth that Jupiter had raped Io and then had transformed her into a cow to avoid having his adulterous behavior detected by his jealous spouse, Juno.

Christine insists that the Ovidian version of Io be read allegorically so that her metamorphosis authorizes Io's scribal practice: "She became a cow, for just as the cow gives milk, which is sweet and nourishing, she gave by the letters that she invented sweet nourishment for the mind" [Elle devint vache, car sicomme la vache donne laict, le quel est doulx et nourrissant, elle donna par les lettres que elle trouva doulce nourriture a l'entendement] (29.15–18). In the column next to this *glose,* the miniature to the next chapter (30) depicts Io as a cow being freed by Mercury from the custody of the hundred-eyed Argus, appointed by Juno to guard her (fig. 5.14). The somnambulant Argus stands at the left while Mercury leans down from a cloud to enchant him. Io's embodied status as a cow replete with nourishing milk is visually emphasized by a posture that gives prominence to her unusually full udders, a detail not found in the *Ovide moralisé*

Fig. 5.13. Io directing scriptorium, *Epistre Othea*, BL, Harley 4431, fol. 109r.
(By permission of the British Library.) ☙

Fig. 5.14. Mercury, Argus, and Io, *Epistre Othea*, BL, Harley 4431, fol. 109v. (By permission of the British Library.) ঙ৭

Fig. 5.15. Mercury, Argus, and Io, *Ovide moralisé,* Rouen, Bibl. mun., MS O.4, fol. 38r. (Collections de la Bibliothèque municipale de Rouen. Photographies Thierry Ascencio-Parvy.) ☙

illustrations of Io (fig. 5.15). The *glose* from the previous chapter directs the reader/viewer to see Io's lactation as an analogue for the production of letters, so that the female body as the lactating body becomes the most suitable for textual activity. In the process, this image inverts the cultural assumptions that the female body is the appropriate object of scribal practice rather than the subject. The montage arrangement allows the reader to see Io both as a cow and as the director of a scriptorium without having to choose between them: the Christian allegory of Io as the inventor of letters thus reinterprets the classical fable of Io as cow to establish a foundational myth in which female corporeality becomes the basis for humanist activity. Later in the *Livre de la cité des dames,* Raison cites the *Othea* to establish the authority of this version of Io's story (1.36.1).

The image of Io seated in her scriptorium evokes and perhaps even cites the representations of sibyls found in the French manuscripts of Boccaccio's *Des cleres et nobles femmes.* Among the sibyls depicted in the illustrations of Boccaccio's text, the Cumaean Sibyl Amalthea (fig. 5.16) shares placement, posture,

Fig. 5.16. Sibyl Amalthea, Boccaccio, *Des cleres et nobles femmes,* BnF, fr. 598, fol. 37r. (Photo Bibliothèque nationale de France, Paris.) ✇

activity, and dress with the Io in the *Othea*. The similarity between the two illustrations emphasizes the authority claimed for Io in the composition that situates her as a director of a scriptorium. Indeed, a figure Christine called the "Cumaean" Sibyl later became critical to the text and images of Christine's *Livre du chemin de long estude* and to the text of her *Cité des dames*. Yet Christine employs this figure of the "Cumaean" Sibyl for the first time at the end of the *Othea* where the sibyl's function becomes a synthetic image for all of the ways women's interpretive gestures might achieve authority.

The prophetic authority of the sibyl allows Christine to envision a gendered intervention in the course of history. The last chapter of the *Othea* depicts a sibyl interpreting for the Roman emperor Augustus his vision of the Virgin and Child known as the *ara coeli* (figs. 5.1 and 5.17). Insistently directing his adoring gaze toward the vision, the sibyl teaches the emperor how to read history and his place in it: as a secular ruler he must kneel in adoration before the vision of the Virgin and Child in acknowledgment of Christ's presence on earth. In this tableau, Augustus represents the pre-Christian past, while the Virgin and Child represent the Christian future; all historical temporality is compressed into this one scene. Although according to tradition it is the Tiburtine Sibyl who appears in the *ara coeli*, Christine calls the sibyl who instructs Augustus the Cumaean Sibyl.[32] Long viewed as a female prophet, the figure of the sibyl forms a bridge between ancient and Christian cultures. In Virgil the Cumaean Sibyl guides Aeneas to the underworld; Augustine understood the Cumaean Sibyl's prophecy in Virgil's Fourth Eclogue as a reference to the birth of Christ.[33] Both the Rouen and Arsenal manuscripts of the *Ovide moralisé* illustrate sibyls, including the Tiburtine Sibyl, who instructs the Romans in the prophecy of Christ (fig. 5.18), and the Cumaean Sibyl, who leads Aeneas to the underworld.[34] Although these figures of female prophetic authority animate the last sections of the *Ovide moralisé*, the final images in the manuscripts reinscribe Roman imperial rule in a masculine form. For example, the last miniature in Rouen O.4, which introduces a textual celebration of Julius Caesar's conquests, depicts Caesar seated on a throne, gesturing authoritatively with one hand and holding a sword with the other (fig. 5.19).

Although sibyls are found repeatedly in illustrations to Boccaccio's *Des cleres femmes* and in the *Ovide moralisé*, the image of the sibyl and the *ara coeli* that closes the *Othea* was not drawn from these traditions but from the visual programs found in books of hours. Augustus's vision of the Virgin and Child appears in an initial in the *Brussels Hours* (fig. 5.20) made in Paris around 1395–1400.[35] The sibyl's authority, encoded in her gesture as well as her scroll, dominates the initial. This image is the first of several renditions of this subject in manuscripts commissioned by Jean, duke of Berry. According to Meiss, the

Fig. 5.17. The sibyl instructing Augustus, *Epistre Othea*, BnF, fr. 606, fol. 46r.
(Photo Bibliothèque nationale de France, Paris.) ⟆

Fig. 5.18. Tiburtine Sibyl telling prophecy of Christ to kings, *Ovide moralisé*, Rouen, Bibl. mun., MS O.4, fol. 357r. (Collection de la Bibliothèque municipale de Rouen. Photographies Thierry Ascencio-Parvy.) ✏

duke of Berry "liked to associate himself with" Augustus and consequently had a sustained interest in the image of the sibyl and the *ara coeli*,[36] versions of which are found in his *Belles Heures* and *Très Riches Heures,* dating respectively from the first and second decades of the fifteenth century (figs. 5.21 and 5.22). In the devotional context of books of hours, these two images accompany a prayer to the Virgin Mary. The composition aligns the devout gaze of the reader/viewer with that of the praying emperor, who venerates the prominent image of the Virgin and Child.

In the *Belles Heures* the sibyl wears a form-fitting dress under her mantle and a loosely arranged veil that reveals her hair; her halo suggests that she is a type of female saint. Yet the masculine economy of the page overrides any authority the sibyl might have. Augustus's sword and luxuriant beard secure his phallic authority, and the Virgin is beneath the surveillance of an ever-present Father-God. By contrast, in both the Duke's and the Queen's manuscripts, the

Fig. 5.19. Homage to Julius Caesar, *Ovide moralisé*, Rouen, Bibl. mun., MS O.4, fol. 400v. (Collection de la Bibliothèque municipale de Rouen. Photographies Thierry Ascencio-Parvy.) ❧

sibyl's heavily draped form and loose wimple assign her the authority that comes with age. The kneeling figure of Augustus lacks a sword; his large brown cloak and submissive piety further subdue his masculinity. Though the image of the *ara coeli* must have come to Christine's attention in the devotional context of a book of hours, its placement in the concluding chapter of the *Othea* situates it in an interpretive context for thinking about secular history and culture. This single Christian image concludes the extensive sequence of chapters on subjects drawn from ancient myth and Trojan history that constitutes the *Othea*. Its placement as the final image creates an evocative relationship among the sibyl and the female figures of learning and prophecy treated in the *Othea* such as Io, Diana, and Cassandra.[37]

The miniature of the sibyl and Augustus in the Duke's manuscript addresses several larger issues of patronage. The presentation pages of early *Othea* manuscripts encode the patronage of Louis of Orleans, brother of Charles VI. When Louis was assassinated in 1407 the *Othea* in the Duke's manuscript was

Fig. 5.20. The sibyl instructing Augustus, detail of initial, *Brussels Hours,* BR, MS 11060-1, p. 83. (Foto Marburg/Art Resource, New York.)

almost certainly not complete, and the duke of Berry must have assumed the patronage of the manuscript. This change of patronage also coincided with a change of artist. With the exception of this image of Augustus and the sibyl, all of the miniatures in the duke's copy of the *Othea* have been attributed to the anonymous artists known as the Epître Master and the Saffron Master; a different artist, the Egerton Master, executed this final miniature.[38] As noted above, the duke of Berry was especially partial to the image of Augustus and the sibyl, and its concluding status in a manuscript of which he became patron suggests that Christine perhaps exploited the duke's interests in her production of this luxury manuscript. If Christine used this means of bringing the *Othea* to

Fig. 5.21. The sibyl instructing Augustus, *Belles Heures of Jean, duke of Berry,* New York, The Metropolitan Museum of Art, The Cloisters, fol. 26v.

m̄e... ...temerata et
me... ...ternum bene
dicta... ...singularis at
qꝫ incomparabi lis uirgo dei geni
tur maria gratissimum dei templum spiritus sā
sacrarium ianua regni celorum. per quam post
deum totus uiuit orbis terrarum de te dei genitur
filius dei uerus et omnipotens deus suam sacratis
simam fecit matrem assumens de illa sacratissiā
carnē per quem mundus qui perditus erat salua
tus est. Cuius preciosissimo sanguine suo mundꝰ
redemptus est. et
omnia peccata
et remissa sunt
formans eam in
preciosissimo sā
guine tuo munēs
eam eterne et in
commutabili
diuinitatis sue
a quo bona cūc
ta procedunt p

Fig. 5.22. The sibyl instructing Augustus, *Très Riches Heures*, Chantilly, Musée Condé, Ms 65, fol. 22r. (Giraudon/Art Resource, New York.)

the duke's attention, she appears to be especially interested in tutoring him in her feminist view of history and myth. Likewise, in adapting material from the *Legenda aurea* for the *glose* to this chapter, Christine emphasizes Augustus's need to recognize that divine agency brought about the world peace of the Pax Romana. Like the sibyl tutoring Augustus, Christine tutors the duke of Berry in the politics of peace. Indeed, in 1410 when Christine addressed her *Lamentacion sur les maux de la France* to the duke of Berry, she sought to persuade him to seek an end to the conflict that was becoming a civil war between the Burgundians and the Armagnacs.[39]

The image of the sibyl represents the final gesture in the visual rhetoric of the *Othea*. The sibyl's assertive and didactic posture encapsulates the authoritative potential of female guidance since it metaphorically sets in motion all of Christian history. The *texte* directly below this eloquent image clarifies Christine's interventionist view when Othea makes her final statement to Hector:

I have written one hundred authorities for you, so don't be disparaging of them, because Augustus learned from a woman who admonished him for having himself worshipped.

[Cent auctoritez t'ay escriptes,
Si ne soient de toy despites,
Car Augustus de femme apprist,
Qui d'estre aouré le reprist.]
(100.2–5)

The text and image of the sibylline prophecy envision a feminist rhetoric more persuasive than anger and more effective than the heroic gestures of the Trojan heroes.

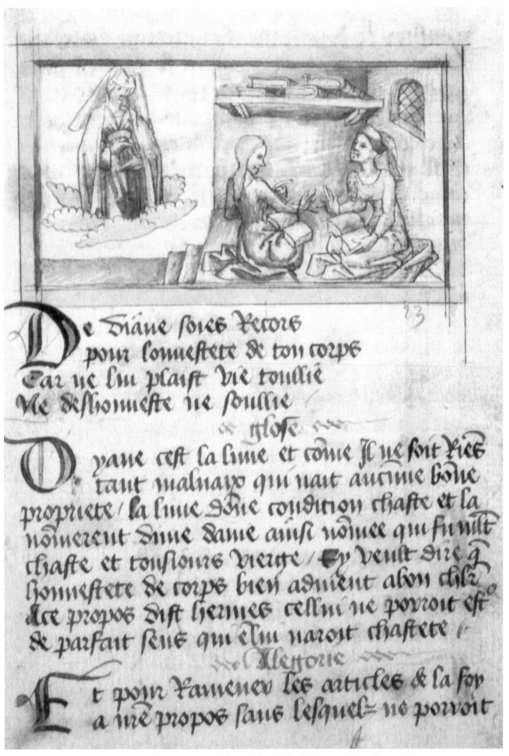

De Diane soies recors
pour conneste de ton corps
Car ne lui plaist vie touillié
Ne deshonneste ne souillie

Glose

Dyane cest la lune et come il ne soit riens
tant malvaiz qui nait aucune bone
propriete / la lune dune condition chaste et la
nomerent dune dame ainsi nomee qui fu mult
chaste et tousiours vierge / Et veult dire q
honnestete de corps bien advient a bon chl'z
A ce propos dist hermes cellui ne porroit est'
de parfait sens qui elm naroit chastete

Allegorie

Et pour ramener les articles de la foy
a nre propos sans lesquelz ne porroit

Fig. A.1. Diana and her women, *Epistre Othea*, Lille, Bibl. mun. Jean Levy, MS 175, fol. 26r. (Bibliothèque municipale Jean Levy.) ☙

Afterword

The *Epistre Othea* was by far Christine's most popular work. During the course of the fifteenth century it was repeatedly copied, and ten manuscripts with full programs of illustration survive.[1] While the *Othea* had emerged from Parisian manuscript culture at the beginning of the fifteenth century, it had a second life in Burgundian court culture half a century later. By 1500, the mechanical reproduction of the printing press transformed the visual program of the *Othea* by enabling exact duplication of its images as woodcuts. The full visual potential of the *Othea* is only partially legible at any given moment in its reception history. Any one exemplar—whether in manuscript or print—only partially realizes the visuality of the *Othea;* as we have seen, the images are never simply illustrations of the text. Not only does the visual component escape language, it also eludes interpretive closure. But that which escapes continues to exist, and it haunts future copies.

As we saw in chapter 2, the reception of the *Othea* in the court of Philip the Good erases the more radical aspect of the visual program evident in the Duke's and the Queen's manuscripts. Although many of the Burgundian manuscripts of the *Othea* similarly reinterpret its visual content, a discernible iconographic tradition persists throughout fifteenth-century copies. Yet the subtle implications of an image in either the Duke's or the Queen's manuscript may not survive even when the iconography does. For instance, in The Hague, MS 74 G 27 (fig. A.2), the miniature of Medea giving her jewelry box to Jason preserves the early composition of this scene (fig. I.3), yet alters the gender politics.[2] In the Hague image, Jason towers over a simpering Medea, who looks up at him submissively. This more stereotypically gendered image robs the encounter of all nuance. Likewise, the image of Diana and her followers in The Hague manuscript

Fig. A.2. Medea handing her casket to Jason, *Epistre Othea*, The Hague, Koninklijke Bibliotheek, 74 G 27, fol. 54v. (Koninklijke Bibliotheek.) ❧

(fig. A.3) resembles the miniature in the Queen's and the Duke's manuscripts to the extent that both depict the goddess with a group of mortal women (fig. 3.16), but the connection between chastity and reading was otherwise illegible to the designer of The Hague program. In both the Queen's and the Duke's manuscripts, the women were united by the act of reading, and the depiction of reading took on a particularly erotic meaning in relation to the text. The Hague manuscript, on the other hand, depicts Diana and her followers standing with arms folded in front of them and with their hands hidden in their sleeves. Neither engaged nor at ease, their lack of activity or involvement with one another conforms to a conventional vision of feminine decorum.

All of the fifteenth-century manuscripts of the *Othea* omit the books from the Diana image except one, a small paper manuscript with color-washed pen drawings made in Lille in the 1460s. In general, the illustration in this manuscript preserves the iconography from the *Othea* in the Duke's and the Queen's manuscripts.[3] The expressive style renders the prominent gestures and the informal, active poses in a manner typical of Lille painters of this generation.[4] In the image of Diana and her women (fig. A.1), the Lille artist has represented

Fig. A.3. Diana and her women, *Epistre Othea*, The Hague, Koninklijke Bibliotheek, 74 G 27, fol. 26r. (Koninklijke Bibliotheek.) ☙

books as the conduit for an intimacy between two female readers. In a horizontal adaptation of the Children of the Planets iconography, the goddess Diana hovers on a cloud at the left, and her women sit in a room at the right, books open on their laps and hands raised in eloquent speaking gestures. The small room, an enclave for female literacy, is furnished only with a shelf of books. By representing literacy as a form of intimacy, this image preserves and even develops further the association of reading and homoeroticism that the Diana chapter enabled in the Duke's and Queen's manuscripts.

The standard Christian iconography of the *ara coeli* usually appears in the final chapter of the *Othea* on the sibyl. However, in the mid-fifteenth-century Erlangen-Nürnberg manuscript (fig. A.4), the *ara coeli* is replaced by an image of Augustus enthroned, an image reminiscent of the final miniature of Julius Caesar in the Rouen *Ovide moralisé* (fig. 5.19).[5] As the last illustration in the Erlangen-Nürnberg manuscript, this image celebrates masculine authority and overshadows the female prophecy that is the focus of the chapter. This final miniature is unique in the reception history of the *Othea;* by contrast, some manuscripts intensify the vision of female authority in this final chapter. For

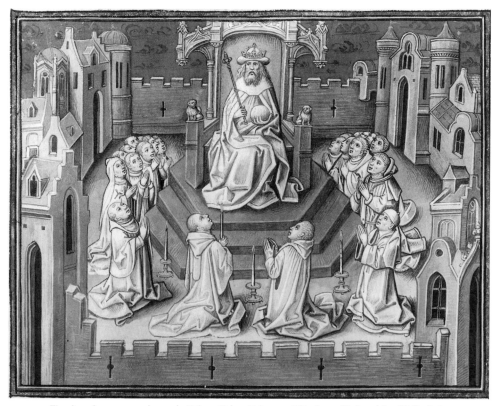

Fig. A.4. Augustus enthroned, *Epistre Othea*, Erlangen-Nürnberg, Universitäts-Bibliothek, MS 2361, fol. 125r. (Universitäts-Bibliothek.) ◑§

example, in the *Othea* in Waddesdon Manor, this final image depicts Augustus kneeling before the Virgin and Child (fig. A.5).[6] Having placed both crown and scepter on the ground beside him, Augustus swings a censer in veneration of the Virgin and Child. In his willing subjection to the Christian future, this Augustus defers to the female authority of the sibyl.

In addition to manuscripts that contain or were designed for full one-hundred-miniature cycles, some illustrated manuscripts of the *Othea* display only a frontispiece. In single-image versions of the *Othea*, the visual program is frequently limited to some variant of the standard illustration to chapter 1, the goddess Othea delivering her letter to Hector (I.2).[7] Even such a limited program of illustration conditions a reader's perception of the entire *Othea*, as we can see from two single-image copies that belonged to Philip the Good. In addition to his splendidly illustrated Miélot exemplar, Philip the Good owned several other copies of the *Othea;* among them are two produced in the workshop of Guillebert de Metz, one a copy of the other, and each containing only one miniature (Brussels, Bibl. Royale, MS 9559–64 and Brussels, Bibl. Royale,

Fig. A.5. The sibyl instructing Augustus, *Epistre Othea*, Waddesdon Manor, MS 8, fol. 54v. (The National Trust, Waddesdon Manor; photographer: Mike Fear.)

MS IV 1114).[8] The original image and its copy are remarkably similar, and both point to an ethical rather than a mythological understanding of Christine's *Othea*. In the miniature, a personification of justice, a woman holding a sword in one hand and an open book in the other, sits within an elaborate architectural setting (fig. A.6). The architecture frames Justice between two slender columns that support the vaulted ceiling as if it were a canopy over her throne. The two men who flank her, a bishop and a monk-scribe, are subordinated to her by their placement and body language. The men and the architectural elements are labeled with the names of abstract virtues. Such a visualization of Justice as the primary virtue elicits a reading of the *Othea* that emphasizes the *glose* and the *allegorie* of each chapter; these prose portions offer lessons about the virtue to be learned from each chapter, whereas the verse *texte* encapsulates the mythological matter from which the lesson is drawn. A full pictorial cycle of mythical and historical illustrations would only have distracted from this moral level.

The visuality of the *Othea* made it an attractive text for printers; in Paris, Philippe Pigouchet, Philippe Le Noir, and the widow Trepperel all published

Fig. A.6. Justice, *Epistre Othea*, BR, MS 9559-64, fol. 7r. (Brussels, Royal Library of Belgium.) 🔖

editions of the *Othea*.[9] Printers in general selected texts such as the *Othea* that had been illustrated in manuscript in order to attract book buyers who may have been minimally literate or had not hitherto been able to afford illustrated books. The earliest printed edition of the *Othea*, which employed a design of one chapter per page, appeared from the Parisian workshop of Philippe Pigouchet under the title *Les cent histoires de Troye* in 1499/1500. The text is set in three columns, the wider center column headed by a rectangular woodcut; this position signals the centrality of the visual to the reading of each chapter (figs. A.7 and A.8). As we have seen, in manuscripts of the *Othea* included in the collected works, the miniatures were inserted into the columns of the continuous text. This layout does not focus attention on the images and does not result in a uniform page design; nonetheless, the images attract the reader by means of color, light, and illusionism. Since the woodcut in a printed book is in the same black and white as the surrounding text, its placement on the page becomes critical. The design of early *Othea* manuscripts such as BnF, fr. 848 positions the grisaille miniatures at the upper center portion of the page and focuses the reader/viewer's attention on the visual element. Only two other early manuscripts, Newnham, MS 900 (5) and Beauvais, MS. 9 follow the *ordinatio* of a centrally placed *texte* framed by the *glose* and *allegorie* in columns on each side.[10] The survival of this page design in Pigouchet's printed *Othea* suggests the efficacy of a layout that situates the image as the central focus of the page.

Pigouchet's edition testifies to the visual legacy of the manuscript tradition of the *Othea*. Within the limits of the medium, the compositions of the woodcuts in Pigouchet's edition often resemble those of the miniatures in 4431 and fr. 606, even though the woodcuts have a horizontal format in which the narrative content sometimes reads more clearly than in the vertically shaped miniatures of these manuscripts. For example, Pigouchet's woodcut for chapter 29 (fig. A.7) eliminates the somewhat distracting architectural setting and preserves the basic composition in which Io, seated in a position of authority, supervises male scribes who hold scrolls (see fig. 5.13). The woodcut, like many in Pigouchet's program, reverses the composition from Harley 4431 and fr. 606. However, at least one-third of the woodcuts in Pigouchet's edition closely resemble miniatures in another copy of the *Othea*, Bodley 421, a northern French manuscript from the late fifteenth century. The resemblance is strongest for major compositional elements—usually reversed as mirror images—not necessarily for background and minor figures or for details of iconography. Indeed, Bodley 421 appears to be an intermediary between the manuscripts made during Christine's lifetime and Pigouchet's printed version. Bodley 421, however, cannot account for Pigouchet's text or layout. Pigouchet's edition testifies to the dynamic features of the fifteenth-century reception of the *Othea*, a

y Ðfut
Ðne da/
moifelle fille du
ꝛoy ꝑnacus qui
moult fut de gꝛãt
fcauoit et trouua
maintes manie:
res de lettres qui
deuant nauoi ent
efte veues/ com
biẽ que aulcunes
fables difent que
ꝓo fut ãpꝑe iupi
ter ꝗ que vacfe de
uint ꝗ puis fẽme
commune fut/
mais comme les
poetes aient muf
fe verite foubz
couuerture de fa
ble peult eftre en/
tendu que iupiter
fapma/ceft a en/
tendꝛe les vertus
de iupiter ꝗ en ef/
le furẽt elle deuĩt

ꝓꝛix   Texte
m   Ðult te delictes au fcauoir
ꝓo/ plus quen nul aultre auoir
Car par ce pourras moult apꝛendꝛe
Et du bien largement compꝛendꝛe.

y Ðꝗ eft
notee par
lettres ꝗ efcriptu
res nous pouuonſ
entẽdꝛe que le bõ
efpetit fe doibt de
lictet a lyꝛe les
fainctes efcriptu
res ꝗ les auoir ef
criptes en fa pen/
fee ꝗ par ce pours
ra apꝑendꝛe a
monter au ciel a/
uec iefuchꝛift par
bõnes oeuuꝛes et
faincte cõtempla
tion/et croire fe di
gne article ꝗ dift
fainct Barthele
my.

C Afcendit ad celos
fedet ad dexterã dei
patris omnipotẽtis.

Vacfe/car ficomme la vacfe qui donne lait lequel eft doulx ꝗ nourrif
fant elle dõna par les lettres ꝗ elle trouua doulce nourriture a lentẽde/
ment/ce que elle fut femme cõmune peult eftre entẽdu que fon fens fut
commun a tous cõme lettres font cõmunes a toutes gens. Pource dit
que le bon cheualier doibt moult aymer ꝓo qui peult eftre entendu pout
lettres ꝗ efcriptures ꝗ les hyftoires des bons que le bon cheualier doibt
voulentiers ouyꝛ racõpter ꝗ lyꝛe ꝗ dont lexemple luy peult eftre vail/
fable. A ce ꝓpos dit Hermes. Qui fefforce de acquerir fcience ꝗ bõ/
nes meuts/il trouue ce qui luy plaift en ce monde ꝗ en lautre.

cᵗ

Fig. A.7. Io directing scriptorium, Philippe Pigouchet, *Les cent histoires de troye*, chap. 29.
(By permission of the British Library.)

G Elayne
fut fême
au roy menelaus
et tauie par paris
en grece/ et quant
les grecz fu/
rent venus sur
troye a grant ar/
mee pour la ven
geance dicelluy
fait/ ains quilz
meffeiffent a la
terre ilz requirent
que helayne leur
fuft redue et ainé
de leur fuft faicte
de ceffe offêce ou
si non ilz deftrui/
roient le pays/ et
pource que riens
nen voulurêt fai

G Elayne
qui doit
eftre rendue peult
eftre entêdu le cô
mandement q̃ dit
Tu ne defireras
point la fême de
ton prochain par
quoy eft deffêdu
ce dit faict augu/
ftin la penfee:
et la voulente de
faire fornication
dôt le fait eft def/
fendu deuant par
le. Si. cômande/
ment/ car dit no/
ftre feigneur en le
uangile.

C Qui viderit mulie
rem ad côcupifcêdã
eam iam mechatus
eft in cozde fuo. Mat
thei.vi.capitulo.

pliii   Tepte
r   Ens helaine fon la demande
      Car en grant meffait gift amende
Et mieulp vault toft paip confentir
Que tard venir au repentir

re les troyês sen enfuyuit le grât mefchief qui depuis leur aduint/pour
ce veult dire au bon cheualier que se il a folie encouuenâcee mieulp lui
vault la delaiffer et faire paip que la pourfuyure q̃ mal ne luy en auié/
tgne.pour ce dit le philofophe platon. Se tu as fait iniure a qui que ce
foit tu ne doibs eftre aife iufques a tant q̃ tu fopes a luy accozde et fait
paip.

Fig. A.8. The Greeks asking Priam for the return of Helen, Philippe Pigouchet,
Les cent histoires de troye, chap. 43. (By permission of the British Library.) ✒

reception marked by different realizations of text, image, and page design in each exemplar. The aesthetically pleasing layout in Pigouchet's *Les cent histoires de troye* exploits the potential of print as a medium to integrate visuality into the reading experience.

As a process of mechanical reproduction, print offers the possibility of a new kind of error. The production of a fully illustrated *Othea* required sustained attention to detail, since the one hundred separate units of type and of woodcut had to be flawlessly matched. Even though all of Pigouchet's woodcuts had been made with the correct subjects, in the production of the book two pairs of woodcuts were interchanged, and as a result there is no meaningful relationship between text and image in four chapters.[11] Two decades later, in 1522, another Parisian printer, Philippe Le Noir, published an illustrated edition of the *Othea* for which he used Pigouchet's blocks. Le Noir apparently had only thirty-nine of Pigouchet's original one hundred blocks, the rest of which must have been broken, lost, or removed from the set to use in another project. Le Noir worked from an exemplar of the Pigouchet edition, and when he lacked the correct block he either substituted one of a handful of others,[12] or he reused one of the thirty-nine Pigouchet blocks, so that the same woodcut appears in more than one chapter in Le Noir's edition.

Attentive to the text-image relationship that Pigouchet laid out, Le Noir made some effort to employ compositionally appropriate woodcuts even when he did not have the same block that Pigouchet had used; for example, Le Noir apparently did not have Pigouchet's block for chapter 29, "Io directing a scriptorium" (fig. A.7), in which Io sits on a high-backed wooden chair facing left. From the available woodblocks he selected the block for chapter 43, "The Greeks demand the return of Helen," which includes a figure seated in a very similar chair in the same position (fig. A.8). In each case three figures occupy the left half of the image. Even though the action in the Helen woodcut differs from the action in the Io woodcut, some of the visual elements correspond closely. In order to substitute the Helen block for the Io, Le Noir would have had to consult a complete copy of the Pigouchet edition. Throughout he chose substitute blocks for their compositional similarity to the blocks Pigouchet used for particular chapters rather than for their relationship to the narrative in the *texte* or the *glose* of that chapter. Consequently, the substituted images in the Le Noir edition do not illustrate the chapters in which they appear, and in these chapters there is no relationship between text and image. Thus, when the text-image relationship survives in Le Noir, it is a residue of the visual tradition, not an informed response to the textual material. Indeed Le Noir responded to the visuality of the Pigouchet edition, not to the textual material of the *Othea*, so that his respect for the Pigouchet exemplar actually resulted in the illegibility of the text-image relationship in nearly two-thirds of the chapters in the Le Noir edition.

The text-image relationship in Robert Wyer's English translation of the *Othea,* the *C. Hystoryes of Troye* (ca. 1540), is even less legible than in Le Noir's. Wyer, however, worked from a Pigouchet edition. In the first half of the text he frequently copies Pigouchet's woodcuts, even when Le Noir had not, and Wyer faithfully reproduces several of Pigouchet's errors.[13] In the second half of the text, Wyer's woodcuts appear to be completely miscellaneous insertions. In the mechanical reproduction of printed books, the text-image relationship in the *Othea* becomes loosened and then illegible in a way that seems inconceivable in a manuscript tradition. Wyer's printed and illustrated edition represents the last of three separate English translations. Stephen Scrope translated the *Othea* circa 1440,[14] and Anthony Babyngton made his own translation in the second half of the fifteenth century.[15] Taken together, these three separate English translations attest to the popularity of the *Othea* in England in addition to France and Burgundy. In its English permutations, the *Othea* retains its legibility as a chivalric treatise that mediates between the mythic past and the demands of the present.[16]

The manuscripts, printed books, and translations that make up the reception history of the *Othea* testify to the continued appeal of this text for more than a century after its original composition. The reception history also demonstrates the extent to which the montage quality of the *Othea* makes it responsive to diverse cultural contexts. In developing a theory of montage, Eisenstein insists that montage is a principle of image making generally and of painting and cinema in particular. Warburg's *Mnemosyne* also relies on a montage principle of juxtaposition, in his case in order to construct his history of visual expressions of motion and emotion. In some sense, the montage arrangement of a text like the *Othea* anticipated cinematic juxtaposition as a technique that generates visual meaning. As complex intertextual and intervisual artifacts, manuscripts and early printed books of the *Epistre Othea* offer visions of identity, sexuality, desire, and emotions that remain legible and eloquent.

Notes

༄༅༄

Introduction

1. The Munich manuscript (ca. 1410) represents the second stage of illustration of the *Livre de la Mutacion de Fortune;* four manuscripts were illustrated in 1403 and two others in the second decade of the fifteenth century. In the first group, this part of the text is illustrated with miniatures depicting wall paintings and no viewer; in the second group, the artists create a volume of space and place a viewer of the wall paintings within it. For a description of the miniatures in the illustrated manuscripts of the *Mutacion,* see Lucie Schaefer, "Die Illustrationen zu den Handschriften der Christine de Pizan," *Marburger Jahrbuch für Kunstwissenschaft* 10 (1937): 119–208; and Millard Meiss, *French Painting in the Time of Jean de Berry: The Limbourgs and Their Contemporaries,* 2 vols. (London: Thames and Hudson, 1974).

2. For a discussion of the ekphrasis in the *Mutacion,* see Kevin Brownlee, "The Image of History in Christine de Pizan's *Livre de la Mutacion de Fortune,*" in the special issue "Contexts: Styles and Values in Medieval Art and Literature," ed. Daniel Poirion and Nancy Regalado, *Yale French Studies* 1991:44–56.

3. Michael Camille, "Before the Gaze: The Internal Senses and Late Medieval Practices of Seeing," in *Visuality before and beyond the Renaissance,* ed. Robert S. Nelson (Cambridge: Cambridge University Press, 2000), 203.

4. Ivan Illich, *In the Vineyard of the Text: A Commentary to Hugh's "Didascalicon"* (Chicago: University of Chicago Press, 1993), 20.

5. Maureen Turim, "The Place of Visual Illusions," in *The Cinematic Apparatus,* ed. Teresa de Lauretis and Stephen Heath (New York: St. Martin's, 1985), 147.

6. Patrick M. de Winter, *La Bibliothèque de Philippe le Hardi, duc de Bourgogne (1364–1404): Étude sur les manuscrits à peintures d'une collection princière a l'époque du "style gothique international"* (Paris: Editions du CNRS, 1985), 95–102; Charles Sterling, *La Peinture médiévale à Paris 1300–1500,* 2 vols. (Paris: Bibliothèque des Arts, 1987); Millard Meiss, *French Painting in the Time of Jean de Berry: The Late XIV Century and the Patronage of the Duke,* 2d ed. (New York: Phaidon, 1969), 140–46.

7. Paul Saenger, *Space between Words: The Origins of Silent Reading* (Stanford: Stanford University Press, 1997), 256–76.

8. For manuscripts and early printed editions of the *Epistre Othea*, see Gianni Mombello, *La tradizione manoscritta dell' "Epistre Othéa" di Christine de Pizan. Prolegomeni all'edizione del testo*, Memorie dell'Accademia delle Scienze di Torino, Classe di Scienze Morali, Storiche e Filologiche, series 4, no. 15 (Turin: Accademia delle Scienze, 1967); for an updating of Mombello's list of manuscripts, see Christine de Pizan, *Epistre Othea. Edition critique*, ed. Gabriella Parussa (Geneva: Droz, 1999), 87–88; for a recent overview of early printed editions, see Cynthia J. Brown, "The Reconstruction of an Author in Print: Christine de Pizan in the Fifteenth and Sixteenth Centuries," in *Christine de Pizan and the Categories of Difference*, ed. Marilynn Desmond (Minneapolis: University of Minnesota Press, 1998), 215–35; for editions of the English translations, see Christine de Pizan, *The Epistle of Othea*, trans. Stephen Scrope, ed. Curt F. Bühler, Early English Text Society 264 (London: Oxford University Press, 1970); Christine de Pizan, *The Epistle of Othea to Hector: a "lytil bibell of knyghthod,"* ed. James D. Gordon (Philadelphia: University of Pennsylvania, 1942); Christine de Pizan, *The C. Hystoryes of Troye* (Charing Cross: Robert Wyer, 1536–45).

9. For an overview of the multiple dedicatees, see the introduction to Christine de Pizan, *Epistre Othea*, ed. Parussa, 83–85. See also Gianni Mombello, "Per un'edizione critica dell'*Epistre Othea* di Christine de Pizan," *Studi Francesi* 25 (1965): 1–12.

10. For the largest selection of published images from *Othea* manuscripts, see Sandra L. Hindman, *Christine de Pizan's "Epistre Othéa": Painting and Politics at the Court of Charles VI* (Toronto: Pontifical Institute of Mediaeval Studies, 1986) (hereafter *Painting and Politics*). For black-and-white reproductions of the one-hundred-miniature cycle in BR, MS 9392, see J. van den Gheyn, *Christine de Pizan. Epitre d'Othéa, déesse de la prudence, à Hector, chef des Troyens. Réproductions des 100 miniatures du MS 9392 de Jean Miélot* (Brussels: Vromant and Co., 1913); for a facsimile on microfiche of the one-hundred-miniature cycle in Erlangen-Nürnberg, Universitäts-Bibliothek, MS 2361, see Christine de Pizan, *L'Epistre d'Othéa*, color microfiche edition of manuscript Erlangen-Nürnberg, Universitäts-Bibliothek, Ms. 2361, introduction by Helga Lengenfelder, Codices illuminati medii aevi 31 (Munich: Edition Helga Lengenfelder, 1996). For discussion of the relationships among manuscripts with one-hundred-miniature cycles, see Charlotte Schoell-Glass, "Aspekte der Antikenrezeption in Frankreich und Flandern im 15. Jahrhundert: Die Illustrationen der *Epistre Othea* von Christine de Pizan," Ph.D. diss., Universität Hamburg, 1993. For an edition of the text of the *Othea*, see Christine de Pizan, *Epistre Othea*, ed. Parussa; for a transcription of the *Othea* in BL, Harley 4431, see Halina Didycky Loukopoulos, "Classical Mythology in the Works of Christine de Pisan, with an Edition of *L'Epistre Othea* from the Manuscript Harley 4431," Ph.D. diss., Wayne State University, 1977. For a discussion of editing problems, see Eric Hicks, "Pour une édition génétique de l'*Epistre Othea*," in *Pratiques de la culture écrite en France au XVe siècle*, ed. Monique Ornato and Nicole Pons (Louvain-La-Neuve: Collège Thomas More, 1995), 151–59.

11. For a discussion of the derivation of the name *Othea*, see the introduction in Christine de Pizan, *Epistre Othea*, ed. Parussa, 20–21; and Gianni Mombello, "Recherches sur l'origine du nom de la Déesse Othea," *Atti della accademia delle Scienze di Torino*, 2, Classe di Scienze Morali, Storiche e Filologiche 103 (1969): 343–75.

12. For a discussion of the organization of the textual material in the *Othea*, see Judith L. Kellogg, "Christine de Pizan as Chivalric Mythographer," in *The Mythographic Art: Classical Fable and the Rise of the Vernacular in Early France and England*, ed. Jane Chance (Gainesville: University of Florida Press, 1990), 100–123; see also Mary Ann Ignatius, "Christine de Pizan's *Epistre Othea:* An Experiment in Literary Form," *Medievalia et Humanistica* 9 (1979): 127–42. In her dissertation, Schoell-Glass suggests that Francesco da Barbarino's *Documenti d'Amore*, both in its textual components and in the crucial importance of the visual to the whole, offers a possible model for the structure of the *Othea* ("Aspekte der Antikenrezeption," 22–23). On the *Documenti d'Amore*, see Sterling, *La Peinture médiévale*, 1:76–85; and Bernhard Degenhart and Annegrit Schmitt, *Corpus der italienischen Zeichnungen, 1300–1450*, pt. 1, *Süd- und Mittelitalien*, vol. 1, *Katalog* (Berlin: Mann, 1968), 31–38 and pls. 29–33.

13. All quotations from the *Othea* are from Christine de Pizan, *Epistre Othea*, ed. Parussa, and all references are in a form in which the number before the period indicates the chapter in the *Othea* and the number or numbers after the period indicate the lines of text as in the Parussa edition; translations from Christine's French are our own. Numerous errors mar the translation in *Christine de Pizan's Letter of Othea to Hector*, trans. Jane Chance (Newburyport, Mass.: Focus Information Group, 1990). There are good translations of three chapters of the *Othea* ("Cassandra," "Medea," and "The Judgment of Paris") by Earl Jeffrey Richards in *The Writings of Christine de Pizan*, ed. Charity Cannon Willard (New York: Persea Books, 1994), 96–103, and of the "Prologue" and the chapters on Pygmalion, Arachne, Achilles, Fortune, and the Cumaean Sibyl in *The Selected Writings of Christine de Pizan*, ed. Renate Blumenfeld-Kosinski (New York: W. W. Norton, 1997), 29–40. Also useful is the Middle English version in Christine de Pizan, *Epistle of Othea*, trans. Scrope.

14. Kaja Silverman, *World Spectators* (Stanford: Stanford University Press, 2000), 33. For a related discussion on the relation between death and responsibility, see Jacques Derrida, *The Gift of Death*, trans. David Wills (Chicago: University of Chicago Press, 1995), 35–52.

15. On humanism as a central aspect of Christine's cultural milieu, see Gilbert Ouy, "Paris: L'un des principaux foyers de l'humanisme en Europe au début du XVᵉ siècle," *Bulletin de la société de l'histoire de Paris et de l'Ile de France* 94–95 (1967–68): 71–98. On Christine's different engagement with Latin and vernacular texts, see Thelma Fenster, "'Perdre son latin': Christine de Pizan and Vernacular Humanism," in Desmond, *Christine de Pizan*, 91–107. For the standard work on Christine's textual sources for the *Othea*, see Percy G. C. Campbell, *L'Épître d'Othéa: Étude sur les sources de Christine de Pisan* (Paris: Honoré Champion, 1924). In her edition of the *Epistre Othea*, Parussa offers many significant revisions of Campbell's assertions. Although Campbell identifies textual sources as such, he does not note the extent to which Christine revises her source material, particularly in relation to the *Ovide moralisé*. For a consideration of the *Othea* as an intertextual revision of its sources, see Gabriella Parussa, "Le Concept d'intertextualité comme hypothèse interprétative d'une oeuvre: L'exemple de l'*Epistre Othea* de Christine de Pizan," *Studi Francesi* 111 (1993): 471–93.

16. For illustrations in *Ovide moralisé* manuscripts, see Carla Lord, "Three Manuscripts of the *Ovide moralisé*," *Art Bulletin* 57 (1975): 161–75. For a study of the

first illuminated cycle of Boccaccio's *Des cleres et nobles femmes*, see Brigitte Buettner, *Boccaccio's Des cleres et nobles femmes: Systems of Signification in an Illuminated Manuscript*, College Art Association Monograph on the Fine Arts 53 (Seattle: University of Washington Press, 1996).

17. For an edition, see *Ovide moralisé. Poème du commencement du quatorzième siècle, publié d'après tous les manuscrits connus*, ed. Cornelius de Boer et al., *Verhandelingen der Koninklijke Akademie van Wetenschappen te Amsterdam, Afdeeling Letterkunde*, Nieuwe Reeks 15 (1915): 1–374; 21 (1920): 1–394; 30 (1931): 1–303; 37 (1936): 1–478; 43 (1938): 1–429; reprint in 5 vols. (Wiesbaden: Martin Sändig, 1966–68).

18. We use the following edition and translation: Guillaume de Lorris and Jean de Meun, *Le Roman de la rose*, ed. Félix Lecoy, 3 vols., Classiques Français du Moyen Age (Paris: Champion, 1966–75); Guillaume de Lorris and Jean de Meun, *The Romance of the Rose*, trans. Frances Horgan (Oxford: Oxford University Press, 1994).

19. For information about this text, see Paul Meyer, "Les premières Compilations françaises d'histoire ancienne. 1. Les faits des romains. 11. Histoire ancienne jusqu'à César," *Romania* 14 (1885): 1–81. For the visual tradition, see Doris Oltrogge, *Die Illustrationszyklen zur "Histoire ancienne jusqu'à César" (1250–1400)* (Frankfurt am Main: Peter Lang, 1989).

20. For the Latin text, see Giovanni Boccaccio, *Tutte le opere di Giovanni Boccaccio*, ed. Vittore Branca, vol. 10, *De mulieribus claris*, ed. and trans. V. Zaccaria, 2d ed. (Milan: Mondadori, 1970). For an English translation of the Latin text, see Giovanni Boccaccio, *Famous Women*, ed. and trans. Virginia Brown, I Tatti Renaissance Library 1 (Cambridge: Harvard University Press, 2001). For the text of the French translation, see Giovanni Boccaccio, *"Des Cleres et Nobles Femmes," Ms. Bibl. Nat. 112420*, ed. Jeanne Baroin and Josiane Haffen (Paris: Belles Lettres, 1993–95). For information regarding manuscripts of translations into French, see Carla Bozzolo, "Manuscrits des traductions françaises d'oeuvres de Boccace dans les Bibliothèques de France," *Italia medioevale e umanistica* 11 (1968): 1–69. On the pictorial component, see Buettner, *Boccaccio's Des cleres*. For Christine's use of Boccaccio as a source in the *Othea*, see Christine de Pizan, *Epistre Othea*, ed. Parussa, 64–66.

21. On Tommaso's family as members of the rural nobility from the *contado* of Bologna, see Nikolai Wandruszka, "The Family Origins of Christine de Pizan: Noble Lineage between City and *Contado* in the Thirteenth and Fourteenth Centuries," in *Au Champ des escriptures. IIIe Colloque international sur Christine de Pizan*, ed. Eric Hicks (Paris: Honoré Champion, 2000), 111–30. Wandruszka corrects and expands this article in "Familial Traditions of the *de Piçano* at Bologna," in *Contexts and Continuities*, ed. Kennedy, Brown-Grant, Laidlaw, and Müller, 3:889–906. On astrology in the French court, see Edgar Laird, "Astrology in the Court of Charles V of France, as Reflected in Oxford, St John's College, MS 164," *Manuscripta* 34 (1990): 167–76; and Laird, "Christine de Pizan and the Controversy Concerning Star-Study in the Court of Charles V," *Allegorica* 18 (1997): 21–30.

22. The duke of Berry's manuscript, now PML, M. 785, is a copy of BL, Sloane 3983, which is a copy of BnF, lat. 7330, the earliest illustrated copy of a Latin translation of Abū Ma'šar's astrological text. For a thorough discussion of illustrations of the planetary deities in the pictorial arts of western Europe, see Dieter Blume, *Regenten des*

Himmels. Astrologische Bilder in Mittelalter und Renaissance, Studien aus dem Warburg-Haus 3 (Berlin: Akademie, 2000). For Christine's knowledge of the astrological tradition and her use of it in the *Othea,* see Charity Cannon Willard, "Christine de Pizan: The Astrologer's Daughter," in *Mélanges à la mémoire de Franco Simone,* ed. Jonathan Beck and Gianni Mombello (Geneva: Slatkine, 1980), 95–111.

23. Claude Lévi-Strauss, *The Savage Mind* (Chicago: University of Chicago Press, 1966), 19. On the implications of Lévi-Strauss's suggestion that "[m]ythical thought appears to be an intellectual form of 'bricolage'" (21), see Karlheinz Stierle, "Mythos als 'Bricolage' und zwei Endstufen des Prometheusmythos," in *Terror und Spiel: Probleme der Mythenrezeption,* ed. Manfred Fuhrmann, Poetik und Hermeneutik 4 (Munich: Wilhelm Fink Verlag, 1971), 455–72. In the introduction to her *Reading Myth: Classical Mythology and Its Interpretations in Medieval French Literature* (Stanford: Stanford University Press, 1997), Renate Blumenfeld-Kosinski offers an overview of theoretical approaches to medieval uses of classical myth that we have found very useful. She discusses segmentation and *bricolage* in relation to myth, and in her chap. 4 she employs the concept of *bricolage* to analyze the *dits* of Froissart, a poet whose work Christine certainly knew. Mieke Bal proposes a different relationship between a myth and later reworkings of it: "The work's genesis in a preexistent narrative helps to sever the tie between the two and to produce another narrative, irreducibly alien to it, void of the deceptive meaning the pre-text brought along" (*Reading "Rembrandt": Beyond the Word-Image Opposition* [Cambridge: Cambridge University Press, 1991], 20).

24. Since Lévi-Strauss introduced the concept of *bricolage* in 1962, it has been taken up in a number of discourses. In 1965 Gérard Genette claimed that the analysis of *bricolage* could be applied almost word for word to literary criticism ("Structuralisme et critique littéraire," *L'Arc* 26 [1965]: 37–49). In 1971 Gerald Garvey used the term to refer to the ongoing process of constitutional *bricolage* (*Constitutional "Bricolage"* [Princeton: Princeton University Press, 1971]). Also in 1971, Stierle modified the idea of myth as *bricolage* to analyze the twentieth-century reception of ancient myth ("Mythos als 'Bricolage'"). In 1977, Jasper Halfmann and Clod Zillich discussed *bricolage* as a technique by which marginal social groups might produce "reduced models," for example, of a neighborhood, as part of a process of empowerment ("Reality and Reduced Model," *Studio International* 193, no. 986 [March–April 1977]: 99–104). In 1978 Jacques Derrida observed that "every discourse is bricoleur . . . if one calls *bricolage* the necessity of borrowing one's concepts from the text of a heritage which is more or less coherent or ruined" (Jacques Derrida, "Structure, Sign, and Play in the Discourse of the Human Sciences," in *Writing and Difference,* trans. Alan Bass [Chicago: University of Chicago Press, 1978], 285). In 1983 Rainer Crone used *bricolage* as a concept for analyzing the paintings of Jiři Georg Dokoupil ("Jiři Georg Dokoupil: The Imprisoned Brain," *Artforum* 21, no. 7 [1983]: 50–55). Janet Berlo, writing in 1992, saw *bricolage* as a rather derogatory term that anthropologists had applied to the indigenous textiles of postcolonial Latin America ("Beyond Bricolage: Women and Aesthetic Strategies in Latin American Textiles," *Res* 22 [autumn 1992]: 128). In 1993 Bruce W. Ferguson wrote that Klaus vom Bruch uses "the techniques of a media *bricoleur,*" in a video combining documentary footage of World War II American bombing of Aachen, the Krupp factory, and Cologne, with superimposed images of himself (Bruce W. Ferguson,

"Video? Art? History?" in *Künstlerischer Austausch. Artistic Exchange,* ed. Thomas W. Gaehtgens, 3 vols. [Berlin: Akademie, 1993], 3:213–22). Medieval art historians employ the term *bricolage* to describe the reuse of either antique subject matter or the fragments of antique artifacts called *spolia* (see Annabel Jane Wharton, "Good and Bad Images from the Synagogue of Dura Europos: Contexts, Subtexts, Intertexts," *Art History* 17 [1994]: 1–25; and Jane Hawkes, "The Rothbury Cross: An Iconographic Bricolage," *Gesta* 35 [1996]: 77–94). Finally, *bricolage* has been associated with postmodernity (Martin Roberts, *Michel Tournier: "Bricolage" and Cultural Mythology,* Stanford French and Italian Studies 79 [Saratoga, Calif.: ANMA Libri and Stanford: Department of French and Italian, 1994], 12). The term is employed in this sense by Homi K. Bhabha: "the absence of the dialectic of depth—inside/outside—is now replaced by a lateral 'side-by-sideness' (collage, bricolage) of the postmodern as palimpsest" ("Postmodernism/Postcolonialism," in *Critical Terms for Art History,* ed. Robert S. Nelson and Richard Shiff [Chicago: University of Chicago Press, 1996], 316).

In a special issue of the *Journal of Medieval and Early Modern Studies* edited by Kathleen Ashley and Véronique Plesch and entitled "The Cultural Processes of 'Appropriation,'" Claire Sponsler discusses *bricolage* as one of those cultural processes ("In Transit: Theorizing Cultural Appropriation in Medieval Europe," *Journal of Medieval and Early Modern Studies* 32 [2002]: 17–39).

25. Blumenfeld-Kosinski, "*Bricolage,* as used by Lévi-Strauss, implies a segmentation," by which she means a division "into segments seen as suitable for interpretation" (*Reading Myth,* n. 38, 224–25; 7). *Segmentation,* however, also implies the preservation of narrative sequence, whereas *bricolage* or *fragmentation* does not, and therefore the latter terms seem to us to be more applicable to the *Othea.* Also applicable to the *Othea* is Liliane Dulac's term, *rupture* ("Travail allégorique et ruptures du sens chez Christine de Pizan: *L'Epistre d'Othea,*" in *Continuités et ruptures dans l'histoire et la littérature. Actes du colloque franco-polonais. Montpellier, 1987* [Paris: Champion; Geneva: Slatkine, 1988], 24–32).

One could argue that Christine's *Othea* goes "beyond *bricolage*" in Janet Berlo's sense. Berlo writes, "In regard to women's arts of the Euroamerican tradition, Meyer and Schapiro have termed a similar aesthetic impulse 'femmage,' which combines aspects of collage, assemblage, improvisation, recycling, and personal history, all within the context of a woman-centered art form. Feminist art historians and literary critics of the past two decades have explored the notion of a female aesthetic that is separate from the dominant, patriarchal culture. This has, of course, been a controversial enterprise. Although for the most part these inquiries have been defined for and by the arts and letters of white Euroamerican women, occasionally a wider application is realized: 'What we here have been calling (the) female aesthetic turns out to be a specialized name for any practices available to those groups—nations, genders, sexualities, races, classes—all social practices which wish to criticize, to differentiate from, to overturn the dominant forms of knowing and understanding with which they are saturated'" (Berlo, "Beyond Bricolage," n. 3, 115, quoting Rachel Blau DuPlessix).

26. Scholars have found it important to identify a structure that unifies the *Othea.* Loukopoulos argued that unity was to be found in the epistolary frame: "We are con-

fronted by a juggling act in which mythology, medieval exegesis, moralizing, and Christian spirituality are manipulated within a collection of diverse and achronologically assembled stories. At this point, it is necessary to refer to the overall framework, which has the form, *mutatis mutandis,* of an initiatory paradigm and which acts as a cohesive force underlying the entire conglomerate" ("Classical Mythology," 109). Beginning with Rosemond Tuve, others have emphasized the allegorical level, pointing out that from chap. 1 through chap. 44 the allegories appear to determine the sequence of chapters in the *Othea* (Rosemond Tuve, *Allegorical Imagery: Some Mediaeval Books and Their Posterity* [Princeton: Princeton University Press, 1966]). Tuve suggests that "sets not so readily recognized" probably structure the rest of the *Othea* as well (286) and concludes that the *Othea* is "an ingenious little classical *Somme le roi* with adornments" (286). This view continues to be put forward; Renate Blumenfeld-Kosinski argues, "It is important to see that the whole text is structured not by the fables but by the allegories, which, at least initially, follow the scheme of series, such as the Seven Deadly Sins or the Twelve Articles of the Creed. This arrangement shows that the spiritual level of the allegory was the most important" (Christine de Pizan, *Selected Writings,* ed. Blumenfeld-Kosinski, 30). It follows for William Wells that Christine had little interest in the received tradition: "It is obvious that Christine de Pisan was interested in her classical sources only in so far as they supplied her with a peg for the moralisation. She pays no attention to the chronology of the Trojan War; the works of Ovid and Homer as transformed by their mediaeval interpreters—the anonymous authors of the *Ovide moralisé,* and the *Histoire ancienne jusqu'à César*—have been dissected, mingled and rearranged according to a theological plan" (William Wells, "A Simile in Christine de Pisan for Christ's Conception," *Journal of the Warburg and Courtauld Institutes* 2 [1938–39]: 68). Hindman sought to recuperate the unity of the *Othea* by means of a political interpretation; she reads the sequence of chapters as an attempt to develop a lesson on good government for Louis of Orleans (*Painting and Politics,* 24–60).

27. Chap. 75 is the second chapter of the *Othea* devoted to the story of Paris and Helen, since chap. 43 instructs Hector that the Trojans should have given up Helen rather than fighting a war over her. As an illustration, the miniature to chap. 75 actually fits better with the textual material in chap. 43, which discusses the implications of Helen's abduction by Paris. Even the *allegorie* of chap. 43—"you ought not to desire the wife of your neighbor" [Tu ne desireras point la femme de ton prochain]—addresses itself to the implications of adultery in a way that suits the image of Paris and Helen's embrace in chap. 75. But when image is combined with text, chap. 75 works to suggest a different interpretation of the most famous adultery of all time. See the discussion of chap. 75 in our chap. 3.

28. Sergei Eisenstein, *Towards a Theory of Montage,* vol. 2, *Selected Works,* ed. Michael Glenny and Richard Taylor (London: British Film Institute, 1991), 83.

29. Laura Mulvey and Peter Wollen, "Penthesilea, Queen of the Amazons," interview by Claire Johnston and Paul Willemen, *Screen* 15 (1974): 120–34; Laura Mulvey and Peter Wollen, "Riddles of the Sphinx: Script," *Screen* 18 (1977): 61–77. For Mulvey's classic statement on structures of visual pleasure in Hollywood cinema, see "Visual Pleasure and Narrative Cinema," first published in 1975; see also "Afterthoughts on 'Visual

Pleasure and Narrative Cinema' Inspired by King Vidor's *Duel in the Sun* (1946)," which first appeared in 1981. Both are reprinted in Mulvey's *Visual and Other Pleasures* (Bloomington: Indiana University Press, 1989).

30. "The myth of the Sphinx took on new life after Napoleon's campaigns in Egypt, when the Great Sphinx at Gizeh was disclosed once again to Western eyes. The Egyptian Sphinx is male, but on its blank face, resonant with mystery and with death, the spectator could project the image of the Greek Sphinx. Once again the Sphinx could enter popular mythology, in the image of male fears and fantasies, the cannibalistic mother, part bestial, part angelic, indecipherable" (Mulvey and Wollen, "Riddles," 62).

31. Mulvey and Wollen, "Riddles," 62.

32. Mulvey and Wollen, "Penthesilea," 120.

33. See Lucy Fischer, *Shot/Countershot: Film Tradition and Women's Cinema* (Princeton: Princeton University Press, 1989), 49–62. For another analysis of *Riddles of the Sphinx,* see E. Ann Kaplan, *Women and Film: Both Sides of the Camera* (London: Routledge, 1983), 171–81. For a general discussion of aesthetics and feminist filmmaking, see Teresa de Lauretis, "Rethinking Women's Cinema: Aesthetics and Feminist Theory," in *Multiple Voices in Feminist Film Criticism,* ed. Diane Carson, Linda Dittmar, and Janice R. Welsch (Minneapolis: University of Minnesota Press, 1994), 140–61.

34. Mulvey describes "Visual Pleasure and Narrative Cinema" as "written in 1973, polemically and without regard for context or nuances of argument" (*Visual and Other Pleasures,* vii). In the introduction to *Visual and Other Pleasures,* Mulvey contextualizes her early writing within feminist politics. However, when one reads "Visual Pleasure and Narrative Cinema" in conjunction with a viewing of the film *The Riddles of the Sphinx*—produced within a few years of "Visual Pleasure and Narrative Cinema"—it becomes clear that Mulvey's theory of the male gaze is a description of a particular historical moment, not a universalizing theory of all cinematic contracts. *The Riddle of the Sphinx* is in every way a refusal of the paradigm described in "Visual Pleasure."

35. Mulvey, "Film, Feminism, and the Avant-Garde," in *Visual and Other Pleasures,* 120–21; see also de Lauretis, "Rethinking Women's Cinema."

36. Kaja Silverman, *The Acoustic Mirror: The Female Voice in Psychoanalysis and Cinema* (Bloomington: Indiana University Press, 1988), 48.

37. Silverman, *World Spectators,* especially 85–100.

38. For an edition of Oresme's translation, see Nicole Oresme, *Le Livre de ethiques d'Aristote,* ed. Albert Douglas Menut (New York: Stechert, 1940). For a list of manuscripts, see 46–53. For a study of the illustrated manuscripts, see Claire Richter Sherman, *Imaging Aristotle: Verbal and Visual Representation in Fourteenth-Century France* (Berkeley and Los Angeles: University of California Press, 1995).

39. "C'est a dire, par acoustumance et frequentacion de bonnes operacions" [That is to say, through habit and the regular performance of good actions] (Oresme, *Livre de ethiques,* ed. Menut, book 2, chap. 1).

40. Pierre Bourdieu, *Outline of a Theory of Practice,* trans. Richard Nice (Cambridge: Cambridge University Press, 1977).

41. On spectatorship, see Linda Williams, "Corporealized Observers: Visual Pornographies and the 'Carnal Density of Vision,'" in *Fugitive Images: From Photography to Video,* ed. Patrice Petro (Bloomington: Indiana University Press, 1995), 3–41; Janet

Staiger, *Perverse Spectators: The Practices of Film Reception* (New York: New York University Press, 2000). Although film theory was critical to the development of the feminist theories of the 1970s and 1980s, since the 1990 publication of Judith Butler's *Gender Trouble* feminism has been animated more by the discourses of performance theory (Judith Butler, *Gender Trouble: Feminism and the Subversion of Identity* [London: Routledge, 1990]). Butler's essay "Performative Acts and Gender Constitution: An Essay in Phenomenology and Feminist Theory" appeared in *Performing Feminisms: Feminist Critical Theory and Theatre*, ed. Sue-Ellen Case (Baltimore: Johns Hopkins University Press, 1990), 270–82, a collection that signaled, in a sense, the creation of feminist performance theory. For feminist performance theory, see *The Performance of Power: Theatrical Discourse and Politics*, ed. Sue-Ellen Case and Janelle Reinelt (Iowa City: University of Iowa Press, 1991); *Gender in Performance: The Presentation of Difference in the Performing Arts*, ed. Laurence Senelick (Hanover, N.H.: University Press of New England, 1992); Jill Dolan, *Presence and Desire: Essays on Gender, Sexuality, Performance* (Ann Arbor: University of Michigan Press, 1993); *Performativity and Performance*, ed. Andrew Parker and Eve Kosofsky Sedgwick (London: Routledge, 1995); and *Performance and Cultural Politics*, ed. Elin Diamond (London: Routledge, 1996).

42. Bernard J. Hibbitts, "Coming to Our Senses: Communication and Legal Expression in Legal Cultures," *Emory Law Journal* 41 (1992): 882–83. We wish to thank Carol Weisbrod for bringing this article to our attention.

43. Catherine M. Soussloff, "Like a Performance: Performativity and the Historicized Body, from Bellori to Mapplethorpe," in *Acting on the Past: Historical Performance across the Disciplines*, ed. Mark Franko and Annette Richards (Hanover, N.H.: University Press of New England, 2000), 91.

44. Christine de Pizan, "The God of Love's Letter," trans. Kevin Brownlee, in Christine de Pizan, *Selected Writings*, ed. Blumenfeld-Kosinski, 23.

45. Christine de Pizan, "L'epistre au Dieu d'Amours," in *Oeuvres poétiques de Christine de Pisan*, ed. Maurice Roy (Paris: Firmin Didot, 1891), 2:1–26; see also Christine de Pizan, *Epistre au dieu d'Amours* in *Poems of Cupid, God of Love*, ed. Thelma Fenster and Mary Carpenter Erler (Leiden: Brill, 1990).

46. For the various traditions of Medea, see Ruth Morse, *The Medieval Medea* (Woodbridge, Suffolk: Boydell and Brewer, 1996). See also Christine Reno, "Feminist Aspects of Christine de Pizan's 'Epistre d'Othea a Hector,'" *Studi francesi* 71 (1980): 271–76. Carol M. Meale compares the treatments of Medea in Chaucer, Boccaccio, and Christine's *Le Livre de la Cité des Dames* (1405), but she does not discuss the *Othea*. See Carole M. Meale, "Legends of Good Women in the European Middle Ages," *Archiv für das Studium der neueren Sprachen und Literaturen* 229 (1992): 55–70.

47. Hindman, *Painting and Politics*, 97.

48. This is not the only place in the *Othea* that Christine uses this verb. See, for example, 3.4–5: "Vers Herculés te faut virer / Et ses vaillances remirer"; 5.2: "Aprés te mire en Perseüs"; 37.5: "Et en Leomedon te mire."

49. On memory in the Middle Ages, see Mary Carruthers, *The Book of Memory: A Study of Memory in Medieval Culture* (Cambridge: Cambridge University Press, 1990). For the useful concept of the "memorial center," see V. A. Kolve, *Chaucer and the Imagery of Narrative: The First Five Canterbury Tales* (Stanford: Stanford University Press,

1984). For a study emphasizing the central roles of vision and memory in the medieval interpretation of allegory, see Susan K. Hagen, *Allegorical Remembrance: A Study of "The Pilgrimage of the Life of Man" as a Medieval Treatise on Seeing and Remembering* (Athens: University of Georgia Press, 1990).

50. Hindman considers three sorts of evidence—"information on manuscript production in Paris, Christine's writings on art, and the sources for the miniatures in the *Epistre Othéa*"—on the basis of which she concludes that the miniaturists "worked under Christine's direction, following her verbal instructions" (*Painting and Politics,* 98). In a later article on Harley 4431 coauthored with Stephen Perkinson, the authors conclude that "the autograph Harley codex . . . represents the latest and most complete versions of Christine's . . . works, with respect to their text and illustrations, and, since it was produced at the height of her career when presumably her financial difficulties had abated, it seems reasonable to suppose that the number and placement of illustrations in this work were intentional" (Sandra Hindman and Stephen Perkinson, "Insurgent Voices. Illuminated Versions of Christine de Pizan's 'Le Livre du Duc des vrais amans,'" in *The City of Scholars: New Approaches to Christine de Pizan,* ed. Margarete Zimmermann and Dina De Rentiis, European Cultures: Studies in Literature and the Arts, ed. Walter Pape, 2 [Berlin: de Gruyter, 1994], 228 n. 30). See also Meiss, *Limbourgs,* 40.

51. Sherman, *Imaging Aristotle,* xxii.

52. A comprehensive list was published by Lucie Schaefer ("Die Illustrationen") as early as 1937.

53. Gilbert Ouy and Christine M. Reno, "Identification des autographes de Christine de Pizan," *Scriptorium* 34 (1980): 221–38. Scholars have recently begun to question several of the premises regarding the autograph status of the manuscripts of the Christine corpus. See Gabriella Parussa, "Autographes et orthographe: Quelques considérations sur l'orthographe de Christine de Pizan," *Romania* 117 (1999): 143–59; Gabriella Parussa and Richard Trachsler, "*Or sus, alons ou champ des escriptures.* Encore sur l'orthographe de Christine de Pizan: l'intérêt des grandes corpus," in *Contexts and Continuities,* ed. Kennedy, Brown-Grant, Laidlaw, and Müller, 3:621–43; James C. Laidlaw, "Christine's Lays—Does Practice Make Perfect?" in *Contexts and Continuities,* ed. Kennedy, Brown-Grant, Laidlaw, and Müller, 2:467–81. For a response to Laidlaw's critique in "Christine's Lays" as well as additional evidence in support of their conclusion that "Christine's manuscripts provide abundant evidence of the interchangeable roles of [scribal hands] X and X' and clearly link both with the author" (730), see Christine Reno and Gilbert Ouy, "X + X' = 1," in *Contexts and Continuities,* ed. Kennedy, Brown-Grant, Laidlaw, and Müller, 3:723–30.

54. Tuve, *Allegorical Imagery.*

55. Meiss notes, "More than any other text by Christine the *Epître* was designed for miniatures" (*Limbourgs,* 23).

56. Hindman, *Painting and Politics.* Parussa's attention to the intertextual qualities of the *Othea* implies its intervisuality as well; as she puts it, "L'image parle aussi bien que le texte au lecteur" ("Le concept d'intertextualité," 485). For a recent example of a study giving serious attention to visual content, see Rosalind Brown-Grant, "Illumination as Reception: Jean Miélot's Reworking of the 'Epistre Othea,'" in *City of Scholars,* ed. Zimmerman and De Rentiis, 260–71, figs. 25–32.

57. For a thorough description of this manuscript, see Mombello, *La tradizione manoscritta,* cat. 73, 23–31, who suggests that fr. 848 must be one of the first if not the first manuscript of the *Othea* (24 n. 1). For a discussion of the miniature cycle, see Schoell-Glass, "Aspekte der Antikenrezeption," 52–60. For a reproduction of fol. 2r, see Hindman, *Painting and Politics,* pl. 2.

58. James Laidlaw, "Christine de Pizan—a Publisher's Progress," *Modern Language Review* 82 (1987): 42. See also Laidlaw, "Christine de Pizan: From Scriptorium to Database and Back Again," *Journal of the Institute of Romance Studies* 1 (1992): 59–67.

59. We thus disagree with Laidlaw, who attributes the lack of fit between text and image to "poor planning or inexperience" ("Publisher's Progress," 41). For Stephanie Gibbs, the irregular text length in these first six chapters results from this early page design. See "Christine de Pizan's *Epistre Othea* in England: The Manuscript Tradition of Stephen Scrope's Translation," in *Contexts and Continuities,* ed. Kennedy, Brown-Grant, Laidlaw, and Müller, 2:397–408.

60. See Charity Cannon Willard, who comments that the arrangement of the Othea constitutes a "format recalling legal texts and their commentaries," including a gloss on Dante (Willard, *Christine de Pizan: Her Life and Works* [New York: Persea, 1984], 95); on this point, see also Laidlaw: "The layout is . . . modeled on the standard biblical or theological manuscripts of the period" ("Publisher's Progress," 41).

61. Ignatius, "Christine de Pizan's *Epistre Othea,*" 133. Margaret J. Ehrhart concludes: "The arrangement of the text on the page in B. N. fr. 848 suggests too that Christine initially conceived the *Othea* as a text to be apprehended visually rather than aurally" ("Christine de Pizan and the Judgment of Paris: A Court Poet's Use of the Mythographic Tradition," in Chance, *Mythographic Art,* 139–40).

62. Schoell-Glass, "Aspekte der Antikenrezeption," 99–112; Mombello, *La tradizione manoscritta,* nos. 46 and 24.

63. Both Chantilly, MS 492–93 and BnF, fr. 12779 are dated soon after 1400. Another manuscript of the same date and layout, BnF, fr. 604, has spaces for the same number of miniatures. For the "Livre de Christine," see James Laidlaw, "Christine de Pizan—an Author's Progress," *Modern Language Review* 78 (1983): 544–46, and for descriptions of these manuscripts, see Mombello, *La tradizione manoscritta,* nos. 21, 11, and 1 respectively.

64. Laidlaw describes the *Othea*'s relationship to the rest of the collection: "Although it is exceptionally well illustrated by comparison to the other works [in the Duke's manuscript], the *Epistre Othea* was none the less designed to fit within the collection. That can be seen from the fact that the miniature, the introductory capital, and the associated borders which precede the prologue are similar in size and style to those which introduce earlier items" ("Publisher's Progress," 56–57).

65. Hindman concluded that the Queen's manuscript was compiled of separately written texts gathered together in one codex. She observed that the *Othea* in the Queen's manuscript is written on leaves whose size has been enlarged by the very careful addition of vellum borders and concluded that this was done in order to make them larger so that the *Othea* would be of uniform size with the other parts of the Queen's manuscript. See Sandra L. Hindman, "The Composition of the Manuscript of Christine de Pizan's Collected Works in the British Library: A Reassessment," *British Library Journal*

9 (1983): 93–123. The hypothesis is faulty: the columns throughout the Queen's manuscript are identical, which demonstrates that the *Othea* was produced for this collection. James Laidlaw sees no evidence that the *Othea* in the Queen's manuscript was ever intended to circulate separately from the collected works (Laidlaw, "Publisher's Progress," 66).

66. Deborah McGrady, "What Is a Patron? Benefactors and Authorship in Harley 4431, Christine de Pizan's Collected Works," in Desmond, *Christine de Pizan,* 198. See also Brigitte Buettner, "Profane Illuminations, Secular Illusions: Manuscripts in Late Medieval Courtly Society," *Art Bulletin* 74 (1992): 75–90.

67. Jonathan J. G. Alexander, "Art History, Literary History, and the Study of Medieval Illuminated Manuscripts," *Studies in Iconography* 18 (1997): 56. Meiss postulates a series of drawings from which fr. 606 was made and argues that the miniatures in 4431 are copies of those in 606 (*Limbourgs,* 39); Laidlaw considers the textual relationship between the *Othea* in the Duke's and in the Queen's manuscripts and concludes that the text in the Queen's manuscript is a later version that represents the author's improvements on her earlier texts ("Author's Progress," 544–46; "Publisher's Progress," 60–66).

68. Jonathan J. G. Alexander, *Medieval Illuminators and Their Methods of Work* (New Haven: Yale University Press, 1992), 138. Alexander defines "twin manuscripts": "for some special reason, two identical or nearly identical manuscripts were made at the same time, or perhaps after a very short interval, rather than that one manuscript aimed to copy another exactly after a longer interval. In the later Middle Ages there are examples of a new text or newly translated text being made in two or even multiple copies" (105). Alexander identifies the two *Othea* manuscripts under discussion here as twin manuscripts (138). Early on, Schaefer argued that 4431 and fr. 606 were copied from the same manuscript ("Die Illustrationen," 172).

69. Meiss, *Limbourgs,* 23–41; Sterling, *La Peinture médiévale,* 1:311–17. Fr. 606 is no. 2 in Mombello's catalogue (*La tradizione manoscritta*).

70. Meiss, *Limbourgs,* 39. The *Othea* in Harley 4431 is no. 38 in Mombello's catalogue (*La tradizione manoscritta*).

71. As Schoell-Glass points out, the verticality of the miniatures in fr. 606 and Harley 4431 is unusual in this period; within double-column formats, miniatures usually tend to be roughly square. Schoell-Glass takes this feature as further evidence for Christine's personal involvement in manuscript design and suggests that she herself left these spaces for the miniatures. For Schoell-Glass, the verticality enabled the inclusion of the allegorical content of each chapter in its miniature, an inclusion that Christine intended ("Aspekte der Antikenrezeption," 84–90). In our reading of these manuscripts, neither the format of the miniatures nor their iconography refers in any direct way to the interpretations set forth in the *allegories.*

72. See Louisa Dunlop, "Pigments and Painting Materials in Fourteenth- and Early Fifteenth-Century Parisian Manuscript Illumination," in *Artistes, Artisans et production artistique au Moyen Age,* vol. 3, *Fabrication et consommation de l'oeuvre,* ed. Xavier Barral i Altet (Paris: Picard, 1990), 271–93. See also Meiss, *Late Fourteenth Century,* 140–46.

73. On the shift in the meanings associated with the color blue and the great rise in its popularity that became particularly evident in the late fourteenth century, see Michel

Pastoureau, *Blue: The History of a Color*, trans. Markus I. Cruse (Princeton: Princeton University Press, 2001).

74. Eric Wolf, *Europe and the People without History*, 2d ed. (Berkeley and Los Angeles: University of California Press, 1997), 38–39.

75. Rosalind Brown-Grant identifies the *Othea* as a text that promotes an ethical program, but she does not see this as a response to the visuality of the text in its manuscript context. See *Christine de Pizan and the Moral Defence of Women: Reading beyond Gender* (Cambridge: Cambridge University Press, 1999), 52–88.

76. We have found especially useful Hal Foster's distinction between vision and visuality: "Although vision suggests sight as a physical operation, and visuality sight as a social fact, the two are not opposed as nature to culture: vision is social and historical too, and visuality involves the body and the psyche. Yet neither are they identical: here, the difference between the terms signals a difference within the visual—between the mechanism of sight and its historical techniques, between the datum of vision and its discursive determinations" (Hal Foster, ed., *Vision and Visuality* [Seattle: Bay Press, 1988], ix).

77. "[T]he texist valuation of art would have images follow, not lead. They are seen as intrinsically subordinate, their inferiority deriving from the same cause as that of subjected woman" (Leo Steinberg, *The Sexuality of Christ in Renaissance Art and in Modern Oblivion*, 2d ed. [Chicago: University of Chicago Press, 1996], 386).

Chapter 1

1. Erwin Panofsky and Fritz Saxl, "Classical Mythology in Mediaeval Art," *Metropolitan Museum Studies* 4 (1932–33): 228–80.

2. Panofsky and Saxl, "Classical Mythology," 240. This essay has had such an enduring influence that a translation into French was published in book form as recently as 1990: *La mythologie classique dans l'art médiéval*, trans. Sylvie Girard (Saint-Pierre-de-Salerne: Monfort, 1990). These ideas were further developed by Panofsky in *Renaissance and Renascences in Western Art* (1960; reprint, New York: Harper and Row, 1969).

3. "Transforming the ancient prototypes in such a way that they became almost unrecognizable, [the illuminators] decomposed the representational tradition of mythological figures" (Panofsky and Saxl, "Classical Mythology," 237). "This decomposition of the classical type was not the result of any increasing respect for the scientific and true position of the stars (which were still placed as arbitrarily as ever) but was due to a purely stylistic and intellectual evolution" (238). "As the scimitar is an Oriental weapon it suggests that the painter of this fifteenth-century miniature, which in all other respects is only a peculiarly degenerate descendant of the widespread Western tradition, had been influenced by representations deriving from the Arabian East" (238). For another critique of this Panofskyan "principle of disjunction," see Michael Camille, *The Gothic Idol: Ideology and Image-Making in Medieval Art* (Cambridge: Cambridge University Press, 1989), 102. For a consideration of Panofsky's cultural politics as shaped by Europe in the early twentieth century, see Carl Landauer, "Erwin Panofsky and the Renascence of the Renaissance," *Renaissance Quarterly* 47 (1994): 255–81.

4. Panofsky and Saxl, "Classical Mythology," fig. 16 and p. 238.

5. Panofsky and Saxl, "Classical Mythology," 240, referring to Morgan Library manuscript M. 284. They based their theory of separation and reunion largely on representations of the constellations and planets in astrological manuscripts. Dieter Blume has undercut this theory by making a very strong case for the independent development of astrological representation in the East and the West (*Regenten des Himmels*, 201–4).

6. Jean Seznec, *The Survival of the Pagan Gods: The Mythological Tradition and Its Place in Renaissance Humanism and Art*, trans. Barbara F. Sessions (1953; reprint, New York: Harper and Row, 1961), 6. Seznec undoes his erasure of the medieval visual tradition by reproducing a number of illustrations of medieval works of art with mythological content.

7. Of course the *Othea* is not the only medieval manuscript to challenge Panofsky's principle of disjunction. Illuminated manuscripts of the *Ovide moralisé*, one or more of which Christine de Pizan knew well, also do so. Carla Lord registers her critique of the dismissive treatment of these illustrated Ovidian manuscripts by scholars who subscribe to the value judgments inherent in the principle of disjunction when she comments: "the strictly contemporary costuming of the miniatures, gracefully disjoined from the proper Classical mode, has been analyzed somewhat superciliously" ("Three Manuscripts," 170).

8. "The history of a discipline, like the history of, say, politics or art, requires for its telling the identification and understanding of major events. In the history of modern art history, the primary 'event' is undoubtedly the work of Erwin Panofsky" (Michael Ann Holly, *Panofsky and the Foundations of Art History* [Ithaca, N.Y.: Cornell University Press, 1984]: 10). Holly also calls Panofsky "arguably the most influential historian of art in the twentieth century" (23). Among the events marking the one hundredth anniversary of Panofsky's birth was a colloquium held at the Institute for Advanced Study in Princeton. The papers delivered at that colloquium were subsequently edited by Irving R. Lavin, the colloquium organizer, and published as *Meaning in the Visual Arts: Views from the Outside: A Centennial Commemoration of Erwin Panofsky (1892–1968)* (Princeton: Institute for Advanced Study, 1995). In his essay in that volume entitled "Panofsky's History of Art," Lavin writes, "It was [his] insistence on, and search for, meaning—especially meaning in places where no one suspected there was any—that led Panofsky to understand art, as no previous historian had, as an intellectual endeavor on a par with the traditional liberal arts like literature and music; and in so doing he made art history into something it had never been before, a humanistic discipline" (6). For a perceptive analysis of the contribution of the generation of German scholars before Panofsky, see Kathryn Brush, *The Shaping of Art History: Wilhelm Vöge, Adolph Goldschmidt, and the Study of Medieval Art* (Cambridge: Cambridge University Press, 1996).

9. For a description of cinema in Germany in the first three decades of the twentieth century, see Siegfried Kracauer, *From Caligari to Hitler: A Psychological History of the German Film* (Princeton: Princeton University Press, 1947). Kracauer specifically notes the popularity of Hollywood films in Germany throughout this period, though no Hollywood films were shown during the First World War, and they were eventually banned by the Nazis.

10. Thomas Y. Levin notes, "Panofsky's engagement with the cinema extended well beyond the immediate context of the various versions of [the] film essay and included, for example, his discussion of 'the "cinematographic" drawings of the Codex Huygens,' his inaugural address at the first meeting of The Society of Cinematologists in 1960, and his not infrequent discussions of films well into the 1960s ("Iconology at the Movies: Panofsky's Film Theory," in Lavin, *Meaning in the Visual Arts,* 314). His lively correspondence with Siegfried Kracauer is one indication that his interest in the cinema continued throughout his life (*Siegfried Kracauer—Erwin Panofsky Briefwechsel,* ed. Volker Breidecker (Berlin: Akademie, 1996).

11. The iconographic method that came to be identified with Panofsky, especially in the United States, seems to be a synthesis of ideas in circulation in Hamburg in the 1920s, originating in "a relatively circumscribed problem of method which was at the heart of Aby Warburg's research and reflections, and which has been revived and variously applied by his followers, namely the use of iconographic evidence as a historical source" (Carlo Ginzburg, "From Aby Warburg to E. H. Gombrich: A Problem of Method," in *Clues, Myths, and the Historical Method,* trans. John Tedeschi and Anne C. Tedeschi [Baltimore: Johns Hopkins University Press, 1989], 18). Panofsky's debts to Warburg are fundamental; see also Landauer, "Panofsky and the Renascence." In addition, as Joan Hart has demonstrated, "Panofsky adopted far more from Mannheim's theory of interpretation than he credited to him" (Joan Hart, "Erwin Panofsky and Karl Mannheim: A Dialogue on Interpretation," *Critical Inquiry* 19 [1993]: 553). Others to whom Panofsky owed significant intellectual debts include Ernst Cassirer and G. J. Hoogewerff, "who first gave the method of 'iconology' its definition, differentiating it from the traditional method of iconography" (Jan Bialostocki, "Iconography and Iconology," *Encyclopedia of World Art,* vol. 7, col. 774). For a discussion of Panofsky in the context of the Warburgian method, see Ginzburg, "Warburg to Gombrich." Recent German scholarship is highly critical of Panofsky's formulations regarding iconography and sharply differentiates Warburg's iconography from Panofsky's: "Warburgs Werk wurde sehr häufig ohne weitere Berücksichtigung seiner eigenen Ideen anhand der ikonologischen Methode bewertet, wie sie Panofsky in der berühmten Einleitung zu den 'Studies in Iconologie' definiert hat. Zahlreiche Anhaltspunkte erlauben jedoch die Behauptung, dass Warburgs kulturgeschichtliche Methode sich grundlegend von Panofskys Ideen in seiner Einführung unterscheidet" (Peter van Huisstede, "Der Mnemosyne-Atlas. Ein Laboratorium der Bildgeschichte," in *Aby M. Warburg. "ekstatische Nymphe—trauerender Flussgott." Porträt eines Gelehrten,* ed. Robert Galitz and Brita Reimers [Hamburg: Dölling and Galitz, 1995], 136).

12. In *Panofsky and the Foundations of Art History,* Holly clarifies Panofsky's systematization of the iconological approach: "A 'preiconographical description,' on the basis of 'practical experience,' interprets 'primary or natural subject matter.' An 'iconographic analysis' ('in the narrow sense of the word') is interested in the 'secondary or conventional meanings' that can be discovered by a knowledge of literary sources. An iconological interpretation ('iconography in a deeper sense') directs itself to Panofsky's original concern with 'intrinsic meaning or content.' To reveal the meaning of a work of art on this level, we must familiarize ourselves with the 'essential tendencies of the human mind' as they are conditioned by cultural predispositions and personal psychology"

(159–60). "Iconological analysis is based upon the posing of one major question; that is, it persistently asks why this image has assumed this shape at this historical moment" (185). However, as Holly acknowledges, "Panofsky's own practical art history often contradicted—or, more affirmatively, only rarely fulfilled—the challenge of his theoretical work" (185). In the 1994 edition of the widely used *History of Art: A Students' Handbook* Marcia Pointon indicates the extent to which the term *iconography* has subsumed *iconology* in the current understanding of these concepts in the discipline of art history (88–89, 107–10). Although we are aware of the distinctions drawn by Panofsky and analyzed in detail by Holly, we here follow current usage in employing *iconography* as the general term. For a consideration of the status of iconography, see the colloquium proceedings *Iconography at the Crossroads,* ed. Brendan Cassidy (Princeton: Index of Christian Art and Department of Art and Archaeology, 1993). The iconographic method is deeply entrenched; Roelof van Straten's *An Introduction to Iconography* (trans. Patricia de Man [Amsterdam: Gordon and Breach, 1994]) relies very heavily on Panofsky. See, however, Brendan Cassidy's critical review in *Studies in Iconography* 17 (1996): 432–35.

13. Many art historians no longer subscribe to this definition of iconography. As Jonathan Alexander observes, "[S]hifts in the field of art history have . . . led to a questioning of older definitions of what constitutes iconographic study. We can now admit that meanings in images could vary for different spectators, that they are not static over time, and also that they may often be sites of contested and conflicting meanings. As such these meanings are only intelligible in the social contexts in which they were created, semiotically in other words" ("Art History," 54).

14. Willibald Sauerländer, "Struggling with a Deconstructed Panofsky," in Lavin, *Meaning in the Visual Arts,* 394.

15. Panofsky wrote this piece as a lecture, which he delivered numerous times. Lavin describes its publication history: "The article was published in three versions: initially in 1936 with the title 'On Movies'; again the following year, slightly enlarged and with a new title, 'Style and Medium in the Moving Pictures'; and a decade later in the definitive version, extensively revised and expanded and with the word 'Moving' in the title changed to 'Motion,' when it was described as 'one of the most significant introductions to the aesthetics of the motion picture yet to be written'" (Irving Lavin, introduction to Erwin Panofsky, *Three Essays on Style,* ed. Lavin [Cambridge: MIT Press, 1995], 9–10).

16. Our references are to the following edition: "Style and Medium in the Motion Pictures," in Panofsky, *Three Essays on Style,* 91–125. For a review of *Three Essays,* see E. H. Gombrich, "Icon," *New York Review of Books,* February 15, 1996, 29–30. For a careful analysis of the changes Panofsky made in the various versions of this essay, see Regine Prange, "Stil und Medium. Panofsky's 'On Movies,'" in *Erwin Panofsky. Beiträge des Symposions Hamburg 1992,* ed. Bruno Reudenbach (Berlin: Akademie, 1994), 171–90.

17. "What Panofsky never could swallow was the modern separation of form and expression from content, content in the most traditional, iconographic sense" (Sauerländer, "Struggling," 394). William S. Heckscher, a student of Panofsky's in Hamburg, followed Panofsky's lead. He gives several examples of the iconographic decoding of film in "*Petites perceptions:* An Account of *sortes Warburgianae,*" in *Art and Literature: Studies in Relationship,* ed. Egon Verheyen (Durham: Duke University Press, 1985),

435–68 and figs. 1–17. As professor of medieval art and iconography at the University of Utrecht, Heckscher was chiefly responsible for the installation there of a copy of the Princeton Index of Christian Art (Dirk Jacob Jansen, "Princeton Index of Christian Art: The Utrecht Copy," *Visual Resources: An International Journal of Documentation* 13 [1998]: 253–85).

18. "Vor allem aber, weil der Erzählfilm zeichenhaft bleibt, Sprache und Handlung durch Bilder illustriert und insofern ikonographischer Entschlüsselung offensteht, findet er bei Panofsky volle Anerkennung als einzig legitimer Nachfolger der traditionellen Bildkunst" (Prange, "Stil und Medium," 180–81). We thank Margareth Taube Clayton for assistance with the translation.

19. Lavin, introduction to Panofsky, *Three Essays on Style*, 10.

20. "Style and Medium" had a tremendous influence on the development of film theory as a discipline. Seminal works in film theory frequently cite Panofsky's essay and often treat the theoretical categories posed in "Style and Medium" as the received wisdom of the discipline, to be tested, revised, or discarded. For two examples see Stanley Cavell (*The World Viewed: Reflections on the Ontology of Film* [New York: Viking, 1971]), who takes Panofsky's essay as his point of departure (see esp. 16 and 29–37) and Gerald Mast, *Film/Cinema/Movie: A Theory of Experience* (New York: Harper and Row, 1977; reprint, Chicago: University of Chicago Press, 1983), who cites Panofsky throughout and implicitly ranks him with S. M. Eisenstein and Siegfried Kracauer.

21. Levin, "Iconology at the Movies," 314. As Martin Warnke warns, this refusal to see film studies as part of the art historical project is increasingly dangerous for art history: "One wonders whether the discipline of art history is capable of surviving if it fails to take account of this formative medium of visual experience" (quoted in Levin, "Iconology at the Movies," 329).

22. Vivian Sobchack, "Phenomenology and the Film Experience," in *Viewing Positions: Ways of Seeing Film*, ed. Linda Williams (New Brunswick, N.J.: Rutgers University Press, 1995), 37. For a sociological discussion of the location of pornographic movie theaters, see Peter Donnelly, "Running the Gauntlet: The Moral Order of Pornographic Movie Theaters," *Urban Life* 10 (1981): 239–64.

23. Sigmund Freud, "The 'Uncanny,'" in *The Standard Edition of the Complete Psychological Works of Sigmund Freud*, ed. James Strachey, vol. 17 (London: Hogarth Press, 1955), 217–56.

24. Freud, "The 'Uncanny,'" 237.

25. Linda Williams, *Hard Core: Power, Pleasure, and the "Frenzy of the Visible,"* rev. ed. (Berkeley and Los Angeles: University of California Press, 1999), 45. See also Williams's discussion in chap. 2, "Pre-History," of how "a cinematic hard core" is indebted to the "optical inventions of the late nineteenth-century" (53).

26. Williams, *Hard Core*, 45.

27. Cavell, *World Viewed*, 45.

28. "Style and Medium" was originally delivered at the Museum of Modern Art to a "group of Princeton amateurs intent on founding a film archive" (Lavin, introduction to Panofsky, *Three Essays on Style*, 10). William Heckscher notes that "in 1946–7 [Panofsky] traveled to various places in and around Princeton, to give his talk as a *tema con variazioni* (William S. Heckscher, "Erwin Panofsky: A Curriculum Vitae," in Panofsky,

Three Essays on Style, 219 n. 12). In this context, it is perhaps interesting that Panofsky referred to Princeton as the "last Indian Reserve for gentlemen (because a gentleman is a gentleman only in a womanless atmosphere)" (quoted by Heckscher in Panofsky, *Three Essays*, 183). "Anyone educated in Germany prior to World War I would have studied philology in depth. Panofsky testified to his love of his teachers of Latin and Greek. . . . He said he learned 'method' from them" (Hart, "Panofsky and Mannheim," 554).

29. Erwin Panofsky, "Three Decades of Art History in the United States," in *Meaning in the Visual Arts* (1955; reprint, Chicago: University of Chicago Press, 1982), 343. Panofsky contrasts his all-male educational environment to American educational institutions: "The American theory of education requires that the teachers of the young—a vast majority of them females—know a great deal about 'behavior patterns,' 'group integration,' and 'controlled aggression drives,' but does not insist too much upon what they may know of their subject, and cares even less for whether they are genuinely interested or actively engaged in it" (343). In his gratuitous comment about the "vast majority" of teachers being women, Panofsky disdainfully associates the presence of women as teachers with the weaknesses he perceives in the American educational system, particularly its almost complete lack of emphasis on classical philology.

For a discussion of the Renaissance study of Latin as "a relatively violent puberty rite setting, a sense of existence on a threshold, within a marginal environment (associated with forced seclusion from the company of women and to a certain extent from one's own family), in an atmosphere of continuous excitement," see Walter J. Ong, S.J., "Latin Language Study as a Renaissance Puberty Rite," *Studies in Philology* 56 (1959): 122. See also Ong's "Latin and the Social Fabric," in *The Barbarian within and Other Fugitive Essays and Studies* (New York: Macmillan, 1962), 206–19.

On the notion of the homosocial as a critical category, see Eve Kosofsky Sedgwick, *Epistemology of the Closet* (Berkeley and Los Angeles: University of California Press, 1990). On homosociality and pornographic film, see Thomas Waugh, "Homosociality in the Classical American Stag Film: Off-Screen, On-Screen," *Sexualities* 4 (2001): 275–91.

30. For a discussion of how "the reading of the *Aeneid*—as part of Latin training— has been associated with a class-specific performance of masculinity," see Marilynn Desmond, *Reading Dido: Gender, Textuality, and the Medieval "Aeneid"* (Minneapolis: University of Minnesota Press, 1994), 7–11.

31. Frances Ferguson, "Pornography: The Theory," *Critical Inquiry* 21 (1995): 690.

32. This is one of two woodcuts that were added to the second edition of *Underweysung der Messung mit dem Zirckel und Richtscheyt. . .* , an edition published in 1538, a decade after Dürer died. An editor apparently took both the woodcut and additions to the text from material left by the artist himself. See *Dürer in America: His Graphic Work,* ed. Charles W. Talbot (Washington, D.C.: National Gallery of Art, 1971), no. 215, 353–55. It is relevant to note here that Panofsky repeatedly returned to the study of Dürer. During his first semester as a university student of law, Panofsky attended a lecture by Wilhelm Vöge on a painting by Dürer that "sparked his move into the study of art" (Carl Hollis Landauer, "The Survival of Antiquity: The German Years of the Warburg Institute," Ph.D. diss., Yale University, 1984, 229). Panofsky's *The Life and Art of Albrecht Dürer,* 4th ed. (Princeton: Princeton University Press, 1955) is considered a classic work on the artist.

33. For a discussion of this woodcut, see Lynda Nead, *The Female Nude: Art, Obscenity, and Sexuality* (London: Routledge, 1992), 11. Barbara Freedman interprets this woodcut from the model's point of view: "Once we adopt the woman's perspective, the picture neatly reverses itself. The woman lies comfortably relaxed; the artist sits upright, rigidly constrained by his fixed position. The woman knows that she is seen; the artist is blinded by his viewing apparatus, deluded by his fantasy of objectivity. The draftsman's need to order visually and to distance himself from that which he sees suggests a futile attempt to protect himself from what he would (not) see. Yet the cloth draped between the woman's legs is not protection enough; neither the viewing device nor the screen can delineate or contain his desire. The perspective painter is transfixed in this moment, paralyzed, unable to capture the sight that encloses him. Enclosing us as well, Dürer's work draws our alarm" (*Staging the Gaze: Postmodernism, Psychoanalysis, and Shakespearean Comedy* [Ithaca, N.Y.: Cornell University Press, 1991], 2). We disagree with this reading for a number of reasons: with her knees bent at a sharp angle reminiscent of that required by gynecologist's stirrups, the woman does not appear to be comfortable, and the way the artist's forearms rest on his drawing table suggests that he is more relaxed than constrained. But our fundamental disagreement is with the way that such a reading removes the woodcut from its historical context: not only is the woodcut's placement in a handbook for artists and draftsmen evidence that the viewer was intended to take the artist's point of view in the woodcut, but, in addition, artists of the early sixteenth century were virtually all male. Though the reading that Freedman posits may be available to a modern audience—just as the same kind of reading of a Shakespearean comedy might be, especially in a contemporary production—we conclude that it would be extremely unlikely as the response of a sixteenth-century male artist.

34. Charles Musser, *The Emergence of Cinema: The American Screen to 1907* (New York: Scribner, 1990), 16–54. As "screen practice," cinema situates the observer in an embodied, corporeal capacity. Jonathan Crary has demonstrated the extent to which cinema and photography have decentered the viewer and thereby mark a break with classical theories of vision; see *Techniques of the Observer: On Vision and Modernity in the Nineteenth Century* (Cambridge: MIT Press, 1990). Recent film theory, however, has emphasized embodiment; see Linda Williams, "Film Bodies: Gender, Genre, and Excess," *Film Quarterly* 44 (1991): 2–13; Williams, "Corporealized Observers: Visual Pornographies and the 'Carnal Density of Vision,'" in Petro, *Fugitive Images,* 3–41. On the "fetishized vision of the voyeur," see Elena del Río, "The Body of Voyeurism: Mapping a Discourse of the Senses in Michael Powell's *Peeping Tom,*" *Camera Obscura* 15 (2000): 115–49. On the "carnal foundations of cinematic intelligibility," see Vivian Sobchack, "What My Fingers Knew: The Cinesthetic Subject, or Vision in the Flesh," revised version of a paper delivered at the Special Effects/Special Affects: Technologies of the Screen symposium held on the University of Melbourne, March 2000, http://www.senseofcinema.com/contents/00/5/fingers.html, cited 24 June 2001.

35. André Bazin, *What Is Cinema?* trans. Hugh Gray (Berkeley and Los Angeles: University of California Press, 1967), 10.

36. Landauer, "Erwin Panofsky and the Renascence," 265. Panofsky's essay "Die Perspektive als 'symbolische Form'" appeared in the *Vorträge der Bibliothek Warburg*

volume for 1924–25. According to Christopher Wood, who published a fine translation of the essay, Panofsky's project in "Perspective as Symbolic Form" was "to write the history of Western art as a history of perspective" (Erwin Panofsky, *Perspective as Symbolic Form*, trans. Christopher S. Wood [New York: Zone Books, 1991], 13). "To some extent the perspective essay collapses" the "distinction between artistic perception and cognition" (13). When he describes perspective as "an objectification of the subjective" (66) or "the carrying over of artistic objectivity into the domain of the phenomenal" (72), Panofsky reveals the extent to which perspective was intrinsic to his own viewing practices.

37. Panofsky, "Style and Medium," 112.

38. Panofsky, "Style and Medium," 119.

39. For the classic statement regarding the visual politics of the cinema, see Mulvey, "Visual Pleasure"; see also Teresa de Lauretis, *Alice Doesn't: Feminism, Semiotics, Cinema* (Bloomington: Indiana University Press, 1984), 12–36; Stephen Heath, "Difference," in *The Sexual Subject: A Screen Reader in Sexuality* (London: Routledge, 1992), 47–106; Jacqueline Rose, *Sexuality and the Field of Vision* (London: Verso, 1986), 216–33. The paradigm of the "male gaze" has proven useful enough to be critiqued and refined. See Mulvey, "Afterthoughts"; Carol J. Clover, *Men, Women, and Chain Saws: Gender in the Modern Horror Film* (Princeton: Princeton University Press, 1992). Perhaps Kaja Silverman's formulation of the relationship between identity and the gaze is most productive: "all subjects, male or female, rely for their identity upon the repertoire of culturally available images, and upon a gaze which . . . is not theirs to deploy." In Silverman's view, the gaze, like the phallus, belongs to the symbolic order. See Kaja Silverman, *Male Subjectivity at the Margins* (London: Routledge, 1992), 153.

40. For essays that demonstrate "the possibilities of alternative pleasures" by "trac[ing] the spaces for multiple readings within the text," see *Outlooks: Lesbian and Gay Sexualities and Visual Cultures*, ed. Peter Horne and Reina Lewis (London: Routledge, 1996), 5. This quotation is from the editors' introduction.

41. Prange, "Stil und Medium," refers to the "euphorische Ton" of this essay (172).

42. Walter Benjamin, "The Work of Art in the Age of Mechanical Reproduction," in *Illuminations*, ed. Hannah Arendt, trans. Harry Zohn (New York: Harcourt, 1955), 219–53. For two among many interpretive studies of Benjamin's influential essay, see Joel Snyder, "Benjamin on Reproducibility and Aura: A Reading of 'The Work of Art in the Age of Its Technical Reproducibility,'" in *Benjamin: Philosophy, Aesthetics, History*, ed. Gary Smith (Chicago: University of Chicago Press, 1989), 158–74; and J. Hillis Miller, *Illustration* (London: Reaktion, 1992), 19–31.

43. Benjamin, "Work of Art," 221–22.

44. On the relationship of lantern shows to the development of film, see Musser, *The Emergence of Cinema*, 20–54. On the presence of magic lantern shows in early screenings of film, see Noël Burch, *Life to Those Shadows*, trans. and ed. Ben Brewster (London: British Film Institute, 1990), 85.

45. On the "lecturer," see Burch, *Life to Those Shadows*, 154–55; Musser, *The Emergence of Cinema*, 38–42; and Tom Gunning, "'Primitive' Cinema: A Frame-up? Or, The Trick's on Us," in *Early Cinema: Space, Frame, Narrative*, ed. Thomas Elsaesser and Adam Baker (London: British Film Institute, 1990), 101.

46. Holly notes, "In 1930, nine years before his well-known exposition of the 'iconological method' in *Studies in Iconology,* Panofsky was already refining Warburg's ideas with reference to categories of content" (*Panofsky and Foundations,* 111); according to Hart, while he was associated with the Warburg, "Panofsky produced a number of purely theoretical papers and a large group of iconological essays and books" ("Panofsky and Mannheim," 539).

47. In her article, "Saxl, Warburg, Panofsky. Lectures in the Library and a Link to the University," in the *Warburg Institute Newsletter* 7 (winter 1997): 2, archivist D[orothea McE[wan] notes Panofsky's close involvement with Saxl in the 1920s in support of Saxl's efforts to develop a lecture program at the Warburg.

48. On the relationship between Warburg's scholarship and his development of the library, see Kurt Forster, "Aby Warburg's History of Art: Collective Memory and the Social Mediation of Images," *Daedalus* 105 (1976): 169–76. In an essay written in 1975, Giorgio Agamben describes Warburg's deeper purpose as follows: "one can say that the entire work of Warburg the 'art historian,' including the famous library that he began to put together in 1886, is meaningful only if understood as a unified effort, across and beyond art history, directed toward a broader science for which he could not find a definite name but on whose configuration he tenaciously labored until his death" ("Warburg and the Nameless Science," in *Potentialities: Collected Essays in Philosophy,* ed. and trans. Daniel Heller-Roazen [Stanford: Stanford University Press, 1999], 91).

49. In his history of Warburg's library, Fritz Saxl mentions the presence of photographs from the very beginning of the collection, though they become critical later in the 1920s (Fritz Saxl, "The History of Warburg's Library (1886–1944)," in E. H. Gombrich, *Aby Warburg: An Intellectual Biography* [London: Warburg Institute, 1970], 330–34). See also Warburg's early letter in which he expresses the importance of taking photographs as part of his collecting endeavor (Gombrich, *Aby Warburg,* 132), and the early years of the Warburg-Saxl correspondence, in which the acquisition of photographs is a recurrent theme (*Ausreiten der Ecken. Die Aby Warburg-Fritz Saxl Korrespondenz 1910 bis 1919,* ed. Dorothea McEwan [Hamburg: Dölling und Galitz, 1998]).

50. When the time came to design a purpose-built structure to house the library, the capacity to show slides was a primary concern; the project plan of architect Gerhard Langmaack included a screen that could be pulled up out of the floor, rolling blinds to darken the room, and an "epdiaskop" specially produced by Zeiss. The institute occupied this building from 1926 until it was forced to leave Hamburg for London in 1933. For photographs and a transcription of Langmaack's plan, see Tilmann von Stockhausen, *Die Kulturwissenschaftliche Bibliothek Warburg. Architektur, Einrichtung und Organisation* (Hamburg: Dölling und Galitz, 1992), 139–43 and figs. 50, 60.

51. For an account of the move to London, see Eric M. Warburg, "The Transfer of the Warburg Institute to England in 1933," *The Warburg Institute Annual Report, 1952–3,* 13–16. Eric Warburg describes the dramatic circumstances in which "the physical removal of about 60,000 books, thousands of slides, photographs and furniture" took place on 12 December 1933. A survey of the existing slide collection at the Warburg Institute reveals that approximately twelve thousand bear the imprint of the Hamburg library.

52. William Heckscher, "The Genesis of Iconology," in *Stil und Überlieferung in der*

Kunst des Abendlandes: Akten des 21. Internationalen Kongresses für Kunstgeschichte in Bonn 1964, 3 vols. (Berlin: Gebr. Mann, 1967), 3:239–62.

53. "Kommilitonen! Die Auflösung eines Bilderrätsels—noch dazu wenn man nicht einmal ruhig beleuchten, sondern nur kinematographisch scheinwerfen kann—war selbstverständlich nicht Selbstzweck meines Vortrages" (Aby Warburg, "Italienische Kunst und Internationale Astrologie im Palazzo Schifanoja zu Ferrara," *Die Erneuerung der heidnischen Antike: Kulturwissenschaftliche Beiträge zur Geschichte der europäischen Renaissance,* sec. 1, vol. 1, pt. 2 of *Gesammelte Schriften herausgeben von der Bibliothek Warburg,* ed. Gertrud Bing [Leipzig: B. G. Teubner, 1932; reprint, Berlin: Akademie, 1998], 478). For the English translation, see Aby Warburg, "Italian Art and International Astrology in the Palazzo Schifanoia, Ferrara," in *The Renewal of Pagan Antiquity: Contributions to the Cultural History of the European Renaissance,* trans. David Britt, intro. Kurt W. Forster (Los Angeles: Getty Research Institute for the History of Art and the Humanities, 1999), 585.

54. Robert S. Nelson makes a related but more general point when he observes that before projection the art history lecture relied on ekphrastic rhetoric—the speaker's effort to make an absent work of art present—and deductive reasoning, but that the new ability to project slides, so that the artwork was "present in the discursive space," enabled a shift to inductive reasoning in the art history lecture: "Wölfflin, Warburg, and Goldschmidt built their visual arguments upon carefully observed particulars, be they iconographic motifs or formal characteristics" (Robert S. Nelson, "The Slide Lecture, or The Work of Art *History* in the Age of Mechanical Reproduction," *Critical Inquiry* 26 [2000]: 432).

55. Warburg, "Italian Art," 565; "zweifache mittelalterliche Überlieferung der antiken Götterbilderwelt. Hier können wir sowohl die Einwirkung der systematichen olympischen Götterlehre, wie sie jene gelehrten mittelalterlichen Mythographen von Westeuropa überlieferten, als auch den Einfluß astraler Götterlehre, wie sie sich in Wort und Bild der astrologischen Praktik ungestört erhielt, bis ins einzelne quellenmäßig klarlegen" ("Italienische Kunst," 463).

56. Warburg, "Italian Art," 563; "die halbdunkeln Regionen des Gestirnaberglaubens" ("Italienische Kunst," 461).

57. Warburg, "Italian Art," 572; "Über die unterste Schicht des griechischen Fixsternhimmels hatte sich zunächst das ägyptisierende Schema des Dekankultes gelagert. Auf dieses setzte sich die Schicht indischer mythologischer Umformung ab, die sodann—wahrscheinlich durch persische Vermittlung—das arabische Milieu zu passieren hatte. Nachdem weiter durch die hebräische Übersetzung eine abermalige trübende Ablagerung stattgefunden hatte, mündete, durch französische Vermittlung in Pietro d'Abanos lateinische Übersetzung des Abû Ma'schar, der griechische Fixsternhimmel schließlich in die monumentale Kosmologie der italienischen Frührenaissance ein, in der Gestalt eben jener 36 rätselhaften Figuren des mittleren Streifens aus den Fresken von Ferrara" ("Italienische Kunst," 468–69).

58. For a discussion of the centrality of astrology to the Warburg project, see Martin Warnke, "Die Bibliothek Warburg und ihr Forschungsprogramm," in *Porträt aus Büchern. Bibliothek Warburg und Warburg Institute. Hamburg—1933—London* (Ham-

burg: Dölling und Galitz, 1993), 29–34. For a thorough revision of the development of astrological iconography, see Blume, *Regenten des Himmels.*

59. Hans Robert Jauss, "Allegorese, Remythisierung und neuer Mythos. Bemerkungen zur christlichen Gefangenschaft der Mythologie im Mittelalter," in Fuhrmann, *Terror und Spiel,* 187–209.

60. Giorgio Agamben, *Infancy and History: Essays on the Destruction of Experience,* trans. Liz Heron (London: Verso, 1993), 21.

61. At the end of his piece on the Schifanoia frescoes, Warburg concludes, "It was with this desire to restore the ancient world that 'the good European' began his battle for enlightenment, in that age of internationally migrating images that we—a shade too mystically—call the Age of the Renaissance" (Warburg, "Italian Art," 586); "Mit diesem Willen zur Restitution der Antike begann 'der gute Europäer' seinen Kampf um Aufklärung in jenem Zeitalter internationaler Bilderwanderung, das wir—etwas allzu mystisch—die Epoche der Renaissance nennen" ("Italienische Kunst," 479). It is the category of "the good European" that increasingly became insupportable during the course of Warburg's lifetime, and the category became increasingly more suspect throughout the twentieth century, so that when, on the seventieth anniversary of Warburg's death, 26 October 1999, Gombrich delivered a lecture under the auspices of the Warburg Institute, he commented: "Alas, in the seventy years that have passed since Warburg's death, our pride in being Europeans has been dealt a devastating blow. At the same time we have also had to learn utterly to distrust national, racial or cultural stereotypes. This is also the reason why I here ventured, in this lecture, to criticise Warburg's faith in the 'historical psychology of human expression.' It was this faith that led him to interpret the images of Oriental astrology which he had encountered at Ferrara as tell-tale symptoms of cultural decline, as a perversion of the classical heritage from which the Renaissance had to rescue mankind" (E. H. Gombrich, "Aby Warburg: His Aims and Methods: An Anniversary Lecture," *Journal of the Warburg and Courtauld Institutes* 62 [1999]: 278–79). On Warburg's notion of "the good European," see also Agamben, "Warburg and the Nameless Science," 96.

62. Fritz Saxl, "Die Bibliothek Warburg und Ihr Ziel," *Vorträge der Bibliothek Warburg* 1 (1921–22): "An ihnen konnte er das Zentralproblem seiner Forschungen in seiner ganzen Vielseitigkeit darstellen: was bedeutet die Antike für den Frührenaissance-menschen?" (5).

63. As Gertrude Koch comments, "Film's effects are more directly related to the social environments in which the films are presented than to the film's form and content" ("The Body's Shadow Realm," in *Dirty Looks: Women, Pornography, Power,* ed. Pamela Church Gibson and Roma Gibson [London: British Film Institute, 1993], 26). On the representation of a desired feminine type, see Terry J. Prewitt, "Like a Virgin: The Semiotics of Illusion in Erotic Performance," *American Journal of Semiotics* 6 (1989): 137–52.

64. Gombrich, *Aby Warburg,* 261.

65. Forster, introduction to Warburg, *Renewal,* 31. Although Warburg himself had planned to publish *Mnemosyne,* he was unable to bring it to closure. Plans to publish it as part of his collected works were realized only at the end of the twentieth century;

see Aby Warburg, *Gesammelte Schriften. Studienausgabe,* pt. 2, vol. 2.1, *Der Bilderatlas Mnemosyne,* ed. Martin Warnke with C. Brink (Berlin: Akademie, 2000). On the picture atlas, see also Dorothee Bauerle, *Gespenstergeschichten für ganz Erwachsene: Ein Kommentar zu Aby Warburgs Bilderatlas Mnemosyne* (Münster: Lit Verlag, 1988); Michaela Glashoff, Andrea Neumann, and Martin Deppner, "Bilderatlas zwischen Talmud und Netzwerk," Ein Beitrag zum INSEA-Kongress, (Hamburg, 1987; unpublished; copy in the Warburg Library); van Huisstede, "Der Mnemosyne-Atlas."

66. Giorgio Agamben, "Notes on Gesture," in *Means without End: Notes on Politics,* trans. Vincenzo Binetti and Cesare Casarino (Minneapolis: University of Minnesota Press, 2000), 54. By "De Jorio" in this quotation Agamben refers to a treatise on gesture; see Andrea de Jorio, *Gesture in Naples and Gesture in Classical Antiquity,* trans. Adam Kendon (Bloomington: Indiana University Press, 2000).

67. Eisenstein, *Towards a Theory of Montage,* 311.

68. Warburg, "Italian Art," 585; "Aus der engumsponnenen burgundischen Raupe entpuppt sich der florentinische Schmetterling, die 'Nynfa' mit dem Flügelkopfputz und der flatternden Gewandung der griechischen Mänade oder römischen Victoria" ("Italienische Kunst," 477).

69. "The figure of the nymph enters Warburg's work from the very start with his dissertation in 1893. . . . Even the pages of the *Mnemosyne* reflected his obsession with the nymph" (Landauer, "Survival of Antiquity," 23–24).

70. Gombrich, *Aby Warburg,* 113. For a fuller discussion of Warburg's interest in the nymph, see 105–27.

71. Agamben, "Warburg and the Nameless Science," 100.

72. Gombrich, *Aby Warburg,* 283. For a description of Warburg's dependence on this method of displaying photographs, see 260–85. Gombrich notes that "this device was especially suited to Warburg's needs. The method of pinning photographs to a canvas presented an easy way of marshalling the material and reshuffling it in ever new combinations, just as Warburg had been used to rearranging his index cards and his books whenever another theme became dominant in his mind" (284).

73. The Warburg Library under Saxl's leadership continued to sponsor photographic exhibitions after its move to London in 1933. For a discussion of Saxl's longstanding interest in photography, see Gertrud Bing, "A Memoir," in *Fritz Saxl (1890–1948): A Volume of Memorial Essays from His Friends in England* (London: Thomas Newson and Sons, 1957), 1–46, esp. 30–33. A notable activity of the Warburg Library during World War II was the mounting of "large scale photographic exhibitions" under the direction of Fritz Saxl. "For Saxl the making of these exhibitions was not stopgap but a matter of conviction. During the last thirty years modern techniques of visual representation in the form of posters, illustration and the cinema, had accustomed the public to use their eyes more than at any other time. Saxl felt that here was a chance for the art historian to come in with his own message; having been trained to read images he should also be able to make them speak to others. Saxl did not think of his exhibitions in terms of 'education to art.' That was an aim which could only be achieved through originals, and there was no easy way to it. He wanted to convey a historical message, and in each case a great deal of thorough research went into its preparation. But he relied on an appeal through the eye. He insisted on a very high quality of pho-

tography and brought the beauty or significance of the objects home by an unusual choice of enlarged details. Only a minimum of verbal information was added. It was left to the spectator's perceptiveness to read the message, without necessarily noticing how his understanding was guided by the control of relevant material and the choice and combination of pictures" (31). The first of these exhibitions, mounted in 1939, was "The Visual Approach to the Classics" (31).

74. Michael Ann Holly emphasizes the differences between Warburg's practice of art history and what has come to be thought of as the iconographical method of traditional art history. "To put the matter in contemporary critical terms, Warburg considered the language of Renaissance art as always subject to dislocating forces at work, despite its illusions of framing. Representational meaning, he well knew, is always in process. If ever it can be said to be a product, it is a product of intertextual conflict and stylistic features in the process of differentiation—between the work's expressive mythopoeic 'substratum' and its historical symbolization—and not the result of any one-to-one iconographic correspondence between a classical text and a domesticated image" (Michael Ann Holly, "Unwriting Iconology," in Cassidy, *Iconography at the Crossroads,* 23).

75. Charlotte Schoell-Glass, who turns to the *Tagebuch der K. B. W.* for information about the ways that Warburg worked on *Mnemosyne,* points out that Warburg "saw his research institute (and the atlas) as a *laboratory.* . . . An atlas, of course, is an instrument to *reduce* the world and information about it to the size of a book. . . . Now the art historian dominates what had dominated *him* before" ("'Serious Issues': The Last Plates of Warburg's Picture Atlas *Mnemosyne,*" in *Art History as Cultural History: Warburg's Projects,* ed. Richard Woodfield [Amsterdam: G and B Arts International, 2001], 186). Warburg's failure to complete the atlas—most of the commentary texts intended to accompany each plate were never written—suggests an intuitive realization that such a project would produce only fragments. Strikingly, lack of closure is the interpretive key to the last plate of *Mnemosyne:* according to Schoell-Glass, it is "*ambivalence* and *ambiguity* which emerge. . . . In developing a model which is centered on an unresolvable ambiguity, Warburg begins a move from the 19th century Nietzschean concept [of polarity] to one which becomes immensely influential in 20th century thought" (198).

76. Barbara E. Savedoff, "Looking at Art through Photographs," *Journal of Aesthetics and Art Criticism* 51 (1993): 461.

77. Holly, *Panofsky and Foundations,* 14.

78. Erwin Panofsky, "Blind Cupid," in *Studies in Iconology: Humanistic Themes in the Art of the Renaissance* (1939; reprint, New York: Harper and Row, 1962), 95–129.

79. As Hart comments, "The goal of the theories concerning *Kunstwollen* and weltanschauung was a totalizing, harmonizing, and comprehensive whole, unified in meaning. These aims resembled God. In discussing their theories, Mannheim and Panofsky produced images of an organic, self-contained universe laden with meaning. That both men adopted hermeneutics to attain this godlike totalizing whole is not surprising, since hermeneutics was developed for the exegesis of biblical texts in the seventeenth century" ("Panofsky and Mannheim," 560–61). For a similar assessment of Panofsky's "fantasy of a fixed and universalizable point of view," see Margaret Iversen, "Retrieving Warburg's Tradition," *Art History* 16 (1993): 54.

80. See Norman Bryson, "Art in Context," in *Studies in Historical Change,* ed. Ralph Cohen (Charlottesville: University Press of Virginia, 1992), 18–42. See also Michael Camille, "Art History in the Past and Future of Medieval Studies," in *The Past and Future of Medieval Studies,* ed. John Van Engen (Notre Dame: University of Notre Dame Press, 1994), 362.

81. Donald Preziosi, *Rethinking Art History: Meditations on a Coy Science* (New Haven: Yale University Press, 1989), 72–73.

82. Kaja Silverman, *The Threshold of the Visible World* (London: Routledge, 1996), 101.

83. Mast, *Film/Cinema/Movie,* 142–43.

84. Benjamin, "Work of Art," 223. For an analysis of the role of the photographic facsimile in relation to issues of connoisseurship, see Michael Camille, "The *Très Riches Heures:* An Illuminated Manuscript in the Age of Mechanical Reproduction," *Critical Inquiry* 17 (1990): 72–107.

85. Karen Michels situates the rise of the iconographic method within the political climate of nineteenth- and early-twentieth-century Germany. She points out that German Jewish art historians of the early twentieth century absorbed "humanistic educational principles" as part of the gymnasium education crucial to their assimilation into bourgeois German society and therefore were drawn, as scholars, "to deal predominantly with the source of humanistic ideals, that is, with Renaissance topics" (168). Their interest in tracing these ideals contributed to the development of the iconographic method by such art historians in the milieu of the Kulturwissenschaftliche Bibliothek Warburg. "The success of iconology and the perception of Renaissance art that emerged through the iconological perspective are thus closely linked to the emigration of Jewish art historians to America and to America's acceptance of the innovative methodology they brought with them. The difficulties of Jewish emancipation in Germany had engendered an intellectual and emotional investment on the part of these Jewish scholars in the ideals and values that had driven the emancipation process. Its catastrophic demise in Nazi Germany did little to change their fundamental attitudes" (Karen Michels, "Art History, German Jewish Identity, and the Emigration of Iconology," in *Jewish Identity in Modern Art History,* ed. Catherine M. Soussloff [Berkeley and Los Angeles: University of California Press, 1999], 175).

86. Panofsky, "Three Decades," 328.

87. Sauerländer, "Struggling," 393–94.

88. Erwin Panofsky, *Early Netherlandish Painting: Its Origins and Character* (1953; reprint, New York: Harper and Row, 1971), 1:36. For a general critique of Panofsky's approach to book illustration in *Early Netherlandish Painting,* see Sandra Hindman, "The Illustrated Book: An Addendum to the State of Research in Northern European Art," *Art Bulletin* 68 (1986): 536–42.

89. Panofsky, "Style and Medium," 120.

90. Even a casual user of the photo archive finds it easy to distinguish between photographs from the Hamburg years, with their German inscriptions on the back, and those added after the archive moved to London. Fritz Saxl went on photographing journeys to the libraries of Europe, where he himself photographed manuscript and

prints in accordance with Warburg's instructions. See, for example, a letter from Warburg to Saxl (17 October 1911) in *Ausreiten der Ecken,* ed. McEwan, 73–74.

91. For a photograph of Warburg's panel 55, which includes the "Judgment of Paris" from the *Epistre Othea* in BR, MS 9392, see van Huisstede, "Der Mnemosyne-Atlas," 145.

92. See Abū Ma'šar, *The Abbreviation of the Introduction to Astrology together with the Medieval Latin Translation of Adelard of Bath,* ed. and trans. Charles Burnett, Keiji Yamamoto, and Michio Yano (Leiden: Brill, 1994). Georgius Zaparus Zorotus Fendulus claimed that he translated from this Arabic text into Latin, but he actually only selected excerpts from an earlier translation by Hermann the Dalmatian.

93. On BnF, lat. 7330, see François Avril, Marie-Thérèse Gousset, and Claudia Rabel, *Manuscrits enluminés d'origine italienne,* vol. 2, *XIIIᵉ siècle* (Paris: Bibliothèque nationale, 1984), 160–62; Blume, *Regenten des Himmels,* 204–5, pls. 1–11, figs. 13–46; and Raymond Klibansky, Erwin Panofsky, and Fritz Saxl, *Saturn and Melancholy: Studies in the History of Natural Philosophy, Religion, and Art* (London: Thomas Nelson and Sons, 1964), figs. 19–22. On BL, Sloane 3983, see Blume, 149ff. and figs. 153–56; on M 785, see Blume, 150ff. and figs. 157–58; Klibansky, Panofsky, and Saxl, *Saturn and Melancholy,* 24.

94. In the astrological manuscripts, the signs of the zodiac, often personifications, are drawn to a smaller scale than the planetary deities and usually placed below them, in the same compositional relationship as the Children of the Planets in the *Othea* miniatures.

95. In the notes to her edition of the *Othea,* Parussa summarizes Eliana Carrara's suggestions for iconographic sources for Mercury's flower, neither of which she finds convincing (397–98).

96. Blume identifies the influence of the astrological tradition in Christine's series on the planets, but he traces the specific arrangement of the figure to the iconography of the allegorical triumph as developed in Italy rather than to the iconography of the ascendant planet invented by Fendulus (*Regenten des Himmels,* 157).

97. In his edition, Angus Kennedy dates this text to 1406–7 (Christine de Pizan, *Le Livre du corps de policie,* ed. Angus J. Kennedy [Paris: Honoré Champion, 1998], xvii–xx). We quote the French text from Kennedy's edition and the translation from Christine de Pizan, *The Book of the Body Politic,* ed. and trans. Kate Langdon Forhan (Cambridge: Cambridge University Press, 1994).

98. Kristen Lippincott, "*Urania redux:* A View of Aby Warburg's Writings on Astrology and Art," in Woodfield, *Art History as Cultural History,* 151–82, especially 158–65.

99. Fendulus's claim that he invented the illustrations to visualize that text appears to be correct. For a transcription of Fendulus's text, see Blume, *Regenten des Himmels,* 216–23; for Blume's discussion of the illustrations and their originality, see 36–45. Blume points out that the illustrations correspond closely to the descriptions in the text and lack any indications of Islamic iconography that might suggest they had been copied.

100. Panofsky and Saxl, "Classical Mythology," 246.

101. Panofsky and Saxl, "Classical Mythology," 246.

102. See Eliana Carrara, "Bacco e Nettuno nell'*Epistre d'Othéa* di Christine de Pizan: Scene di vita quotidiana e figurazioni religiose in temi mitologici," *Ricerche di storia dell'arte* 55 (1995): 83–88; Carrara, "Mitologia antica in un trattato didattico-allegorico della fine del Medioevo: L'*Epistre d'Othéa* di Christine de Pizan," *Prospettiva* 66 (1992): 67–86; Sylvie Jeanneret, "Text et enluminures dans l'*Epistre othea* de Christine de Pizan: Une lecture politique?" in Hicks, *Au champ des escriptures,* 723–36; and Charlotte Schoell-Glass, "Verwandlungen der Metamorphosen. Christliche Bildformen in Ovid-Illustrationen bei Christine de Pizan," in *Die Rezeption der "Metamorphosen" des Ovid in der Neuzeit: Der Antike Mythos in Text und Bild,* Internationales Symposion der Werner Reimers-Stiftung Bad Homburg v. d. H. (22. bis 25. April 1991), ed. Hermann Walter and Hans-Jürgen Horn [Berlin: G. Mann, 1995], 36–47, pls. 7–11. Schoell-Glass's approach is set out at greater length in her dissertation, "Aspekte der Antikenrezeption."

103. Panofsky and Saxl, "Classical Mythology," 247, 248.

104. We thus disagree with Leonard Barkan, who clearly follows Panofsky and Saxl when he complains that the illustrations of the gods and goddesses in the *Othea* have "nothing to do with pagan antiquity at all, since the figures of gods and men have all been assimilated into medieval Christian tradition" (Leonard Barkan, *The Gods Made Flesh: Metamorphosis and the Pursuit of Paganism* [New Haven: Yale University Press, 1986], 173).

105. For a detailed description of the organization of the library in its various locations, see Salvatore Settis, "Warburg *continuatus*. Description d'une bibliothèque," in *Le Pouvoir des bibliothèques: La mémoire des livres en Occident,* ed. Marc Baratin and Christian Jacob (Paris: Albin Michel, 1996), 122–73.

Chapter 2

1. We have used the edition in Christine de Pizan, *Oeuvres poétiques,* ed. Roy, and the translation by Brownlee in Christine de Pizan, *Selected Writings,* ed. Blumenfeld-Kosinski.

2. For discussions of the intertextual relations between the *Rose* and medieval literatures, see Sarah Kay, "Sexual Knowledge: The Once and Future Texts of the *Romance of the Rose,*" in *Textuality and Sexuality: Reading Theories and Practices,* ed. Judith Still and Michael Worton (Manchester: Manchester University Press, 1993), 69–86. See also Nancy Freeman Regalado, "'Des Contraires choses': La fonction poétique de la citation et des *exempla* dans le 'Roman de la Rose' de Jean de Meun," *Littérature* 41 (1981): 62–81.

3. As Thelma Fenster has noted, "Christine . . . seems to have read and grasped the thrust of the entire [*Rose*]" ("Did Christine Have a Sense of Humor? The Evidence of the *Epistre au Dieu d'Amours,*" in *Reinterpreting Christine de Pizan,* ed. Earl Jeffrey Richards [Athens: University of Georgia Press, 1992], 35 n. 13).

4. In response to the charge that Gerson was "a puritanical Christian out to burn books that we today value for their literary quality, subtlety, and humor," Brian Patrick McGuire writes, "[I]f one believes in marriage as a sacrament and the only proper and right context for sexual union, as Gerson did, then *The Romance of the Rose* is indeed a

questionable work. Its very cleverness and intelligence hide what it is all about: the naked physical conquest of a woman by a man, popularly known in late-twentieth-century America as 'scoring,' and perhaps even rape" (introduction to Jean Gerson, *Early Works*, trans. Brian Patrick McGuire [New York: Paulist Press, 1998], 54–55). Whether Christine de Pizan and Jean Gerson, one of the leading preachers in Paris, a doctor of theology, and chancellor of the University of Paris, were personally acquainted and if so, whether their relationship involved intellectual exchange, have been much debated questions. Earl Jeffrey Richards argues for "an intellectual friendship" throughout Christine's career as a writer ("Christine de Pizan and Jean Gerson: An Intellectual Friendship," in *Christine de Pizan 2000: Studies on Christine de Pizan in Honour of Angus J. Kennedy*, ed. John Campbell and Nadia Margolis [Amsterdam: Rodopi, 2000], 197–208, 328–30). McGuire, however, points out that Gerson "generally ignored" Christine's contributions to the Rose debate (introduction to Gerson, *Early Works*, 55) and, based on his extensive knowledge of Gerson's life and writing, McGuire concludes that "Gerson kept a careful distance from Christine—as from all other women except for his sisters" (private communication, 4 April 2001).

5. For an edition of the French and Latin texts, see Christine de Pizan, Jean Gerson, Jean de Montreuil, Gontier and Pierre Col, *Le Débat sur le Roman de la Rose,* ed. and trans. Eric Hicks (1977; reprint, Geneva: Slatkine Reprints, 1996), 63. Unless otherwise noted, translations from the Rose debate documents are our own; translations are available in Christine de Pizan, Jean Gerson, Jean de Montreuil, Gontier and Pierre Col, *La Querelle de la Rose: Letters and Documents,* trans. Joseph L. Baird and John R. Kane (Chapel Hill: University of North Carolina Press, 1978); Gerson's treatise is also translated by McGuire in Gerson, *Early Works,* 378–98. For a discussion of the dating of Montreuil's letters, see Eric Hicks and Ezio Ornato, "Jean de Montreuil et le débat sur le *Roman de la Rose,*" *Romania* 98 (1977): 34–64, 186–219. On the *Rose* debate, see Joseph L. Baird and John R. Kane, "*La Querelle de la Rose:* In Defense of the Opponents," *French Review* 48 (1974): 298–307; Eric Hicks, "The 'Querelle de la Rose' in the *Roman de la Rose,*" *Les bonnes feuilles* 3 (1974): 152–69; Eric Hicks, "De l'histoire littéraire comme cosmogonie: La Querelle du *Roman de la Rose,*" *Critique* 32 no. 348 (1976): 511–19; Pierre-Yves Badel, *Le Roman de la rose au XIVe siècle: Etude de la réception de l'oeuvre* (Geneva: Droz, 1980), 411–91. J. L. Baird, "Pierre Col and the *Querelle de la Rose,*" *Philological Quarterly* 60 (1981): 273–86; Karen Sullivan, "At the Limit of Feminist Theory: The Architectonics of the Querelle de la Rose," *Exemplaria* 3 (1991): 435–66; Eric Hicks, "Situation du débat sur le RR," in *Une femme de lettres au Moyen Age: Études autour de Christine de Pizan,* ed. Liliane Dulac and Bernard Ribémont (Orléans: Paradigme, 1995), 51–67; Helen Solterer, "Flaming Words: Verbal Violence and Gender in Pre-Modern Paris," *Romanic Review* 86 (1995): 355–78; David F. Hult, "Words and Deeds: Jean de Meun's *Romance of the Rose* and the Hermeneutics of Censorship," *New Literary History* 28 (1997): 345–66; Helen Solterer, "States of Siege: Violence, Place, Gender: Paris around 1400," *New Medieval Literatures* 2 (1998): 95–132; Helen Solterer, "Fiction vs Defamation: The Quarrel over the *Romance of the Rose,*" *Medieval History Journal* 2 (1999): 111–41; Brown-Grant, *Christine,* 7–51; Jennifer Monahan, "*Querelles:* Medieval Texts and Modern Polemics," in *Contexts and Continuities,* ed. Kennedy, Brown-Grant, Laidlaw, and Müller, 2:575–84; and Marilynn

Desmond, "The *Querelle de la Rose* and the Ethics of Reading," in *Christine de Pizan: A Casebook*, ed. Barbara Altmann and Deborah McGrady (New York: Routledge, 2003).

6. Translation from Gerson, *Early Works*, 384–85. In a letter to Pierre Col, Gerson characterizes his treatise as "against writings, words, and pictures that encourage, stimulate, and excite forbidden loves, which are more bitter than death" (Gerson, *Early Works*, 213–14). McGuire concludes that Gerson's "main concern was the way such clever tracts and alluring illustrations made young men feel that their interior passions had a right to express themselves in sexual activity outside marriage" (Brian Patrick McGuire, "Sexual Control and Spiritual Growth in the Late Middle Ages: The Case of Jean Gerson," in *Tradition and Ecstasy: The Agony of the Fourteenth Century*, ed. Nancy van Deusen, Clermont Cultural Studies, Musicological Studies, vol. 62.3 [Ottawa: Institute of Mediaeval Music, 1997], 128).

7. For an analysis of the uses of myth in the *Rose* that focuses on "the allegorical characters turned interpreters and glossators of myth," and especially the way that Jean de Meun "managed to recast the myths' meanings and substitute his own glosses" (89), see chap. 2, "The Myths of the *Roman de la Rose*," in Blumenfeld-Kosinski, *Reading Myth*, 52–89.

8. Sylvia Huot, *The "Romance of the Rose" and Its Medieval Readers: Interpretation, Reception, Manuscript Transmission* (Cambridge: Cambridge University Press, 1993).

9. Léopold Delisle, *Recherches sur la Librairie de Charles V.*, 2 vols. (Paris: Honoré Champion, 1907). For the duke of Berry, see Delisle, "Librairie du duc de Berry—1402–1424," in *Le Cabinet des manuscrits de la Bibliothèque nationale* (Paris, 1881), 3:170–94. For an analysis employing theories of Gilles Deleuze and Jean Laplanche to conclude that "Jean de Berry's polymorphous sexual desire was embodied and articulated through his collection" (191), see Michael Camille, "'For Our Devotion and Pleasure': The Sexual Objects of Jean, Duc de Berry," *Art History* 24 (2001): 169–94.

10. According to the entry in the card files of the Pierpont Morgan Library, this manuscript was produced for Charles V or someone at his court.

11. For a reproduction of the ex libris, see Meiss, *Late Fourteenth Century*, pl. 845; see also Meiss, *Late Fourteenth Century*, 313.

12. In *Les Manuscrits du Roman de la Rose. Description et classement* (Paris: Honoré Champion, 1910), Ernest Langlois tentatively identifies his no. 275 as fr. 12595, which would place it in the duke's library at the time of the 1402 inventory.

13. Patrick de Winter dates this manuscript to 1403–4; de Winter indicates that Christine had employed this artist to illustrate two manuscripts of her *Chemin de long estude*, one presented to Jean, duke of Berry, in March 1403 and the other to the duke of Burgundy at about the same time. De Winter indicates that the artist of the València *Rose* manuscript also illustrated BnF, fr. 1188, which is the *Chemin de long estude*, dated 1403. He also illustrated BR 10982, another *Chemin*, also dated 1403. Millard Meiss had incorrectly dated the València *Rose* "after 1420" (*Limbourgs*, 433 n. 55), and John Fleming follows the Meiss dating. See de Winter, *La Bibliothèque de Philippe le Hardi*, 51, 100, 218, 298–99; no. 57. See also François Avril, "La Peinture française au temps de Jean de Berry," *Revue de l'art* 28 (1977): 40–52.

14. According to Pächt and Alexander, this manuscript is "[r]elated to a group of

manuscripts of Christine de Pisan executed for Philippe le Hardi in 1402–3, particularly Brussels, bibl. Roy., MS. 10982 and MS. 10983." See Otto Pächt and Jonathan Alexander, *Illuminated Manuscripts in the Bodleian Library*, 5 vols. (Oxford: Clarendon Press, 1966–73), 2:49.

15. Meradith McMunn takes 1399, the date of Christine's *Epistre au dieu d'Amours*, as the terminus ante quem for the production of any *Rose* manuscript that influenced Christine's response to the *Rose;* consequently, she draws conclusions about Christine's response to *Rose* illustration that do not take into account the dynamic context in which *Rose* manuscripts were being produced while the letters in the *querelle* were circulating. See Meradith T. McMunn, "Programs of Illustration in *Roman de la Rose* Manuscripts Owned by Patrons and Friends of Christine de Pizan," in Hicks, *Au Champ des escriptures*, 737–53.

16. In addition to the examples discussed below, two images in the València manuscript appear to have served as models for illustrations in the *Othea* in the Duke's and Queen's manuscripts: a section of the large miniature illustrating the labors of Hercules on fol. 65r reappears in reverse as the miniature to chap. 27 of the *Othea;* likewise the illustration of Jason and the dragon on fol. 92r is compositionally similar to and a reversed version of the miniature to chap. 54 of the *Othea.*

17. Simon Gaunt, "Bel Acueil and the Improper Allegory of the *Romance of the Rose*," *New Medieval Literatures* 2 (1998): 65–93.

18. On same-sex desire in the *Roman de la rose*, see Jo Ann Hoeppner Moran, "The *Roman de la Rose* and the Thirteenth-Century Prohibitions of Homosexuality," *Cultural Frictions: Medieval Studies in Postmodern Contexts* (1995), http://www.georgetown.edu/labyrinth/conf/cs95/papers/moran.html, 22 Nov. 1996. Also published as "Literature and the Medieval Historian," *Medieval Perspectives* 10 (1995): 49–66. See also Marta Harley, "Narcissus, Hermaphroditus, and Attis: Ovidian Lovers at the Fontaine d'Amors in Guillaume de Lorris's *Roman de la Rose*," *PMLA* 101 (1986): 324–37.

19. BnF, fr. 380 likewise visualizes homoeroticism in a sequence of four interactions between the God of Love and Amant early in the manuscript. In "Bel Acueil and the Improper Allegory" Simon Gaunt points to a confusion of gender in Bel Acueil himself and cites another example, BL Egerton 881, in which Bel Acueil and Amant, both represented as men, kiss one another. Gaunt argues that the *Rose* "evinces an interest in sexual deviance on the more profound level of allegorical discourse itself" (85).

For the range of meanings assigned to the kiss in medieval culture, see Carolyn Dinshaw, "A Kiss Is Just a Kiss: Heterosexuality and Its Consolations in *Sir Gawain and the Green Knight*," *Diacritics* 24, nos. 2–3 (1994): 205–26; Yannick Carré, *Le Baiser sur la bouche au moyen age: Rites, symboles, mentalités à travers les textes et les images, XIᵉ–XVᵉ siècles* (Paris: Léopard d'Or, 1992); Michael Camille, "Gothic Signs and the Surplus: The Kiss on the Cathedral," in the special issue "Contexts: Styles and Values in Medieval Art and Literature," ed. Daniel Poirion and Nancy Regalado, *Yale French Studies* 1991:151–70. Our discussion of the ways in which heterosexuality can act as a conduit for male desire is indebted to Eve Kosofsky Sedgwick's formulations in *The Epistemology of the Closet.*

20. John V. Fleming, "The *Roman de la Rose* and Its Manuscript Illustrations," Ph.D. diss., Princeton University, 1963.

21. Though seldom rendered in such explicit visual terms, the image is only a thinly veiled metaphor in the poem; Leslie Cahoon suggests that "the architectural imagery for the female genitalia" derives from Ovid's *Amores* ("the military metaphor for erotic conquest, the architectural imagery for the female genitalia, and the religious imagery for the emotions of love are all conspicuous features of the *Amores*, as is, for that matter, the whole conception of a lover's progress seen largely from the lover's own point of view" [Leslie Cahoon, "Raping the Rose: Jean de Meun's Reading of Ovid's *Amores*," *Classical and Modern Literature* 6 (1986): 270]). Michael Camille reproduces the miniature on fol. 146v as his figure 173 and entitles it "the climax of the lover's pilgrimage." He points to the "very thin line between parody and perversity" (324) that the illuminators had to walk in visualizing "an interplay that is at the basis of the whole poem's parodic sacral discourse," that is, "calling the vagina a shrine" (323). To Camille, "[T]he architectural detail [of the loophole] is a hilarious reversal of the normal sacralization of allegory" (*The Gothic Idol*, 322). Camille does not recognize the violence in these images, and he does not discuss the miniature on fol. 147v.

22. This is the gesture by which a feudal lord receives a vassal's offer of fealty, a description of which may be found in chap. 56 of Galbert of Bruges, *The Murder of Charles the Good, Count of Flanders*, trans. James Bruce Ross (1960; reprint, Toronto: University of Toronto Press, 1982); see François L. Ganshof, *Feudalism*, trans. Philip Grierson, 2d. ed. (New York: Harper, 1961), 65–67. For representations, see François Garnier, *Le Langage de l'image au Moyen Age*, vol. 1, *Signification et symbolique* (Paris: Léopard d'Or, ca. 1982), 206–8.

23. H. Marshall Leicester Jr. shows that Guillaume de Lorris's God of Love is "quite close to Ovid's original *magister amoris*." Leicester sees this God of Love as "comically and ineffectually asserting an authority over love that his own performance will not sustain" (H. Marshall Leicester Jr., "Ovid Enclosed: The God of Love as *Magister Amoris* in the *Roman de la Rose* of Guillaume de Lorris," *Res publica litterarum* 7 [1984]: 127).

24. For an analysis demonstrating that "[i]n the *Epistre au Dieu d'Amours*, Christine confronts and displaces the *Rose*'s Ovidian Cupid with a corrected Cupid of her own" (236), see Kevin Brownlee, "Discourses of the Self: Christine de Pizan and the *Romance of the Rose*," in *Rethinking the "Romance of the Rose": Text, Image, Reception*, ed. Kevin Brownlee and Sylvia Huot (Philadelphia: University of Pennsylvania Press, 1992), 234–61.

25. See Fenster, "Sense of Humor."

26. In the Queen's manuscript, the God of Love wears a metal crown and grasps a bow and arrows; there is a small fountain next to him (Harley 4431, fol. 51r). In the Duke's manuscript his crown is a leafy wreath and he holds two enormous arrows (fig. 2.2).

27. For this interpretation of the handshake, see Garnier, *Le Langage de l'image*, 1:208. For a further discussion of the semiotics of the handshake and additional bibliography, see Diane Wolfthal, ed., *Peace and Negotiation: Strategies for Coexistence in the Middle Ages and Renaissance* (Turnhout: Brepols, 2000), xxiv–xxv.

28. Silverman, *Male Subjectivity*, 52.

29. Silverman, *Male Subjectivity*, 42.

30. On the status of castration in medieval society and culture, see Mathew S.

Kuefler, "Castration and Eunuchism in the Middle Ages," in *Handbook of Medieval Sexuality,* ed. Vern L. Bullough and James A. Brundage (New York: Garland, 1996), 279–306.

31. For a study of the Saturn myth in the Middle Ages reaching the conclusion that "Jean de Meun occupe donc une place parfaitement originale dans la mythographie médiévale du dieu Saturne" (54), see Jean Marie Fritz, "Du Dieu émasculateur au roi émasculé: Metamorphoses du Saturne au Moyen Age," in *Pour une Mythologie du Moyen Age,* ed. Laurence Harf-Lancner and Dominique Boutet, Collection de l'Ecole Normale Supérieure de Jeunes Filles, 41 (Paris: Ecole Normale Supérieure, 1988), 43–60. For Saturn in medieval mythography, see Theresa Tinkle, "Saturn of the Several Faces: A Survey of the Medieval Mythographic Traditions," *Viator* 18 (1987): 289–302. For a discussion of the role of Venus in relation to the castration of Saturn, see Sarah Kay, "The Birth of Venus in the Roman de la rose," *Exemplaria* 9 (1997): 7–37.

32. The castration of Saturn is an unusual subject for *Rose* illustration; Fleming ("Roman de la Rose") cites only three examples of the castration, of which this is the earliest. The València manuscript would appear to be unique among early *Rose* manuscripts in this respect.

33. For a discussion of Raison as an interpreter of myth, including this use of the myth of Saturn's castration, see Blumenfeld-Kosinski, *Reading Myth,* 68–72.

34. Silverman, *Male Subjectivity,* 63.

35. Silverman, *Male Subjectivity,* 65.

36. On the positive construction of Saturn's slowness in the *Othea* as a unique interpretation of the tradition, see Klibansky, Panofsky, and Saxl, *Saturn and Melancholy,* 194.

37. Several manuscripts made in northern Europe derive ultimately from BnF, lat. 7330, Georgius Fendulus's abridgement of the Latin translation of Abū Ma'šar, including BnF, lat. 7331, BL, Sloane 3983, and Morgan, M. 785. Our study of the miniatures in lat. 7331 and M. 785 reveals that they are twin manuscripts.

38. Abū Ma'šar, *Abbreviation of the Introduction to Astrology,* 125. This phrase does not appear in the Morgan manuscript.

39. In a wall painting in the Palazzo della Ragione in Padua, Giotto painted Saturn in the house of Capricorn. The aged deity holds his left hand, fingers straight, parallel to and in front of his closed mouth. What Blume calls a completely incomprehensible gesture (*Regenten des Himmels,* 82) must refer to his taciturn nature. Thus there was a visual tradition of the silent Saturn that Christine could have known. For a color illustration, see Blume, *Regenten des Himmels,* pl. 20.

40. Helen Solterer, *The Master and Minerva: Disputing Women in French Medieval Culture* (Berkeley and Los Angeles: University of California Press, 1995), 156–57.

41. "Par force d'armes et de guerre / Le desherita de sa terre; / Les genitaires li trencha, / Et dedens la mer les lança" (1.649–52). *Genitaires,* derived from Latin *genitalia,* is certainly less colorful than *coilles,* derived from Latin *culleus* (leather bag), a more metaphorical and less clinical term.

42. For a color illustration of "Atropos," see Meiss, *Limbourgs,* plate vol., pl. 62.

43. The classical Atropos, who cuts the thread of human life, is one of the three Fates. Atropos does not appear in Ovid. Later manuscripts of the *Othea* consistently

follow the traditional iconography for Death by representing Atropos as a partially decayed or skeletal body. For example, Newnham College Library 900 (5), fol. 18v, shows a male rider on a gray horse, invoking the Apocalypse tradition; The Hague, MS 74 G 27, fol. 34v, mid–fifteenth century, depicts death as a naked man with skeletal head; both Waddesdon Manor, MS 8, fol. 35, ca. 1455, and BR, MS 9392, fol. 37v, portray Atropos as a skeletal figure with a long dart (see Hindman, *Painting and Politics,* fig. 89).

44. Christine's Atropos may be the source for the mention of Atropos in the Dutch Rederijker play *Mariken van Nieumeghen,* written between 1471 and 1516–18. In this play Mariken's uncle responds to seeing her lying senseless after having been thrown from the sky by a demon: "Because I want to die in sorrow! Oh, Atropos, Goddess of Death, come quickly and shoot me dead!" [Om steruen dat ic in deser noot wensch / Och antropos coem en doerschiet mi lichte]. See *Mariken van Nieumeghen: A Bilingual Edition,* ed. and trans. Therese Decker and Martin W. Walsh (Columbia, S.C.: Camden House, 1994), 109.

45. Meiss, *Limbourgs,* 31–32. Meiss eliminates the València *Rose* as a possible influence because he mistakenly dates that manuscript too late. However, in general Meiss looks to Italy as the source of any innovation in French art of this period and especially tends to equate any form of classicizing impulse with influence from Italy.

46. This is actually the second image of Atropos in the València manuscript. She also appears with her two sisters in a representation of the three Fates on fol. 134v. The miniature is accompanied by the rubric, "Des troiz suers nommees clotho lachesis et atropos." Below the miniature is line 19733 of the text.

47. Meiss, *Limbourgs,* 30.

48. "Do not allow yourselves to be defeated; you have styluses, so put your mind to using them. Do not keep your arms muffled up: hammer, forge, and blow, help Clotho and Lachesis, so that if base-born Atropos cuts six threads, a dozen more may spring from them" [Ne vos lessiez pas desconfire, / greffes avez, pansez d'escrire. / N'aiez pas les braz anmouflez: / martelez, forgiez et souflez; / aidiez Cloto et Lachesis, / si que, se des fils cope .VI. / Atropos, qui tant est vilaine, / qu'il an resaille une dozaine] (19763–70).

49. The question as to whether Amant repeats or transcends the experience of Narcissus has long been debated in *Rose* scholarship; for some recent contributions, see Phillip McCaffrey, "*Le Roman de la Rose* and the Sons of Narcissus," *Mediaevalia* 11 (1985): 101–20; Harley, "Narcissus, Hermaphroditus, and Attis"; Eric M. Steinle, "Versions of Authority in the Roman de la Rose: Remarks on the Use of Ovid's Metamorphoses by Guillaume de Lorris and Jean de Meun," *Mediaevalia* 13 (1989): 189–206.

50. The Narcissus story in BnF, fr. 12595 is presented in five miniatures:

12v: In the upper left Narcissus stands before a fountain; in the lower left he kneels and looks at his image (two miniatures).

13r: Amant stands by a fountain.

13v: Amant stands and looks into fountain, inside of which is a rosebush.

14r: Amant stands and grasps the rose from the rosebush.

51. Almost every illustrated version of the *Roman de la rose* includes illustrations of Narcissus at the fountain. These miniatures tend to depict the fountain as an architectural structure—sometimes complete with carvings and spouts. Such illustration

responds to the specific description of the fountain in the *Rose*, which emphasizes that Amant comes to a fountain on which is engraved an identifying label. In BnF fr. 380, the fountain is represented as a large stone basin around the rim of which is carved, "Here is the fountain where Narcissus perished." By comparison to *Rose* illustration, the illustrated versions of the *Ovide moralisé*, in keeping with its text, depict the well of Narcissus as a spring rising up from the ground.

52. For a discussion of how Guillaume's Narcissus fails to learn from Ovid's Narcissus, see Harley, "Narcissus, Hermaphroditus, and Attis."

53. At line 1336 of the *Ovide moralisé*, Narcissus is described as "Plains d'orgueil et d'outrecuidance," terms that are repeated in the gloss (1903–64). In the *Rose*, by contrast, Narcissus is characterized by his "desdaing" and his "fierte." In the *texte* of the *Othea*, Narcissus is described as "Par trop grant orgueil affubler, / Car chevalier outrecuidez" (16.3–4); the *glose* states that "c'est a entendre l'oultrecuidance de lui meismes, ou il se mira" (16.12–14).

54. Echo plays a very minor role in the version of the Narcissus story told in the *Roman de la rose*; consequently, she almost never appears in *Rose* illustration. The only exception we have identified is Bodleian, e. Mus. 65, fol. 12v, a depiction of Narcissus that includes Echo in the background.

55. On the relationship between Narcissus and Pygmalion, see Martin Thut, "Narcisse versus Pygmalion: Un lecture du *Roman de la Rose*," *Vox romanica* 41 (1982): 104–32; and Herman Braet, "Narcisse et Pygmalion: Mythe et intertexte dans le 'Roman de la Rose,'" in *Mediaeval Antiquity*, ed. Andries Welkenhuysen, Herman Braet, and Werner Verbeke (Leuven: Leuven University Press, 1995), 237–54. For a thorough discussion of the placement of Pygmalion in relation to the overall organization of the *Rose*, see Jean M. Dornbush, *Pygmalion's Figure: Reading Old French Romance* (Lexington, Ky.: French Forum, 1990), 49–98.

56. Meradith T. McMunn uses the term "freeze frame" to describe this moment in the text and observes that it is frequently illustrated: "I have found 37 examples in 130 illustrated manuscripts. It is thus one of the more frequently illustrated distinctive scenes in the extant *Rose* manuscripts" ("Representations of the Erotic in Some Illustrated Manuscripts of the *Roman de la Rose*," *Romance Languages Annual* 4 [1992]: 127). The illustration of this scene in the *Rose* manuscript in the Getty Museum (Ludwig XV 7) virtually removes the veil of allegory in its graphic representation of violence against the depersonalized female body. This manuscript with its 101 miniatures was made in Paris around 1405 and has been associated in various ways with workshops and libraries that Christine frequented. See Anton von Euw and Joachim M. Plotzek, *Die Handschriften der Sammlung Ludwig* (Cologne: Schnütgen Museum, 1979–85), 4: 228–38, pls. 143–74.

57. As Rosemond Tuve observes, the Pygmalion story "is allowed to seem as if it were casually brought in on the wing of a comparison of statues, but it both mocks pretended delicacy and slyly joins the nearby image of luxurious Venus's part (disguised, or not) in taking the fortress, all the fortresses" (*Allegorical Imagery*, 278). For a discussion of the literary function of the Pygmalion story as one of the three endings of the *Rose*, see Kevin Brownlee, "Pygmalion, Mimesis, and the Multiple Endings of the *Roman de la Rose*," in *Rereading Allegory: Essays in Memory of Daniel Poirion*, ed. Sahar

Amar and Noah D. Guynn, Yale French Studies 95 (New Haven: Yale University Press, 1999), 193–211. Brownlee concludes, "The dialectical juxtaposition of the three endings of the *Rose* . . . constitutes in the last analysis an extended authorial meditation on the processes and the problems, the possible successes and the built in limitations of mimetic art as such: of verbal signifying activity and its capacities for transmitting values" (210).

Blumenfeld-Kosinski points out that this narrative is "the most elaborate myth told in *Rose II*" even though it "exists only in a kind of ellipsis with respect to the diegesis" (66). She discusses the function of the myth of Pygmalion in relation to the allegory of the *Rose* (*Reading Myth*, 62–67).

58. Braet observes that the Pygmalion story is one of the most frequently illustrated and often the last. He gives a provisional list of manuscripts in which this is the case (Braet, "Narcisse et Pygmalion," 238–39 n. 5).

59. Virginia Wylie Egbert, "Pygmalion as Sculptor," *Princeton University Library Chronicle* 28 (1966–67): 21. See this article also for photographs of six other *Rose* miniatures of Pygmalion carving his statue.

60. BnF, fr. 12595, fols. 150v, 152, 152v, etc.; BnF, fr. 380, fol. 132v; Bodleian, Douce 371, fol. 136r.

61. For the connection between femininity and death in the Western aesthetic, see Elisabeth Bronfen, *Over Her Dead Body: Death, Femininity, and the Aesthetic* (London: Routledge, 1992).

62. Michael Camille illustrates his discussion of this chapter of the *Othea* with a miniature from a manuscript of the *Othea* made for Philip the Good, duke of Burgundy, about 1460 (BR, MS 9392, fol. 25v). As we show later in this chapter, Loyset Liédet, the miniaturist, departs from Christine's program of miniatures to move his subjects closer to the chivalric ideals of the Burgundian court. Thus the miniature of Pygmalion in BR, 9392, which includes the scene of Pygmalion carving his statue, is not responsive to the question that Camille poses, "What does a late-medieval woman writer make of the Pygmalion story?" (*Gothic Idol*, 333; for the miniature see fig. 178, p. 335).

63. Sullivan, "At the Limits," 442.

64. See Willard, *Life and Works*, 169–71; Muriel J. Hughes, "The Library of Philip the Bold and Margaret of Flanders, First Valois Duke and Duchess of Burgundy," *Journal of Medieval History* 4 (1978): 145–88; Richard Vaughan, *Philip the Good: The Apogee of Burgundy* (London: Longmans, 1970), 155–57; Otto Cartellieri, *The Court of Burgundy: Studies in the History of Civilization* (London: Kegan, Paul, Trench, 1929), 166–72; Georges Doutrepont, *La Littérature française à la cour des ducs de Bourgogne* (Paris: Champion, 1909), 290–319.

65. See Charity Cannon Willard, "Christine de Pizan on the Art of Warfare," in Desmond, *Christine de Pizan*, 3–15.

66. On the court of Philip the Good, see Vaughan, *Philip the Good;* Johan Huizinga, *The Autumn of the Middle Ages,* trans. Rodney J. Payton and Ulrich Mammitzsch (Chicago: University of Chicago Press, 1996). On Flanders in the period of Philip's rule, see David Nicholas, *Medieval Flanders* (London: Longman, 1992), 317–56; Wim Blockmans and Walter Prevenier, *The Promised Lands: The Low Countries under Burgundian Rule, 1369–1530,* trans. Elizabeth Fackelman, ed. Edward Peters (Philadelphia:

University of Pennsylvania Press, 1999); Jean C. Wilson, *Painting in Bruges at the Close of the Middle Ages: Studies in Society and Visual Culture* (University Park: Pennsylvania State University Press, 1998).

67. There is a vast literature on the Order of the Golden Fleece. See the catalog for the exhibition *L'Ordre de la Toison d'or de Philippe le Bon à Philippe le Beau (1430–1505): Idéal ou reflet d'une société?* ed. Christiane Van den Bergen-Pantens (Brussels: Brepols, 1996); Walter Prevenier and Wim P. Blockmans, *The Burgundian Netherlands* (Cambridge: Cambridge University Press, 1986), 131–40; Morse, *Medieval Medea*, 148–84.

68. Burr Wallen emphasizes the promotion of neochivalric ethics based on magnanimity to glorify Philip the Good. He sees this glory in a psychomachia with vainglory, the sin for which the revival of chivalry was condemned ("Burgundian *Gloire* vs. *Vaine Gloire:* Patterns of Neochivalric *Psychomachia*," in Gregory T. Clark et al., *A Tribute to Robert A. Koch: Studies in the Northern Renaissance* [Princeton: Department of Art and Archaeology, 1994], 147–75).

69. Jacques Paviot, "L'ordre de la Toison d'or et la Croisade," in Van den Bergen-Pantens, *L'Ordre de la Toison d'or,* 74.

70. BR, MS 9242, fol. 1r. The miniature opens the first of three volumes containing Jean Wauquelin's French translation of the *Chroniques.* Since Wauquelin and his scribe Jacotin du Bois were paid for the transcription of the first volume in March of 1448 and scholars think that the miniatures are contemporary with the text, they are also dated to 1448. See Frédéric Lyna, *Les principaux Manuscrits à peintures de la Bibliothèque royale de Belgique III,* ed. Christiane Pantens (Brussels: Bibliothèque royale Albert 1er, 1984), 9–25 and 409–12, no. 245; and Anne van Buren-Hagopian, "The Date of the Miniatures," in *Les Chroniques de Hainaut ou les ambitions d'un Prince Bourguignon,* ed. Christiane Van den Bergen-Pantens (Turnhout: Brepols, 2000), 61–64. For Van Buren-Hagopian's conclusion that Rogier Van der Weyden is very likely to have made the preparatory drawing for this painting, which was transferred to the manuscript and executed by a "close associate" of Rogier, see her "Artists of Volume 1," in *Les Chroniques,* 65–73.

71. Margaret Scott, *Late Gothic Europe, 1400–1500,* History of Dress Series, ed. Aileen Ribeiro (Atlantic Highlands, N.J.: Humanities Press, 1980), 48. For a description of Philip drawn from textual sources, see Vaughan, *Philip the Good,* 127–28.

72. Scott, *Late Gothic Europe,* 159. For a precise and detailed description of this miniature, "a major document for the history of late medieval fashion," see Anne van Buren-Hagopian, "Dress and Costume," in *Les Chroniques de Hainaut,* ed. Van den Bergen-Pantens, 111–17.

73. Richard Dyer, "Don't Look Now: The Male Pin-Up," in *The Sexual Subject: A Screen Reader in Sexuality* (London: Routledge, 1992), 269.

74. Norman Bryson, "Géricault and 'Masculinity,'" in *Visual Culture: Images and Interpretations,* ed. Norman Bryson, Michael Ann Holly, and Keith Moxey (Hanover, N.H.: University Press of New England, 1994), 231.

75. Bryson, "Géricault and Masculinity," 231.

76. BR, MS 9392. For reproductions of most of the miniatures, see J. van den Gheyn, *Christine de Pizan. Epitre d'Othéa.* For Miélot, see Doutrepont, *La Littérature*

française, 274–78; and P. Perdrizet, "Jean Miélot, l'un des traducteurs de Philippe le Bon," *Revue d'Histoire littéraire de la France* 14 (1907): 472–82. In the more traditional presentation miniature to BR, MS 9392 (see van den Gheyn, fig. 1), Philip the Good is seated on a dais and beneath a brocade canopy. He wears a loose fur-trimmed, full-length gown. Although he still displays the broad shoulders and pointed toes of the presentation miniature in BR, MS 9242, the format of this presentation image does not allow for the display of his figure.

Loyset Liédet was a native of Hesdin. After an apprenticeship in Valenciennes under Simon Marmion he returned to Hesdin. Sometime after 1460 he entered into a collaboration with David Aubert in Bruges, where their workshop produced large numbers of books, among them luxury manuscripts for Philip the Good. See Dorothy Miner, "Hesdin, Atelier of Loyset Liédet, 1455–60," in *Flanders in the Fifteenth Century: Art and Civilization,* catalog of the exhibition "Masterpieces of Flemish Art: Van Eyck to Bosch," organized by the Detroit Institute of Fine Arts and the City of Bruges (Detroit: Detroit Institute of Arts, 1960), 384–86. For Liédet, see also Georges Dogaer, *Flemish Miniature Painting in the Fifteenth and Sixteenth Centuries* (Amsterdam: B. M. Israel, 1987), 106–12.

77. In a few chapters that were too long to fit his page design, Miélot reduced the number of lines in the *texte;* for an overview of Miélot's adaptation of the text of the *Othea,* see Campbell, *L'Épître d'Othéa,* 58–62.

78. See Évelyne van den Neste, *Tournois, joutes, pas d'armes dans les villes de Flandre à la fin du Moyen Âge (1300–1486)* (Paris: École des Chartes, 1996).

79. Charity Cannon Willard, "Christine de Pizan on Chivalry," in *The Study of Chivalry: Resources and Approaches,* ed. Howell Chickering and Thomas H. Seiler (Kalamazoo, Mich.: Medieval Institute Publications, 1988), 516.

80. Rosalind Brown-Grant observes that the miniature follows closely the details that Miélot added to the *glose* ("Illumination as Reception: Jean Miélot's Reworking of the 'Epistre Othea,'" in Zimmermann and De Rentiis, *The City of Scholars,* 268).

Chapter 3

1. Beverly Brown, "A Feminist Interest in Pornography: Some Modest Proposals," *m/f* 5–6 (1981): 11.

2. For a range of views on the politics of pornography, see Williams, *Hard Core;* Catherine Itzin, *Pornography: Women, Violence, and Civil Liberties* (Oxford: Oxford University Press, 1992), 1–24; Robin West, "Pornography as a Legal Text," in *For Adult Users Only: The Dilemma of Violent Pornography,* ed. Susan Gubar and Joan Huff (Bloomington: Indiana University Press, 1989), 108–30; Catherine MacKinnon, *Only Words* (Cambridge: Harvard University Press, 1993); Andrea Dworkin, *Pornography: Men Possessing Women* (New York: Perigee, 1981); John B. McConahay, "Pornography: The Symbolic Politics of Fantasy," *Law and Contemporary Problems* 5, no. 1 (winter 1988): 32–69; Joseph W. Slade, "Violence in the Hard-Core Pornographic Film: A Historical Survey," *Journal of Communication* 34 (1984): 148–63; Karen Boyle, "The Pornography Debates: Beyond Cause and Effect," *Women's Studies International Forum* 23 (2000): 187–95.

3. Williams, "Film Bodies," 12.

4. Judith Butler, *Excitable Speech: A Politics of the Performative* (New York: Routledge, 1997), 67.

5. Paul Saenger notes that the privatization of reading emphasized its erotic potential and, indeed, made possible the voyeurism of pornography: "Before the thirteenth century, erotic decorations in books were usually oblique, suggesting the repressed illicit desires of the chaste, rather than artfully crafted graphic fantasies intended to excite the reader. In fifteenth-century France . . . private reading encouraged the production of illustrated salacious writings intended for the laity, writings that were tolerated precisely because they could be disseminated in secret" (*Space between Words*, 274).

6. See Blumenfeld-Kosinski's overview of the allegoresis of the *Ovide moralisé* in *Reading Myth*, chap. 3, "The Hermeneutics of the *Ovide moralisé*." See also James R. Simpson, *Fantasy, Identity, and Misrecognition in Medieval French Narrative* (Oxford: Peter Lang, 2000), 133–90.

7. This phrase is taken from Williams, *Hard Core.*

8. For the medieval Orpheus the most important authors were Ovid, Virgil, and Boethius, along with commentaries on their texts. Of these three only Ovid explicitly discusses Orpheus's homosexuality; see Thomas Bein, "Orpheus als Sodomit. Beobachtungen zu einer mhd. Sangspruchstrophe mit (literar) historischen Exkursen zur Homosexualität im hohen Mittelalter," *Zeitschrift für deutsche Philologie* 109 (1990): 33–55. For an overview of Orpheus in the classical tradition, see W. S. Anderson, "The Orpheus of Virgil and Ovid: *Flebile nescio quid*," in *Orpheus: The Metamorphoses of a Myth,* ed. John Warden (Toronto: University of Toronto Press, 1982), 25–50. For appropriations of Orpheus in the early Christian period, see Eleanor Irwin, "The Songs of Orpheus and the New Song of Christ," in Warden, *Orpheus,* 51–62; and Patricia Vicari, "*Sparagmos:* Orpheus among the Christians," in Warden, *Orpheus,* 63–83.

For a survey of the range of uses of the Orpheus myth in the Middle Ages, see John B. Friedman, *Orpheus in the Middle Ages* (Cambridge: Harvard University Press, 1970); Klaus Heitmann, "Orpheus im Mittelalter," *Archiv für Kulturgeschichte* 45 (1963): 253–94; Klaus Heitmann, "Typen der Deformierung antiker Mythen im Mittelalter am Beispiel der Orpheussage," *Romanistisches Jahrbuch* 14 (1963): 45–77.

9. For Orpheus in the *Roman de la Rose,* see Kevin Brownlee, "Orpheus's Song Re-sung: Jean de Meun's Reworking of *Metamorphoses,* X," *Romance Philology* 36 (1982): 201–9. For an excellent discussion of language, gender, and sexuality in the *Rose* that focuses on the interactions of Nature, Reason, Genius, and Amant and concludes that Jean de Meun explores in the poem the "irreducible complexity" of heterosexual union as an aspect of "the impossibility, in a Fallen world, of any truly rational sexuality" (59), see Sylvia Huot, "Bodily Peril: Sexuality and the Subversion of Order in Jean de Meun's *Roman de la Rose,*" *Modern Language Review* 95 (2000): 41–61.

10. For an analysis of the structure of book 10 in the *Ovide moralisé,* see Blumenfeld-Kosinski, *Reading Myth,* 94–98.

11. Since the *Ovide moralisé* was composed after 1309, Rouen O.4, which is dated 1315–20, may be the first manuscript. On this manuscript, see Lord, "Three Manuscripts." François Avril has identified Rouen O.4 with an entry in the inventory of the estate of Clemence of Hungary, the widow of Louis X of France, which indicates that

the manuscript was purchased by Philip VI of France (François Avril, catalog entry in *Les Fastes du Gothique: Le siècle de Charles V* [Paris: Galeries nationales du Grand Palais, 1981], no. 230, pp. 284–85). Building on the work of Alison Stones, Avril attributed this manuscript to the Fauvel Artist or his workshop (Edward H. Roesner, François Avril, and Nancy Freeman Regalado, *Le Roman de Fauvel in the Edition of Mesire Chaillou de Pesstain: A Reproduction in Facsimile of the Complete Manuscript, Paris, Bibliothèque Nationale, Fonds Français 146* [New York: Broude Brothers, 1990], 42–48). Carla Lord has added evidence that the manuscript was made for Clemence and Louis ("Marks of Ownership in Medieval Manuscripts: The Case of the Rouen *Ovide moralisé*," *Source* 18 [1998]: 7–11). Richard A. Rouse and Mary A. Rouse conclude that all of the miniatures in Rouen O.4 (which they cite as 1044) were made by the Fauvel Master, whose work progressively deteriorates in quality (*Manuscripts and Their Makers: Commercial Book Producers in Medieval Paris, 1200–1500* [London: Harvey Miller, 2000], 2: 208–11). For a collation of these Ovidian images with the same subjects in the *Othea*, see the tables in Hindman, *Painting and Politics*, 194–203.

12. For a codicological study of Arsenal 5069 and conclusions about the number of missing miniatures, see Lord, "Three Manuscripts," 164. Lord notes what she calls a "proportional lessening of enthusiasm for religious themes" (169). Avril attributes this manuscript to the Fauvel Artist or his workshop; with regard to the rather loose style and impression of hasty work, Avril comments, "If anything, his work came to be executed more expeditiously as the years passed—as if the artist, harassed by his work and weighed down by years, heedlessly rushed his projects to completion" (Roesner, Avril, and Regalado, *Le Roman de Fauvel*, 46; see also Rouse and Rouse, *Manuscripts and Their Makers*, 213).

13. As to the relationships among these three manuscripts, although Arsenal was made by one of the artists who worked on Rouen, Lord has shown that only slightly over one-fifth of the Arsenal miniatures demonstrate a close relationship to this model ("Three Manuscripts," 166–67). The Lyon miniatures show an awareness of the tradition rather than a close dependence upon it.

14. The subjects of the five miniatures in Arsenal 5069 are as follows: marriage of Orpheus and Eurydice, fol. 132v; Orpheus in Hades, fol. 132v; Hellmouth as illustration to allegory, fol. 133; Christ in Majesty as illustration to the allegory, fol. 140r; death of Orpheus, fol. 145r. In Lyon 742 the five subjects are marriage of Orpheus and Eurydice, fol. 165v; Eurydice bitten by the serpent, fol. 166r; Orpheus and Eurydice in Hades, fol. 166v; Orpheus in the forest playing to trees and animals, fol. 167; death of Orpheus, fol. 178v.

15. For Christine's negative attitude toward the social institution of courtly love, see Charity Cannon Willard, "Christine de Pizan's *Cent ballades d'amant et de dame*: Criticism of Courtly Love," in *Court and Poet*, ed. Glyn S. Burgess (Liverpool: Cairns, 1981), 357–64; Roberta Krueger, *Women Readers and the Ideology of Gender in Old French Verse Romance*, Cambridge Studies in French 43 (Cambridge: Cambridge University Press, 1993), 217–46; Diane Bornstein, *Ideals for Women in the Works of Christine de Pizan*, Medieval and Renaissance Monograph Series 1 (Ann Arbor: Michigan Consortium for Medieval and Early Modern Studies, 1981), 117–28.

16. Bein, "Orpheus als Sodomit." Bein notes that *harfen* survives as a sexual metaphor in modern German usage (36).

17. For the classic formulation of this view, see John Boswell, *Christianity, Social Tolerance, and Homosexuality* (Chicago: University of Chicago Press, 1980). Boswell has been criticized for painting a more positive picture than the sources support. For the view that there was a general turn toward persecution in the high Middle Ages, see R. I. Moore, *The Formation of a Persecuting Society: Power and Deviance in Western Europe 950–1250* (Oxford: Oxford University Press, 1987); for the formation of the category of sodomy in the high Middle Ages, see Mark D. Jordan, *The Invention of Sodomy in Christian Theology* (Chicago: University of Chicago Press, 1997).

18. On Christine and Machaut, see Johanna Schilperoort, *Guillaume de Machaut et Christine de Pizan: Etude comparative* (n.p., 1936).

19. Guillaume de Machaut, *Le Confort d'ami (Comfort for a Friend)*, ed. and trans R. Barton Palmer (New York: Garland, 1992).

20. For the clerical tradition, see Boswell, *Christianity, Social Tolerance, and Homosexuality*, and note Panofsky's comment, "In the Middle Ages Ganymede was so typical a representative of homosexuality that a prelate so inclined could be ridiculed as 'ganimedior Ganimede'" (*Renaissance and Renascences*, 78, citing von Bezold, 58, 101). For a manifestation of the clerical tradition of pederasty in medieval drama, see V. A. Kolve, "Ganymede/*Son of Getron*: Medieval Monasticism and the Drama of Same-Sex Desire," *Speculum* 73 (1998): 1014–67. For vernacular texts, see especially the mid-twelfth-century *Roman d'Enéas*, a French adaptation of Virgil's *Aeneid*. In an exchange between Lavine and her mother about Lavine's love for Enéas, her mother tries to dissuade Lavine by characterizing Enéas as a sodomite. Lavine later decides that her mother is right: "He has his Ganymede with him and so cares nothing for me; he is a long time rutting and he has his pleasure with a boy" [Son Ganimede a avec soi, / asez li est or po de moi; / il est molt longuement an ruit, / a garçon moine son deduit] (J.-J. Salverda de Grave, *Enéas: Roman du XIIᵉ siècle* [Paris, Champion, 1983], 9135–38). See Simon Gaunt's perceptive discussion of the function served by the homophobia evident in the *Enéas* in *Gender and Genre in Medieval French Literature* (Cambridge: Cambridge University Press, 1995), 75–85; for translation quoted above, see p. 78. On Ganymede in visual culture, see Gerda Kempter, *Ganymed: Studien zur Typologie, Ikonographie und Ikonologie*, Dissertationen zur Kunstgeschichte 12 (Cologne: Böhlau, 1980). For the explicit association of Ganymede with homosexuality, see James M. Saslow, *Ganymede in the Renaissance: Homosexuality in Art and Society* (New Haven: Yale University Press, 1986), and Saslow, *Pictures and Passions: A History of Homosexuality in the Visual Arts* (New York: Penguin, 1999).

21. Campbell reads this as a mistake on Christine's part (*L'Épître d'Othéa*, 126).

22. The idea that desire enters through the eye is based in the optical theory called "intromission theory," which says that "the agent responsible for vision passes from the observed object to the eye" (David C. Lindberg, *The Beginnings of Western Science: The European Scientific Tradition in Philosophical, Religious, and Institutional Context, 600 B.C. to A.D. 1450* [Chicago: University of Chicago Press, 1992], 308). Argued by Aristotle and developed further by Alhazen, whose *Optics* was translated into Latin by the early thirteenth century, intromission theory was dominant in medieval optics (Lindberg, 307–15).

23. For a very similar representation of a courtier dressed in a short, form-fitting

doublet, parti-colored hose, and a garter worn on the left leg, see the frontispiece to Royal 20 B. VI, as illustrated in Scott, *Late Gothic Europe*, fig. 35, p. 85. Scott considers such costume to be an extreme example of "foppishness" in men's dress in this era; by the first decade of the fifteenth century excessively long sleeves were part of such costume (85–87).

24. Translation from Henry Charles Lea, *Materials toward a History of Witchcraft*, ed. Arthur C. Howland, 3 vols. (Philadelphia: University of Pennsylvania Press, 1939; reprint, New York: AMS Press, 1986), 1:178–79. The Latin text reads: "quaedam sceleratae mulieres retro post Satanam conversae daemonum illusionibus et phantasmatibus seductae, credunt se et profitentur nocturnis horis cum Diana paganorum dea et innumera multitudine mulierum equitare super quasdam bestias, et multa terrarum spatia intempestae noctis silentio pertransire, eiusque iussionibus velut dominae obedire, et certis noctibus ad eius servitium evocari" (Joseph Hansen, *Quellen und Untersuchungen zur Geschichte des Hexenwahns und der Hexenverfolgung im Mittelalter* [Bonn, 1901; reprint, Hildesheim: G. Olms, 1963], 38).

25. Jeffrey Burton Russell, *Witchcraft in the Middle Ages* (Ithaca, N.Y.: Cornell University Press, 1972), 77–82; see also the chapter "Following the Goddess," in Carlo Ginzburg, *Ecstasies: Deciphering the Witches' Sabbath*, trans. Raymond Rosenthal (New York: Penguin, 1991), 89–121; and D. Lesourd, "Diane et les sorcières. Études sur les survivances," *Anagrom* 1 (1972): 55–74. We owe our awareness of this material to Patricia Simons, "Lesbian (In)Visibility in Italian Renaissance Culture: Diana and Other Cases of *donna con donna*," *Journal of Homosexuality* 27 (1994): 81–122.

26. Ginzburg, *Ecstasies*, 122.

27. Giovanni Boccaccio, *Diana's Hunt, Caccia di Diana: Boccaccio's First Fiction* ed. and trans. Anthony K. Cassell and Victoria Kirkham (Philadelphia: University of Pennsylvania Press, 1991), 101–2.

28. "It is difficult to imagine a miniaturist creating this imagery for Diana. Like the iconography of the seven planets [for which Christine provided instructions], it is entirely extratextual. It is, moreover, self-referential of the author, referring as it does to book-writing and -reading. Rather, having developed her iconography of the planets and being familiar with miniatures in *Des Cleres femmes* where a similar formula was used throughout, Christine adapted the schema to different subjects, such as this one of Diana" (Hindman, *Painting and Politics*, 93).

29. "[T]here are no fourteenth-century or fifteenth-century miniatures depicting classroom scenes of students taking down verbatim transcriptions of professorial lectures. . . . Instead the illuminations typically show the professor lecturing from his text to students, who, with the occasional exception of the recording scribe, either had no pens or books or more usually were holding already written books" (Saenger, *Space between Words*, 260). For an image of students seated on the floor holding open books while a lecturer, seated above, speaks, see the drawing in the lecture notes of George Lichton, taken while he was a university student in Leuven in 1467, reproduced in Lorne Campbell, *The Fifteenth Century Netherlandish Schools* (New Haven: Yale University Press, 1998), 49, fig. 3. For a miniature of a king and his counselors seated in front of a lecturer and holding open books, see Nicole Oresme, *Les éthiques d'Aristote*, Brussels,

Bibl. Royale Albert Ier, MS 9505-06, fol. 2v, reproduced in Sherman, *Imaging Aristotle*, fig. 7.

30. Saenger, *Space between Words*, 258–59. "In 1259, the Dominican house of the University of Paris required that students, if possible, bring to class a copy of the text expounded upon in public lectures. . . . Regulations requiring students to bring books to class also existed in Paris at the College of Harcourt and at the universities of Vienna and Ingolstadt. In 1309, Pierre Dubois, the most celebrated of the legists in the service of Philip the Fair, observed that students who did not have a copy of the text before them could profit little from university lectures. Students too poor to purchase their own copies could borrow them from libraries like that of the Cathedral of Notre Dame of Paris, which received bequests especially for this purpose. The statutes of the Sorbonne provided for lending books against security deposits" (259).

31. Margaret L. King, "Book-Lined Cells: Women and Humanism in the Early Italian Renaissance," in *Beyond Their Sex: Learned Women of the European Past*, ed. Patricia H. Labalme (New York: New York University Press, 1980), 66–90; Lisa Jardine, "Women Humanists: Education for What?" in *From Humanism to the Humanities: Education and the Liberal Arts in Fifteenth- and Sixteenth-Century Europe*, ed. Anthony Grafton and Lisa Jardine (Cambridge: Harvard University Press, 1986), 29–57.

32. Christine Reno interprets Christine's revision, in which it is not Daphne's father Peneus who saves her from Apollo's pursuit, but the goddess Diana, as follows: "What is the net effect of the substitution Christine has made? As a result of her modification a female character, Diana, plays a more active role in the narrative; correspondingly, although less significantly perhaps, a male character's role is reduced. The modification is slight, to be sure, but when it is added to the other changes Christine makes in material from the *Ovide moralisé* as well as other sources, the combined effect is a very definite shift in the literary portrait of women this work presents. And the shift is quite definitely in the direction of feminism" (Reno, "Feminist Aspects," 272).

33. The explicit nature of this image is in sharp contrast to the illustration in an *Ovidius moralizatus* manuscript made in Italy later in the fifteenth century (Bergamo, Biblioteca Civica Angelo Mai MS, Cassaf. 3.4, fol. 22), where, as Carla Lord remarks, "The portrayal of Jupiter and Callisto resembles a sedate Visitation rather than an unusual carnal adventure" ("Illustrated Manuscripts of Berchorius before the Age of Printing," in Walter and Horn, *Die Rezeption der Metamorphosen*, 6–7). Lord attributes the "strait-laced" nature of the scene to its having been made "in an era when religious imagery still dominated iconography and classical myths were not yet widespread" (6).

34. See François Garnier, *Le Langage de l'image au Moyen Age*, vol. 2, *Grammaire des gestes* (Paris: Léopard d'Or, 1989), "Main sous le menton d'autrui," 120–26.

35. See Ruth Mazo Karras, "Sex and the Singlewoman," in *Singlewomen in the European Past, 1250–1800*, ed. Judith M. Bennett and Amy M. Froide (Philadelphia: University of Pennsylvania Press, 1999), 128. See also Francesca Canadé Sautman and Pamela Sheingorn, "Introduction: Charting the Field," in *Same-Sex Love and Desire among Medieval Women*, ed. Sautman and Sheingorn (New York: Palgrave, 2001).

36. Simons, "Lesbian (In)Visibility," 109. In spite of her title, some of Simons's

examples are drawn from late medieval northern Europe; others come from a humanist milieu, elements of which were familiar to Christine.

37. Valerie Traub, "The Perversion of 'Lesbian' Desire," *History Workshop Journal* 41 (1996): 24.

38. Sally O'Driscoll, "Outlaw Readings: Beyond Queer Theory," *Signs* 22 (1996): 34.

39. O'Driscoll, "Outlaw Readings," 37. For discussions of queer theory, see Teresa de Lauretis, "Queer Theory: Lesbian and Gay Sexualities, an Introduction," *differences* 3, no. 2 (1991): iii–xviii; Eve Kosofsky Sedgwick, "Queer and Now," in *Tendencies* (Durham: Duke University Press, 1993), 1–20; Louise Fradenberg and Carla Freccero, "Introduction: Caxton, Foucault, and the Pleasures of History," in *Premodern Sexualities,* ed. Louise Fradenberg and Carla Freccero (London: Routledge, 1995), xiii–xxiv; Harriet Malinowitz, "Lesbian Studies and Postmodern Queer Theory," in *The New Lesbian Studies: Into the Twenty-First Century,* ed. Bonnie Zimmerman and Toni A. H. McNaron (New York: Feminist Press, 1996), 262–68; William B. Turner, *A Genealogy of Queer Theory* (Philadelphia: Temple University Press, 2000); and Glenn Burger and Steven F. Kruger, eds., *Queering the Middle Ages* (Minneapolis: University of Minnesota Press, 2001), xi–xxiii.

40. O'Driscoll, "Outlaw Readings," 37.

41. The *Ovide moralisé* obsessively returns to this point: "He is able to see her uncovered" [Veoir la puet sans couverture] (6640).

42. Texts describing constellations as complete human figures form a distinct tradition traced back to Aratus and/or Hyginus. For a survey of some astrology manuscripts and their illustrations, see Fritz Saxl and Hans Meier, *Verzeichnis astrologischer und mythologischer illustrierter Handschriften des lateinischen Mittelalters III. Handschriften in englischen Bibliotheken,* 2 vols. (London: Warburg Institute, 1953).

43. For a description of this manuscript and a bibliography, see catalog entry no. 8 in C. M. Kauffmann, *Romanesque Manuscripts, 1066–1190,* Survey of Manuscripts Illuminated in the British Isles, 3, general editor, J. J. G. Alexander (London: Harvey Miller, 1975), 77–78. For a representation of Andromeda similarly tied, though clothed, in a manuscript from the second half of the fourteenth century that is probably French, see Berlin, Staatsbibliothek Preussischer Kulturbesitz MS. lat. oct. 44, fol. 4v (*Glanz alter Buchkunst: Mittelalterliche Handschriften der Staatsbibliothek Preussischer Kulturbesitz Berlin* [Wiesbaden: Ludwig Reichert Verlag, 1988], 129). An Italian astrology manuscript dated ca. 1400 shows Andromeda in a transparent gown, hands tied at shoulder-height to trees (Munich, Bayerische Staatsbibliothek clm 10268, fol. 81v).

44. For a discussion of the *Othea* image in relation to earlier treatments of the subject, see Meiss, *Limbourgs,* 27–29. Meiss emphasizes the role of the artist: "This representation by the Epître Master is historically important not only for its novel drama but also for its iconography" (27). We would argue that the innovations in the image of Perseus and Andromeda are demonstrably consistent with the overall revisionary nature of the *Othea* and should therefore be attributed to Christine as well as to the artist with whom she worked.

45. On the visual similarities between images of Perseus rescuing Andromeda and

St. George slaying a dragon to rescue a princess, see Samantha Riches, *St. George: Hero, Martyr, and Myth* (Phoenix Mill: Sutton, 2000).

46. Marina Warner, *From the Beast to the Blonde: On Fairy Tales and Their Tellers* (London: Vintage, 1994), 259.

47. "[Q]ui est a entendre que tous chevaliers doivent secourir femmes qui besoing de leur ayde aront" (5.34–36).

48. O'Driscoll, "Outlaw Readings," 36.

49. Arsenal 5069 illustrates the marriage of Perseus and Andromeda on fol. 62v and Rouen O.4 on fol. 129v. See figures 4 and 6 in Marilynn Desmond and Pamela Sheingorn, "Queering Ovidian Myth: Bestiality and Desire in Christine de Pizan's *Epistre Othea*," in Burger and Kruger, *Queering the Middle Ages*.

50. "Riding Pegasus the marvelous horse, he flew through the air, and in flight, delivered Andromeda from the monster, taking her from him by force" [Pegasus, li chevaulx appers, / Chevaucha par l'air en volant, / Et Andromada en alant / Il delivra de la belue, / Si lui a a force tolue] (5.5–9).

51. Dante, *Purgatorio*, canto 26, quoted from the translation by Charles S. Singleton in Dante Alighieri, *The Divine Comedy, Purgatorio*, vol. 1, Italian Text and Translation (Princeton: Princeton University Press, 1973; Bollingen Series 80), 285. In his notes on this canto, Singleton observes that Thomas Aquinas considered bestiality a more serious sin than sodomy.

52. For a survey of medieval attitudes toward bestiality, see Joyce E. Salisbury, "Bestiality in the Middle Ages," in *Sex in the Middle Ages: A Book of Essays,* ed. Joyce E. Salisbury (New York: Garland, 1991), 173–86.

53. Erwin Panofsky, "Letter to the Editor," *Art Bulletin* 30 (1948): 242. We would like to thank Diane Wolfthal for bringing this letter to our attention.

54. As with the modern French *fou*, the middle French word *fole* denotes a wide range of meanings from mad or insane to foolish, licentious, or silly.

55. For a detailed study of the academic tradition of Ovid texts, see Ralph Hexter, *Ovid and Medieval Schooling. Studies in Medieval School Commentaries on Ovid's Ars amatoria, Epistulae ex Ponto, and the Epistulae Heroidum* (Munich: Arbeo-Gesellschaft, 1986). For the pervasive influence of Ovid in medieval culture, including the Latin texts of Ovid in the schools, see the special issue "Ovid in Medieval Culture," ed. Marilynn R. Desmond, *Mediaevalia* 13 (1989, for 1987). For a thorough consideration of the relationship between Ovidian texts and discourses on sexuality, see John W. Baldwin, *The Language of Sex: Five Voices from Northern France around 1200* (Chicago: University of Chicago Press, 1994).

56. For a summary and analysis of this passage, see Renate Blumenfeld-Kosinski, "The Scandal of Pasiphae: Narration and Interpretation in the *Ovide moralisé*," *Modern Philology* 93 (1995): 307–26.

57. In Arsenal 5069, the miniature accompanying this passage on fol. 108v shows Pasiphaë looking out of a tower and pointing at a bull that frolics flirtatiously before her.

58. The *Ovide moralisé* thus recapitulates the Roman visual tradition, which repeatedly represents the moment when Pasiphaë selects the actual heifer the great technician

is to replicate so that she can position herself inside it. For an example, see Gilbert Picard, *Roman Painting* (Greenwich, Conn.: New York Graphic Society, 1968), pl. 40.

59. The Second Vatican Mythographer (ca. 800–900) recounts that Pasiphaë had sexual relations with Taurus, the *notarius* of Minos, which led to the birth of twins, one a son of Minos and the other of Taurus, instead of the Minotaur (*Mythographi Vaticani I et II*, ed. Péter Kulcsár, CCSL no. 91c [Turnhout: Brepols, 1987], 149/126). In his gloss on a reference to Pasiphaë at lines 10–12 in the First Satire of Juvenal, William of Conches writes, "Minos had a secretary by the name of Taurus whom Pasiphaë loved" [Minos habebat cancellarium nomine Taurum quem Pasiphaë adamavit] (Guillaume de Conches, *Glosae in Iuvenalem*, ed. Bradford Wilson [Paris: J. Vrin, 1980], 111). In his commentary on Dante's *Inferno*, 12.12–13, Guido da Pisa (1328–33) writes, "The truth of the story is this: In the realm of Crete, there was a certain secretary of King Minos named Taurus whom Queen Pasiphaë loved, and she slept with him within the labyrinth" [Veritas ystorie est ista: In regno namque Cretensi fuit quidam notarius regis Minois, nomine Taurus, quem regina Pasiphe dilexit et cum eo in domo Dedali occulte concubuit] (Guido da Pisa, *Expositiones et Glose super Comediam Dantis or Commentary on Dante's Inferno*, ed. Vincenzo Cioffari [Albany: State University of New York Press, 1974], 222).

60. Blumenfeld-Kosinski, "Scandal of Pasiphae," 314–15.

61. For an analysis of the gesture of dominant embrace and the power relationship it encodes, see Pamela Sheingorn, "The Bodily Embrace or Embracing the Body: Gesture and Gender in Late Medieval Culture," in *The Stage as Mirror: Civic Theatre in Late Medieval Europe*, ed. Alan E. Knight (Cambridge: D. S. Brewer, 1997), 51–89.

62. J. E. Robson, "Bestiality and Bestial Rape in Greek Myth," in *Rape in Antiquity*, ed. Susan Deacy and Karen F. Pierce (London: Duckworth, 1997), 81.

63. *The Life of Christina of Markyate: A Twelfth-Century Recluse*, ed. and trans. C. H. Talbot (Oxford: Oxford University Press, 1959), 99.

64. Elizabeth Grosz, "Animal Sex: Libido as Desire and Death," in *Sexy Bodies: The Strange Carnalities of Feminism*, ed. Elizabeth Grosz and Elspeth Probyn (London: Routledge, 1995), 293. See also Alphonso Lingis, "Bestiality," *Symplokē* 6 (1998): 56–71.

65. Grosz, "Animal Sex," 283.

66. For a discussion of Circe as she is treated elsewhere in Christine's corpus, see Blumenfeld-Kosinski, *Reading Myth*, 176–81.

67. For a survey of literary treatments of Circe, see Judith Yarnall, *Transformations of Circe: The History of an Enchantress* (Urbana: University of Illinois Press, 1994).

68. This representation differs significantly in the episode from this narrative selected for visualization in Roman painting, as exemplified by the Odyssey frieze. Here Circe opens the gate of her palace to welcome Odysseus, then pleads for her life after he fails to succumb to her magic potion and exposes her stratagem. Even in its setting, the interior of Circe's palace, the Odyssey painting implies Circe's penetration by the male power visibly signaled in Odysseus's drawn sword. For a representation of this painting as well as a generously illustrated discussion of Circe in ancient art, see Diana Buitron, Beth Cohen, Norman Austin, George Dimock, Thomas Gould, William Mullen, Barry B. Powell, and Michael Simpson, *The Odyssey and Ancient Art: An Epic in Word and Image* (Annandale-on-Hudson: Bard College, 1992), fig. 6 and pp. 77–94.

For a discussion of the Odyssey frieze, see Roger Ling, *Roman Painting* (Cambridge: Cambridge University Press, 1991), 107–12.

69. For a color reproduction of "The Burning of Ilion" in fr. 606, see Meiss, *Limbourgs*, plate vol., pl. 61.

70. Elspeth Probyn, "Queer Belongings: The Politics of Departure," in Grosz and Probyn, *Sexy Bodies*, 9.

71. O'Driscoll, "Outlaw Readings," 36.

72. See Judith L. Kellogg, "Transforming Ovid: The Metamorphosis of Female Authority," in Desmond, *Christine de Pizan*, 181–94.

73. See Sheingorn, "Bodily Embrace."

74. For an overview of ideas about the hermaphrodite through the twelfth century, see Cary J. Nederman and Jacqui True, "The Third Sex: The Idea of the Hermaphrodite in Twelfth-Century Europe," *Journal of the History of Sexuality* 6 (1996): 497–517.

75. "Drawing at once on the *Metamorphoses* of Ovid and the *Achilleid* of Statius, the *Placides et Timéo* confers on the character of Hermaphrodite the power to reveal to men the secrets of women" (Danielle Jacquart and Claude Thomasset, *Sexuality and Medicine in the Middle Ages,* trans. Matthew Adamson [Cambridge: Polity Press, 1988], 141–42). For an edition of *Placides et Timéo,* see *Placides et Timéo ou Li secrés as philosophes,* ed. Claude Thomasset, Textes littéraires français (Geneva: Droz, 1980), along with the commentary volume: Claude Thomasset, *Une Vision du monde à la fin du XIIIᵉ siècle. Commentaire du Dialogue de Placides et Timéo* (Geneva: Droz, 1982). Jacquart and Thomasset emphasize the cultural role of the medieval hermaphrodite: "We would point out that it was clearly stated in the Middle Ages that the character who established and legitimized knowledge concerning women was Hermaphrodite" (216 n. 23).

76. Closest to Christine's understanding would seem to be emblems in later emblem books in which the hermaphrodite is a symbol for marriage. For an example, see "Emblem of Marriage," a woodcut from Bartholemy Aneau, *Picta Poesis* (Lyon, 1552), illustrated in Andrea Raehs, *Zur Ikonographie des Hermaphroditen: Begriff und Problem von Hermaphroditismus und Androgynie in der Kunst,* Europäische Hochschulschriften: Reihe 28, Kunstgeschichte, vol. 113 (Frankfurt am Main: Peter Lang, 1990), fig. 16.

77. For a reproduction of the miniature in the Arsenal manuscript, see Diane Wolfthal, *Images of Rape: The "Heroic" Tradition and Its Alternatives* (Cambridge: Cambridge University Press, 1999), fig. 77.

78. Williams, "Film Bodies," 10.

79. See Sharon Marcus, "Fighting Bodies, Fighting Words: A Theory and Politics of Rape Prevention," in *Feminists Theorize the Political,* ed. Judith Butler and Joan Scott (London: Routledge, 1992), 385–403. For a revisionary treatment of visual images of abduction that mask the violence of rape, see Wolfthal, *Images of Rape.* Wolfthal's reading of Helen in the *Othea,* however, sees Helen as complicit in a way that we do not.

Chapter 4

1. The two manuscripts are BL, Stowe 54 and BnF fr. 301; see George F. Warner and Julius P. Gilson, *Catalogue of Western Manuscripts in the Old Royal and King's Collections,* vol. 2, *Royal Mss. 12 A. I to 20 E. X and App. 1–89* (London: British Museum,

1921), 375–77; François Avril, "Trois manuscrits napolitains des collections de Charles V et de Jean de Berry," *Bibliothèque d'École des Chartes* 127 (1969): 291–328; Hugo Buchthal, *Historia Troiana: Studies in the History of Mediaeval Secular Illustration,* Studies of the Warburg Institute 32 (London: Warburg Institute, 1971); Saxl and Meier, *Verzeichnis astrologischer und mythologischer illustrierter Handschriften;* and Meiss, *Limbourgs.* For a detailed consideration of the relationship between Royal 20 D. I and its copies, see Rouse and Rouse, *Manuscripts and Their Makers,* 293–96.

Royal 20 D. I, fr. 301, and Stowe 54 all belong to the second redaction of the *Histoire ancienne.* See Oltrogge, *Die Illustrationszyklen,* 327.

2. Christiane Raynaud, *La Violence au Moyen Age XIIIe–XVe siècle d'après les Livres d'Histoire en Français* (Paris: Léopard d'or, 1990), 54–56. In a legal context, the presence of blood was often a determining factor in the definition of and judgment of a violent act; see A. J. Finch, "The Nature of Violence in the Middle Ages: An Alternative Perspective," *Historical Research* 70 (1997): 249–68. On the role of law in defining violence as a cultural category, see Lauro Martines, ed., *Violence and Civil Disorder in Italian Cities, 1200–1500* (Berkeley and Los Angeles: University of California Press, 1972), 3–18. In his early-sixteenth-century notebooks Leonardo da Vinci emphasizes that blood signifies a corpse: "make the dead, some half-buried in dust, others with the blood oozing and changing into crimson mud, and let the line of the blood be discerned by its colour, flowing in a sinuous stream from the corpse to the dust" ("The Way to Represent a Battle," *Notebooks of Leonardo da Vinci,* trans. Edward MacCurdy [London: Jonathan Cape, 1938], 2:269–71).

3. Dunlop, "Pigments and Painting Materials," 285.

4. Raynaud, *La Violence,* 56.

5. In *La Violence,* Raynaud notes that head wounds are particularly numerous in manuscripts of this period as a way of acknowledging the unrelenting fierceness of battles by the late fourteenth century, especially during the Hundred Years' War.

6. Warner and Gilson, *Catalogue of Western Manuscripts,* 2:376.

7. The sequence opens with a full-page miniature on fol. 134v showing the city of Troy in the upper half and the battle outside its walls in the lower half. Penthesilea appears in each of the two registers devoted to this battle. In addition to the miniatures reproduced in figs. 4.3 to 4.6, there is another miniature of Penthesilea in battle on fol. 136r.

8. Eisenstein, *Towards a Theory of Montage,* 110.

9. Stephen Prince, *Screening Violence* (New Brunswick, N.J.: Rutgers University Press, 2000), 177.

10. On the instrumentality of violence, see Hannah Arendt, *On Violence* (London: Penguin, 1969).

11. BnF fr. 301, fol. 35v.

12. Eisenstein, *Towards a Theory of Montage,* 145.

13. Teresa de Lauretis, "The Violence of Rhetoric: Considerations on Representation and Gender," in *The Violence of Representation: Literature and the History of Violence,* ed. Nancy Armstrong and Leonard Tennenhouse (London: Routledge, 1989), 249, 250.

14. William Ian Miller discusses the idea that the perception of violence is tied up

with the notions of force; see his *Humiliation and Other Essays on Honor, Social Discomfort, and Violence* (Ithaca, N.Y.: Cornell University Press, 1993), 68.

15. Miller, *Humiliation*, 65; see also Mary Douglas, *Purity and Danger: An Analysis of Concepts of Pollution and Taboo* (London: Routledge and Kegan Paul, 1966).

16. Johann Huizinga, *Homo Ludens: A Study of the Play Element in Culture* (London: Routledge and Kegan Paul, 1949), chap. 5, "Play and War," 89; on the specific rituals of violence in late medieval culture, see Charles V. Phythian-Adams, "Rituals of Personal Confrontation in Late Medieval England," *Bulletin of the John Rylands University Library of Manchester* 73 (1991): 65–90; Juliet Vale, "Violence and the Tournament," in *Violence in Medieval Society,* ed. Richard W. Kaeuper (Woodbridge: Boydell and Brewer, 2000), 143–58.

On approaches to the topic of violence as a theoretical category in medieval culture, see J. R. Hale, "Violence in the Late Middle Ages: A Background," in Martines, *Violence and Civil Disorder,* 19–37; Phillippa C. Maddern, "Viewing Violence: The Conceptual Context of Violence in Fifteenth-Century England," in *Violence and the Social Order: East Anglia, 1422–1442* (Oxford: Oxford University Press, 1992), 75–110; Peter Haidu, *The Subject of Violence: The Song of Roland and the Birth of the State* (Bloomington: Indiana University Press, 1993); Richard W. Kaeuper, *Chivalry and Violence in Medieval Europe* (Oxford: Oxford University Press, 1999); Richard W. Kaeuper, "Chivalry and the Civilising Process," in *Violence in Medieval Society,* ed. Kaeuper, 21–35. See also Jody Enders, *The Medieval Theater of Cruelty: Rhetoric, Memory, Violence* (Ithaca, N.Y.: Cornell University Press, 1999). For Enders, the category of violence is largely confined to torture.

For theoretical approaches to violence, see David Riches, "The Phenomenon of Violence," in *The Anthropology of Violence,* ed. David Riches (Oxford: Oxford University Press, 1987), 2–27; see also Arthur Kleinman, "The Violences of Everyday Life: The Multiple Forms and Dynamics of Social Violence," in *Violence and Subjectivity,* ed. Veena Das, Arthur Kleinman, Mamphela Ramphele, and Paula Reynolds (Berkeley and Los Angeles: University of California Press, 2000), 226–41; and Beatrice Hanssen, *Critique of Violence: Between Poststructuralism and Critical Theory* (London: Routledge, 2000).

17. René Girard, *Violence and the Sacred,* trans. Patrick Gregory (Baltimore: Johns Hopkins University Press, 1977).

18. De Lauretis, "The Violence of Rhetoric," 250. For a further critique of Girard's lack of attention to gender as well as of the monolithic character of his formulations, see Nancy Jay, *Throughout Your Generations Forever: Sacrifice, Religion, and Paternity* (Chicago: University of Chicago Press, 1992), 130–31.

19. For a discussion of Daphne's metamorphosis in the *Othea,* see Diane Wolfthal, "'Douleur sur toutes autres': Revisualizing the Rape Script in the *Epistre Othea* and the *Cité des dames,*" in Desmond, *Christine de Pizan,* 41–70; see also Wolfthal, *Images of Rape,* 127–50.

20. Giorgio Agamben, *Homo Sacer: Sovereign Power and Bare Life,* trans. Daniel Heller-Roazen (Stanford: Stanford University Press, 1998), 89.

21. Agamben excludes from the political sphere "the power to kill, which lies within the competence of the father or the husband who catches his wife or daughter in the act of adultery." For him, this power "concern[s] the domestic jurisdiction of the head

of the family and therefore remain[s], in some way, within the sphere of the *domus*" (*Homo Sacer*, 88). The *Othea* insistently recognizes that the domestic, or personal, is political. As Henrietta Moore frames the question: "Is violence between the sexes instrumental in converting gender difference into gender hierarchy?" ("The Problem of Explaining Violence in the Social Sciences," in *Sex and Violence: Issues in Representation*, ed. Penelope Harvey and Peter Gow [London: Routledge, 1994], 138).

22. For another example, Memnon attacking Achilles, see the illustrations to chap. 36 in the Duke's and the Queen's manuscripts (Hindman, *Painting and Politics*, figs. 32 and 33).

23. Specifically, the attack to the head while the victim is kneeling at an altar recalls the martyrdom of Thomas Becket; see Tancred Borenius, *St. Thomas Becket in Art* (1932; reprint, Port Washington, N.Y.: Kennikat Press, 1970).

24. For a reproduction of this folio in the Queen's manuscript, see Hindman, *Painting and Politics*, fig. 35. Hindman reads the image of Hecuba as a lesson in "bad queenship" (122). However, in the context of the strategies required in a city under siege, Hecuba's role in the murder of Achilles would seem to be an example of excellent queenship, since she manages to have the foremost enemy of Troy killed.

25. The relationship of this miniature to the *Othea* Busiris has been overlooked; in her concordance of subjects, Hindman provides no visual analogue for the Busiris image (*Painting and Politics*, 199).

26. Nicole Oresme employs the term *homicide* in his translation of Aristotle's *Politics;* see his gloss to chap. 9. Nicole Oresme, *Le Livre de Politiques d'Aristote*, ed. Albert Douglas Menut, Transactions of the American Philosophical Society (Philadelphia, 1970), 87.

27. Meyer Schapiro, *Words, Script, and Pictures: Semiotics of Visual Language* (New York: George Braziller, 1996): "[The profile] is, broadly speaking, like the grammatical form of the third person, the impersonal 'he' or 'she' with its concordantly inflected verb; while the face turned outward is credited with intentness, a latent or potential glance directed to the observer, and corresponds to the role of 'I' in speech, with its complementary 'you'" (73). Schapiro refers to "the duality of profile and frontal as paired carriers of opposed meanings" (75), and remarks, "Throughout medieval Christian art [the frontal form] marks what I have called the theme of state and is applied not only in theophanies but to royal persons as well" (76).

28. On the Amazons as one of the monstrous races, see John Block Friedman, *The Monstrous Races in Medieval Art and Thought* (Cambridge: Harvard University Press, 1981), 8–9.

29. In the *Livre de la cité des dames*, Christine explains that the word *Amazon* denotes a woman who has "had her breast removed" (book 1, 16). For a discussion of the location of the Amazons at the border between civilization and the barbarians (as guardians of the gate that Alexander the Great constructed across the Caspian mountains) and the related notion of the Amazons' involvement in the end time (because among those behind the gate are Gog and Magog, whose release signals the beginning of Armageddon), see Vincent DiMarco, "The Amazons and the End of the World," in *Discovering New Worlds: Essays on Medieval Exploration and Imagination*, ed. Scott D. Westrem (New York: Garland, 1991), 69–90.

30. As Anne Derbes shows, the versions of the *Histoire ancienne* produced in Acre in the late thirteenth century show an intense interest in the Amazons, which Derbes reads as the result of crusader appropriation of Trojan mythology. Anne Derbes and Mark Sandona, "Amazons and Crusaders: The *Histoire Universelle* in Flanders and the Holy Land," in *France and the Holy Land: Frankish Culture at the End of the Crusades,* ed. Daniel Weiss (Baltimore: Johns Hopkins University Press, 2003).

31. On the appropriation of the Trojan myth to justify the Crusades, see Colette Beaune, *The Birth of an Ideology: Myths and Symbols of Nation in Late-Medieval France,* trans. Susan Ross Huston, ed. Fredric L. Cheyette (Berkeley and Los Angeles: University of California Press, 1991), 234–40.

32. A miniature in Royal 20 D. I (fol. 218v) also depicts Thamyris in profile at the far right of a page, gesturing toward Cyrus, who stands before her with his hands tied.

33. See, for example, the death of Holofernes in *Histoire ancienne,* Copenhagen, Thott 431, vol. 2, fol. 112; and Judith decapitating Holofernes in *Histoire ancienne,* BnF fr. 301, fol. 118v; both of these manuscripts were in libraries accessible to Christine, one in the royal library of Charles V and the other purchased by the duke of Berry in 1402.

34. For medieval representations of Judith, see Leslie Abend Callahan, "Ambiguity and Appropriation: The Story of Judith in Medieval Narrative and Iconographic Traditions," in *Telling Tales: Medieval Narratives and the Folk Tradition,* ed. Francesca Canadé Sautman, Diana Conchado, and Giuseppe Carlo Di Scipio (New York: St. Martin's, 1998), 79–99 and the bibliography cited there.

35. Of course, the tent appears in other contexts as well. For example, in representations of God the Father enthroned, and specifically in the Throne of Grace Trinity, he may be seated within a tent that signifies the tent of the Covenant, with its sides pulled back by angels to reveal him. For examples see Gyöngyi Török, "Beiträge zur Verbreitung einer Niederländischen Dreifaltigkeitsdarstellung im 15. Jahrhundert. Eine Elfenbeintafel aus dem Besitze Philipps des Guten von Burgund," *Jahrbuch der kunsthistorischen Sammlungen in Wien* 81 (1985): 7–31, figs. 1, 15–17. Török attributes the innovation of the holy tent to the Master of Flemalle (17–18).

36. Miller, *Humiliation,* 220.

37. Campbell, *L'Épître d'Othéa,* 90.

38. See Willard, "Art of Warfare," 14.

39. Christine de Pizan, *The Book of Fayttes of Armes and of Chyualrye: Translated and Printed by William Caxton from the French Original by Christine de Pisan,* ed. A. T. P. Byles, Early English Text Society 189 (London: Oxford University Press, 1932), 7. For the translation, see Christine de Pizan, *The Book of Deeds of Arms and of Chivalry,* trans. Sumner Willard, ed. Charity Cannon Willard (University Park: Pennsylvania State University Press, 1999).

Chapter 5

1. Although she does not include the *Othea* in her discussion, Liliane Dulac identifies a concrete, visual quality in Christine's writing that is exemplified in her use of gesture; textual descriptions of gestures function as signs, revealing a person's inner thoughts, true nature, or emotion ("La Gestuelle chez Christine de Pizan: Quelques

aperçus," in Hicks, *Au Champ des escriptures,* 609–26). A similar attention to gesture in the miniatures of the *Othea* underscores the interrelation of text and image in the early manuscripts of the *Othea.*

2. Jody Enders emphasizes the performative dimension of gesture: "In the all too discrete histories of rhetoric and drama, a vast body of evidence attests to the status of gesture as a highly dramatic, metadramatic, and potentially performative language. It was a language, moreover, in which the Middle Ages was both knowledgeable and fluent, for it counted amongst its most expert practitioners orators, lawyers, artists, dramatists, and actors" (Jody Enders, "Of Miming and Signing: The Dramatic Rhetoric of Gesture," in *Gesture in Medieval Drama and Art,* ed. Clifford Davidson (Kalamazoo, Mich.: Medieval Institute Publications, 2001), 2.

3. In her introduction to *Anger's Past: The Social Uses of an Emotion in the Middle Ages* (Ithaca, N.Y.: Cornell University Press, 1998), editor Barbara H. Rosenwein describes the collection as "the first book explicitly devoted to the history of anger in the medieval West" (1). In her concluding essay, "Controlling Paradigms," she acknowledges that the category of gender was not explored in the collection, although "we are justified in speaking of male and female anger if by that we intend to understand how gendered emotion is constructed" (246). See also Rosenwein's review essay, "Worrying about Emotions in History," *American Historical Review* 107 (2002): 821–45.

4. Jean de Montreuil's treatise does not survive; in his introduction to Christine de Pizan et al., *Le Débat,* Eric Hicks states that Christine's *Epistre au dieu d'Amours* "n'a rien d'un *document polémique*" (xxxii) and identifies de Montreuil's lost treatise as the first document in the *querelle.*

5. Joan W. Scott, "'Experience,'" in Butler and Scott, *Feminists Theorize the Political,* 22–40.

6. Satya P. Mohanty, "The Epistemic Status of Cultural Identity: On *Beloved* and the Postcolonial Condition," in *Reclaiming Identity: Realist Theory and the Predicament of Postmodernism,* ed. Paula M. L. Moya and Michael R. Hames-García (Berkeley and Los Angeles: University of California Press, 2000), 55.

7. Christine de Pizan et al., *Le Débat,* 11–22. For a discussion of Christine's prose style, see Fenster, "Perdre son latin"; and for an analysis of the *querelle* in the tradition of disputing women, see Solterer, *Master and Minerva,* 151–61.

8. For the topos of assumed modesty, see Ernst Robert Curtius, *European Literature and the Latin Middle Ages,* trans. Willard R. Trask (New York: Pantheon, 1953), 83–85.

9. Our translation; the translation offered by Baird and Kane (Christine de Pizan, et al., *La Querelle*) generally softens the anger and critique in Christine's contributions to the debate.

10. Solterer, *Master and Minerva,* 154.

11. In the Duke's manuscript, the *Epistles* on the *Rose* appear just before the *Othea;* in the Queen's manuscript, the *Epistles* appear later. See Laidlaw, "Publisher's Progress," 70–73.

12. In contemporary discourse, a parallel and equally dismissive move to the accusation of anger is the accusation of censorship. Thus in an analysis of Christine's and Jean Gerson's participation in the *Rose* debate, David F. Hult writes, "So whereas Christine's overt motivations cannot be flatly assimilated to those of a 1990s feminist such as

MacKinnon, whose aim first and foremost is to protect women as a class, what I will be attempting to show is that the impulse to censor itself displays deeply rooted similarities in the two authors" ("Words and Deeds: Jean de Meun's *Romance of the Rose* and the Hermeneutics of Censorship," *New Literary History* 28 [1997]: 356). Hult attacks Christine's "assumed modesty," commenting that it "can be read as a model of bad faith" (356), which fails to recognize that it was virtually the only rhetorical strategy available to a woman writer. For an explication of the rhetorical constraints operative in the epistolary structures of the debate, see Desmond, "Ethics of Reading."

13. For a photograph of the miniature of Temperance in fr. 606, see Meiss, *Limbourgs,* fig. 127. Meiss points out that the clock is not mentioned in the text of the *Othea* and attributes its presence in the miniature in fr. 848 to "explicit instructions of Christine. . . . She formulated the analogy, in other words, after writing the text of fr. 848 but before she gave instructions to the illuminator. She incorporated the explanation of the new iconography in her text when, shortly afterward, she revised the *Epître* and added the long descriptive rubrics before several miniatures" (Meiss, *Limbourgs,* 34).

14. As Campbell points out (*L'Epître d'Othéa,* 111–12), all of Christine's material in this chapter could come either from the *Ovide moralisé* or from Ovid, with the exception of the detail about Arachne's work. In both Ovid and the *Ovide moralisé,* Pallas emphasizes that Arachne and all her descendants will always be spiders.

15. In Ovid, the situation in which humans behave inhumanly is rectified by their transformation; as William S. Anderson puts it, "The inhuman reaction of the rustics earns them their loss of humanity by metamorphosis" (Ovid, *Ovid's Metamorphoses,* 199). In the *Othea* the contrast is between nobility and peasantry, and since the base behavior of the peasants correlates with their class from the beginning, there is no need for metamorphosis to rectify the situation. The *allegorie* of this chapter tells the good spirit that the "vilains" who became frogs signify the sin of avarice. Schoell-Glass offers an explanation for the change from the moralization of the frogs as the sin of gluttony in the *Ovide moralisé* and argues that there are visual references to avarice in the miniatures to this chapter of the *Othea* ("Verwandlungen der Metamorphosen," 40–41).

16. "Let us now allegorize for our purpose the seven deadly sins" [Or ferons allegorie a nostre propos, applicant aux .vij. pechez mortieulx] (16.20–21). In this chapter Narcissus is read as an example of the sin of pride, initiating the sequence of the seven deadly sins that continues through the next six chapters.

17. The Douce Medea appears to be based on the same pattern as an illustration of Medea in a mid-fourteenth-century manuscript of the *Rose,* Paris, Bib. Ste.-Geneviève 1126, fol. 95r.

18. This image incorporates a folklore motif regarding the inefficacy of planting boiled grain seed that enters the Ino story in the *Ovide moralisé* version. See Stith Thompson, *Motif-Index of Folk-Literature,* 6 vols. (Bloomington: Indiana University Press, 1955), H1023.1.1. Countertask: sowing cooked seeds and harvesting the crop; J1932.1. Numbskulls sow cooked grain.

19. For a discussion of medieval theological responses to anger, see Maureen Flynn, "Taming Anger's Daughters: New Treatment for Emotional Problems in Renaissance Spain," *Renaissance Quarterly* 51, no. 3 (1998): 864–72.

20. For copies of the *Éthiques* accessible to Christine in Paris, and for evidence that

Christine had read Oresme's translations of Aristotle, see Sylvie Lefèvre, "Christine de Pizan et l'Aristote oresmien," in Hicks, *Au Champ des escriptures,* 231–50, esp. 235.

21. "Car quiconques ne se courrouce pour les causes pour quoy il se convient courroucier et qui ne se courrouce en la maniere que il se convient courroucier, et qui ne le fait quant il appartient et qui ne le fait contre ceuls contre lesquelz il appartient, ce est fait et condicion de fol et de non scené, pour ce qu'il semble que tel homme ne sente ne apparçoive mal qui le adviengne et que il ne ait pour ce quelconques tristece. Item, quiconques ne se courrouce aucune fois, il ne veult nulle venjance. Item, soustenir celui qui est injurieus et fait injures et despite ses familiers, c'est condicion miserable et servile" (Oresme, *Livre de éthiques,* ed. Menut, book 4, chap. 20).

22. D. W. Robertson Jr., *Preface to Chaucer* (Princeton: Princeton University Press, 1962), 264. Irving Lavin's reference to Christine as "the famous fourteenth-century suffragette" is no less dismissive, and given the association in the popular mind of women involved in the suffrage movement with aggression and lack of femininity, it is arguable that Lavin also meant to characterize Christine as an angry woman (Irving Lavin, "Cephalus and Procris: Transformations of an Ovidian Myth," *Journal of the Warburg and Courtauld Institutes* 17 [1954]: 264).

23. Susan Noakes, *Timely Reading: Between Exegesis and Interpretation* (Ithaca, N.Y.: Cornell University Press, 1988), 118.

24. On medieval rewritings of the Troy story, especially those that understood the Trojans to be descendants of various European peoples, see František Graus, "Troja und trojanische Herkunftssage im Mittelalter," in *Kontinuität und Transformation der Antike im Mittelalter. Veröffentlichung der Kongressakten zum Freiburger Symposion des Mediävistenverbandes,* ed. Willi Erzgräber (Sigmaringen: Jan Thorbecke Verlag, 1989), 25–43. On the appropriation of this material into French history, see Gabrielle M. Spiegel, *Romancing the Past: The Rise of Vernacular Prose Historiography in Thirteenth-Century France* (Berkeley and Los Angeles: University of California Press, 1993). On its political uses, see Beaune, *Birth of an Ideology,* 226–44.

25. Agamben, "Notes on Gesture," 56.

26. For Hindman (*Painting and Politics*) the Trojan material from chap. 88 to the end in the Queen's manuscript (Harley 4431) takes on a clear political message for Isabeau regarding good government. On this point see also Patrick M. de Winter, "Christine de Pizan: Ses enlumineurs et ses rapports avec le milieu bourguignon," in *Actes du 104ᵉ Congrès National des Sociétés Savantes* (Bordeaux 1979) (Paris: Bibliothèque Nationale, 1982), 335–75. Susan Noakes argues that the Hector biography is not the point of the *Othea;* she suggests rather that a "new continuity, a new reading time" emerges from the allegorical level, which distances the reader from the seductions of the text (*Timely Reading,* 128). Roberta Krueger sees the death of Hector as "the central irony" of the *Othea* because Hector as the addressee does not heed the lessons of Othea ("Christine's Anxious Lessons: Gender, Morality, and the Social Order from the *Enseignemens* to the *Avison*," in Desmond, *Christine de Pizan,* 21).

27. Spiegel, *Romancing the Past,* 116.

28. Hindman, *Painting and Politics,* 89–97.

29. On the function of the fantasy scenario in the construction of identity, see Joan

Scott, "Fantasy Echo: History and the Construction of Identity," *Critical Inquiry* 27 (2001): 284–304.

30. Campbell notes that Christine used both the *Ovide moralisé* and the *Histoire ancienne* as sources for her Io material (*L'Épître d'Othéa*, 129–30). Guyart des Moulins's *Bible historiale* identifies Isis as the goddess who taught the Egyptians the letters of the alphabet and the art of writing (Seznec, *Survival*, 16).

31. See Christine de Pizan, *Epistre Othea*, ed. Parussa, 409 n. a.

32. For an explanation of Christine's naming of her sibyl, see Parussa's edition of the *Othea*, 453–55.

33. Medieval Latin drama rehearses the authority of sibylline prophecy as a gendered interpretive tradition. Dramatic performances of a type of text known as the *Ordo Prophetarum* were based on a sermon attributed to Augustine entitled *Contra Judaeos, Paganos, et Arianos Sermo de Symbolo*. A sibyl is included among the prophets. See Karl Young, *The Drama of the Medieval Church*, 2 vols. (Oxford: Clarendon, 1933), vol. 2, chap. 21. For an argument that the 360-line sibylline prophecy in the manuscript of the Anglo-Norman play *Jeu d'Adam* should be understood as "poetically and dramatically a true culmination" rather than extraneous to an unfinished playtext, see Peter Dronke, "Medieval Sibyls: Their Character and Their 'Auctoritas,'" *Studi Medievali*, 3d ser. 36 (1995): 581–615.

34. Images of a sibyl appear in the Arsenal manuscript on the following folios: Cumaean Sibyl, 199r, 199v, 203r; the ten sibyls, 200r; Tibertine Sibyl, 201r, 203r. For representations of sibyls in the Rouen manuscript, see the Cumaean Sibyl, 355v, and the ten sibyls, 357r.

35. For an extensive discussion of the *Brussels Hours*, see Meiss, *Late Fourteenth Century*, 194–246, and for a discussion of the *ara coeli*, see 233–35.

36. "This vision began to be represented in France in the late fourteenth century, and the duke of Berry became its chief sponsor. He introduced it into his Books of Hours, beginning with the one now in Brussels, and in the *Belles Heures* it provides a novel illustration for one of the two common prayers to the Virgin. Its connection with this prayer—*O Intemerata*—confirms our thought that the Duke favored the subject because he liked to associate himself with the Emperor Augustus, for the illustration of the prayer often showed the donor, not the Emperor, kneeling before the Virgin." See the commentary to fol. 26v in Millard Meiss and Elizabeth H. Beatson, *The Belles Heures of Jean, Duke of Berry* (New York: Braziller, 1974); see also Meiss, *Late Fourteenth Century*, 232–35.

37. For Cassandra, see Hindman, *Painting and Politics*, 130.

38. On the styles of the artists who participated in painting the Othea miniatures, Charles Sterling's comments are helpful: "L'illustration du ms. fr. 606 a été dirigée et en grande partie exécutée par le Maître de *L'Epître d'Othéa*. La dernière miniature représentant l'*Ara Coeli* est de la main de l'artiste que R. Schilling baptisa le Maître du Egerton 1070 (Londres, British Library), enlumineur sans doute néerlandais établi à Paris, dont l'art est intéressant mais sans rapport avec celui du Maître de l'Epître. Tel n'est pas le cas d'un peintre que M. Meiss a fini par appeler le *Maître au safran* (the Saffron Master) à cause de sa prédilection pour cette tonalité du jaune. M. Meiss lui

attribue une dizaine de miniatures dans le ms. fr. 606 (1974, p. 36). Après l'avoir considéré comme un 'associate' du Maître de l'Epître (M. Meiss 1968, Fig. 478), il l'en éloigna. Ce divorce ne me paraît pas heureux. L'esprit de liberté technique et picturale qui a permis au *Maître au safran* de créer la frappante image de *L'Aurore amenant le soleil* est celui qu'introduisit à Paris le grand enlumineur de Christine. Originaire très probablement de Pays-Bas, le *Maître au safran* était nourri d'un naïf appétit du réalisme et de l'expression lyrique au mépris de toute stylisation" (*La Peinture médiévale,* 1:315–16).

39. For an edition of this text, see Angus J. Kennedy, ed., "*La Lamentacion sur les maux de la France* de Christine de Pisan," in *Mélanges de langue et littérature françaises du Moyen Age et de la Renaissance offerts à Charles Foulon* (Rennes: Université de Haute-Bretagne, 1980), 1:177–85. For a translation, see "The Lamentation on the Evils That Have Befallen France," in Christine de Pizan, *Selected Writings,* ed. Blumenfeld-Kosinski, 224–29.

Afterword

1. These are BnF, fr. 606; BL, Harley 4431; Cambridge, Newnham College Library, MS 900 (5); Erlangen-Nürnberg, Universitäts-Bibliothek, MS 2361; Aylesbury, Buckinghamshire, Waddesdon Manor, MS 8; BR, MS 9392; Oxford, Bodleian Library, Bodley 421; Lille, Bibl. mun. Jean Levy, MS 175; Cologny, Foundation Bodmer, MS 49; and The Hague, Koninklijke Bibliotheek, MS 74 G 27. Beauvais, Bibl. mun., MS 9, was planned for one hundred illustrations, of which only forty were drawn in ink. On these manuscripts, see the relevant catalog entries in Mombello, *La tradizione manoscritta* and the discussions in Schoell-Glass, "Aspekte der Antikenrezeption."

2. On this manuscript, see Mombello, *La tradizione manoscritta,* 182–86; and Schoell-Glass, "Aspekte der Antikenrezeption," 145–55.

3. On Lille, MS 175, see Schoell-Glass, "Aspekte der Antikenrezeption," 157–63; Patrick M. de Winter, "Manuscrits à peintures produits pour le mécénat Lillois sous les règnes de Jean sans Peur et de Philippe le Bon," in *Actes du 101ᵉ Congrès National des Sociétés Savantes* (Lille 1976) (Paris: Bibliothèque Nationale, 1978), 254–56. De Winter observes that the artist knew well the work he was illustrating (254). See also Jacques Lemaire, "Les manuscrits Lillois de Christine de Pizan. Comparaison matérielle entre les copies Lille, Bibliothèque Municipale 175 et Oxford, Bodley 421," in *Contexts and Continuities,* ed. Kennedy, Brown-Grant, Laidlaw, and Müller, 2:531–48.

4. See François Avril, "Le dessin colorié dans le nord de la France," in François Avril and Nicole Reynaud, *Les manuscrits à peintures en France, 1440–1520* (Paris: Flammarion-Bibliothèque Nationale, 1993), 98–103.

5. For Erlangen-Nürnberg, Universitäts-Bibliothek, MS 2361, see Christine de Pizan, *L'Epistre d'Othéa,* intro. Lengenfelder; Mombello, *La tradizione manoscritta,* 186–89; and Schoell-Glass, "Aspekte der Antikenrezeption," 115–29. Schoell-Glass suggests that Isabelle of Portugal, duchess of Burgundy, may have commissioned this manuscript as a gift for her son, the future Charles the Bold (120–21).

6. Waddesdon Manor, MS 8 contains the Miélot version of the text, which was copied into the manuscript as early as ca. 1455, and a visual program dating from the

end of the fifteenth century; a number of the images in this manuscript are reversed copies of Liédet's illustrations in BR, MS 9392. On MS 8 see the catalog entry by James Marrow in L. M. J. Delaissé, James Marrow, and John de Wit, *The James A. de Rothschild Collection at Waddesdon Manor: Illuminated Manuscripts* (Fribourg: Office du Livre, 1977), 154–80; Schoell-Glass, "Aspekte der Antikenrezeption," 138–40; Mombello did not see this manuscript and knew only that it had been sold at Sotheby's in 1825 (*La tradizione manoscritta*, 221–22).

7. For example, BnF fr. 1185, which was made in Bruges during the 1460s, contains only the *Othea* (in the text version classified by Mombello as D III). Its only miniature shows the goddess Othea presenting her book to Hector. For a photograph of this miniature, see Schaefer, "Die Illustrationen," 175, fig. 88. A manuscript made in Ghent or Bruges and preserving a closely related version of the *Othea* text, BnF fr. 25559, also has only one miniature. In this scene, the goddess Othea gestures from a castle toward two figures, one of whom—apparently her page—presents a book to a knight. For a photograph, see Schaefer, "Die Illustrationen," 175, fig. 89.

8. On MS 9559-64, see Mombello, *La tradizione manoscritta*, 153–64. On MS IV 1114, see catalog entry 38 in *Cinq Années d'acquisitions 1974–1978: Exposition organisée à la Bibliothèque Royale Albert Ier du 24 Septembre au 31 octobre 1979* (Brussels: Bibliothèque Albert Ier, 1979), 81–86.

9. For a comprehensive overview that demonstrates the significance of printed versions of Christine de Pizan's works, see Brown, "Reconstruction of an Author."

10. Further, as Mombello points out, the text in Pigouchet shares many errors and variants with Newnham and Beauvais.

11. The cuts for chaps. 31 and 92 are interchanged, as are the cuts for chaps. 66 and 94.

12. Le Noir uses non-Pigouchet cuts for seven chapters.

13. For instance, for chap. 37 (Laomedon) Pigouchet uses a block that belongs to chap. 46 (Thydeus and Polinices) and that is repeated there; Wyer does likewise; for chap. 69 (Actaeon seeing Diana in bath), Wyer has a woodcut of a woman in a bath, as does Pigouchet, whereas Le Noir uses a block from Pigouchet's chap. 86 (Narcissus and Echo).

14. Christine de Pizan, *The Epistle of Othea*, trans. Scrope, ed. Bühler. For a description of manuscripts of Scrope's translation, see xiv–xvi.

15. Christine de Pizan, *The Epistle of Othea to Hector*, ed. Gordon.

16. See Percy G. C. Campbell, "Christine de Pisan en Angleterre," *Revue de littérature comparée* 5 (1925): 659–70; Laurie A. Finke, "Christine de Pizan in England," in *Women's Writing in English: Medieval England* (London: Longman's, 1999); see also Jennifer Summit, *Lost Property: The Woman Writer and English Literary History, 1380–1589* (Chicago: University of Chicago Press, 2000). Summit's analysis of Scrope's translation fails to see how much Scrope's interest in chivalry and masculinity derives from the French original that he undertook to translate.

Bibliography

৩৭৩৫

Manuscripts

Aylesbury, Buckinghamshire, Waddesdon Manor, MS 8.

Besançon, Bibliothèque municipale, MS 677.

Brussels, Bibliothèque royale de Belgique, MS 9242, MS 9392, MS 11060-1.

Cambridge, Newnham College, MS 900 (5).

Copenhagen, Kongelige Bibliotek, Thott 431.

Erlangen-Nürnberg, Universitäts-Bibliothek, MS 2361.

The Hague, Koninklijke Bibliotheek, MS 74 G 27.

Lille, Bibliothèque municipale Jean Levy, MS 175.

London, British Library, Add. 10324, Harley 219, Harley 4431, Royal 14 E. II, Royal 16 G. V, Royal 17 E. IV, Royal 20 D. I, Stowe 54.

Los Angeles, J. Paul Getty Library, 83.MR.177 (Ludwig XV 7).

Lyon, Bibliothèque municipale, MS 742.

Munich, Bayerisches Staatsbibliothek, ms. gall. 11.

New York, Metropolitan Museum of Art, Cloisters Collection, *Belles Heures of Jean, duke of Berry,* Pierpont Morgan Library, M.48, M.785.

Oxford, Bodleian Library, Bodley 421, Bodley 614, Douce 371.

Paris, Bibliothèque de l'Arsenal, MS 5069.

Paris, Bibliothèque nationale de France, fr. 246, fr. 301, fr. 380, fr. 598, fr. 606, fr. 848, fr. 12420.

Rouen, Bibliothèque municipale, O.4.

València, Universitat de València, Biblioteca Històrica, MS 1327.

Primary Sources

Abū Maʿšar. *The Abbreviation of the Introduction to Astrology together with the Medieval Latin Translation of Adelard of Bath.* Ed. and trans. Charles Burnett, Keiji Yamamoto, and Michio Yano. Leiden: Brill, 1994.

Boccaccio, Giovanni. *Diana's Hunt, Caccia di Diana: Boccaccio's First Fiction.* Ed. and trans. Anthony K. Cassell and Victoria Kirkham. Philadelphia: University of Pennsylvania Press, 1991.

———. *"Des Cleres et Nobles Femmes," Ms. Bibl. Nat. 112420.* Ed. Jeanne Baroin and Josiane Haffen. Paris: Belles Lettres, 1993–95.

———. *Famous Women.* Ed. and trans. Virginia Brown. I Tatti Renaissance Library 1. Cambridge: Harvard University Press, 2001.

———. *Tutte le opere di Giovanni Boccaccio.* Ed. Vittore Branca. Vol. 10, *De mulieribus claris.* Ed. and trans. V. Zaccaria. 2d ed. Milan: Mondadori, 1970.

Christine de Pizan. *The Book of Deeds of Arms and of Chivalry.* Trans. Sumner Willard. Ed. Charity Cannon Willard. University Park: Pennsylvania State University Press, 1999.

———. *The Book of Fayttes of Armes and of Chyualrye: Translated and Printed by William Caxton from the French Original by Christine de Pisan.* Ed. A. T. P. Byles. Early English Text Society 189. London: Oxford University Press, 1932.

———. *The Book of the Body Politic.* Ed. and trans. Kate Langdon Forhan. Cambridge: Cambridge University Press, 1994.

———. *The C. Hystoryes of Troye.* Charing Cross: Robert Wyer, 1536–45.

———. *Les cent Histoires de Troye.* Paris: Philippe Pigouchet, 1499/1500.

———. *The Epistle of Othea.* Trans. Stephen Scrope. Ed. Curt F. Bühler. Early English Text Society 264. London: Oxford University Press, 1970.

———. *The Epistle of Othea to Hector: A 'lytil bibell of knyghthod'.* Ed. James D. Gordon. Philadelphia: University of Pennsylvania, 1942.

———. *Epistre au dieu d'Amours* in *Poems of Cupid, God of Love.* Ed. Thelma Fenster and Mary Carpenter Erler. Leiden: Brill, 1990.

———. *L'Epistre d'Othéa.* Color microfiche edition of the manuscript Erlangen-Nürnberg, Universitäts-Bibliothek, Ms. 2361. Intro. Helga Lengenfelder. Codices illuminati medii aevi 31. Munich: Edition Helga Lengenfelder, 1996.

———. *Epistre Othea. Edition critique.* Ed. Gabriella Parussa. Geneva: Droz, 1999.

———. *"La Lamentacion sur les maux de la France* de Christine de Pisan." Ed. Angus J. Kennedy. In *Mélanges de langue et littérature françaises du Moyen Age et de la Renaissance offerts à Charles Foulon,* 1:177–85. Rennes: Université de Haute-Bretagne, 1980.

———. *Le Livre de la cité des dames/La citt'delle dame.* Ed. Earl Jeffrey Richards. Italian translation by Patricia Caraffi. Milan: Luna editrice, 1997.

———. *Le Livre du corps de policie.* Ed. Angus J. Kennedy. Paris: Honoré Champion, 1998.

———. *Oeuvres poétiques de Christine de Pisan.* Ed. Maurice Roy. 3 vols. Paris: Firmin Didot, 1886–96.

———. *The Selected Writings of Christine de Pizan.* Trans. Renate Blumenfeld-Kosinski and Kevin Brownlee. Ed. Renate Blumenfeld-Kosinski. New York: Norton, 1997.

———. *The Writings of Christine de Pizan.* Ed. Charity Cannon Willard. New York: Persea Books, 1994.

Christine de Pizan, Jean Gerson, Jean de Montreuil, Gontier and Pierre Col. *Le Débat sur le Roman de la Rose.* Ed. and trans. Eric Hicks. 1977; reprint, Geneva: Slatkine Reprints, 1996.

———. *La Querelle de la Rose: Letters and Documents.* Trans. Joseph L. Baird and John R. Kane. Chapel Hill: University of North Carolina Press, 1978.

Dante Alighieri. *The Divine Comedy. Purgatorio,* vol. 1, Italian text and translation. Trans. Charles S. Singleton. Bollingen Series 80. Princeton: Princeton University Press, 1973.

Dürer, Albrecht. *Underweysung der Messung mit dem Zirckel und Richtscheyt....* 1538.

Galbert of Bruges. *The Murder of Charles the Good, Count of Flanders.* Trans. James Bruce Ross. 1960; reprint, Toronto: University of Toronto Press, 1982.

Gerson, Jean. *Early Works.* Trans. Brian Patrick McGuire. New York: Paulist Press, 1998.

Guido da Pisa. *Expositiones et Glose super Comediam Dantis or Commentary on Dante's Inferno.* Ed. Vincenzo Cioffari. Albany: State University of New York Press, 1974.

Guillaume de Conches. *Glosae in Iuvenalem.* Ed. Bradford Wilson. Paris: J. Vrin, 1980.

Guillaume de Lorris and Jean de Meun. *Le Roman de la rose.* Ed. Félix Lecoy. 3 vols. Classiques Français du Moyen Age. Paris: Champion, 1966–75.

———. *The Romance of the Rose.* Trans. Frances Horgan. Oxford: Oxford University Press, 1994.

Leonardo da Vinci. "The Way to Represent a Battle." In *Notebooks of Leonardo da Vinci,* trans. Edward MacCurdy. 2 vols. London: Jonathan Cape, 1938.

The Life of Christina of Markyate: A Twelfth-Century Recluse. Trans. and ed. C. H. Talbot. Oxford: Oxford University Press, 1959.

Loukopoulos, Halina Didycky. "Classical Mythology in the Works of Christine de Pisan, with an Edition of *L'Epistre Othea* from the Manuscript Harley 4431." Ph.D. diss., Wayne State University, 1977.

Machaut, Guillaume de. *Le Confort d'ami (Comfort for a Friend).* Trans. and ed. R. Barton Palmer. New York: Garland, 1992.

———. *Le Livre dou Voir Dit (The Book of the True Poem).* Trans. R. Barton Palmer. Ed. Daniel Leech-Wilkinson. New York: Garland, 1998.

Mariken van Nieumeghen: A Bilingual Edition. Trans. and ed. Therese Decker and Martin W. Walsh. Columbia, S.C.: Camden House, 1994.

Meyer, Paul. "Les Premières Compilations françaises d'histoire ancienne. 1. Les faits des romains. 11. Histoire ancienne jusqu'à César." *Romania* 14 (1885): 1–81.

Mythographi Vaticani I et II. Ed. Péter Kulcsár. CCSL no. 91c. Turnhout: Brepols, 1987.

Oresme, Nicole. *Le Livre de éthiques d'Aristote.* Ed. Albert Douglas Menut. New York: Stechert, 1940.

———. *Le Livre de Politiques d'Aristote.* Ed. Albert Douglas Menut. Transactions of the American Philosophical Society, Philadelphia, 1970.

Ovid. *Metamorphoses.* Ed. William S. Anderson. Leipzig: Teubner, 1977.

Ovide moralisé. Poème du commencement du quatorzième siècle, publié d'après tous les manuscrits connus. Ed. Cornelius de Boer et al. *Verhandelingen der Koninklijke Akademie van Wetenschappen te Amsterdam. Afdeeling Letterkunde.* Nieuwe Reeks 15 (1915), 1–374; 21 (1920): 1–394; 30 (1931): 1–303; 37 (1936): 1–478; 43 (1938): 1–429. Reprint in 5 vols., Wiesbaden: Martin Sändig, 1966–68.

Placides et Timéo ou Li secrés as philosophes. Textes littéraires français. Ed. Claude Thomasset. Geneva: Droz, 1980.

Roesner, Edward H., François Avril, and Nancy Freeman Regalado. *Le Roman de Fauvel in the Edition of Mesire Chaillou de Pesstain: A Reproduction in Facsimile of the Complete Manuscript, Paris, Bibliothèque Nationale, Fonds Français 146.* New York: Broude Brothers, 1990.

Salverda de Grave, J.-J. *Enéas: Roman du XIIe siècle.* Paris: Champion, 1983.

Secondary Sources

Agamben, Giorgio. *Homo Sacer: Sovereign Power and Bare Life.* Trans. Daniel Heller-Roazen. Stanford: Stanford University Press, 1998.

———. *Infancy and History: Essays on the Destruction of Experience.* Trans. Liz Heron. London: Verso, 1993.

———. *Means without End: Notes on Politics.* Trans. Vincenzo Binetti and Cesare Casarino. Minneapolis: University of Minnesota Press, 2000.

———. "Notes on Gesture." In *Means without End.*

———. *Potentialities: Collected Essays in Philosophy.* Trans. and ed. Daniel Heller-Roazen. Stanford: Stanford University Press, 1999.

———. "Warburg and the Nameless Science." In *Potentialities.*

Alexander, Jonathan J. G. "Art History, Literary History, and the Study of Medieval Illuminated Manuscripts." *Studies in Iconography* 18 (1997): 51–66.

———. *Medieval Illuminators and Their Methods of Work.* New Haven: Yale University Press, 1992.

Anderson, W. S. "The Orpheus of Virgil and Ovid: *Flebile nescio quid.*" In *Orpheus,* ed. Warden.

Arendt, Hannah. *On Violence.* London: Penguin, 1969.

Avril, François. Catalogue Entry no. 230. In *Les Fastes du Gothique: Le siècle de Charles V.* Paris: Galeries nationales du Grand Palais, 1981.

———. "La Peinture française au temps de Jean de Berry." *Revue de l'art* 28 (1975): 40–52.

———. "Trois manuscrits napolitains des collections de Charles V et de Jean de Berry." *Bibliothèque d'Ecole des Chartes* 127 (1969): 291–328.

Avril, François, Marie-Thérèse Gousset, and Claudia Rabel. *Manuscrits enluminés d'origine italienne.* Vol. 2, *XIIIe siècle.* Paris: Bibliothèque nationale, 1984.

Avril, François, and Nicole Reynaud. *Les Manuscrits à peintures en France, 1440–1520.* Paris: Flammarion-Bibliothèque Nationale, 1993.

Badel, Pierre-Yves. *Le Roman de la Rose au XIVe siècle: Etude de la recéption de l'oeuvre.* Geneva: Droz, 1980.

Baird, Joseph L. "Pierre Col and the *Querelle de la Rose.*" *Philological Quarterly* 60 (1981): 273–86.

Baird, Joseph L., and John R. Kane. "*La Querelle de la Rose:* In Defense of the Opponents." *French Review* 48 (1974): 298–307.

Bal, Mieke. *Reading "Rembrandt": Beyond the Word-Image Opposition.* Cambridge: Cambridge University Press, 1991.

Baldwin, John W. *The Language of Sex: Five Voices from Northern France around 1200.* Chicago: University of Chicago Press, 1994.

Barkan, Leonard. *The Gods Made Flesh: Metamorphosis and the Pursuit of Paganism.* New Haven: Yale University Press, 1986.

Bauerle, Dorothee. *Gespenstergeschichten für ganz Erwachsene: Ein Kommentar zu Aby Warburgs Bilderatlas Mnemosyne.* Münster: Lit Verlag, 1988.

Bazin, André. *What Is Cinema?* Trans. Hugh Gray. Berkeley and Los Angeles: University of California Press, 1967.

Beaune, Colette. *The Birth of an Ideology: Myths and Symbols of Nation in Late-Medieval France.* Trans. Susan Ross Huston. Ed. Fredric L. Cheyette. Berkeley and Los Angeles: University of California Press, 1991.

Bein, Thomas. "Orpheus als Sodomit. Beobachtungen zu einer mhd. Sangspruchstrophe mit (literar)historischen Exkursen zur Homosexualität im hohen Mittelalter." *Zeitschrift für deutsche Philologie* 109 (1990): 33–55.

Benjamin, Walter. "The Work of Art in the Age of Mechanical Reproduction." In *Illuminations,* ed. Hannah Arendt, trans. Harry Zohn. New York: Harcourt, 1955.

Berlo, Janet. "Beyond Bricolage: Women and Aesthetic Strategies in Latin American Textiles." *Res* 22 (autumn 1992): 115–34.

Bhabha, Homi K. "Postmodernism/Postcolonialism." In *Critical Terms for Art History,* ed. Nelson and Shiff.

Bialostocki, Jan. "Iconography and Iconology." *Encyclopedia of World Art,* vol. 7, cols. 769–85.

Bing, Gertrud. "A Memoir." In *Fritz Saxl (1890–1948): A Volume of Memorial Essays from His Friends in England.* London: Thomas Nelson and Sons, 1957.

Blockmans, Wim, and Walter Prevenier. *The Promised Lands: The Low Countries under Burgundian Rule, 1369–1530.* Trans. Elizabeth Fackelman. Ed. Edward Peters. Philadelphia: University of Pennsylvania Press, 1999.

Blume, Dieter. *Regenten des Himmels. Astrologische Bilder in Mittelalter und Renaissance.* Studien aus dem Warburg-Haus 3. Berlin: Akademie, 2000.

Blumenfeld-Kosinski, Renate. *Reading Myth: Classical Mythology and Its Interpretations in Medieval French Literature.* Stanford: Stanford University Press, 1997.

———. "The Scandal of Pasiphae: Narration and Interpretation in the *Ovide moralisé.*" *Modern Philology* 93 (1996): 307–26.

Borenius, Tancred. *St. Thomas Becket in Art.* 1932; reprint, Port Washington, N.Y.: Kennikat Press, 1970.

Bornstein, Diane. *Ideals for Women in the Works of Christine de Pizan.* Medieval and Renaissance Monograph Series 1. Ann Arbor: Michigan Consortium for Medieval and Early Modern Studies, 1981.

Boswell, John. *Christianity, Social Tolerance, and Homosexuality.* Chicago: University of Chicago Press, 1980.

Bourdieu, Pierre. *Outline of a Theory of Practice.* Trans. Richard Nice. Cambridge: Cambridge University Press, 1977.

Boyle, Karen. "The Pornography Debates: Beyond Cause and Effect." *Women's Studies International Forum* 23 (2000): 187–95.

Bozzolo, Carla. "Manuscrits des traductions françaises d'oeuvres de Boccace dans les Bibliothèques de France." *Italia medioevale e umanistica* 11 (1968): 1–69.

Braet, Herman. "Narcisse et Pygmalion: Mythe et intertexte dans le 'Roman de la Rose.'" In *Mediaeval Antiquity,* ed. Andries Welkenhuysen, Herman Braet, and Werner Verbeke. Leuven: Leuven University Press, 1995.

Bredekamp, Horst, Michael Diers, and Charlotte Schoell-Glass, eds. *Aby Warburg: Akten des internationalen Symposions, Hamburg 1990.* Schriften des Warburg-Archivs im Kunstgeschichtlichen Seminar der Universität Hamburg 1. Weinheim: VCH, Acta Humaniora, 1991.

Breidecker, Volker, ed. *Siegfried Kracauer–Erwin Panofsky Briefwechsel.* Berlin: Akademie Verlag, 1996.

Bronfen, Elisabeth. *Over Her Dead Body: Death, Femininity, and the Aesthetic.* London: Routledge, 1992.

Brown, Beverly. "A Feminist Interest in Pornography: Some Modest Proposals." *m/f* 5–6 (1981): 5–18.

Brown, Cynthia J. "The Reconstruction of an Author in Print: Christine de Pizan in the Fifteenth and Sixteenth Centuries." In *Christine de Pizan and the Categories of Difference,* ed. Desmond.

Brown-Grant, Rosalind. *Christine de Pizan and the Moral Defense of Women: Reading beyond Gender.* Cambridge: Cambridge University Press, 1999.

———. "Illumination as Reception. Jean Miélot's Reworking of the 'Epistre Othea.'" In *City of Scholars,* ed. Zimmermann and De Rentiis.

Brownlee, Kevin. "Discourses of the Self: Christine de Pizan and the *Romance of the Rose.*" In *Rethinking the "Romance of the Rose,"* ed. Brownlee and Huot.

———. "The Image of History in Christine de Pizan's *Livre de la Mutacion de Fortune.*" In "Contexts," ed. Poirion and Regalado.

———. "Orpheus's Song Re-sung: Jean de Meun's Reworking of *Metamorphoses,* X." *Romance Philology* 36 (1982): 201–9.

———. "Pygmalion, Mimesis, and the Multiple Endings of the *Roman de la Rose.*" In *Rereading Allegory: Essays in Memory of Daniel Poirion,* ed. Sahar Amar and Noah D. Guynn. Yale French Studies 95. New Haven: Yale University Press, 1999.

Brownlee, Kevin, and Sylvia Huot, eds. *Rethinking the "Romance of the Rose": Text, Image, Reception.* Philadelphia: University of Pennsylvania Press, 1992.

Brush, Kathryn. *The Shaping of Art History: Wilhelm Vöge, Adolph Goldschmidt, and the Study of Medieval Art.* Cambridge: Cambridge University Press, 1996.

Bryson, Norman. "Art in Context." In *Studies in Historical Change,* ed. Ralph Cohen. Charlottesville: University Press of Virginia, 1992.

———. "Géricault and 'Masculinity.'" In *Visual Culture: Images and Interpretations,* ed. Norman Bryson, Michael Ann Holly, and Keith Moxey. Hanover, N.H.: University Press of New England, 1994.

Buchthal, Hugo. *Historia Troiana: Studies in the History of Mediaeval Secular Illustration.* Studies of the Warburg Institute 32. London: Warburg Institute, 1971.

Buettner, Brigitte. *Boccaccio's Des cleres et nobles femmes: Systems of Signification in an Illuminated Manuscript.* College Art Association Monographs on the Fine Arts 53. Seattle: University of Washington Press, 1996.

———. "Profane Illuminations, Secular Illusions: Manuscripts in Late Medieval Courtly Society." *Art Bulletin* 74 (1992): 75–90.

Buitron, Diana, Beth Cohen, Norman Austin, George Dimock, Thomas Gould, William Mullen, Barry B. Powell, and Michael Simpson. *The Odyssey and Ancient Art: An Epic in Word and Image*. Annandale-on-Hudson: Bard College, 1992.

Burch, Noël. *Life to Those Shadows*. Trans. and ed. Ben Brewster. London: British Film Institute, 1990.

Burger, Glenn, and Steven F. Kruger, eds. *Queering the Middle Ages*. Minneapolis: University of Minnesota Press, 2001.

Butler, Judith. *Excitable Speech: A Politics of the Performative*. New York: Routledge, 1997.

———. *Gender Trouble: Feminism and the Subversion of Identity*. London: Routledge, 1990.

———. "Performative Acts and Gender Constitution: An Essay in Phenomenology and Feminist Theory." In *Performing Feminisms*, ed. Case.

Butler, Judith, and Joan Scott, eds. *Feminists Theorize the Political*. London: Routledge, 1992.

Cahoon, Leslie. "Raping the Rose: Jean de Meun's Reading of Ovid's *Amores*." *Classical and Modern Literature* 6 (1986): 261–85.

Callahan, Leslie Abend. "Ambiguity and Appropriation: The Story of Judith in Medieval Narrative and Iconographic Traditions." In *Telling Tales: Medieval Narratives and the Folk Tradition*, ed. Francesca Canadé Sautman, Diana Conchado, and Giuseppe Carlo Di Scipio. New York: St. Martin's, 1998.

Camille, Michael. "Art History in the Past and Future of Medieval Studies." In *The Past and Future of Medieval Studies*, ed. Van Engen.

———. "Before the Gaze: The Internal Senses and Late Medieval Practices of Seeing." In *Visuality before and beyond the Renaissance*, ed. Nelson.

———. "The Book of Signs: Writing and Visual Difference in Gothic Manuscript Illumination." *Word and Image* 1 (1985): 133–48.

———. "'For Our Devotion and Pleasure': The Sexual Objects of Jean, Duc de Berry." *Art History* 24 (2001): 169–94.

———. *The Gothic Idol: Ideology and Image-Making in Medieval Art*. Cambridge: Cambridge University Press, 1989.

———. "Gothic Signs and the Surplus: The Kiss on the Cathedral." In "Contexts," ed. Poirion and Regalado.

———. "Seeing and Reading: Some Visual Implications of Medieval Literacy and Illiteracy." *Art History* 8, no. 1 (1985): 26–49.

———. "The *Très Riches Heures*: An Illuminated Manuscript in the Age of Mechanical Reproduction." *Critical Inquiry* 17 (1990): 72–107.

Campbell, John, and Nadia Margolis, eds. *Christine de Pizan 2000: Studies on Christine de Pizan in Honour of Angus J. Kennedy*. Amsterdam: Rodopi, 2000.

Campbell, Lorne. *The Fifteenth Century Netherlandish Schools*. New Haven: Yale University Press, 1998.

Campbell, Percy G. C. "Christine de Pisan en Angleterre." *Revue de littérature comparée* 5 (1925): 659–70.

———. *L'Épître d'Othéa: Étude sur les sources de Christine de Pisan*. Paris: Honoré Champion, 1924.

Carrara, Eliana. "Bacco e Nettuno nell'*Epistre d'Othéa* di Christine de Pizan: Scene di vita quotidiana e figurazioni religiose in temi mitologici." *Ricerche di storia dell'arte* 55 (1995): 83–88.

———. "Mitologia antica in un trattato didattico-allegorico della fine del Medioevo: L'*Epistre d'Othéa* de Christine di Pizan." *Prospettiva* 66 (1992): 67–86.

Carré, Yannick. *Le Baiser sur la bouche au moyen age: Rites, symboles, mentalités à travers les textes et les images, XIe–XVe siècles*. Paris: Léopard d'Or, 1992.

Carruthers, Mary. *The Book of Memory: A Study of Memory in Medieval Culture*. Cambridge: Cambridge University Press, 1990.

Carson, Diane, Linda Dittmar, and Janice R. Welsch, eds. *Multiple Voices in Feminist Film Criticism*. Minneapolis: University of Minnesota Press, 1994.

Cartellieri, Otto. *The Court of Burgundy: Studies in the History of Civilization*. London: Kegan, Paul, Trench, 1929.

Case, Sue-Ellen, ed. *Performing Feminisms: Feminist Critical Theory and Theatre*. Baltimore: Johns Hopkins University Press, 1990.

Case, Sue-Ellen, and Janelle Reinelt, eds. *The Performance of Power: Theatrical Discourse and Politics*. Iowa City: University of Iowa Press, 1991.

Cassidy, Brendan. Review of *An Introduction to Iconography*, by Roelof van Straten. *Studies in Iconography* 17 (1996): 432–35.

———, ed. *Iconography at the Crossroads*. Index of Christian Art Occasional Papers 2. Princeton: Index of Christian Art and Department of Art and Archaeology, 1993.

Cavell, Stanley. *The World Viewed: Reflections on the Ontology of Film*. New York: Viking, 1971.

Chance, Jane, ed. *The Mythographic Art: Classical Fable and the Rise of the Vernacular in Early France and England*. Gainesville: University of Florida Press, 1990.

Chartier, Roger. "General Introduction: Print Culture." In *The Culture of Print: Power and the Uses of Print in Early Modern Europe*, trans. Lydia G. Cochrane, ed. Roger Chartier. Princeton: Princeton University Press, 1989.

Cinq Années d'acquisitions, 1974–1978: Exposition organisée à la Bibliothèque Royale Albert Ier du 24 Septembre au 31 octobre 1979. Brussels: Bibliothèque Albert Ier, 1979.

Clover, Carol J. *Men, Women, and Chain Saws: Gender in the Modern Horror Film*. Princeton: Princeton University Press, 1992.

Crary, Jonathan. *Techniques of the Observer: On Vision and Modernity in the Nineteenth Century*. Cambridge: MIT Press, 1990.

Crone, Rainer. "Jiři Georg Dokoupil: The Imprisoned Brain." *Artforum* 21, no. 7 (1983): 50–55.

Curtius, Ernst Robert. *European Literature and the Latin Middle Ages*. Trans. Willard R. Trask. New York: Pantheon, 1953.

Degenhart, Bernhard, and Annegrit Schmitt. *Corpus der italienischen Zeichnungen, 1300–1450*. Pt. 1, *Süd-und Mittelitalien*, vol. 1, *Katalog*. Berlin: Mann, 1968.

de Jorio, Andrea. *Gesture in Naples and Gesture in Classical Antiquity: A Translation of "La Mimica Degli Antichi Investigata Nel Gestire Napoletano."* Trans. Adam Kendon. Bloomington: Indiana University Press, 2000.

Delaissé, L. M. J., James Marrow, and John de Wit. *The James A. de Rothschild Collection at Waddesdon Manor: Illuminated Manuscripts.* Fribourg: Office du Livre, 1977.

de Lauretis, Teresa. *Alice Doesn't: Feminism, Semiotics, Cinema.* Bloomington: Indiana University Press, 1984.

———. *The Practice of Love: Lesbian Sexuality and Perverse Desire.* Bloomington: Indiana University Press, 1994.

———. "Queer Theory: Lesbian and Gay Sexualities, an Introduction." *Differences* 3, no. 2 (1991): iii–xviii.

———. "Rethinking Women's Cinema: Aesthetics and Feminist Theory." In *Multiple Voices,* ed. Carson, Dittmar, and Welsch.

———. "The Violence of Rhetoric: Considerations on Representation and Gender." In *The Violence of Representation: Literature and the History of Violence,* ed. Nancy Armstrong and Leonard Tennenhouse. London: Routledge, 1989.

Delisle, Léopold. "Librairie du duc de Berry—1402–1424." In *Le Cabinet des manuscrits de la Bibliothèque nationale.* 3 vols. Paris, 1881.

———. *Recherches sur la Librairie de Charles V.* 2 vols. Paris: Honoré Champion, 1907.

del Río, Elena. "The Body of Voyeurism: Mapping a Discourse of the Senses in Michael Powell's *Peeping Tom.*" *Camera Obscura* 15 (2000): 115–49.

Derbes, Anne, and Mark Sandona. "Amazons and Crusaders: The *Histoire Universelle* in Flanders and the Holy Land." In *France and the Holy Land: Frankish Culture at the End of the Crusades,* ed. Daniel Weiss. Baltimore: Johns Hopkins University Press, 2003.

Derrida, Jacques. *The Gift of Death.* Trans. David Wills. Chicago: University of Chicago Press, 1995.

———. "Structure, Sign, and Play in the Discourse of the Human Sciences." In *Writing and Difference,* trans. Alan Bass. Chicago: University of Chicago Press, 1978.

Desmond, Marilynn. "The *Querelle de la Rose* and the Ethics of Reading." In *Christine de Pizan: A Casebook,* ed. Barbara K. Altmann and Deborah L. McGrady. London: Routledge, 2003.

———. *Reading Dido: Gender, Textuality, and the Medieval "Aeneid."* Minneapolis: University of Minnesota Press, 1994.

———, ed. *Christine de Pizan and the Categories of Difference.* Minneapolis: University of Minnesota Press, 1998.

Desmond, Marilynn, and Pamela Sheingorn. "Queering Ovidian Myth: Bestiality and Desire in Christine de Pizan's *Epistre Othea.*" In *Queering the Middle Ages,* ed. Burger and Kruger.

Diamond, Elin, ed. *Performance and Cultural Politics.* London: Routledge, 1996.

DiMarco, Vincent. "The Amazons and the End of the World." In *Discovering New Worlds: Essays on Medieval Exploration and Imagination,* ed. Scott D. Westrem. New York: Garland, 1991.

Dinshaw, Carolyn. "A Kiss Is Just a Kiss: Heterosexuality and Its Consolations in *Sir Gawain and the Green Knight.*" *Diacritics* 24, nos. 2–3 (1994): 205–26.

Dogaer, Georges. *Flemish Miniature Painting in the Fifteenth and Sixteenth Centuries.* Amsterdam: B. M. Israel, 1987.

Dolan, Jill. *Presence and Desire: Essays on Gender, Sexuality, Performance.* Ann Arbor: University of Michigan Press, 1993.

Donnelly, Peter. "Running the Gauntlet: The Moral Order of Pornographic Movie Theaters." *Urban Life* 10 (1981): 239–64.

Dornbush, Jean M. *Pygmalion's Figure: Reading Old French Romance.* Lexington, Ky.: French Forum, 1990.

Douglas, Mary. *Purity and Danger: An Analysis of Concepts of Pollution and Taboo.* London: Routledge and Kegan Paul, 1966.

Doutrepont, Georges. *La Littérature française à la cour des ducs de Bourgogne.* Paris: Champion, 1909.

Driver, Martha W. "Christine de Pisan and Robert Wyer: The .C. Hystoryes of Troye, of L'Epistre d'Othea Englished." *Gutenberg-Jahrbuch* 72 (1997): 125–39.

Dronke, Peter. "Medieval Sibyls: Their Character and Their 'Auctoritas.'" *Studi Medievali,* 3d ser. 36 (1995): 581–615.

Dulac, Liliane. "La Gestuelle chez Christine de Pizan: Quelques aperçus." In *Au Champ des escriptures,* ed. Hicks.

———. "Travail allégorique et ruptures du sens chez Christine de Pizan: *L'Epistre d'Othea.*" In *Continuités et ruptures dans l'histoire et la littérature. Actes du colloque franco-polonais. Montpellier, 1987.* Paris: Champion; Geneva: Slatkine, 1988.

Dunlop, Louisa. "Pigments and Painting Materials in Fourteenth- and Early Fifteenth-Century Parisian Manuscript Illumination." In *Artistes, Artisans et production artistique au Moyen Age,* vol. 3, *Fabrication et consommation de l'oeuvre,* ed. Xavier Barral i Altet. Paris: Picard, 1990.

Dworkin, Andrea. *Pornography: Men Possessing Women.* New York: Perigee: 1981.

Dyer, Richard. "Don't Look Now: The Male Pin-Up." In *The Sexual Subject: A Screen Reader in Sexuality.* London: Routledge, 1992.

Egbert, Virginia Wylie. "Pygmalion as Sculptor." *Princeton University Library Chronicle* 28 (1966–67): 20–23.

Ehrhart, Margaret J. "Christine de Pizan and the Judgment of Paris: A Court Poet's Use of the Mythographic Tradition." In *The Mythographic Art,* ed. Chance.

Eisenstein, Sergei. *Towards a Theory of Montage.* Vol. 2, *Selected Works,* ed. Michael Glenny and Richard Taylor. London: British Film Institute, 1991.

Enders, Jody. *The Medieval Theater of Cruelty: Rhetoric, Memory, Violence.* Ithaca, N.Y.: Cornell University Press, 1999.

———. "Of Miming and Signing: The Dramatic Rhetoric of Gesture." In *Gesture in Medieval Drama and Art,* ed. Clifford Davidson. Kalamazoo, Mich.: Medieval Institute Publications, 2001.

Fenster, Thelma. "Did Christine Have a Sense of Humor? The Evidence of the *Epistre au Dieu d'Amours.*" In *Reinterpreting Christine de Pizan,* ed. Earl Jeffrey Richards. Athens: University of Georgia Press, 1992.

———. "'Perdre son latin': Christine de Pizan and Vernacular Humanism." In *Christine de Pizan and the Categories of Difference,* ed. Desmond.

Ferguson, Bruce W. "Video? Art? History?" In *Künstlerischer Austausch. Artistic Exchange,* ed. Thomas W. Gaehtgens. 3 vols. Berlin: Akademie, 1993.

Ferguson, Frances. "Pornography: The Theory." *Critical Inquiry* 21 (1995): 670–95.

Finch, A. J. "The Nature of Violence in the Middle Ages: An Alternative Perspective." *Historical Research* 70 (1997): 249–68.

Finke, Laurie A. "Christine de Pizan in England." In *Women's Writing in English: Medieval England.* London: Longman's, 1999.

Fischer, Lucy. *Shot/Countershot: Film Tradition and Women's Cinema.* Princeton: Princeton University Press, 1989.

Fleming, John V. *The "Roman de la Rose": A Study in Allegory and Iconography.* Princeton: Princeton University Press, 1969.

———. "The *Roman de la Rose* and Its Manuscript Illustrations." Ph.D. diss., Princeton University, 1963.

Flynn, Maureen. "Taming Anger's Daughters: New Treatment for Emotional Problems in Renaissance Spain." *Renaissance Quarterly* 51, no. 3 (1998): 864–86.

Forster, Kurt. "Aby Warburg's History of Art: Collective Memory and the Social Mediation of Images." *Daedalus* 105 (1976): 169–76.

Foster, Hal, ed. *Vision and Visuality.* Seattle: Bay Press, 1988.

Fradenberg, Louise, and Carla Freccero. "Introduction: Caxton, Foucault, and the Pleasures of History." In *Premodern Sexualities,* ed. Louise Fradenberg and Carla Freccero. London: Routledge, 1995.

Franko, Mark, and Annette Richards, eds. *Acting on the Past: Historical Performance across the Disciplines.* Hanover, N.H.: University Press of New England, 2000.

Freedman, Barbara. *Staging the Gaze: Postmodernism, Psychoanalysis, and Shakespearean Comedy.* Ithaca, N.Y.: Cornell University Press, 1991.

Freud, Sigmund. "The 'Uncanny.'" In *The Standard Edition of the Complete Psychological Works of Sigmund Freud,* ed. James Strachey, vol. 17. London: Hogarth Press, 1955.

Friedman, John Block. *The Monstrous Races in Medieval Art and Thought.* Cambridge: Harvard University Press, 1981.

———. *Orpheus in the Middle Ages.* Cambridge: Harvard University Press, 1970.

Fritz, Jean Marie. "Du Dieu émasculateur au roi émasculé: Metamorphoses du Saturne au Moyen Age." In *Pour une Mythologie du Moyen Age,* ed. Laurence Harf-Lancner and Dominique Boutet. Collection de l'Ecole Normale Supérieure de Jeunes Filles 41. Paris: Ecole Normale Supérieure, 1988.

Fuhrmann, Manfred, ed. *Terror und Spiel: Probleme der Mythenrezeption.* Poetik und Hermeneutik 4. Munich: Wilhelm Fink Verlag, 1971.

Galitz, Robert, and Brita Reimers, eds. *Aby M. Warburg: "Ekstatische Nymphe—trauernder Flussgott." Porträt eines Gelehrten.* Hamburg: Dölling und Galitz, 1995.

Ganshof, François L. *Feudalism.* 2d. ed. New York: Harper, 1961.

Garnier, François. *Le Langage de l'image au Moyen Age.* Vol. 1, *Signification et symbolique;* vol. 2, *Grammaire des gestes.* Paris: Léopard d'Or, ca. 1982–89.

Garvey, Gerald. *Constitutional "Bricolage."* Princeton: Princeton University Press, 1971.

Gaunt, Simon. "Bel Acueil and the Improper Allegory of the *Romance of the Rose.*" *New Medieval Literatures* 2 (1998): 65–93.

———. *Gender and Genre in Medieval French Literature.* Cambridge: Cambridge University Press, 1995.

Genette, Gérard. "Structuralisme et critique littéraire." *L'Arc* 26 (1965): 37–49.

Gibbs, Stephanie Viereck. "Christine de Pizan's *Epistre d'Othea* in England: The Manuscript Tradition of Stephen Scrope's Translation." In *Contexts and Continuities,* ed. Kennedy, Brown-Grant, Laidlaw, and Müller, 2.

Gibson, Pamela Church, and Roma Gibson, eds. *Dirty Looks: Women, Pornography, Power.* London: British Film Institute, 1993.

Ginzburg, Carlo. *Ecstasies: Deciphering the Witches' Sabbath.* Trans. Raymond Rosenthal. New York: Penguin, 1991.

———. "From Aby Warburg to E. H. Gombrich: A Problem of Method." In *Clues, Myths, and the Historical Method,* trans. John Tedeschi and Anne C. Tedeschi. Baltimore: Johns Hopkins University Press, 1989.

Girard, René. *Violence and the Sacred.* Trans. Patrick Gregory. Baltimore: Johns Hopkins University Press, 1977.

Glanz alter Buchkunst: Mittelalterliche Handschriften der Staatsbibliothek Preussischer Kulturbesitz Berlin. Wiesbaden: Ludwig Reichert Verlag, 1988.

Glashoff, Michaela, Andrea Neumann, and Martin Deppner. "Bilderatlas zwischen Talmud und Netzwerk." Ein Beitrag zum INSEA-Kongress, Hamburg, 1987. Unpublished, copy in the Warburg Library.

Gombrich, E. H. *Aby Warburg: An Intellectual Biography.* London: Warburg Institute, 1970.

———. "Aby Warburg: His Aims and Methods. An Anniversary Lecture." *Journal of the Warburg and Courtauld Institutes* 62 (1999): 268–82.

———. "Icon." *New York Review of Books,* 15 February 1996, 29–30.

Graus, František. "Troja und trojanische Herkunftssage im Mittelalter." In *Kontinuität und Transformation der Antike im Mittelalter. Veröffentlichung der Kongressakten zum Freiburger Symposion des Mediävistenverbandes,* ed. Willi Erzgräber. Sigmaringen: Jan Thorbecke Verlag, 1989.

Gray, Douglas. "'A Fulle Wyse Gentyl-Woman of Fraunce': *The Epistle of Othea* and Later Medieval English Literary Culture." In *Medieval Women: Texts and Contexts in Late Medieval Britain: Essays for Felicity Riddy,* ed. Jocelyn Wogan-Browne, Rosalynn Voaden, Arlyn Diamond, Ann Hutchison, Carol M. Meale, and Lesley Johnson. Turnhout: Brepols, 2000.

Grosz, Elizabeth. "Animal Sex: Libido as Desire and Death." In *Sexy Bodies,* ed. Grosz and Probyn.

Grosz, Elizabeth, and Elspeth Probyn, eds. *Sexy Bodies: The Strange Carnalities of Feminism.* London: Routledge, 1995.

Gunning, Tom. "'Primitive' Cinema: A Frame-up? Or, The Trick's on Us." In *Early Cinema: Space, Frame, Narrative,* ed. Thomas Elsaesser and Adam Baker. London: British Film Institute, 1990.

Hagen, Susan K. *Allegorical Remembrance: A Study of "The Pilgrimage of the Life of Man" as a Medieval Treatise on Seeing and Remembering.* Athens: University of Georgia Press, 1990.

Haidu, Peter. *The Subject of Violence: The Song of Roland and the Birth of the State.* Bloomington: Indiana University Press, 1993.

Hale, J. R. "Violence in the Late Middle Ages: A Background." In *Violence and Civil Disorder,* ed. Martines.

Halfmann, Jasper, and Clod Zillich. "Reality and Reduced Model." *Studio International* 193, no. 986 (March–April 1977): 99–104.

Hansen, Joseph. *Quellen und Untersuchungen zur Geschichte des Hexenwahns und der Hexenverfolgung im Mittelalter.* Bonn, 1901; reprint, Hildesheim: G. Olms, 1963.

Hanssen, Beatrice. *Critique of Violence: Between Poststructuralism and Critical Theory.* London: Routledge, 2000.

Harley, Marta Powell. "Narcissus, Hermaphroditus, and Attis: Ovidian Lovers at the Fontaine d'Amors in Guillaume de Lorris's *Roman de la Rose*." *PMLA* 101 (1986): 324–37.

Hart, Joan. "Erwin Panofsky and Karl Mannheim: A Dialogue on Interpretation." *Critical Inquiry* 19 (1993): 534–66.

Hawkes, Jane. "The Rothbury Cross: An Iconographic Bricolage." *Gesta* 35 (1996): 77–94.

Heath, Stephen. "Difference." In *The Sexual Subject: A Screen Reader in Sexuality.* London: Routledge, 1992.

Heckscher, William S. "Erwin Panofsky: A Curriculum Vitae." In Panofsky, *Three Essays.*

———. "The Genesis of Iconology." In *Stil und Überlieferung in der Kunst des Abendlandes: Akten des 21. Internationalen Kongresses für Kunstgeschichte in Bonn 1964.* 3 vols. Berlin: Gebr. Mann, 1967.

———. "*Petites perceptions:* An Account of *sortes Warburgianae.*" In *Art and Literature,* ed. Verheyen.

Heitmann, Klaus. "Orpheus im Mittelalter." *Archiv für Kulturgeschichte* 45 (1963): 253–94.

———. "Typen der Deformierung antiker Mythen im Mittelalter am Beispiel der Orpheussage." *Romanistisches Jahrbuch* 14 (1963): 45–77.

Hexter, Ralph. *Ovid and Medieval Schooling. Studies in Medieval School Commentaries on Ovid's Ars amatoria, Epistulae ex Ponto, and Epistulae Heroidum.* Munich: Arbeo-Gesellschaft, 1986.

Hibbitts, Bernard J. "Coming to Our Senses: Communication and Legal Expression in Legal Cultures." *Emory Law Journal* 41 (1992): 873–960.

Hicks, Eric. "Pour une édition génétique de l'*Epistre Othea*." In *Pratiques de la culture écrite en France au XVe siècle,* ed. Monique Ornato and Nicole Pons. Louvain-La-Neuve: Collège Thomas More, 1995.

———. "The 'Querelle de la Rose' in the *Roman de la Rose*." *Les bonnes feuilles* 3 (1974): 152–69.

———. "De l'histoire littéraire comme cosmogonie: La Querelle du *Roman de la Rose*." *Critique* 32, no. 348 (1976): 511–19.

———. "Situation du débat sur le RR." In *Une femme de lettres au Moyen Age: Études autour de Christine de Pizan,* ed. Liliane Dulac and Bernard Ribémont. Orléans: Paradigme, 1995.

———, ed. *Au Champ des escriptures. IIIᵉ Colloque international sur Christine de Pizan.* Paris: Honoré Champion, 2000.

Hicks, Eric, and Ezio Ornato. "Jean de Montreuil et le débat sur le *Roman de la Rose*." *Romania* 98 (1977): 34–64, 186–219.

Hindman, Sandra L. *Christine de Pizan's "Epistre Othéa": Painting and Politics at the Court of Charles VI.* Toronto: Pontifical Institute of Mediaeval Studies, 1986.

———. "The Composition of the Manuscript of Christine de Pizan's Collected Works in the British Library: A Reassessment." *British Library Journal* 9 (1983): 93–123.

———. "The Illustrated Book: An Addendum to the State of Research in Northern European Art." *Art Bulletin* 68 (1986): 536–42.

Hindman, Sandra, and Stephen Perkinson. "Insurgent Voices: Illuminated Versions of Christine de Pizan's 'Le Livre du Duc des vrais amans.'" In *The City of Scholars,* ed. Zimmermann and De Rentiis.

Holly, Michael Ann. *Panofsky and the Foundations of Art History.* Ithaca, N.Y.: Cornell University Press, 1984.

———. "Unwriting Iconology." In *Iconography at the Crossroads,* ed. Cassidy.

Horne, Peter, and Reina Lewis, eds. *Outlooks: Lesbian and Gay Sexualities and Visual Cultures.* London: Routledge, 1996.

Hughes, Muriel J. "The Library of Philip the Bold and Margaret of Flanders, First Valois Duke and Duchess of Burgundy." *Journal of Medieval History* 4 (1978): 145–88.

Huizinga, Johan. *The Autumn of the Middle Ages.* Trans. Rodney J. Payton and Ulrich Mammitzsch. Chicago: University of Chicago Press, 1996.

———. *Homo Ludens: A Study of the Play-Element in Culture.* London: Routledge and Kegan Paul, 1949.

Hult, David F. "Words and Deeds: Jean de Meun's *Romance of the Rose* and the Hermeneutics of Censorship." *New Literary History* 28 (1997): 345–66.

Huot, Sylvia. "Bodily Peril: Sexuality and the Subversion of Order in Jean de Meun's *Roman de la Rose.*" *Modern Language Review* 95 (2000): 41–61.

———. *The "Romance of the Rose" and Its Medieval Readers: Interpretation, Reception, Manuscript Transmission.* Cambridge: Cambridge University Press, 1993.

Ignatius, Mary Ann. "Christine de Pizan's *Epistre Othea:* An Experiment in Literary Form." *Medievalia et Humanistica* 9 (1979): 127–42.

Illich, Ivan. *In the Vineyard of the Text: A Commentary to Hugh's "Didascalicon."* Chicago: University of Chicago Press, 1993.

Irwin, Eleanor. "The Songs of Orpheus and the New Song of Christ." In *Orpheus,* ed. Warden.

Itzin, Catherine. *Pornography: Women, Violence, and Civil Liberties.* Oxford: Oxford University Press, 1992.

Iversen, Margaret. "Retrieving Warburg's Tradition." *Art History* 16 (1993): 541–53.

Jacquart, Danielle, and Claude Thomasset. *Sexuality and Medicine in the Middle Ages.* Trans. Matthew Adamson. Cambridge: Polity Press, 1988.

Jansen, Dirk Jacob. "Princeton Index of Christian Art: The Utrecht Copy." *Visual Resources: An International Journal of Documentation* 13 (1998): 253–85.

Jardine, Lisa. "Women Humanists: Education for What?" In *From Humanism to the Humanities: Education and the Liberal Arts in Fifteenth- and Sixteenth-Century Europe,* ed. Anthony Grafton and Lisa Jardine. Cambridge: Harvard University Press, 1986.

Jauss, Hans Robert. "Allegorese, Remythisierung und neuer Mythos. Bemerkungen zur christlichen Gefangenschaft der Mythologie im Mittelalter." In *Terror und Spiel,* ed. Fuhrmann.

Jay, Nancy. *Throughout Your Generations Forever: Sacrifice, Religion, and Paternity.* Chicago: University of Chicago Press, 1992.

Jeanneret, Sylvie. "Text et enluminures dans l'*Epistre othea* de Christine de Pizan: Une lecture politique?" In *Au champ des escriptures,* ed. Hicks.

Jordan, Mark D. *The Invention of Sodomy in Christian Theology.* Chicago: University of Chicago Press, 1997.

Kaeuper, Richard W. "Chivalry and the Civilising Process." In *Violence in Medieval Society,* ed. Kaeuper.

———. *Chivalry and Violence in Medieval Europe.* Oxford: Oxford University Press, 1999.

Kaeuper, Richard W., ed. *Violence in Medieval Society.* Woodbridge: Boydell and Brewer, 2000.

Kaplan, E. Ann. *Women and Film: Both Sides of the Camera.* London: Routledge, 1983.

Karras, Ruth Mazo. "Sex and the Singlewoman." In *Singlewomen in the European Past, 1250–1800,* ed. Judith M. Bennett and Amy M. Froide. Philadelphia: University of Pennsylvania Press, 1999.

Kauffmann, C. M. *Romanesque Manuscripts, 1066–1190.* A Survey of Manuscripts Illuminated in the British Isles, 3, general editor, J. J. G. Alexander. London: Harvey Miller, 1975.

Kay, Sarah. "The Birth of Venus in the Roman de la rose." *Exemplaria* 9 (1997): 7–37.

———. "Sexual Knowledge: The Once and Future Texts of the *Romance of the Rose.*" In *Textuality and Sexuality: Reading Theories and Practices,* ed. Judith Still and Michael Worton. Manchester: Manchester University Press, 1993.

Kellogg, Judith L. "Christine de Pizan as Chivalric Mythographer: L'Epistre Othea." In *The Mythographic Art,* ed. Chance.

———. "Transforming Ovid: The Metamorphosis of Female Authority." In *Christine de Pizan and the Categories of Difference,* ed. Desmond.

Kempter, Gerda. *Ganymed: Studien zur Typologie, Ikonographie und Ikonologie.* Dissertationen zur Kunstgeschichte 12. Cologne: Böhlau, 1980.

Kennedy, Angus J., Rosalind Brown-Grant, James C. Laidlaw, and Catherine M. Müller, eds. *Contexts and Continuities: Proceedings of the IVth International Colloquium on Christine de Pizan (Glasgow 21–27 July 2000), published in honour of Liliane Dulac.* Glasgow University Medieval French Texts and Studies 1. 3 vols. Glasgow: University of Glasgow Press, 2002.

King, Margaret L. "Book-Lined Cells: Women and Humanism in the Early Italian Renaissance." In *Beyond Their Sex: Learned Women of the European Past,* ed. Patricia H. Labalme. New York: New York University Press, 1980.

Kleinman, Arthur. "The Violences of Everyday Life: The Multiple Forms and Dynamics of Social Violence." In *Violence and Subjectivity,* ed. Veena Das, Arthur Kleinman, Mamphela Ramphele, and Paula Reynolds. Berkeley and Los Angeles: University of California Press, 2000.

Klibansky, Raymond, Erwin Panofsky, and Fritz Saxl. *Saturn and Melancholy: Studies in the History of Natural Philosophy, Religion, and Art.* London: Thomas Nelson and Sons, 1964.

Koch, Gertrude. "The Body's Shadow Realm." In *Dirty Looks,* ed. Gibson and Gilson.

Kolker, Robert P. "The Film Text and Film Form." In *The Oxford Guide to Film Studies*, ed. John Hill and Pamela Church Gibson. Oxford: Oxford University Press, 1998.

Kolve, V. A. *Chaucer and the Imagery of Narrative: The First Five Canterbury Tales*. Stanford: Stanford University Press, 1984.

———. "*Ganymede / Son of Getron:* Medieval Monasticism and the Drama of Same-Sex Desire." *Speculum* 73 (1998): 1014–67.

Kracauer, Siegfried. *From Caligari to Hitler: A Psychological History of the German Film*. Princeton: Princeton University Press, 1947.

Krueger, Roberta. "Christine's Anxious Lessons: Gender, Morality, and the Social Order from the *Enseignemens* to the *Avison*." In *Christine de Pizan and the Categories of Difference*, ed. Desmond.

———. *Women Readers and the Ideology of Gender in Old French Verse Romance*. Cambridge Studies in French 43. Cambridge: Cambridge University Press, 1993.

Kuefler, Mathew S. "Castration and Eunuchism in the Middle Ages." In *Handbook of Medieval Sexuality*, ed. Vern L. Bullough and James A. Brundage. New York: Garland, 1996.

Laidlaw, James. "Christine de Pizan—an Author's Progress." *Modern Language Review* 78 (1983): 532–50.

———. "Christine de Pizan—a Publisher's Progress." *Modern Language Review* 82 (1987): 35–75.

———. "Christine de Pizan: From Scriptorium to Database and Back Again." *Journal of the Institute of Romance Studies* 1 (1992): 59–67.

———. "Christine's Lays—Does Practice Make Perfect?" In *Contexts and Continuities*, ed. Kennedy, Brown-Grant, Laidlaw, and Müller, 2.

Laird, Edgar. "Astrology in the Court of Charles V of France, as Reflected in Oxford, St John's College, MS 164." *Manuscripta* 34 (1990): 167–76.

———. "Christine de Pizan and the Controversy Concerning Star-Study in the Court of Charles V." *Allegorica* 18 (1997): 21–30.

Landauer, Carl. "Erwin Panofsky and the Renascence of the Renaissance." *Renaissance Quarterly* 47 (1994): 255–81.

———. "The Survival of Antiquity: The German Years of the Warburg Institute." Ph.D. diss., Yale University, 1984.

Langlois, Ernest. *Les Manuscrits du Roman de la Rose. Description et classement*. Paris: Honoré Champion, 1910.

Lavin, Irving. "Cephalus and Procris: Transformations of an Ovidian Myth." *Journal of the Warburg and Courtauld Institutes* 17 (1954): 260–87.

———. "Panofsky's History of Art." In *Meaning in the Visual Arts*, ed. Lavin.

———, ed. *Meaning in the Visual Arts: Views from the Outside: A Centennial Commemoration of Erwin Panofsky (1892–1968)*. Princeton: Institute for Advanced Study, 1995.

Lea, Henry Charles. *Materials toward a History of Witchcraft*. Ed. Arthur C. Howland. 3 vols. Philadelphia: University of Pennsylvania Press, 1939, reprint, New York: AMS Press, 1986.

Lefèvre, Sylvie. "Christine de Pizan et l'Aristote oresmien." In *Au Champ des escriptures*, ed. Hicks.

Leicester, H. Marshall, Jr. "Ovid Enclosed: The God of Love as *Magister Amoris* in the *Roman de la Rose* of Guillaume de Lorris." *Res publica litterarum* 7 (1984): 107–29.

Lemaire, Jacques. "Les manuscrits lillois de Christine de Pizan. Comparaison matérielle entre les copies Lille, Bibliothèque Municipale 175 et Oxford, Bodley 421." In *Contexts and Continuities,* ed Kennedy, Brown-Grant, Laidlaw, and Müller, 2.

Lesourd, Dominique. "Diane et les sorcières. Études sur les survivances de *Diana* dans les langues romanes." *Anagrom* 1 (1972): 55–74.

Lévi-Strauss, Claude. *The Savage Mind.* Chicago: University of Chicago Press, 1966.

Levin, Thomas Y. "Iconology at the Movies: Panofsky's Film Theory." In *Meaning in the Visual Arts,* ed. Lavin.

Lindberg, David C. *The Beginnings of Western Science: The European Scientific Tradition in Philosophical, Religious, and Institutional Context,* 600 B.C. to A.D. 1450. Chicago: University of Chicago Press, 1992.

Ling, Roger. *Roman Painting.* Cambridge: Cambridge University Press, 1991.

Lingis, Alphonso. "Bestiality." *Symplokē* 6 (1998): 56–71.

Lippincott, Kristen. "*Urania redux:* A View of Aby Warburg's Writings on Astrology and Art." In *Art History as Cultural History,* ed. Woodfield.

Lord, Carla. "Illustrated Manuscripts of Berchorius before the Age of Printing." In *Die Rezeption der "Metamorphosen" des Ovid in der Neuzeit,* ed. Walter and Horn.

———. "Marks of Ownership in Medieval Manuscripts: The Case of the Rouen *Ovide moralisé.*" *Source* 18 (1998): 7–11.

———. "Three Manuscripts of the *Ovide moralisé.*" *Art Bulletin* 57 (1975): 161–75.

Lyna, Frédéric. *Les principaux Manuscrits à peintures de la Bibliothèque royale de Belgique III.* Ed. Christiane Pantens. Brussels: Bibliothèque royale Albert 1er, 1984.

McCaffrey, Phillip. "*Le Roman de la Rose* and the Sons of Narcissus." *Mediaevalia* 11 (1985): 101–20.

McConahay, John B. "Pornography: The Symbolic Politics of Fantasy." *Law and Contemporary Problems* 5, no. 1 (1988): 32–69.

McE[wan], D[orothea]. "Saxl, Warburg, Panofsky. Lectures in the Library and a Link to the University." In *Warburg Institute Newsletter* 7 (winter 1997): 2.

McEwan, Dorothea. *Ausreiten der Ecken. Die Aby Warburg-Fritz Saxl Korrespondenz 1910 bis 1919.* Hamburg: Dölling und Galitz, [1998].

McGrady, Deborah. "What Is a Patron? Benefactors and Authorship in Harley 4431, Christine de Pizan's Collected Works." In *Christine de Pizan and the Categories of Difference,* ed. Desmond.

McGuire, Brian Patrick. "Sexual Control and Spiritual Growth in the Late Middle Ages: The Case of Jean Gerson." In *Tradition and Ecstasy: The Agony of the Fourteenth Century,* ed. Nancy van Deusen. Clermont Cultural Studies, Musicological Studies, vol. 62.3. Ottawa: Institute of Mediaeval Music, 1997.

MacKinnon, Catherine. *Only Words.* Cambridge: Harvard University Press, 1993.

McMunn, Meradith T. "Programs of Illustration in *Roman de la Rose* Manuscripts Owned by Patrons and Friends of Christine de Pizan." In *Au Champ des escriptures,* ed. Hicks.

———. "Representations of the Erotic in Some Illustrated Manuscripts of the *Roman de la Rose.*" *Romance Languages Annual* 4 (1992): 125–30.

Maddern, Phillippa C. "Viewing Violence: The Conceptual Context of Violence in Fifteenth-Century England." In *Violence and the Social Order: East Anglia, 1422–1442*. Oxford: Oxford University Press, 1992.

Malinowitz, Harriet. "Lesbian Studies and Postmodern Queer Theory." In *The New Lesbian Studies: Into the Twenty-First Century*, ed. Bonnie Zimmerman and Toni A. H. McNaron. New York: Feminist Press, 1996.

Marcus, Sharon. "Fighting Bodies, Fighting Words: A Theory and Politics of Rape Prevention." In *Feminists Theorize the Political*, ed. Butler and Scott.

Martines, Lauro, ed. *Violence and Civil Disorder in Italian Cities, 1200–1500*. Berkeley and Los Angeles: University of California Press, 1972.

Mast, Gerald. *Film/Cinema/Movie: A Theory of Experience*. New York: Harper and Row, 1977. Reprint, Chicago: University of Chicago Press, 1983.

Meale, Carole M. "Legends of Good Women in the European Middle Ages." *Archiv für das Studium der neueren Sprachen und Literaturen* 229 (1992): 55–70.

Meiss, Millard. *French Painting in the Time of Jean de Berry: The Late Fourteenth Century and the Patronage of the Duke*. 2 vols. 2d ed. London: Phaidon, 1969.

———. *French Painting in the Time of Jean de Berry: The Limbourgs and Their Contemporaries*. 2 vols. London: Thames and Hudson, 1974.

Meiss, Millard, and Elizabeth H. Beatson. *The Belles Heures of Jean, Duke of Berry*. New York: Braziller, 1974.

Michels, Karen. "Art History, German Jewish Identity, and the Emigration of Iconology." In *Jewish Identity in Modern Art History*, ed. Catherine M. Soussloff. Berkeley and Los Angeles: University of California Press, 1999.

Miller, J. Hillis. *Illustration*. London: Reaktion, 1992.

Miller, William Ian. *Humiliation and Other Essays on Honor, Social Discomfort, and Violence*. Ithaca, N.Y.: Cornell University Press, 1993.

Miner, Dorothy. "Hesdin, Atelier of Loyset Liédet, 1455–60." In *Flanders in the Fifteenth Century: Art and Civilization*. Catalog of the exhibition "Masterpieces of Flemish Art: Van Eyck to Bosch," organized by the Detroit Institute of Fine Arts and the City of Bruges. Detroit: Detroit Institute of Arts, 1960.

Mohanty, Satya P. "The Epistemic Status of Cultural Identity: On *Beloved* and the Postcolonial Condition." In *Reclaiming Identity*, ed. Moya and Hames-García.

Mombello, Gianni. "Per un'edizione critica dell'*Epistre Othea* di Christine de Pizan." *Studi Francesi* 24 (1964): 401–17, and 25 (1965): 1–12.

———. "Recherches sur l'origine du nom de la Déesse Othea." *Atti della accademia delle Scienze di Torino*, 2, Classe di Scienze Morali, Storiche e Filologiche 103 (1969): 343–75.

———. *La tradizione manoscritta dell' "Epistre Othéa" di Christine de Pizan. Prolegomeni all'edizione del testo*. Memorie dell'Accademia delle Scienze di Torino, Classe di Scienze Morali, Storiche e Filologiche, series 4, vol. 15. Turin: Accademia delle Scienze, 1967.

Monahan, Jennifer. "*Querelles*: Medieval Texts and Modern Polemics." In *Contexts and Continuities*, ed. Kennedy, Brown-Grant, Laidlaw, and Müller, 2.

Moore, Henrietta. "The Problem of Explaining Violence in the Social Sciences." In *Sex and Violence: Issues in Representation and Experience,* ed. Penelope Harvey and Peter Gow. London: Routledge, 1994.

Moore, R. I. *The Formation of a Persecuting Society: Power and Deviance in Western Europe, 950–1250.* Oxford: Oxford University Press, 1987.

Moran, Jo Ann Hoeppner. "The *Roman de la Rose* and the Thirteenth-Century Prohibitions of Homosexuality." *Cultural Frictions: Medieval Studies in Postmodern Contexts* (1995). 22 November 1996, http://www.georgetown.edu/labyrinth/conf/cs95/papers/moran.html. Also published as "Literature and the Medieval Historian." *Medieval Perspectives* 10 (1995): 49–66.

Morse, Ruth. *The Medieval Medea.* Woodbridge, Suffolk: Boydell and Brewer, 1996.

Moxey, Keith. "The Politics of Iconology." In *Iconography at the Crossroads,* ed. Cassidy.

Moya, Paula M. L., and Michael R. Hames-García, eds. *Reclaiming Identity: Realist Theory and the Predicament of Postmodernism.* Berkeley and Los Angeles: University of California Press, 2000.

Mulvey, Laura. "Afterthoughts on 'Visual Pleasure and Narrative Cinema' Inspired by King Vidor's *Duel in the Sun* (1946)." In *Visual and Other Pleasures.*

——. "Film, Feminism and the Avant-Garde." In *Visual and Other Pleasures.*

——. *Visual and Other Pleasures.* Bloomington: Indiana University Press, 1989.

——. "Visual Pleasure and Narrative Cinema." In *Visual and Other Pleasures.*

Mulvey, Laura, and Peter Wollen. "Riddles of the Sphinx: Script." *Screen* 18 (1977): 61–77.

——. "Penthesilea, Queen of the Amazons." Interview by Claire Johnston and Paul Willemen. *Screen* 15, no. 3 (1974): 120–34.

Musser, Charles. *The Emergence of Cinema: The American Screen to 1907.* New York: Scribner, 1990.

Nead, Lynda. *The Female Nude: Art, Obscenity, and Sexuality.* London: Routledge, 1992.

Nederman, Cary J., and Jacqui True. "The Third Sex: The Idea of the Hermaphrodite in Twelfth-Century Europe." *Journal of the History of Sexuality* 6 (1996): 497–517.

Nelson, Robert S. "The Slide Lecture, or The Work of Art *History* in the Age of Mechanical Reproduction." *Critical Inquiry* 26 (2000): 414–34.

——, ed. *Visuality before and beyond the Renaissance.* Cambridge: Cambridge University Press, 2000.

Nelson, Robert S., and Richard Shiff, eds. *Critical Terms for Art History.* Chicago: University of Chicago Press, 1996.

Nicholas, David. *Medieval Flanders.* London: Longman, 1992.

Noakes, Susan. *Timely Reading: Between Exegesis and Interpretation.* Ithaca, N.Y.: Cornell University Press, 1988.

O'Driscoll, Sally. "Outlaw Readings: Beyond Queer Theory." *Signs* 22 (1996): 30–51.

Oltrogge, Doris. *Die Illustrationszyklen zur "Histoire ancienne jusqu'à César" (1250–1400).* Frankfurt am Main: Peter Lang, 1989.

Ong, Walter J., S.J. "Latin Language Study as a Renaissance Puberty Rite." *Studies in Philology* 56 (1959): 103–24.

——. "Latin and the Social Fabric." In *The Barbarian within and Other Fugitive Essays and Studies.* New York: Macmillan, 1962.

Ouy, Gilbert. "Paris: L'un des principaux foyers de l'humanisme en Europe au début du XVᵉ siècle." *Bulletin de la société de l'histoire de Paris et de l'Ile de France* 94–95 (1967–68): 71–98.

Ouy, Gilbert, and Christine M. Reno. "Identification des autographes de Christine de Pizan." *Scriptorium* 34 (1980): 221–38.

"Ovid in Medieval Culture." Ed. Marilynn R. Desmond. Special issue of *Mediaevalia* 13 (1989, for 1987).

Pächt, Otto, and Jonathan Alexander. *Illuminated Manuscripts in the Bodleian Library.* 5 vols. Oxford: Clarendon Press, 1966–73.

Panofsky, Erwin. "Blind Cupid." In *Studies in Iconology.*

———. *Early Netherlandish Painting: Its Origins and Character.* 1953; reprint, New York: Harper and Row, 1971.

———. "Letter to the Editor." *Art Bulletin* 30 (1948): 242–44.

———. *The Life and Art of Albrecht Dürer.* 4th ed. Princeton: Princeton University Press, 1955.

———. *Perspective as Symbolic Form.* Trans. Christopher S. Wood. New York: Zone Books, 1991.

———. *Renaissance and Renascences in Western Art.* 1960; reprint, New York: Harper and Row, 1969.

———. *Studies in Iconology: Humanistic Themes in the Art of the Renaissance.* 1939; reprint, New York: Harper and Row, 1962.

———. "Style and Medium in the Motion Pictures." In *Three Essays on Style.*

———. "Three Decades of Art History in the United States." In *Meaning in the Visual Arts.* 1955; reprint, Chicago: University of Chicago Press, 1982.

———. *Three Essays on Style.* Ed. Irving Lavin. Cambridge: MIT Press, 1995.

Panofsky, Erwin, and Fritz Saxl. "Classical Mythology in Mediaeval Art." *Metropolitan Museum Studies* 4 (1932–33): 228–80.

———. *La mythologie classique dans l'art médiéval.* Trans. Sylvie Girard. Saint-Pierre-de-Salerne: Monfort, 1990.

Parker, Andrew, and Eve Kosofsky Sedgwick, eds. *Performativity and Performance.* London: Routledge, 1995.

Parussa, Gabriella. "Autographes et orthographe: Quelques considérations sur l'orthographe de Christine de Pizan." *Romania* 117 (1999): 143–59.

———. "Le concept d'intertextualité comme hypothèse interprétative d'une oeuvre: L'exemple de l'*Epistre Othea* de Christine de Pizan." *Studi Francesi* 111 (1993): 471–93.

Parussa, Gabriella, and Richard Trachsler. "*Or sus, alons ou champ des escriptures.* Encore sur l'orthographe de Christine de Pizan: l'intérêt des grands corpus." In *Contexts and Continuities,* ed. Kennedy, Brown-Grant, Laidlaw, and Müller, 3.

Pastoureau, Michel. *Blue: The History of a Color.* Trans. Markus I. Cruse. Princeton: Princeton University Press, 2001.

Paviot, Jacques. "L'ordre de la Toison d'or et la Croisade." In *L'ordre de la Toison d'or,* ed. Van den Bergen-Pantens.

Perdrizet, P. "Jean Miélot, l'un des traducteurs de Philippe le Bon." *Revue d'Histoire littéraire de la France* 14 (1907): 472–82.

Petro, Patrice, ed. *Fugitive Images: From Photography to Video.* Bloomington: Indiana University Press, 1995.

Phythian-Adams, Charles V. "Rituals of Personal Confrontation in Late Medieval England." *Bulletin of the John Rylands University Library of Manchester* 73 (1991): 65–90.

Picard, Gilbert. *Roman Painting.* Greenwich, Conn.: New York Graphic Society, 1968.

Pointon, Marcia. *History of Art: A Students' Handbook.* 3d ed. London: Routledge, 1994.

Poirion, Daniel, and Nancy Freeman Regalado, eds. "Contexts: Styles and Values in Medieval Art and Literature." Special issue of *Yale French Studies* 1991.

Prange, Regine. "Stil und Medium. Panofsky's 'On Movies.'" In *Erwin Panofsky. Beiträge des Symposions Hamburg 1992,* ed. Bruno Reudenbach. Berlin: Akademie, 1994.

Prevenier, Walter, and Wim P. Blockmans. *The Burgundian Netherlands.* Cambridge: Cambridge University Press, 1986.

Prewitt, Terry J. "Like a Virgin: The Semiotics of Illusion in Erotic Performance." *American Journal of Semiotics* 6 (1989): 137–52.

Preziosi, Donald. *Rethinking Art History: Meditations on a Coy Science.* New Haven: Yale University Press, 1989.

Prince, Stephen. *Screening Violence.* New Brunswick, N.J.: Rutgers University Press, 2000.

Probyn, Elspeth. "Queer Belongings: The Politics of Departure." In *Sexy Bodies,* ed. Grosz and Probyn.

Raehs, Andrea. *Zur Ikonographie des Hermaphroditen: Begriff und Problem von Hermaphroditismus und Androgynie in der Kunst.* Europäische Hochschulschriften: Reihe 28, Kunstgeschichte, vol. 113. Frankfurt am Main: Peter Lang, 1990.

Raynaud, Christiane. *La Violence au Moyen Age XIIIᵉ–XVᵉ siècle d'après les Livres d'Histoire en Français.* Paris: Léopard d'Or, 1990.

Regalado, Nancy Freeman. "'Des Contraires choses': La fonction poétique de la citation et des *exempla* dans le 'Roman de la Rose' de Jean de Meun." *Littérature* 41 (1981): 62–81.

Reno, Christine. "Feminist Aspects of Christine de Pizan's 'Epistre d'Othea a Hector.'" *Studi francesi* 71 (1980): 271–76.

Reno, Christine, and Gilbert Ouy. "X + X' = 1. Response to James C. Laidlaw." In *Contexts and Continuities,* ed. Kennedy, Brown-Grant, Laidlaw, and Müller, 3.

Richards, Earl Jeffrey. "Christine de Pizan and Jean Gerson: An Intellectual Friendship." In *Christine de Pizan 2000,* ed. Campbell and Margolis.

Riches, David. "The Phenomenon of Violence." In *The Anthropology of Violence,* ed. David Riches. Oxford: Oxford University Press, 1987.

Riches, Samantha. *St. George: Hero, Martyr, and Myth.* Phoenix Mill: Sutton, 2000.

Roberts, Martin. *Michel Tournier: "Bricolage" and Cultural Mythology.* Stanford French and Italian Studies 79. Saratoga, Calif.: ANMA Libri and Stanford, Calif.: Department of French and Italian, 1994.

Robertson, D. W., Jr. *A Preface to Chaucer: Studies in Medieval Perspectives.* Princeton: Princeton University Press, 1962.

Robson, J. E. "Bestiality and Bestial Rape in Greek Myth." In *Rape in Antiquity,* ed. Susan Deacy and Karen F. Pierce. London: Duckworth, 1997.

Rose, Jacqueline. *Sexuality and the Field of Vision.* London: Verso, 1986.

Rosenwein, Barbara H., ed. *Anger's Past: The Social Uses of an Emotion in the Middle Ages.* Ithaca, N.Y.: Cornell University Press, 1998.

———. "Worrying about Emotions in History," *American Historical Review* 107 (2002): 821–45.

Rouse, Richard H., and Mary A. Rouse. *Manuscripts and Their Makers: Commercial Book Producers in Medieval Paris, 1200–1500.* 2 vols. London: Harvey Miller, 2000.

Russell, Jeffrey Burton. *Witchcraft in the Middle Ages.* Ithaca, N.Y.: Cornell University Press, 1972.

Saenger, Paul. *Space between Words: The Origins of Silent Reading.* Stanford: Stanford University Press, 1997.

Salisbury, Joyce E. "Bestiality in the Middle Ages." In *Sex in the Middle Ages: A Book of Essays,* ed. Salisbury. New York: Garland, 1991.

Saslow, James M. *Ganymede in the Renaissance: Homosexuality in Art and Society.* New Haven: Yale University Press, 1986.

———. *Pictures and Passions: A History of Homosexuality in the Visual Arts.* New York: Penguin, 1999.

Sauerländer, Willibald. "Struggling with a Deconstructed Panofsky." In *Meaning in the Visual Arts,* ed. Lavin.

Sautman, Francesca Canadé, and Pamela Sheingorn, eds. *Same-Sex Love and Desire among Women in the Middle Ages.* New York: Palgrave, 2001.

Savedoff, Barbara E. "Looking at Art through Photographs." *Journal of Aesthetics and Art Criticism* 51 (1993): 455–62.

Saxl, Fritz. "Die Bibliothek Warburg und Ihr Ziel." *Vorträge der Bibliothek Warburg* 1 (1921–22): 1–10.

———. "The History of Warburg's Library (1886–1944)." In Gombrich, *Aby Warburg.*

Saxl, Fritz, and Hans Meier. *Verzeichnis astrologischer und mythologischer illustrierter Handschriften des lateinische Mittelalters III. Handschriften in englischen Bibliotheken.* 2 vols. London: Warburg Institute, 1953.

Schaefer, Lucy. "Die Illustrationen zu den Handschriften der Christine de Pizan." *Marburger Jahrbuch für Kunstwissenschaft* 10 (1937): 119–208.

Schapiro, Meyer. *Words, Script, and Pictures: Semiotics of Visual Language.* New York: George Braziller, 1996.

Schilperoort, Johanna. *Guillaume de Machaut et Christine de Pizan: Étude comparative.* n.p., 1936.

Schoell-Glass, Charlotte. "Aspekte der Antikenrezeption in Frankreich und Flandern im 15. Jahrhundert: Die Illustrationen der *Epistre Othea* von Christine de Pizan." Ph.D. diss., Universität Hamburg, 1993.

———. "'Serious Issues': The Last Plates of Warburg's Picture Atlas *Mnemosyne.*" In *Art History as Cultural History,* ed. Woodfield.

———. "Verwandlungen der Metamorphosen. Christliche Bildformen in Ovid-Illustrationen bei Christine de Pizan." In *Die Rezeption der "Metamorphosen" des Ovid in der Neuzeit,* ed. Walter and Horn.

Scott, Joan Wallach. "'Experience.'" In *Feminists Theorize the Political,* ed. Butler and Scott.

———. "Fantasy Echo: History and the Construction of Identity." *Critical Inquiry* 27 (2001): 284–304.

———. "'La Querelle des Femmes' in the Late Twentieth Century." *Differences* 9, no. 2 (1997): 70–92.

Scott, Margaret. *Late Gothic Europe, 1400–1500.* The History of Dress Series. Ed. Aileen Ribeiro. Atlantic Highlands, N.J.: Humanities Press, 1980.

Sedgwick, Eve Kosofsky. *Epistemology of the Closet.* Berkeley and Los Angeles: University of California Press, 1990.

———. "Queer and Now." In *Tendencies.* Durham: Duke University Press, 1993.

Senelick, Laurence, ed. *Gender in Performance: The Presentation of Difference in the Performing Arts.* Hanover, N.H.: University Press of New England, 1992.

Settis, Salvatore. "Warburg *continuatus.* Description d'une bibliothèque." In *Le Pouvoir des bibliothèques: La mémoire des livres en Occident,* ed. Marc Baratin and Christian Jacob. Paris: Albin Michel, 1996.

Seznec, Jean. *The Survival of the Pagan Gods: The Mythological Tradition and Its Place in Renaissance Humanism and Art.* Trans. Barbara F. Sessions. 1953; reprint, New York: Harper and Row, 1961.

Sheingorn, Pamela. "The Bodily Embrace or Embracing the Body: Gesture and Gender in Late Medieval Culture." In *The Stage as Mirror: Civic Theatre in Late Medieval Europe,* ed. Alan E. Knight. Cambridge: D. S. Brewer, 1997.

Sherman, Claire Richter. *Imaging Aristotle: Verbal and Visual Representation in Fourteenth-Century France.* Berkeley and Los Angeles: University of California Press, 1995.

Silverman, Kaja. *The Acoustic Mirror: The Female Voice in Psychoanalysis and Cinema.* Bloomington: Indiana University Press, 1988.

———. *Male Subjectivity at the Margins.* London: Routledge, 1992.

———. *The Threshold of the Visible World.* London: Routledge, 1996.

———. *World Spectators.* Stanford: Stanford University Press, 2000.

Simons, Patricia. "Lesbian (In)Visibility in Italian Renaissance Culture: Diana and Other Cases of *donna con donna.*" *Journal of Homosexuality* 27 (1994): 81–122.

Simpson, James R. *Fantasy, Identity, and Misrecognition in Medieval French Narrative.* Oxford: Peter Lang, 2000.

Slade, Joseph W. "Violence in the Hard-Core Pornographic Film: A Historical Survey." *Journal of Communication* 34 (1984): 148–63.

Snyder, Joel. "Benjamin on Reproducibility and Aura: A Reading of 'The Work of Art in the Age of Its Technical Reproducibility.'" In *Benjamin: Philosophy, Aesthetics, History,* ed. Gary Smith. Chicago: University of Chicago Press, 1989.

Sobchack, Vivian. "Phenomenology and the Film Experience." In *Viewing Positions: Ways of Seeing Film,* ed. Linda Williams. New Brunswick, N.J.: Rutgers University Press, 1995.

———. "What My Fingers Knew: The Cinesthetic Subject, or Vision in the Flesh." Revised version of a paper delivered at the Special Effects/Special Affects: Technologies of the Screen symposium held on the University of Melbourne, March 2000. <http://www.senseofcinema.com/contents/00/5/fingers.html>. Cited 24 June 2001.

Solterer, Helen. "Fiction vs Defamation: The Quarrel over the *Romance of the Rose.*" *Medieval History Journal* 2 (1999): 111–41.

———. "Flaming Words: Verbal Violence and Gender in Pre-modern Paris." *Romanic Review* 86 (1995): 355–78.

———. *The Master and Minerva: Disputing Women in French Medieval Culture.* Berkeley and Los Angeles: University of California Press, 1995.

———. "States of Siege: Violence, Place, Gender: Paris around 1400." *New Medieval Literatures* 2 (1998): 95–132.

Soussloff, Catherine M. "Like a Performance: Performativity and the Historicized Body, from Bellori to Mapplethorpe." In *Acting on the Past,* ed. Franko and Richards.

Spiegel, Gabrielle M. *Romancing the Past: The Rise of Vernacular Prose Historiography in Thirteenth-Century France.* Berkeley and Los Angeles: University of California Press, 1993.

Sponsler, Claire. "In Transit: Theorizing Cultural Appropriation in Medieval Europe." *Journal of Medieval and Early Modern Studies* 32 (2002): 17–39.

Staiger, Janet. *Perverse Spectators: The Practices of Film Reception.* New York: New York University Press, 2000.

Steinberg, Leo. *The Sexuality of Christ in Renaissance Art and in Modern Oblivion.* 2d ed. Chicago: University of Chicago Press, 1996.

Steinle, Eric M. "Versions of Authority in the *Roman de la Rose:* Remarks on the Use of Ovid's Metamorphoses by Guillaume de Lorris and Jean de Meun." *Mediaevalia* 13 (1989): 189–206.

Sterling, Charles. *La Peinture médiévale à Paris, 1300–1500.* 2 vols. Paris: Bibliothèque des Arts, 1987–90.

Stierle, Karlheinz. "Mythos als 'Bricolage' und zwei Endstufen des Prometheusmythos." In *Terror und Spiel,* ed. Fuhrmann.

Sullivan, Karen. "At the Limit of Feminist Theory: The Architectonics of the Querelle de la Rose." *Exemplaria* 3 (1991): 435–66.

Summit, Jennifer. *Lost Property: The Woman Writer and English Literary History, 1380–1589.* Chicago: University of Chicago Press, 2000.

Talbot, Charles W., ed. *Dürer in America: His Graphic Work.* Washington, D. C.: National Gallery of Art, 1971.

Thomasset, Claude. *Une Vision du monde à la fin du XIIIᵉ siècle. Commentaire du Dialogue de Placides et Timéo.* Geneva: Droz, 1982.

Thompson, Stith. *Motif-Index of Folk-Literature.* 6 vols. Bloomington: Indiana University Press, 1955–58.

Thut, Martin. "Narcisse versus Pygmalion: Un lecture du *Roman de la Rose.*" *Vox romanica* 41 (1982): 104–32.

Tinkle, Theresa. *Medieval Venuses and Cupids: Sexuality, Hermeneutics, and English Poetry.* Stanford: Stanford University Press, 1996.

———. "Saturn of the Several Faces: A Survey of the Medieval Mythographic Traditions." *Viator* 18 (1987): 289–302.

Török, Gyöngyi. "Beiträge zur Verbreitung einer Niederländischen Dreifaltigkeitsdarstellung im 15. Jahrhundert. Eine Elfenbeintafel aus dem Besitze Philipps des

Guten von Burgund." *Jahrbuch der kunsthistorischen Sammlungen in Wien* 81 (1985): 7–31.

Traub, Valerie. "The Perversion of 'Lesbian' Desire." *History Workshop Journal* 41 (1996): 23–49.

Turim, Maureen. "The Place of Visual Illusions." In *The Cinematic Apparatus,* ed. Teresa de Lauretis and Stephen Heath. New York: St. Martin's, 1985.

Turner, William B. *A Genealogy of Queer Theory.* Philadelphia: Temple University Press, 2000.

Tuve, Rosemond. *Allegorical Imagery: Some Mediaeval Books and Their Posterity.* Princeton: Princeton University Press, 1966.

Vale, Juliet. "Violence and the Tournament." In *Violence in Medieval Society,* ed. Kaeuper.

van Buren-Hagopian, Anne. "The Date of the Miniatures," "Artists of Volume 1," and "Dress and Costume" in *Les Chroniques de Hainaut,* ed. Van den Bergen-Pantens.

Van den Bergen-Pantens, Christiane, ed. *Les Chroniques de Hainaut ou les ambitions d'un Prince Bourguignon.* Turnhout: Brepols, 2000.

———. *L'ordre de la Toison d'or de Philippe le Bon à Philippe le Beau (1430–1505): Idéal ou reflet d'une société?* Brussels: Brepols, 1996.

van den Gheyn, J. *Christine de Pizan. Epitre d'Othéa, déesse de la prudence, à Hector, chef des Troyens. Réproductions des 100 miniatures du MS 9392 de Jean Miélot.* Brussels: Vromant and Co., 1913.

van den Neste, Évelyne. *Tournois, joutes, pas d'armes dans les villes de Flandre à la fin du Moyen Âge (1300–1486).* Paris: École des Chartes, 1996.

Van Engen, John, ed. *The Past and Future of Medieval Studies.* Notre Dame: University of Notre Dame Press, 1994.

van Huisstede, Peter. "Der Mnemosyne-Atlas. Ein Laboratorium der Bildgeschichte." In *Aby M. Warburg,* ed. Galitz and Reimers.

van Straten, Roelof. *An Introduction to Iconography.* Trans. Patricia de Man. Amsterdam: Gordon and Breach, 1994.

Vaughan, Richard. *Philip the Good: The Apogee of Burgundy.* London: Longmans, Green, 1970.

Verheyen, Egon, ed. *Art and Literature: Studies in Relationship.* Durham: Duke University Press, 1985.

Vicari, Patricia. "*Sparagmos:* Orpheus among the Christians." In *Orpheus,* ed. Warden.

von Euw, Anton, and Joachim M. Plotzek. *Die Handschriften der Sammlung Ludwig.* Cologne: Schnütgen Museum, 1979–85.

von Stockhausen, Tilmann. *Die Kulturwissenschaftliche Bibliothek Warburg. Architektur, Einrichtung und Organisation.* Hamburg: Dölling und Galitz, 1992.

Wallen, Burr. "Burgundian *Gloire* vs. *Vaine Gloire:* Patterns of Neochivalric *Psychomachia.*" In Gregory T. Clark et al., *A Tribute to Robert A. Koch: Studies in the Northern Renaissance.* Princeton: Department of Art and Archaeology, 1994.

Walter, Hermann, and Hans-Jürgen Horn, eds. *Die Rezeption der "Metamorphosen" des Ovid in der Neuzeit: Der Antike Mythos in Text und Bild.* Internationales Symposion der Werner Reimers-Stiftung, Bad Homburg v. d. H. (22. bis 25. April 1991). Berlin: G. Mann, 1995.

Wandruszka, Nikolai. "Familial Traditions of the *de Piçano* at Bologna." In *Contexts and Continuities,* ed. Kennedy, Brown-Grant, Laidlaw, and Müller, 3.

———. "The Family Origins of Christine de Pizan: Noble Lineage between City and *Contado* in the Thirteenth and Fourteenth Centuries." In *Au Champ des escriptures,* ed. Hicks.

Warburg, Aby. *Gesammelte Schriften. Studienausgabe.* Pt. 2, vol. 2.1, *Der Bilderatlas Mnemosyne.* Ed. Martin Warnke with C. Brink. Berlin: Akademie, 2000.

———. "Italian Art and International Astrology in the Palazzo Schifanoia, Ferrara." In *The Renewal of Pagan Antiquity: Contributions to the Cultural History of the European Renaissance,* trans. David Britt, intro. Kurt W. Forster. Los Angeles: Getty Research Institute for the History of Art and the Humanities, 1999.

———. "Italienische Kunst und Internationale Astrologie im Palazzo Schifanoja zu Ferrara." *Die Erneuerung der heidnischen Antike Kulturwissenschaftliche Beiträge zur Geschichte der europäischen Renaissance.* Sec. 1, vol. 1, pt. 2 of *Gesammelte Schriften herausgeben von der Bibliothek Warburg.* Ed. Gertrud Bing. Leipzig: B. G. Teubner, 1932; reprint, Berlin: Akademie, 1998.

———. *The Renewal of Pagan Antiquity: Contributions to the Cultural History of the European Renaissance.* Trans. David Britt. Intro. Kurt W. Forster. Los Angeles: Getty Research Institute for the History of Art and the Humanities, 1999.

Warburg, Eric M. "The Transfer of the Warburg Institute to England in 1933." *Warburg Institute Annual Report, 1952–3: 13–16.*

Warden, John, ed. *Orpheus: The Metamorphoses of a Myth.* Toronto: University of Toronto Press, 1982.

Warner, George F., and Julius P. Gilson. *Catalogue of Western Manuscripts in the Old Royal and King's Collections.* Vol. 2, *Royal Mss. 12 A. I to 20 E. X and App. 1–89.* London: British Museum, 1921.

Warner, Marina. *From the Beast to the Blonde: On Fairy Tales and Their Tellers.* London: Vintage, 1994.

Warnke, Martin. "Die Bibliothek Warburg und ihr Forschungsprogramm." In *Porträt aus Büchern. Bibliothek Warburg und Warburg Institute. Hamburg—1933—London.* Hamburg: Dölling und Galitz, 1993.

Waugh, Thomas. "Homosociality in the Classical American Stag Film: Off-Screen, On-Screen." *Sexualities* 4 (2001): 275–91.

Wells, William. "A Simile in Christine de Pisan for Christ's Conception." *Journal of the Warburg and Courtauld Institute* 2 (1938–39): 68–69.

West, Robin. "Pornography as a Legal Text." In *For Adult Users Only: The Dilemma of Violent Pornography,* ed. Susan Gubar and Joan Huff. Bloomington: Indiana University Press, 1989.

Wharton, Annabel Jane. "Good and Bad Images from the Synagogue of Dura Europos: Contexts, Subtexts, Intertexts." *Art History* 17 (1994): 1–25.

Willard, Charity Cannon. *Christine de Pizan: Her Life and Works.* New York: Persea, 1984.

———. "Christine de Pizan: The Astrologer's Daughter." In *Mélanges à la mémoire de Franco Simone,* ed. Jonathan Beck and Gianni Mombello. Geneva: Slatkine, 1980.

———. "Christine de Pizan on Chivalry." In *The Study of Chivalry: Resources and Ap-*

proaches, ed. Howell Chickering and Thomas H. Seiler. Kalamazoo, Mich.: Medieval Institute Publications, 1988.

———. "Christine de Pizan on the Art of Warfare." In *Christine de Pizan and the Categories of Difference,* ed. Desmond.

———. "Christine de Pizan's *Cent ballades d'amant et de dame:* Criticism of Courtly Love." In *Court and Poet,* ed. Glyn S. Burgess. Liverpool: Cairns, 1981.

Williams, Linda. "Corporealized Observers: Visual Pornographies and the 'Carnal Density of Vision.'" In *Fugitive Images,* ed. Petro.

———. "Film Bodies: Gender, Genre, and Excess." *Film Quarterly* 44 (1991): 2–13.

———. *Hard Core: Power, Pleasure, and the "Frenzy of the Visible."* Rev. ed. Berkeley and Los Angeles: University of California Press, 1999.

Wilson, Jean C. *Painting in Bruges at the Close of the Middle Ages: Studies in Society and Visual Culture.* University Park: Pennsylvania State University Press, 1998.

Winter, Patrick M. de, *La Bibliothèque de Philippe le Hardi, duc de Bourgogne (1364–1404): Étude sur les manuscrits à peintures d'une collection princière à l'époque du "style gothique international."* Paris: Editions du CNRS, 1985.

———. "Christine de Pizan: Ses enlumineurs et ses rapports avec le milieu bourguignon." In *Actes du 104ᵉ Congrès National des Sociétés Savantes (Bordeaux 1979).* Paris: Bibliothèque Nationale, 1982.

———. "Manuscrits à peintures produits pour le mécénat Lillois sous les règnes de Jean sans Peur et de Philippe le Bon." In *Actes du 101ᵉ Congrès National des Sociétés Savantes (Lille 1976).* Paris: Bibliothèque Nationale, 1978.

Wolf, Eric. *Europe and the People without History.* 2d ed. Berkeley and Los Angeles: University of California Press, 1997.

Wolfthal, Diane. "'Douleur sur toutes autres': Revisualing the Rape Script in the *Epistre Othea* and the *Cité des dames.*" In *Christine de Pizan and the Categories of Difference,* ed. Desmond.

———. *Images of Rape: The "Heroic" Tradition and Its Alternatives.* Cambridge: Cambridge University Press, 1999.

———, ed. *Peace and Negotiation: Strategies for Coexistence in the Middle Ages and Renaissance.* Turnhout: Brepols, 2000.

Woodfield, Richard, ed. *Art History as Cultural History: Warburg's Projects.* Amsterdam: G and B Arts International, 2001.

Yarnall, Judith. *Transformations of Circe: The History of an Enchantress.* Urbana: University of Illinois Press, 1994.

Young, Karl. *The Drama of the Medieval Church.* 2 vols. Oxford: Clarendon, 1933.

Zimmermann, Margarete, and Dina De Rentiis, eds. *The City of Scholars: New Approaches to Christine de Pizan.* European Cultures: Studies in Literature and the Arts, ed. Walter Pape, 2. Berlin: de Gruyter, 1994.

Index of the Works of Christine de Pizan

❧❧

Autres Balades, 198

Epistre au dieu d'Amours, 10–12, 47–49,
    48 (fig. 2.2), 50, 53, 74, 97,
    196–97, 211, 273n. 15, 294n. 4
Epistre Othea, passim
  chap. 1, 4, 9 (fig. I.2), 15, 16
    (fig. I.7), 84, 214–16, 234
  chap. 2, 15, 16 (fig. I.7), 198–99, 200
    (fig. 5.2), 295n. 13
  chap. 3, 5, 15, 251n. 48
  chap. 4, 15
  chap. 5, 5, 132–37, 136 (fig. 3.24),
    251n. 48
  chap. 6, 42–43
  chap. 8, 60–62, 61 (fig. 2.10), 65
  chap. 12, 22 (fig. 1.1), 41, 43,
    plate 1.1
  chap. 16, 71–74, 73 (fig. 2.17),
    277n. 53, 295n. 16
  chap. 17, 73 (fig. 2.17), 204–8, 211
  chap. 20, 203–4, 206 (fig. 5.7), 216
  chap. 22, 81–83, 82 (fig. 2.24)
  chap. 23, 123–26, 124 (fig. 3.16),
    128–30, 230 (fig. A.1), 231–33,
    233 (fig. A.3), plate A.1
  chap. 29, 217–22, 218 (fig. 5.13),
    237, 238 (fig. A.7)

  chap. 30, 217–22, 219 (fig. 5.14)
  chap. 34, 66–70, 67 (fig. 2.13)
  chap. 36, 292n. 2
  chap. 37, 251n. 48, 299n. 13
  chap. 40, 173–76, 174 (fig. 4.12), 214
  chap. 41, 174 (fig. 4.12), 176–78
  chap. 43, 90–93, 92 (fig. 2.30), 93
    (fig. 2.31), 237, 239 (fig. A.8),
    249n. 27
  chap. 45, 137–43, 139 (fig. 3.25)
  chap. 46, 299n. 13
  chap. 47, 46 (fig. 2.1), 55–56,
    plate 2.1
  chap. 48, 156 (fig. 4.1), 167–68,
    171–73, 172 (fig. 4.11), plate 4.1
  chap. 51, 60–62, 63 (fig. 2.11)
  chap. 53, 112–14, 113 (fig. 3.8),
    117–18, 216
  chap. 55, 126
  chap. 57, 178–84, 179 (fig. 4.15), 216
  chap. 58, 10–14, 11 (fig. I.3), 207,
    231, 232 (fig. A.2)
  chap. 63, 119, 122 (fig. 3.15)
  chap. 64, 122 (fig. 3.15), 199–203,
    202 (fig. 5.4)
  chap. 67, 98 (fig. 3.1), 108–11, 216
  chap. 69, 119–23, 121 (fig. 3.14),
    299n. 13

Epistre Othea, passim (*continued*)

  chap. 70, 108–11, 109 (fig. 3.7)

  chap. 71, 87–90, 88 (fig. 2.27), 89 (fig. 2.28)

  chap. 75, 150–55, 152 (fig. 3.32), 249n. 27

  chap. 76, 167–69, 170 (fig. 4.10)

  chap. 82, 148–50, 149 (fig. 3.30)

  chap. 84, 94–97, 94 (fig. 2.32), 96 (fig. 2.34)

  chap. 85, 75 (fig. 2.18), 90, 91 (fig. 2.29), 190

  chap. 86, 74–76, 75 (fig. 2.18), 214, 299n. 13

  chap. 87, 126, 214

  chap. 88, 296n. 26

  chap. 89, 192, 214

  chap. 90, 190, 212, 213 (fig. 5.11)

  chap. 91, 184–89, 186 (fig. 4.19), 192

  chap. 92, 184–89, 187 (fig. 4.20)

  chap. 93, 214, 215 (fig. 5.12)

  chap. 94, 190–92

  chap. 96, 190, 191 (fig. 4.23)

  chap. 97, 144–45, 146 (fig. 3.28), 192

  chap. 98, 142–45, 147 (fig. 3.29)

  chap. 99, 204, 209–11, 210 (fig. 5.10)

  chap. 100, 194 (fig. 5.1), 222–29, 223 (fig. 5.17), 233–35, 234 (fig. A.4), 235 (fig. A.5), plate 5.1

Lamentacion sur les maux de la France, 229

Livre de la cité des dames, 4, 119, 199, 220, 222, 292n. 29

Livre de la mutacion de Fortune, xii (fig. I.1), 1–2, 66, 243n. 1, plate I.1

Livre des fais d'armes et de chevalerie, 84, 192–93

Livre du chemin de long estude, 50, 222, 272n. 13

Livre du corps de policie, 43

querelle de la Rose, 49–51, 65, 97, 197–98. *See also* General Index

Index of Manuscripts

❧❧❧

Aylesbury, Buckinghamshire
  Waddesdon Manor
    MS 8, 234, 235 (fig. A.5),
      275n. 43, 298nn. 1, 6

Beauvais
  Bibliothèque Municipale
    MS 9, 16, 237, 298n. 1
Bergamo
  Biblioteca Civica Angelo Mai
    MS Cassaf.3.4, 285n. 33
Berlin
  Staatsbibliothek Preussischer
    Kulturbesitz
    MS lat.oct.44, 286n. 43
Besançon
  Bibliothèque Municipale
    MS 677, 57 (fig. 2.8)
Brussels
  Bibliothèque Royale
    MS 9242, 86 (fig. 2.26), 279nn. 70,
      76
    MS 9392, 85–90, 88 (fig. 2.27),
      91 (fig. 2.29), 93 (fig. 2.31),
      94 (fig. 2.32), 269n. 91,
      275n. 43, 278n. 62, 279n. 76,
      298nn. 1, 6

MS 9559-64, 234, 236 (fig. A.6),
  299n. 8
MS 10982, 272nn. 13, 272n. 14
MS 11060-1, 222–24, 226
  (fig. 5.20)
MS IV 1114, 234–35, 299n. 8

Cambridge
  Newnham College Library
    MS 900 (5), 16, 237, 275n. 43,
      298n. 1
Chantilly
  Musée Condé
    MS 65, 224, 228 (fig. 5.22)
    MS 492-93, 16, 253n. 63
Cologny
  Foundation Bodmer
    MS 49, 298n. 1
Copenhagen
  Kongelige Bibliotek
    MS Thott 341, 165, 175–76, 175
      (fig. 4.13), 177 (fig. 4.14),
      293n. 33

Duke's manuscript. *See* Paris, Bibliothèque Nationale, MS fr. 606, 835,
  836, 605

Erlangen-Nürnberg
  Universitätsbibliothek
    MS 2361, 233, 234 (fig. A.4),
      244n. 10, 298nn. 1, 5

Hague, The
  Koninklijke Bibliotheek
    MS 74 G 27, 231–32, 232
      (fig. A.2), 233 (fig. A.3),
      275n. 43, 298n. 1

Lille
  Bibliothèque Municipale Jean Levy
    MS 175, 230 (fig. A.1), 232–33,
      298nn. 1, 3

London
  British Library
    MS Egerton 881, 273n. 19
    MS Harley 4431 (Queen's manu-
      script), 11 (fig. I.3), 17–19, 22
      (fig. 1.1), 42–43, 45, 46
      (fig. 2.1), 48 (fig. 2.2), 50–52,
      55, 61 (fig. 2.10), 62, 67
      (fig. 2.13), 73 (fig. 2.17), 75
      (fig. 2.18), 82 (fig. 2.24), 84, 87,
      89 (fig. 2.28), 90, 92 (fig. 2.30),
      95, 96 (fig. 2.34), 97, 121
      (fig. 3.14), 122 (fig. 3.15), 124
      (fig. 3.16), 125 (fig. 3.17), 136
      (fig. 3.24), 139 (fig. 3.25), 146
      (fig. 3.28), 147 (fig. 3.29), 152
      (fig. 3.32), 156 (fig. 4.1), 165,
      169, 170 (fig. 4.10), 171–73,
      176, 179 (fig. 4.15), 185, 186
      (fig. 4.19), 187 (fig. 4.20), 190,
      192, 194 (fig. 5.1), 195, 198–99,
      200 (fig. 5.2), 204, 210
      (fig. 5.10), 211, 213 (fig. 5.11),
      215 (fig. 5.12), 217, 218
      (fig. 5.13), 219 (fig. 5.14),
      224–25, 231–33, 237, 252n. 50,
      253n. 65, 254nn. 67, 71,
      273n. 16, 274n. 26, 294n. 11,
      296n. 26, 298n. 1

MS Royal 20 B. VI, 284n. 23
MS Royal 20 D.I, 13 (fig. I.5), 95
  (fig. 2.33), 157–60, 158
  (fig. 4.2), 162–65, 164 (fig. 4.7),
  181, 181 (fig. 4.16), 289n. 1,
  293n. 32
MS Sloane 3983, 42, 246n. 22,
  275n. 37
MS Stowe 54, 159, 165, 289n. 1
Los Angeles
  J. Paul Getty Museum
    MS 83.MR.177 (Ms. Ludwig XV 7),
      77 (fig. 2.20), 277n. 56
Lyon
  Bibliothèque Municipale
    MS 742, 106–8, 127–29 (fig. 3.20),
      282n. 13
    Clm 10268, 286n. 43

Munich
  Bayerisches Staatsbibliothek
    MS Gall. 11, xii (fig. I.1), 243n. 1
    Clm 10268, 286n. 43

New York
  Metropolitan Museum of Art, The
    Cloisters
      Belles Heures of Jean, duke of Berry,
        224–25, 227 (fig. 5.21),
        297nn. 35–36
  Pierpont Morgan Library
    M 48, 50, 78–79, 78 (fig. 2.21),
      79 (fig. 2.22)
    M 284, 256n. 5
    M 785, 42, 62, 64 (fig. 2.12),
      246n. 22, 275n. 37

Oxford
  Bodleian Library
    MS Bodley 421, 237, 298n. 1
    MS Bodley 614, 133, 133
      (fig. 3.21)
    MS Douce 371, 13 (fig. I.6),
      50–51, 52 (fig. 2.3), 53 (fig. 2.4),

54, 56 (fig. 2.7), 71, 72
(figs. 2.15 and 2.16), 208,
278n. 60, 295n. 17
MS e. Mus. 65, 277n. 54

Paris
Bibliothèque de l'Arsenal
MS 5069, 106–8, 115–16, 120
(fig. 3.13), 143, 144 (fig. 3.27),
151 (fig. 3.31), 152–53, 167
(fig. 4.8), 168 (fig. 4.9), 207, 209
(fig. 5.9), 222, 282nn. 12–14,
287nn. 49, 57, 297n. 34
Bibliothèque Nationale de France
MS fr. 246, 165, 182–83, 182
(fig. 4.17), 183 (fig. 4.18)
MS fr. 301, 159, 160 (fig. 4.3),
161, 161 (fig. 4.4), 162 (fig. 4.5),
163 (fig. 4.6), 165, 185, 188
(fig. 4.21), 189 (fig. 4.22),
289n. 1, 290nn. 7, 11, 293n. 33
MS fr. 380, 50, 115 (fig. 3.10),
273n. 19, 276n. 51, 278n. 60
MS fr. 598, 12 (fig. I.4), 199, 201
(fig. 5.3), 221 (fig. 5.16)
MS fr. 604, 253n. 63
MS fr. 606, 835, 836, 605 (Duke's
manuscript), 9 (fig. I.2), 17–19,
42–43, 45, 50–52, 62, 63
(fig. 2.11), 84, 87, 90, 97, 98
(fig. 3.1), 109 (fig. 3.7), 113
(fig. 3.8), 125 (fig. 3.17), 149
(fig. 3.30), 165, 171, 172
(fig. 4.11), 173, 176, 185, 191
(fig. 4.23), 192, 195, 198–99,
202 (fig. 5.4), 204, 206 (fig. 5.7),
211, 217, 223 (fig. 5.17),
224–29, 231–33, 237, 253n. 64,
254nn. 67, 71, 273n. 16,
274n. 26, 289n. 69, 294n. 11,
295n. 13, 297n. 38, 298n. 1
MS fr. 848, 15, 16 (fig. I.7), 199,
237, 252n. 57, 295n. 13
MS fr. 1185, 299n. 7

MS fr. 1188, 272n. 13
MS fr. 12420, 199
MS fr. 12595, 50, 71, 276n. 50,
278n. 60
MS fr. 12779, 16, 253n. 63
MS fr. 25559, 299n. 7
MS lat. 7330, 42, 246n. 22,
275n. 37
MS lat. 7331, 275n. 37
Bibliothèque Ste.-Geneviève
MS 1126, 295n. 17

Queen's manuscript. See London, British
Library, MS Harley 4431

Rouen
Bibliothèque Municipale
MS O.4, 74, 76 (fig. 2.19), 83
(fig. 2.25), 103–6, 104 (fig. 3.2),
105 (fig. 3.3), 106 (fig. 3.4), 107
(fig. 3.5), 108 (fig. 3.6), 115, 116
(fig. 3.11), 117 (fig. 3.12), 127
(fig. 3.18), 128 (fig. 3.19), 134,
134 (fig. 3.22), 135 (fig. 3.23),
140–41, 141 (fig. 3.26), 152–53,
153 (fig. 3.33), 154 (fig. 3.34),
203 (fig. 5.5), 205 (fig. 5.6), 207,
208 (fig. 5.8), 220 (fig. 5.15),
222, 224 (fig. 5.18), 225
(fig. 5.19), 281n. 11, 282n. 13,
287n. 49

Très Riches Heures. See Chantilly, Musée
Condé, MS 65

València
Universitat de València, Biblioteca
Històrica
MS 387, 50–52, 54 (fig. 2.5), 55
(fig. 2.6), 58, 59 (fig. 2.9),
66–69, 68 (fig. 2.14), 79, 80
(fig. 2.23), 81, 114 (fig. 3.9),
272nn. 13–14, 273n. 16,
275n. 32, 276nn. 45–46, 48

General Index

๙ฬ๛

abduction, of Helen of Troy, 150–55, 162–64, 164 (fig. 4.7)

Abū Maʿšar, astrological work, 5, 41–42, 44, 62, 269n. 92

Achilles, 87–90, 88 (fig. 2.27), 89 (fig. 2.28), 292n. 22
   death of, 173–76, 174 (fig. 4.12), 175 (fig. 4.13)

Actaeon, 120 (fig. 3.13), 121 (fig. 3.14)

aesthetics, and ethics, 19

Agamben, Giorgio, 32, 36, 166, 212, 263n. 48, 291n. 21

Ajax, 190–92

Alan de Lille, 101

Alexander, Jonathan, 18, 254n. 68, 258n. 13

allegorie, in Christine's *Othea,* 3

allegory, and astrology, 44

Amazons, 6, 178–84, 181 (fig. 4.16), 292n. 29, 293n. 30. *See also* Penthesilea

Anderson, William S., 295n. 15

Andromeda and Perseus, 100, 131–37, 133 (fig. 3.21), 134 (fig. 3.22), 135 (fig. 3.23), 136 (fig. 3.24), 286n. 41, 287nn. 45–46

anger, 196–212, 294nn. 3, 12, 295n. 15, 296n. 22

antiquity, survival of, 31–32, 34 (fig. 1.3), 35 (fig. 1.4), 40, 44–45

Apollo. *See* Phoebus Apollo

Apostles' Creed, 70

Arachne, 122 (fig. 3.15), 199–203, 201 (fig. 5.3), 203 (fig. 5.5), 295n. 14

ara coeli, 222, 224–25, 233–34

Aristotle, *Nicomachean Ethics,* 7–8, 211. *See also* Oresme, Nicole

ars dictaminis, 7

art history, 256n. 8, 264n. 54, 267n. 74, 268n. 85. *See also* "Panofsky's gaze"
   and cinema, 20, 25–26, 30–31, 259n. 21
   and photography, 33–40, 263nn. 49, 51
   and slide projection, 30–33, 39

artist, female, 201–3

artwork, "original," 38–40

astrology, 4–5, 31–32, 41–45, 60, 62, 64 (fig. 2.12), 133 (fig. 3.21), 265n. 61, 269n. 96, 286nn. 42–43

Athamas and Ino, 204–11, 208 (fig. 5.8), 209 (fig. 5.9), 210 (fig. 5.10)

Athena. *See* Pallas Athena

Atropos, 66–70, 67 (fig. 2.13), 68 (fig. 2.14), 69, 275nn. 42, 43, 276nn. 44, 46

Augustine, Saint, 214, 222
Augustus, Emperor, 222–23, 223
    (fig. 5.17), 224–29, 226 (fig. 5.20),
    227 (fig. 5.21), 228 (fig. 5.22),
    234 (fig. A.4), 235 (fig. A.5),
    297n. 36
author, role in manuscript production,
    14–17
authority, female, 217, 233–34
Avril, François, 281n. 11, 282n. 12

Babyngton, Anthony, 241
Bal, Mieke, 247n. 23
"bare life," 166–73, 176–78, 291n. 21
Barkan, Leonard, 270n. 104
Bazin, André, 30
Belles Heures, 224, 227 (fig. 5.21)
Benjamin, Walter, 30, 39–40
Berlo, Janet, 247n. 24, 248n. 25
bestiality, 131–32, 137–43
Bhabha, Homi K., 247n. 24
Bible, Proverbs, 119–23
blood, 158–60, 164–65, 171, 182,
    290n. 2
Blume, Dieter, 256n. 5, 269nn. 96, 99
Blumenfeld-Kosinski, Renate, 140,
    247n. 23, 248nn. 25, 26, 277n. 57
Boccaccio, Giovanni
    Caccia di Diana, 119
    De claris mulieribus, 4, 181, 199
        (*see also* Laurent de Premierfait)
body, human, 74
    female, 34 (fig. 1.3), 35 (fig. 1.4), 36,
        51, 69, 81, 129, 133–34, 166,
        180–81, 217–20 (*see also* Amazons)
bondage, sexual, 134
books of hours, 214, 222, 224–28,
    297n. 36
Boswell, John, 283n. 17
Bourdieu, Pierre, 8
breast, 69, 180–81
bricolage, 5–6, 247nn. 23–25
Brownlee, Kevin, 277n. 57
Brussels Hours, 222, 226 (fig. 5.20)
Bryson, Norman, 85

Burgundian court culture, 84–97,
    231–32, 234–35, 279n. 76
Burgundy, dukes of. *See* Charles the
    Bold; John the Fearless; Philip
    the Bold; Philip the Good
Busiris, 176–78, 177 (fig. 4.14)
Butler, Judith, 100

Cahoon, Leslie, 274n. 21
Callisto, 126–30, 127 (fig. 3.18), 128
    (fig. 3.19), 129 (fig. 3.20)
Camille, Michael, 2, 274n. 21, 278n. 62
Canon Episcopi, 118
Cassirer, Ernst, 257n. 11
castration, 274n. 30
    crisis, 53–65, 101
    of Saturn, 57–58, 59 (fig. 2.9), 60–62,
        65, 275nn. 32–33
Cavell, Stanley, 27
Cent histoires de Troye, Les, 237–40, 238
    (fig. A.7), 239 (fig. A.8)
Cephalus and Procris, 167–69, 167
    (fig. 4.8), 170 (fig. 4.10)
Charles the Bold, duke of Burgundy,
    298n. 5
Charles V, king of France, 5, 8, 50, 57
    (fig. 2.8), 84, 211, 272n. 10
chastity, 118–31. *See also* Diana
"Children of the Planets," 41, 43–45,
    60, 62, 69, 123, 199, 233, 269n. 94
C. Hystoryes of Troye, 241
chivalric conduct, 3, 7–8, 84–97, 190–93
Christina of Markyate, 142
Christine de Pizan. *See* Index of the
    Works of Christine de Pizan
Chroniques de Hainaut. See Jean
    Wauquelin
chronology, 212–16
cinema, 2, 23–24, 30–31, 39–40, 160,
    256n. 9, 257n. 10, 261n. 34. *See
    also* films; film theory; montage
    and art history, 25–26, 30–31
    Hollywood, 7, 14, 23–27, 57, 256n. 9
Circe, 6, 100, 131–32, 142–45, 144
    (fig. 3.27), 147 (fig. 3.29), 288n. 68

Cité des dames Master, 18

class, 204

classical texts, vernacular adaptations
     of, 4. See also *Ovide moralisé*

Clemence of Hungary, 281n. 11

closet, rhetoric of, 103–12

conduct. *See* chivalric conduct

colonialisms, medieval, 19, 178–80

costume, 74, 85–87, 114, 171, 284n. 23

Crary, Jonathan, 261n. 34

Crone, Rainer, 247n. 24

Crucifixion, 107 (fig. 3.5)

cultural memory, visual, 2

Cupid, 46 (fig. 2.1), 47–49, 48 (fig. 2.2),
     54–56, 56 (fig. 2.7), 95–97, 96
     (fig. 2.34), 196, 274nn. 23–24, 26

Daedalus, 160–61

Dante, *Purgatorio*, 137

Daphne, 166, 282n. 32, 291n. 19

Death. *See* Atropos

death drive, masculinity and, 66–70

deities
     classical, 31–32, 270n. 104 (*see also
         individual deities*)
     planetary, 42–43 (*see also* "Children of
         the Planets")

de Lauretis, Teresa, 163, 165

Derbes, Anne, 293n. 30

Derrida, Jacques, 247n. 24

Diana, 6, 100, 118–31, 120 (fig. 3.13),
     121 (fig. 3.14), 122 (fig. 3.15), 124
     (fig. 3.16), 127 (fig. 3.18), 128
     (fig. 3.19), 129 (fig. 3.20), 230
     (fig. A.1), 231–33, 233 (fig. A.3),
     284n. 28, 285n. 32

Diomede, 94 (fig. 2.32)

domestic violence. *See* violence, against
     women

drama, medieval, 297n. 33

ducal library (Burgundy), 84

Duke's manuscript. *See* Index of
     Manuscripts

Dulac, Liliane, 293n. 1

Dunlop, Louisa, 159

Dürer, Albrecht, 28–30, 29 (fig. 1.2),
     260n. 32, 261n. 33

Echo, 74–76, 75 (fig. 2.18), 76
     (fig. 2.19), 277n. 54

Egbert, Virginia Wylie, 79

Egerton Master, 18, 226

Ehrhart, Margaret J., 253n. 61

Eisenstein, S. M., 6, 36, 160–61, 241

emblems, 289n. 76

Enders, Jody, 294n. 2

Epître Master, 18, 226, 286n. 44

ethics
     and aesthetics, 19
     and temporality, 4

Eurocentrism, 24–25, 32, 40, 45

Eurydice, 103–5, 104 (fig. 3.2), 105
     (fig. 3.3), 109 (fig. 3.7), 110. *See
     also* Orpheus

Fauvel Artist, 282n. 12

Fendulus, Georgius, 269nn. 92, 99
     Liber astrologiae, 41–42, 44

Fenster, Thelma, 270n. 3

Ferguson, Bruce W., 247n. 24

Ferguson, Frances, 28

fetishism, 19, 26, 51, 81, 133

films
     Penthesilea, 6–7
     Riddles of the Sphinx, 6–7, 250nn. 30,
         33

film theory, 8, 250n. 41, 259n. 20,
     261n. 34, 265n. 63

Fleur des Chroniques, 56, 57 (fig. 2.8)

"following the goddess," 118–19,
     130–31, 284n. 24

Forster, Kurt, 36

Foster, Hal, 255n. 76

Freedman, Barbara, 261n. 33

Freud, Sigmund, 26

Ganymede, 100, 112–18, 113 (fig. 3.8),
     116 (fig. 3.11), 283n. 20

Garvey, Gerald, 247n. 24

Gaunt, Simon, 51, 273n. 19

gaze, the. *See also* "Panofsky's gaze"
    female, 135, 137, 140
    male, 85, 109, 262n. 39
    "outlaw," 132, 137, 145
gender, and violence, 161–89
Genette, Gérard, 247n. 24
Gerson, Jean, 49–50, 270n. 4, 272n. 6
gesture, 8, 43, 54–56, 127, 195–96,
        199, 204, 212–16, 222, 232,
        293n. 1, 294n. 2
    embrace, 148, 151–54, 288n. 61
    handclasp, 95
    homage, 54, 274n. 22
Gibbs, Stephanie, 253n. 59
Ginzburg, Carlo, 119, 257n. 11
Giotto, 275n. 39
Girard, René, 165
glose, in Christine's *Othea,* 3
God of Love. *See* Cupid
Golden Fleece, Order of the, 85,
        279n. 67
Gombrich, Ernst, 33, 265n. 61,
        266n. 72
Gontier Col, 197
grisaille, 15
Grosz, Elizabeth, 142
Gui, Bernard, *Fleur des Chroniques,* 56,
        57 (fig. 2.8)
Guido da Pisa, 288n. 59
Guillaume de Lorris, 70. See also *Roman
        de la rose*
Guillaume Machaut, *Confort d'ami,*
        111–12
Guillebert de Metz, 234

habitus, 8
Halfmann, Jasper, 247n. 24
Hamburg, Kulturwissenschaftliche
        Bibliothek Warburg, 31
Hart, Joan, 257n. 11, 263n. 46,
        267n. 79
Hautschild, Lubertus, 41–42
Heckscher, William S., 258n. 17,
        259n. 28
Hector, passim, 75 (fig. 2.18), 91

(fig. 2.29), 188 (fig. 4.21), 213
        (fig. 5.11)
    death of, 184–89, 186 (fig. 4.19), 187
        (fig. 4.20), 189 (fig. 4.22), 212–14,
        215 (fig. 5.12)
    and Patroclus, 158 (fig. 4.2), 164–65,
        190
Hecuba, 173–76, 292n. 24
Helen of Troy, 6, 90–93, 150–55, 152
        (fig. 3.32), 153 (fig. 3.33), 154
        (fig. 3.34), 162–64, 164 (fig. 4.7)
Henry IV, king of England, 3
Hermaphroditus, 100, 148–50, 149
        (fig. 3.30), 151 (fig. 3.31),
        289n. 75
heterosexuality, 100, 148–55
Hibbitts, Bernard J., 8
Hindman, Sandra, 12–15, 123, 214,
        217, 248n. 26, 252n. 50, 253n. 65,
        292n. 24
Histoire ancienne jusqu'à César, 4, 66,
        157–61, 289n. 1
    story of Amazons, 181–84, 181
        (fig. 4.16), 293n. 30
    story of Busiris, 176, 177 (fig. 4.14)
    story of death of Achilles, 175–76, 175
        (fig. 4.13)
    story of Hector, 158 (fig. 4.2), 185,
        188 (fig. 4.21), 189 (fig. 4.22)
    story of Io, 217
    story of Judith and Holofernes,
        182–83, 183 (fig. 4.18), 293n. 33
    story of Medea, 12, 13 (fig. I.5), 14
    story of Paris and Helen, 164 (fig. 4.7)
    story of Penthesilea, 160 (fig. 4.3),
        161 (fig. 4.4), 162 (fig. 4.5), 163
        (fig. 4.6)
    story of Thamyris and Cyrus, 182
        (fig. 4.17)
    story of Troilus and Briseyda, 95
        (fig. 2.33)
Holly, Michael Ann, 38, 257n. 12,
        263n. 46, 267n. 74
homage, 54–55
homoeroticism, 51, 101–12, 115–18,

273n. 19. *See also* Orpheus;
  pederasty; sodomy
women and, 126–31, 178, 184
homosexuality, 101–6, 110–12, 283n. 17
Hoogewerff, G. J., 257n. 11
Hugh of St. Victor, 62
Huizinga, Johann, 165
Hult, David F., 294n. 12
Hundred Years' War, 192, 290n. 5
hunt, the, 119–23, 122 (fig. 3.15)
Huot, Sylvia, 50
Hyacinth, 115, 117–18, 117 (fig. 3.12)

iconography, 25–26, 38–41, 44–45,
  257nn. 11, 12, 258n. 13, 263n. 46,
  267n. 74, 268n. 85
Ignatius, Mary Ann, 15
Illich, Ivan, 2
Ino. *See* Athamas and Ino
intervisuality, 252n. 56. *See also* text and
  image
Io, 217–22, 218 (fig. 5.13), 219
  (fig. 5.14), 220 (fig. 5.15), 238
  (fig. A.7)
Isabeau of Bavaria, queen of France, 17
Isabelle of Portugal, 85, 298n. 5
Isis, 297n. 30

Jacques de Guise, *Chroniques de Hainaut,*
  86 (fig. 2.26)
Jauss, Hans Robert, 32
Jean, duke of Berry, 3, 5, 17, 41, 50, 62,
  199, 222–24, 226–29
Jean de Meun, 49, 65. See also *Roman
  de la rose*
Jean de Montreuil, 83, 196
Jean Wauquelin, *Chroniques de Hainaut,*
  85, 86 (fig. 2.26), 90, 279n. 70
John the Fearless, duke of Burgundy,
  84
Judith and Holofernes, 182–83, 183
  (fig. 4.18), 293n. 33
Julius Caesar, 222, 225 (fig. 5.19)
Jupiter, 127 (fig. 3.18), 285n. 33
Justice, 235, 236 (fig. A.6)

knight, ideal, 83–84. *See also* chivalric
  conduct
Koch, Gertrude, 265n. 63
Kracauer, Siegfried, 256n. 9
Krueger, Roberta, 296n. 26

Laidlaw, James, 15, 253n. 64, 254n. 67
Landauer, Carl, 30, 36
Latona, 203–4, 205 (fig. 5.6), 206
  (fig. 5.7)
Laurent de Premierfait, *Des cleres et
  nobles femmes* (Boccaccio), 4, 12
  (fig. I.4), 123–26, 125 (fig. 3.17),
  165–66, 199, 201 (fig. 5.3),
  220–22, 221 (fig. 5.16)
Lavin, Irving, 26, 256n. 8, 258n. 15,
  296n. 22
Legenda aurea, 229
Leicester, H. Marshall, Jr., 274n. 23
Le Noir, Philippe, 235, 240–41
Leonardo da Vinci, 290n. 2
Levin, Thomas Y., 26, 257n. 10
Lévi-Strauss, Claude, 5
library. *See also* Warburg Institute
  ducal (Burgundy), 84–85
  royal (France), 50, 165
Liédet, Loyset, 52–53, 87–97, 278n. 62,
  279n. 76, 298n. 6
light, theories of. *See* optics
literacy, female, 123–30, 124 (fig. 3.16),
  233
"Livre de Christine," 16
Lord, Carla, 256n. 7, 281n. 11,
  285n. 33
Louis, duke of Orleans, 8, 15, 17,
  225–29

McEwan, Dorothea, 263n. 47
McGrady, Deborah, 17
McGuire, Brian Patrick, 270n. 4
MacKinnon, Catherine, 28
McMunn, Meradith, 273n. 15, 277n. 56
magic lantern, 30–31, 262nn. 44, 45
male lack. *See* castration crisis;
  masculinity

manuscript production, 14–19, 84,
157–60, 217–22, 231–32
Mariken van Nieumeghen, 276n. 44
masculinity
"amorously imperilled male," 143
and castration, 53–65
construction of, 47–49, 84
and death drive, 66–70
ethical, 97
heteronormative, 100
as masquerade, 85–90
performance of, 27–28, 50, 259n. 28,
260n. 29
and reading, 50
Mast, Gerald, 39
Medea, 10–14, 11 (fig. I.3), 12 (fig. I.4),
13 (figs. I.5, I.6), 203, 207–8, 231,
232 (fig. A.2), 295n. 17
Meiss, Millard, 2, 15, 18, 66, 69, 171,
222, 254n. 67, 276n. 45, 286n. 44,
295n. 13
memento mori, 69–70, 212, 214
Mercury, 22 (fig. 1.1), 43, 269n. 95
Michels, Karen, 268n. 85
Miélot, Jean, 52–53, 93, 97, 280nn. 77,
80, 298n. 6
Miller, William Ian, 165, 184, 290n. 14
Minerva, 192–93
misogyny, 47–49, 103, 150
modesty, assumed, 197, 199
Mohanty, Satya, 197
"monstrous races," 180. *See also* Amazons
montage, 6, 36, 45, 87, 110, 159–61,
211–16, 220, 241
Moore, Henrietta, 291n. 21
Mulvey, Laura, 250nn. 30, 34
Musser, Charles, 30
myth. *See names of mythological figures;
Ovide moralisé*

Narcissus, 70–76, 72 (fig. 2.16), 73
(fig. 2.17), 75 (fig. 2.18), 76
(fig. 2.19), 276nn. 49–51,
277nn. 53–55
Nelson, Robert S., 264n. 54

Noakes, Susan, 212, 296n. 26
nudity, female, 133–34

O'Driscoll, Sally, 131–32, 137
Odysseus, 144 (fig. 3.27), 144–45, 147
(fig. 3.29), 288n. 68
optics, 2, 114, 283n. 22
Order of the Golden Fleece, 85,
279n. 67
ordinatio, 3, 15–18, 87, 159, 237
Oresme, Nicole, 14
Livre de ethiques (Aristotle), 8, 211,
250n. 39, 295n. 20, 296n. 21
Livre de politiques (Aristotle), 292n. 26
organization
of manuscript, 3, 15–18
of printed page, 237
orientalism, 24–25, 45, 180–81, 183–84,
265n. 61
Origen, 74
Orpheus, 98 (fig. 3.1), 100–112, 104
(fig. 3.2), 106 (fig. 3.4), 107
(fig. 3.5), 108 (fig. 3.6), 109
(fig. 3.7), 281nn. 5, 8–9, 282n. 14
Othea, passim, 3, 244n. 11
outlaw theory, 131–32, 137–38
Ovid, 138
Metamorphoses, 4, 100–103, 119, 131,
281n. 8, 295n. 15 (see also *Ovide
moralisé*)
Remedia amoris, 49
Ovide moralisé, 4, 66, 100, 165–66, 225
(fig. 5.19), 256n. 7, 281n. 11
story of Actaeon and Diana, 119, 120
(fig. 3.13)
story of Andromeda and Perseus,
132–34, 134 (fig. 3.22), 135
(fig. 3.23), 137
story of Arachne, 201–3, 203
(fig. 5.5), 295n. 14
story of Athamas and Ino, 207–8, 208
(fig. 5.8), 209 (fig. 5.9)
story of Callisto, 126–28, 127
(fig. 3.18), 128, 128 (fig. 3.19),
129 (fig. 3.20)

story of castration of Saturn, 65
story of Cephalus and Procris, 167
    (fig. 4.8), 168–69
story of Circe, 143–44, 144 (fig. 3.27)
story of Ganymede, 116–17, 116
    (fig. 3.11)
story of Hermaphroditus, 151
    (fig. 3.31)
story of Hyacinth, 112, 115, 117
    (fig. 3.12)
story of Io, 220 (fig. 5.15)
story of Latona, 203–4, 205 (fig. 5.6)
story of Narcissus, 71, 74, 76
    (fig. 2.19), 277n. 53
story of Orpheus, 101–8, 104
    (fig. 3.2), 105 (fig. 3.3), 106
    (fig. 3.4), 107 (fig. 3.5), 108
    (fig. 3.6), 110
story of Paris and Helen, 151–53, 153
    (fig. 3.33), 154 (fig. 3.34)
story of Pasiphaë, 138–41, 141
    (fig. 3.26), 286n. 44
story of Phoebus Apollo and Coronis,
    169, 169 (fig. 4.9), 171
story of Pygmalion, 81, 83 (fig. 2.25)
sybils, 222, 224 (fig. 5.18)

Pallas Athena, 122 (fig. 3.15), 199–203,
    202 (fig. 5.4), 211, 295n. 14
Panofsky, Erwin, 20–21, 23–25, 44–45,
    99, 138, 255n. 3, 256n. 8,
    257nn. 10–12, 258n. 15, 259n. 28,
    260nn. 29, 32, 261n. 36,
    263nn. 46–47, 267n. 79
"Panofsky's gaze," 25–41
Paris, as center of manuscript production,
    2, 8, 14, 19, 158–59, 195–96,
    277n. 56
Paris and Helen, 150–55, 152 (fig. 3.32),
    153 (fig. 3.33), 154 (fig. 3.34),
    162–64, 164 (fig. 4.7), 249n. 27
Parussa, Gabriella, 252nn. 53, 56
Pasiphaë, 100, 131–32, 137–43, 139
    (fig. 3.25), 141 (fig. 3.26),
    287n. 58, 288n. 59

patronage, 17, 225–29, 272n. 10,
    298n. 5
peace, politics of, 289
peasantry, 204
pederasty, 112, 283n. 20. See also
    Ganymede
Penthesilea, 160 (fig. 4.3), 161 (fig. 4.4),
    162 (fig. 4.5), 163 (fig. 4.6)
performance, of masculinity, 27–28, 50
performance culture, 8
performance theory, 8, 250n. 41
performativity, gendered, 10–14
Perkinson, Stephen, 252n. 50
Perseus, 133 (fig. 3.21), 134 (fig. 3.22),
    135 (fig. 3.23), 136 (fig. 3.24).
    See also Andromeda and Perseus
perspective, 28–30, 29 (fig. 1.2),
    261nn. 33, 36
    erotic potential of, 28–30
Philip the Bold, duke of Burgundy, 3,
    50–51, 84, 199
Philip the Good, duke of Burgundy, 53,
    85, 86 (fig. 2.26), 87, 97, 231–32,
    234–35, 278n. 62, 279n. 68,
    279n. 76. See also Burgundian
    court culture
philology, training in, 27–28, 259n. 28
Phoebus Apollo, 112–15, 117
    (fig. 3.12), 156 (fig. 4.1)
    and Coronis, 167–71, 168 (fig. 4.9),
    172 (fig. 4.11)
photography, 30–31, 33–40, 261n. 34,
    263nn. 49, 51, 266nn. 72–73,
    268n. 90. See also slide projection
Pigouchet, Philippe, 235, 237–40,
    238 (fig. A.7), 239 (fig. A.8),
    299nn. 10–13
Pliny the Elder, 180
Pointon, Marcia, 257n. 12
pornography, 26–28, 99–100, 154,
    280n. 2, 281n. 5
postcolonial theory, 19, 24–25, 184
Prange, Regine, 25–26
pregnancy, of Callisto, 127–28
Preziosi, Donald, 39

Prince, Stephen, 160
printed books, 235–41
print history, 235–41
Probyn, Elspeth, 145
Pygmalion, 77–84, 78 (fig. 2.21), 79
    (fig. 2.22), 80 (fig. 2.23), 82
    (fig. 2.24), 83 (fig. 2.25),
    277nn. 55, 57, 278nn. 58, 62
Pyrrhus, 163 (fig. 4.6)

queenship, 292n. 24
Queen's manuscript. *See* Index of
    Manuscripts
queer theory, 100, 145, 262n. 40
querelle de la Rose, 49–51, 65, 83, 97,
    195–99, 270n. 4, 273n. 15,
    294nn. 4, 7. *See also* Index of the
    Works of Christine de Pizan

rape, 154, 289n. 79
    of Callisto, 126–30
    in the *Roman de la rose*, 274n. 21
Raynaud, Christiane, 158–59
reader, as spectator, 1–2
reading
    in classroom, 123, 284n. 29, 285n. 30
    and sexuality, 123–30, 232–33, 281n. 5
Renaissance, 24, 33, 36
Reno, Christine, 285n. 32
reproduction. *See* photography; slide
    projection
Richards, Earl Jeffrey, 270–71n. 4
Robertson, D. W., Jr., 212
Robson, J. E., 142
Roman de la rose, 4, 12, 49–50, 53–54,
    57–60, 65–66, 69–71, 77–81, 101,
    112–14, 119, 130–31, 196, 208,
    275n. 32, 277n. 54
    illustrations, 13 (fig. I.6), 52 (fig. 2.3),
        53 (fig. 2.4), 54 (fig. 2.5), 55
        (fig. 2.6), 56 (fig. 2.7), 59 (fig. 2.9),
        68 (fig. 2.14), 72 (figs. 2.15 and
        2.16), 77 (fig. 2.20), 78 (fig. 2.21),
        79 (fig. 2.22), 80 (fig. 2.23), 114
        (fig. 3.9), 115 (fig. 3.10)

Roman d'Enéas, 283n. 20
Rosenwein, Barbara H., 294n. 3
Rouse, Mary A., 281n. 11
Rouse, Richard H., 281n. 11
royal library (France), 50

sacrifice, of Busiris, 176–78, 177 (fig. 4.14)
Saenger, Paul, 2, 123, 281n. 5, 285n. 30
Saffron Master, 18, 171–73, 226
same-sex desire. *See* homoeroticism
Saturn, 61 (fig. 2.10), 63 (fig. 2.11), 64
    (fig. 2.12), 275n. 39
    castration of, 57–58, 59 (fig. 2.9),
        60–62, 65, 275nn. 32–33, 275n. 41
Sauerländer, Willibald, 25, 40
Savedoff, Barbara, 38
Saxl, Fritz, 23–25, 32–33, 34 (fig. 1.3),
    35 (fig. 1.4), 40–41, 44–45,
    255n. 3, 263nn. 47, 49, 266n. 73,
    268n. 90
Schaefer, Lucie, 15, 254n. 68
Schapiro, Meyer, 178, 292n. 27
Schifanoia frescoes (Ferrara), 31–33, 36,
    41, 44, 265n. 61
Schoell-Glass, Charlotte, 254n. 71,
    267n. 75, 295n. 15
Scott, Joan, 196
Scott, Margaret, 85
Scrope, Stephen, 241
Second Vatican Mythographer, 288n. 59
sexuality. *See* heterosexuality;
    homoeroticism
Seznec, Jean, 24, 256n. 6
Sherman, Claire Richter, 14
sibyls, 194 (fig. 5.1), 220–29, 223
    (fig. 5.17), 226 (fig. 5.20), 227
    (fig. 5.21), 228 (fig. 5.22), 235
    (fig. A.5), 297nn. 33–34
    Cumaean Sibyl, 220–22, 297nn. 32, 34
    Sibyl Almathea, 221 (fig. 5.16)
    Tiburtine Sibyl, 222, 224 (fig. 5.18),
        297n. 34
Silverman, Kaja, 4, 7, 39, 56–57, 62,
    262n. 39
Simons, Patricia, 130

slide projection, 30–33, 36, 38–40,
    263n. 51, 264n. 54. *See also* magic
    lantern
Sobchack, Vivian, 26
sodomy, 111, 185
Solterer, Helen, 65, 197
Soussloff, Catherine, 8
spectator
    Christine as, 1–2
    construction of, 8, 36
    embodied, 8, 36
    reader as, 1–2
    spectatorship, 7–8
    construction of, 30, 39–41, 45
Spiegel, Gabrielle, 216
Sponsler, Claire, 247n. 24
statue, woman as, 51–52, 81–83. *See also*
    Pygmalion
Steinberg, Leo, 20
Sterling, Charles, 2, 297n. 38
Stierle, Karlheinz, 247n. 24
Sullivan, Karen, 83

Temperance, 16 (fig. I.7), 198, 200
    (fig. 5.2)
temporality, and ethics, 4
text and image
    in manuscripts, passim
    in printed books, 237–41
texte, in Christine's *Othea,* 3
textism, 20
Thamyris and Cyrus, 178–84, 179
    (fig. 4.15), 182 (fig. 4.17), 293n.
    32
Tommaso da Pizzano, 5
traffic, in women, 90–97, 137
Traub, Valerie, 130
Trepperel, Widow, 235
Tres Riches Heures, 224, 228 (fig. 5.22)
Troilus and Briseyda, 94–97, 94
    (fig. 2.32), 95 (fig. 2.33), 96
    (fig. 2.34)
Trojan Horse, 191 (fig. 4.23)
Trojan War, 87–97, 142–45, 146
    (fig. 3.28), 150–55, 162–65,

173–76, 184–93, 212–17, 292n. 24.
    See also Achilles; Hector; Paris and
    Helen
Troy story, 296nn. 24, 26
Turim, Maureen, 2
Tuve, Rosemond, 15, 248–49n. 26,
    277n. 57
twin manuscripts, 18, 254n. 68

uncanny, the, 26

Van der Weyden, Rogier, 279n. 70
Venus, 77, 77 (fig. 2.20), 81, 82
    (fig. 2.24), 83 (fig. 2.25)
viewer, 2, 173
    disembodied, 36
    embodied, 33, 261n. 34
violence, 155, 290n. 14, 291n. 21.
    See also blood; warfare
    depiction of, 157–65
    and gender, 161–89
    in *Roman de la rose,* 51–52
    subject-object, 165, 167, 171, 173,
        176, 178–80
    against women, 167–73
Virgil, 143, 222, 281n. 8, 283n. 20
vision and visuality, 255n. 76
visual pleasure, 7, 262n. 39
voice-over, 7

Wallen, Burr, 279n. 68
Warburg, Aby, 20–21, 31–36, 38, 44–45,
    265n. 61, 266n. 72
    Mnemosyne, 36, 37 (fig. 1.5), 41, 241,
        265n. 65, 267n. 75
Warburg, Eric, 263n. 51
Warburg Institute (Warburg Library),
    31, 38, 45, 263nn. 48, 50–51,
    266n. 73, 268nn. 85, 90, 270n. 105
warfare, 192–93. *See also* blood; Trojan
    War; violence
    battlefield, 184–89
    depiction of, 157–65
    individual combat, 90
    rules of engagement, 165, 190

Warner, Marina, 135
Warnke, Martin, 259n. 21
warrior
    defeated, 166–67, 185
    female (*see* Amazons)
Wauquelin, Jean. *See* Jean Wauquelin
Wells, William, 248n. 26
"wild ride," 130–31. *See also* "following
    the goddess"
Willard, Charity Cannon, 84, 90, 192,
    253n. 60
William of Conches, 288n. 59
Williams, Linda, 27, 99, 154
Winter, Patrick de, 2, 272n. 13
"wise women," 216–17. *See also* sibyls

Wollen, Peter, 250n. 30
women. *See also* body, human; Diana;
    sibyls
    and anger, 196–212
    as readers, 123–30, 124 (fig. 3.16)
    traffic in, 90–97, 137
    violent, 184
    "wise women," 216–17
Wood, Christopher, 261n. 36
woodcuts, 235–41, 238 (fig. A.7), 239
    (fig. A.8)
Wyer, Robert, 241, 299n. 13

Zillich, Clod, 247n. 24
zodiac, 42, 269n. 94

Plates

Fig. I.1. Christine in the Salle de Fortune, *Mutation de Fortune,* Munich, Bayerische
Staatsbibliothek, Ms. Gall. 11, fol. 53r. (Bayerische Staatsbibliothek, München.)

Fig. 1.1. Mercury and his children, *Epistre Othea*, BL, Harley 4431, fol. 102r. (By permission of the British Library.) ❧

Fig. 2.1. Cupid and a young nobleman, *Epistre Othea*, BL, Harley 4431, fol. 117r.
(By permission of the British Library.)

Fig. 4.1. Phoebus Apollo killing Coronis, *Epistre Othea*, BL, Harley 4431, fol. 117v.
(By permission of the British Library.)

tepte · Cent

Cent auctozitez tay escriptes
si ne soient de toy descrites
Car Augustus de femme apprist

Fig. 5.1. The sibyl instructing Augustus, *Epistre Othea*, BL, Harley 4431, fol. 141r. (By permission of the British Library.)

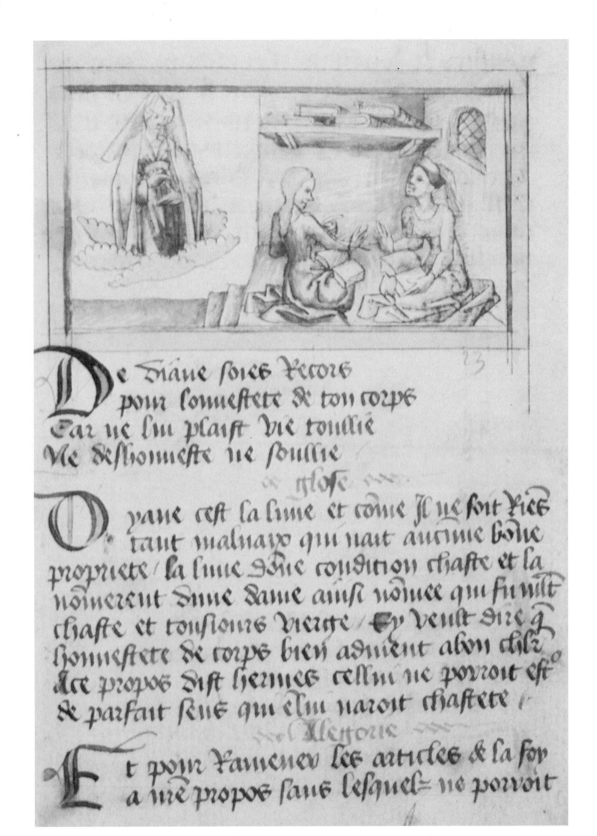

De Diane soies recors
pour honnestete de ton corps
Car ne luy plaist vie souillie
Vie deshonneste ne souillie

Glose

Dyane c'est la lune et come il ne soit riens
tant mauuays qui nait aucune bone
propriete / la lune a une condition chaste et la
nommerent dune dame ainsi nomee qui fu mult
chaste et tousiours vierge / Et veult dire q
honnestete de corps bien aduient a bon chr̅
A ce propos dist hermes cellui ne porroit est
de parfait sens qui en luy naroit chastete /

Allegorie

Et pour ramener les articles de la foy
a mre propos sans lesquel= ne porroit

Fig. A.1. Diana and her women, *Epistre Othea*, Lille, Bibl. mun. Jean Levy, MS 175, fol. 26r. (Bibliothèque municipale Jean Levy.)